Faning 316
Riseley 311
Mathay 285
Stockley 267
Elgar/Strauss IOW. 264
Fauré & Busoni in Manchester 202
Brodsky/Bodden 199
Spark 188
Haydn + Karel /Oxford 161-2
Ole Bull 135
Wagner/London 115
Weber/London 112
Berlioz/London 108/6
Verdi/London 104
Barnett 102
Tchaik/London 101
Liszt/P. of Wales 100
Chopin London-chance 98

A MUSICAL GAZETTEER
OF GREAT BRITAIN & IRELAND

Gerald Norris

A MUSICAL GAZETTEER

of Great Britain
& Ireland

DAVID & CHARLES
Newton Abbot   London   North Pomfret (Vt)

British Library Cataloguing in Publication Data

Norris, Gerald
  A musical gazetteer of Great Britain and
  Ireland.
  I. Music-Great Britain
  I. Title
  780'.914   ML21

  ISBN 0-7153-7845-7

Typeset by Typesetters (Birmingham) Limited
Smethwick, Warley, West Midlands
and printed in Great Britain
by Redwood Burn Limited, Trowbridge, Wiltshire
for David & Charles (Publishers) Limited
Brunel House Newton Abbot Devon

Published in the United States of America
by David & Charles Inc
North Pomfret Vermont 05053 USA

CONTENTS

WALES

THE WEST COUNTRY

PREFACE

When Beethoven was on his deathbed, a friend gave him a picture of Haydn's birthplace. This present so delighted the composer that he kept it close by him and often took it in his hands. He showed it to one of his final visitors, Johann Hummel. 'It affords me much pleasure', he said. 'A lowly peasant dwelling—yet such a great man was born here!'

A fascination in where famous men and women were born and lived is universal, and many books have been devoted to the subject. More than a dozen have documented where poets, novelists, dramatists and other writers had their homes in the British Isles. This book is similar to these literary gazetteers, but is concerned with people like composers, conductors, singers and pianists. Among them are quite a few foreign composers, several of whom were frequent visitors. They came principally to London, which, for more than two centuries, has been the world's most active musical centre. That is why Handel and J. C. Bach chose to live in England and why London today possesses more first-class orchestras than are to be found in practically any other country, apart from the United States and Russia.

The author has been fortunate to receive invaluable help from many people and offers particular thanks to Mrs Ursula Vaughan Williams, Mr Austin Coates, Mr Michael Kennedy, Mr Arthur Jacobs, Mr Adrian Williams, Mrs Norah Kirby, Mr Robert Elliott, Mr Richard Hey Lloyd, Mrs Christine Tratt, Mr Frank Kelsall, Mr Steve Race, Mr and Mrs Jack McKenzie and Elgar's Birthplace Museum, Mr Michael Trott and the Elgar Society, Mr Lowinger Maddison and the Holst Birthplace Museum, Mr Michael Short, Mrs Joy Finzi, Miss Diana McVeagh, Mr Charles Harding, Miss Jill Burrows and the Britten Estate, Mrs Gillian Stormer, Mr Paul E. Bierley, Miss Kathryn Copisarow of Chappell Music, Mr David Stevens of Schott & Co, Mrs Eunice Mistarz and the Liszt Society, Mr H. P. Playford and the Royal Marines Museum, Mrs Frida Knight, Mr Peter Kemp, Miss Margaret McGahon of the Bord Fáilte, Mr Peter Joslin, Miss Elsa V. Matthews, Mr Philip Williams of Holywell, Mr J. Glynn Morris, Mr Gordon Wood, Miss T. P. Holland, Mr Jack Phipps, Mr Frank Warren, Mr Stewart Spencer, Mr Tom Fenton, Mr Richard Langham Smith, Mr Derek Watson, Mr Peter Cox and Mr Robin Johnson of Dartington College of Arts, Mr Barry Russell and Master Toby Price Davies.

Errors and Omissions

Since this book is the first of its kind, there are bound to be errors and omissions, for which the author apologizes. He would be grateful to receive, care of David & Charles, any information that could lead to the correction of these mistakes. The reader should be advised that it is not intended to include details about foreign performing artists, nor, on the whole, anything about native performing artists, other than their places of birth and death. However, an executant who is also a composer, such as Rakhmaninov, qualifies for inclusion.

EAST ANGLIA

CAMBRIDGESHIRE

Burwell Edward Fitzball, librettist of William Wallace's opera *Maritana*, was born here in 1793 and died in Chatham, Kent, on 27 October 1873.

Cambridge William Sterndale Bennett, composer, pianist and conductor, frequently stayed at The Bull Hotel on his visits here during the time he was Professor of Music at the university. Joseph Joachim also regularly stayed at this hotel.

Alban Berg, acting as a juror for the International Society for Contemporary Music, came here during the middle of January 1931 and stayed with Reverend Hugh Stewart at Girton Gate, opposite Girton College. 'This is the oddest town I've ever seen,' he wrote to his wife. He was under the impression that he was staying in 'a genuine old English country house', although Girton Gate was built in 1924. He found the meals in Cambridge plentiful, except that 'the pheasant tastes exactly like a turkey or a chicken', while one meal 'had no taste at all'. Dinner in Trinity College hall, however, made a pleasant and 'unforgettable impression'; the college itself was 'a highly interesting building'. On 15 January, he informed his wife: 'Thank the Lord, Cambridge is over!'

Also serving on the jury were Alfredo Casella, Charles Koechlin and Adrian Boult. Boult conducted the first English performances of Berg's *Three Pieces*, Op 6, and *Lulu-Symphonie*. When *Wozzeck* was played under Boult's direction in a radio broadcast on 14 March 1934, Heinrich Jalowetz wrote to Berg: 'You know well how much I love this work and know, too, that I've heard many performances . . . But I've never been as overpowered as I was yesterday.'

Zoltán Kodály stayed at Girton Gate in 1927, conducting the first English performance of *Psalmus Hungaricus* in Cambridge on 30 November. He wrote in Stewart's visitors' book: 'Cambridge with his habitants who are even in winter sommerly.'

Arthur Honegger was at Girton Gate in 1929, when he conducted *Le Roi David* in Cambridge.

Ferruccio Busoni took part in concerts here in 1903 and 1910; during the later visit, he received an honorary degree. He returned to Cambridge in 1913.

Henry Montagu Butler, author of the hymn ' "Lift Up Your Hearts!" We Lift Them, Lord, to Thee', died here on 14 January 1918.

Roberto Gerhard, composer, was born in Valls, Spain, on 25 September 1896 and died in Cambridge on 5 January 1970. He resided at 14 Madingley Road.

Alexander Glazunov received an honorary doctorate here on 12 June 1907.

Patrick Hadley, composer, was born here on 5 March 1899.

Joseph Haydn visited here in November 1791. 'The King's Chapel is famous because of its stuccoed ceiling, it is made of stone, but so delicate that nothing more beautiful could have been made from wood, it is 400 years old, and everybody thinks it is not more than 10 years old, because the stone is so sound, and because of its special whiteness. The students bear themselves like those at Oxford, but, it is said they have better teachers, there are 800 students in all.'

Petrus Hellendaal, organist, violinist and composer, was born in Rotterdam in 1721 and died here on 26 April 1799.

John Hilton the elder, composer and organist, died here in March 1608.

Paul Hirsch, music collector, was born in Frankfurt-am-Main on 24 February 1881 and died in Cambridge on 25 November 1951. He resided at 10 Adams Road.

Erich von Hornbostel, authority on primitive music, was born in Vienna on 25 February 1877 and died in Cambridge on 28 November 1935.

Ernest Markham Lee, composer and writer on music, was born here on 8 June 1874 and died on 13 November 1956. He resided at 61 Summerdown Road, Eastbourne, East Sussex.

Franz Liszt took part in a concert here on 18 September 1840. He stayed the night at Hoo's Hotel.

Bernard Naylor, organist, composer, music scholar and conductor, was born here in 1907.

Edward Naylor, composer of the hymn tune *From Strength to Strength*, sung to 'Soldiers of Christ, Arise', died here on 7 May 1934.

Robin Orr composed his Sonata for Viola and Piano, *Four Romantic Songs, Spring Cantata* and Rhapsody for String Orchestra at 21 Clarkson Road.

Niccolò Paganini gave a recital in the Theatre Royal on 30 October 1833.

Alan Rawsthorne, composer, died here on 24 July 1971.

Gioachino Rossini came here in July 1824 and took part in concerts in the Senate House and in Great St Mary's, where he played the organ. In the Senate House, he sang a duet, with Angelica Catalani, and *Largo al Factotum* from *The Barber of Seville*.

Camille Saint-Saëns, Piotr Tchaikovsky, Max Bruch, Arrigo Boito and Charles Villiers Stanford took part in a concert here on 12 June 1893. The four foreign composers received honorary degrees on the following day. Saint-Saëns stayed with the provost of King's College. Tchaikovsky stayed with Professor Maitland at West Lodge, Downing College, where Ralph Vaughan Williams was often a visitor around this time. Saint-Saëns also gave an organ recital in the chapel of Trinity College.

Edvard Grieg received an honorary degree here on 10 May 1894; like Saint-Saëns, he stayed at King's Lodge. His English proved to be superior to that of Saint-Saëns, who had confessed, *'Je ne parle pas anglais, sauf avec les cabmen et les waiters'*, but his size—he was not quite five feet tall—was less than ideal for the degree ceremony. 'Like many great composers before him,' wrote *The Musical Times*, 'Grieg's eminence is not to be measured by his height, and some time was spent in adapting to his stature by means of the domestic pin the doctor's gown lent him for the ceremony.' Afterwards, Grieg went straight to the post office and sent a telegram to a doctor friend, in Bergen, whose name was also Grieg. It read: 'Colleague, I greet thee' and was signed 'Doctor Grieg'.

Alexander Skryabin visited the university on 25 March 1914 to acquaint Professor Charles Meyer with his theories on the relationship between sound and colour.

Robert Smith, mathematician and notable writer on harmonics, was born in Cambridge in 1689 and died here in 1768.

Charles Villiers Stanford, composer, conductor, celebrated teacher, pianist, organist and writer on music, was organist of Trinity College 1874–92. He resided at 10 Harvey Road, where he composed *The Revenge*, the *Irish Symphony*, *The Voyage of Maeldune* and *The Battle of the Baltic*.

Antonín Dvořák and his wife stayed with him 14–16 June 1891. Dvořák conducted his Eighth Symphony and *Stabat Mater* at a concert in the Town Hall on the 15th and received an honorary doctorate on the 16th. The degree ceremony caused him agonies of embarrassment. 'All the faces so grave, and it seemed that nobody could speak anything but Latin. I listened to my right and I listened to my left and had no idea where to turn my ear. And when I discovered that it was me they were talking about, I wished I was anywhere but where I was, and I was ashamed that I knew no Latin.'

Dvořák and his wife were very early risers. Stanford was woken by noises one morning, and, looking out of the window, was astonished to see his guests 'sitting under a tree in my garden at 6am'.

Ludwig Straus, violinist and leader of the Hallé Orchestra, was born in Bratislava, Czechoslovakia, on 28 March 1835 and died in Cambridge on 23 October 1899.

Igor Stravinsky came here on 27 October 1961 and had tea with E. M. Forster at King's College.

Thomas Tudway, composer, who was possibly born in Windsor in about 1650, died in Cambridge on 23 November 1726.

Henry Kirke White, author of the hymns 'Oft in Danger, Oft in Woe' and 'When Marshalled on the Nightly Plain', died here on 19 October 1806 at the age of 21. 'Oft in Danger, Oft in Woe' was written during the final minutes of a mathematics examination.

Charles Wood, composer, resided at 17 Cranmer Road from 1898 until his death on 12 July 1926. He is buried in St Giles's Cemetery, Huntingdon Road.

Deeping Gate Robert Fayrfax, composer, was born here in April 1464 and is thought to have died in St Albans, Hertfordshire, on 24 October 1521.

Doddington Christopher Tye, composer, who lived between about 1500 and 1575, resided in Doddington for many years and may have died here.

Ely John Amner, composer and organist, died here in 1641.

Arnold Richardson, organist and composer, was born here on 6 January 1914.

Ludwig Spohr visited here in October 1847. He attended divine service in the cathedral and was greatly moved by 'the finest ecclesiastical psalmody' chanted by sixteen singers. Few hearers could ever have been 'so devoutly attentive and edified', he said.

Huntingdon Franz Liszt played at a concert here on 17 September 1840.

March Martin Peerson, composer, was born here in about 1572 and died in London in December 1650.

14

Meldreth Ralph Vaughan Williams wrote part of his First Symphony at The Warren in July and August 1906.

Peterborough Thomas Armstrong, organist, conductor and composer, was born here on 15 June 1898.

Franz Liszt played at a concert here on 16 September 1840.

Thomas Mudd, composer of the anthem *Let Thy Merciful Ears, O Lord*, who was born in London in about 1560 and possibly died here in 1632, was organist of the cathedral for about a year before his death.

Christopher Robinson, organist, composer and conductor, was born here on 20 April 1936.

St Neots William Tan'sur, composer, died here on 7 October 1783.

ESSEX

Boreham Elizabeth Maconchy, composer, moved to Shottesbrook, Boreham, in 1954. Works written here include String Quartets Nos 7–12, Oboe Quartet, Clarinet Quintet, Sinfonietta, *Ariadne* and *Héloïse and Abelard*.

Buckhurst Hill Reg Connelly, composer of the songs *Show Me the Way To Go Home, Goodnight, Sweetheart* and *Try a Little Tenderness*, was born here in 1895 and died in Bournemouth in 1963.

Chelmsford Franz Liszt played at a concert here on 24 September 1840.

Chipping Ongar Jane Taylor, author of the song 'Twinkle, Twinkle, Little Star', was born in London in 1783 and died in Chipping Ongar in 1824.

Colchester Franz Liszt played at a concert here on 23 September 1840.

John Wilbye, composer, lived here from 1628 until his death in September 1638. He is buried at Holy Trinity Church, opposite the house in which he resided.

Danbury Ralph Vaughan Williams spent the late summer of 1923 here, working on *Sancta civitas*.

Great Baddow Cecil Armstrong Gibbs, composer, was born here on 10 August 1889 and died on 12 May 1960. He resided at The Cottage in the Bush, Danbury.

Great Easton Gustav Holst, composer, resided at Brook End, Easton Park, 1925–8, during which time he wrote *Egdon Heath* and *A Moorside Suite*. He was at The Cottage, Great Easton, 1928–9 and at Hill Cottage 1930–3, when he wrote *Hammersmith* and *Brook Green Suite*.

Great Sampford John Ireland, composer, resided intermittently at The White House 1945–7, during which period he wrote the overture *Satyricon* and music for the film *The Overlanders*.

Harlow Sarah Adams, author of the hymn 'Nearer, My God, to Thee', written in 1840, was born here on 22 February 1805. She died in London on 14 August 1848 and is buried in Harlow. Her elder sister, Eliza Fowler, was an early love of Browning's, inspiring, it is said, the poem 'Pauline', published in 1833, when he was 20. She was born here on 19 April 1803, became a composer and died in London on 12 December 1846.

Little Hallingbury Bernard Rose, organist, music scholar and composer, was born here on 9 May 1915.

Little Sampford John Ireland, composer, resided at Little Sampford Rectory April 1942–March 1945.

Mount End Ethel Smythe, composer, used to visit her sister Mary Hunter at Hill Hall. Charles Hunter, Mary's husband, was 'a great man to hounds' and much liked by Miss Smythe, a keen horsewoman, 'for he mounted me whenever the hunting season found me in England'.
  Percy Grainger, Thomas Beecham, Rodin, Henry James and George Moore also visited Hill Hall. Moore often left or hid when Beecham appeared. Grainger's realization that Beecham understood nothing of Delius's harmonies originated here. Hill Hall is now a prison.

Newport Ernest Longstaffe, composer of *When the Sergeant-Major's on Parade*, was born here in 1888.

Rochford John Georgiadis, violinist, was born here in 1939.

Saffron Walden John Frye, who was born in 1812, was appointed

Alban Berg in January 1931 at Girton Gate, the home in Cambridge of Dr H.F. Stewart. The composer served on the jury for the International Society for Contemporary Music, which met at the university that year. He stayed with the Stewarts, whose daughter, Mrs Frida Knight, was later to become the author of *Beethoven and the Age of Revolution* and the enthralling historical survey, *Cambridge Music* (*Courtesy of Mrs Frida Knight*)

Benjamin Britten with Colin Graham in the composer's Alvis in 1964. Graham was the first to produce many of the later stage works, including *Death in Venice*. The Red House, in Aldeburgh, was Britten's home for the last nineteen years of his life. Among those who visited him here were Zoltán Kodály and Dmitri Shostakovich (*The Britten Estate*)

THE RED HOUSE

Langham Hall, near Bury St Edmunds, where Joseph Haydn stayed with Sir Patrick Blake at the end of November 1791. 'On the 30th I spent 3 days in the country 100 miles from London at the house of Sir Patric Blak [*sic*]; I passed through the little town of Cambridge.' (*Courtesy of T.F. Blackwell*)

Benjamin Britten's birthplace in Kirkley Cliff Road, Lowestoft, his home throughout childhood. The house faces the North Sea, which played such an important part in his life. When we recall that his father was a dental surgeon, it is interesting to note the continuity in the present-day plaque next to the front gate (*The Britten Estate*)

organist of St Mary's at the age of 8, which post he held for sixty-four years. He died here on 23 October 1887.

Sible Hedingham Clive Carey, baritone singer, composer and opera producer, was born here on 30 May 1883 and died on 30 April 1968. He resided at 85 St Marks Road, Kensington, London.

Stapleford Abbotts William Byrd, composer, resided at Battylshall Manor (demolished) during the 1570s.

Stondon Massey William Byrd, composer, who is thought to have been born in Lincolnshire in 1543, resided here, at Stondon Place (demolished), from 1593 until his death on 4 July 1623. He is buried, it is presumed, in Stondon Church.

Thaxted Gustav Holst, composer, resided intermittently at The Cottage (destroyed), Monk Street, 1914–17, during which time he wrote *The Planets*. He was at The Steps (now 25 Town Street) 1917–25, when he wrote *The Hymn of Jesus, Ode to Death* and *The Perfect Fool*.

Thundersley Herbert Bunning, conductor and composer, was born in London on 2 May 1863 and died at Quimperlé, Grasmere Road, on 25 November 1937.

Waltham Abbey Thomas Tallis, composer and organist, was organist of Holy Cross Abbey from an unknown date until 1540, when he was about 35.

Westcliff-on-Sea E. Power Biggs, organist, was born here on 29 March 1906.

Wickham Bishops Elizabeth Maconchy, composer, resided here 1945–54. Works written during this period include the Symphony for Double String Orchestra, Bassoon Concerto and Fifth and Sixth String Quartets.

Witham Thomas Campion, poet and composer, is thought to have been born here, on 12 February 1567. His poems have been set to music by Parry, Stanford, Vaughan Williams, Ireland, Bax and Rubbra.

NORFOLK

Blickling Richard Davy, organist and composer, who was born in about 1467 and died in about 1516, resided at the home of Sir Thomas Boleyn in Blickling from 1506 until probably the time of his death.

Costessey Arthur Sullivan, composer and conductor, stayed at Costessey Park in September 1872 as the guest of Lord Stafford.

Cromer Joan Chissell, music critic, was born here on 22 May 1919.

Diss John Wilbye, composer, was born here in 1574.

East Dereham William Cowper, poet and hymn writer, died here on 25 April 1800.

Great Yarmouth Niccolò Paganini gave a recital here on 2 August 1831.

Heacham Patrick Hadley, composer, who died in December 1973, resided during his final years at Shallcross.

Kimberley John Jenkins, composer, died on 27 October 1678 at Kimberley House and is buried in Kimberley Church.

King's Lynn David Branson, composer, pianist and painter, was born here on 13 July 1909.

George Kiallmark, violinist and composer of *The Old Oaken Bucket*, was born here in February 1781 and died in Islington, London, in March 1835.

Lingwood Ernest John Moeran, composer, resided at Lingwood Lodge during the 1930s.

Norwich Philip Armes, composer and organist, was born here on 15 August 1836. His hymn tune *Galilee* is sung to 'Jesus Shall Reign Where'er the Sun'. When Jenny Lind stayed at the Bishop's Palace in September 1847, Armes, then a junior chorister in the cathedral choir, sang *Where the Bee Sucks* for her.

John Beckwith, composer and organist, was born in Norwich on 25 December 1750 and died here on 3 June 1809.

William Cobbold, organist and composer, was born here on 5 January

1560 and died in Beccles, Suffolk, on 7 November 1639.

William Crotch, organist, pianist, painter and composer of the *Westminster Chimes*, was born in Green's Lane, St George's Colgate, on 5 July 1775. He was ambidextrous and, when composing, often wrote on two staves simultaneously.

Alfred Gaul, organist, conductor and composer, was born here on 30 April 1837 and died in Birmingham on 13 September 1913.

Sarah Glover, music educationist, whose teachings anticipated and greatly influenced those of John Curwen, founder of the tonic sol-fa method, was born here on 13 November 1786 and died in Malvern, Hereford and Worcester, on 20 October 1867.

James Hook, composer, conductor, pianist and organist, was born in the parish of St John, Maddermarket, probably on 3 June 1746 and died in Boulogne in 1827. His most popular songs include *Within a Mile o'Edinbro' Town*, *Lucy Gray of Allendale* and *The Lass of Richmond Hill*.

Johann Nepomuk Hummel took part in a concert here on 14 June 1830.

Herman Klein, music critic and writer on music, was born here on 23 July 1856. He died on 10 March 1934 in London, where he resided at 40 Avenue Road, Hampstead.

Franz Liszt took part in two concerts in the Theatre Royal on 21 September 1840.

Basil Maine, writer on music and novelist, was born in Norwich on 4 March 1894 and died here on 13 October 1972.

Arthur Henry Mann, organist and composer, was born here on 16 May 1850 and died in Cambridge on 19 November 1929.

Edward Miller, composer of the hymn tune *Rockingham*, sung to 'When I Survey the Wondrous Cross', was born here in about 1731.

Antonio Oury, violinist, was probably born in London in 1800 and died in Norwich on 25 July 1883.

Niccolò Paganini gave recitals at the Theatre Royal on 28, 29 and 30 July, and 1 and 3 August 1831, making £800 from the first three engagements.

Osbert Parsley, composer, was born in 1511 and died here in 1585.

George Perry, composer, organist, violinist and conductor, was born here in 1793 and died in London on 4 March 1862.

John Playford, noteworthy music publisher, was born here in 1623 and died in London in 1686.

Samuel Porter, organist and composer, was born here in 1733 and died in Canterbury on 11 December 1810.

Ludwig Spohr stayed with the Mayor of Norwich in September 1839 and took part in the Triennial Festival, playing the violin and conducting his oratorio *Calvary*. A number of people objected to the idea of the oratorio being performed, deeming it profane and sinful to set the sufferings and death of Christ to music. When the composer attended a morning service at the cathedral, the preacher delivered a blistering attack on him from the pulpit. Throughout this diatribe, Spohr, a kindly and uncomplicated man, sat peacefully gazing at the beauties of the cathedral, his total lack of English sparing him any discomfort. The *Monthly Chronicle* later commented: 'We now see the fanatical zealot in the pulpit, and sitting right opposite to him the *great composer*, with ears happily deaf to the English tongue; but with a demeanour so becoming, with a look so full of pure good will, and with so much humility and mildness in the features, that his countenance alone spoke to the heart like a good sermon. Without intending it, we make a comparison, and cannot for a moment doubt in which of the two dwelt the *Spirit* of religion, which denoted the true Christian!'

In 1842, his oratorio *The Fall of Babylon* received its world première in Norwich. He had hoped to conduct it himself, but his employer, the Elector of Cassel, refused him permission to go to England. An enormous petition signed by many citizens of Norwich failed to make the Elector reverse his decision.

Arthur Henry Fox Strangways, writer on music, was born here on 14 September 1859.

Edward Taylor, bass singer, conductor and writer on music, was born here on 22 January 1784 and died in Brentwood, Essex, on 12 March 1863.

Thomas Vaughan, tenor singer, who took part in the first British performance of Beethoven's Ninth Symphony, was born here in 1782 and died in Birmingham on 9 January 1843.

Overstrand Isidore de Lara, opera and song composer, was born in London on 9 August 1858 and died in Paris on 2 September 1935. His famous song *The Garden of Sleep* concerns the church and churchyard on the edge of the cliffs at Overstrand.

Sandringham John Philip Sousa conducted his band at a royal command performance before King Edward VII and Queen Alexandra on the Queen's birthday, 1 December 1901. The King demanded seven encores and awarded Sousa the medal of the Victorian Order. 'Where shall I pin it?' he asked the composer. 'Over my heart,' Sousa replied.

'How American!' said the King. In return, Sousa composed his march *Imperial Edward*, dedicated to the King. This was first performed in Montreal on 21 May 1902; the manuscript is in the British Museum. Sousa later considered the march to be one among his least successful compositions.

Scole Arthur Sullivan, composer and conductor, stayed at Brome Hall in November 1887.

Sheringham Ralph Vaughan Williams began composing his Third Symphony here during the spring of 1919. He resided successively at Sundial and Northern Lights.

Sutton The hymn tune *Stalham*, sung to 'City of Peace, Our Mother Dear', was collected here by Ernest Moeran.

SUFFOLK

Aldeburgh Benjamin Britten, composer, and Peter Pears, tenor singer, resided at Crag House, 4 Crabbe Street, 1947–November 1957, during which time Britten wrote the *Spring Symphony, The Little Sweep, Billy Budd, The Turn of the Screw* and *The Prince of the Pagodas*. They then moved to The Red House, where he wrote *Missa Brevis, Jubilate Deo, A Midsummer Night's Dream*, the *War Requiem*, the Symphony for Cello and Orchestra, *Curlew River, The Burning Fiery Furnace* and *The Prodigal Son*. Britten died here on 4 December 1976, and is buried in Aldeburgh Parish Churchyard.

Kodály visited him here in 1965. Shostakovich and Poulenc were also visitors to The Red House.

Blythburgh William Alwyn, composer, moved to Lark Rise in 1960. Works written here include the Fifth Symphony, *Juan, or the Libertine, Miss Julie*, Sinfonietta for Strings and scores for films such as *In Search of the Castaways*.

Martin Shaw, composer and organist, resided at Farthings during the 1940s.

Bruisyard Simon Tunsted, writer on music, was born in Norwich and is presumed to have died in Bruisyard, in St Clara's Nunnery, in 1369.

Bures Thomas Wood, composer and author, died here on 19 November 1950. He resided at Parsonage Hall.

Bury St Edmunds George Guest, singer, organist and composer, was born here on 1 May 1771 and died in Wisbech, Cambridgeshire, on 10 September 1831.

Charles Kettle, organist and composer, was born here on 28 March 1833 and died in Hove, East Sussex, on 2 March 1895.

Charles King, organist and composer, was born here in 1687 and died in London on 17 March 1748.

George Kirbye, the probable composer of the hymn tune *Winchester Old*, sung to 'While Shepherds Watched Their Flocks By Night', is thought to have been born in Suffolk in about 1565. He resided in Whiting Street towards the end of his life. He died here and was buried in St Mary's on 6 October 1634.

Franz Liszt took part in two concerts here on 19 September 1840.

Henry Percy Smith was vicar of Great Barton, 1868–82, when his hymn tune *Maryton*, usually sung to 'Dear Master, in Whose Life I See', was published in 1874.

Joseph Stammers, author of the hymn 'Breast the Wave, Christian', was born here in 1801 and died in London on 18 May 1885.

Arthur Sullivan, composer and conductor, stayed at Livermere Park in November 1892.

Mary Jane Walker, author of the hymn 'Jesus, I Will Trust Thee, Trust Thee With My Soul', was born here on 27 April 1816 and died in Cheltenham, Gloucestershire, on 2 July 1878.

Hadleigh Mary Shaw, contralto singer, who received the praise of Mendelssohn and appeared in the première of Verdi's first opera, *Oberto*, in Milan on 17 November 1839, was born in Lee, Kent, in 1814 and died at Hadleigh Hall on 9 September 1876.

Hengrave Hall John Wilbye, composer, resided here from about 1595 until 1628.

Horham Benjamin Britten, composer, and Peter Pears, tenor singer, resided intermittently between 1970 and 1976 at Chapel House, where much of *Owen Wingrave* and *Death in Venice* were written.

Ipswich Henry Bird Collins, organist and music scholar, was born here on 13 June 1870 and died in Bromsgrove, Hereford and Worcester, on 19 January 1941.

Mary Anne Keeley, soprano singer, who sang the part of the Mermaid in the first performance of Weber's *Oberon*, was born here on 22 November 1805 and died in London on 12 March 1899.

Franz Liszt played at a concert here on 22 September 1840.

Wilfred Sanderson, composer of the songs *Drake Goes West, Friend o'Mine, Shipmates o'Mine, Up from Somerset* and *Devonshire Cream and Cider,* was born here in 1878.

Guy Woolfenden, conductor and composer, was born here on 12 July 1937.

Langham Joseph Haydn stayed at Langham Hall, the home of Sir Patrick Blake, for three days at the end of November 1791.

Lavenham Henry Westrop, organist, violinist, conductor and composer, was born here on 22 July 1812 and died in London on 23 September 1879.

Lowestoft Benjamin Britten, composer, was born on 22 November 1913 at 21 Kirkley Cliff Road, where he spent his childhood.

Nayland William Jones composed the hymn tune *St Stephen,* often sung to 'The Lord Will Come and Not Be Slow', here, 'for the use of the Church of Nayland'. He died in Nayland on 6 January 1800.

Newmarket Franz Liszt, travelling from Cambridge to Bury St Edmunds, had breakfast here on 19 September 1840.

Snape Benjamin Britten, composer, resided at The Old Mill 1938–9, when *Les Illuminations* was composed, and intermittently between 1942 and 1947, during which latter period he wrote *Peter Grimes, The Young Person's Guide to the Orchestra, Albert Herring* and *Serenade for Tenor, Horn and Strings.*

Lennox Berkeley was a visitor here.

Southwold Martin Shaw, composer and organist, was born in London on 9 March 1875 and died in Southwold on 24 October 1958. He resided at Long Island House. Among his best known hymn tunes are *Marching,* sung to 'There's a Wideness in God's Mercy', and *Pimlico Road,* sung to 'O World Invisible, We View Thee'.

Tostock Roger North, writer on music, was born here on 3 September 1653 and died in Rougham, Norfolk, on 1 March 1734.

Westleton Herbert Heyner, baritone singer, was born in London on 26 June 1881 and died in Westleton on 18 January 1954.

Wetherden Michael Tippett, composer, spent most of his childhood here, 1905–19.

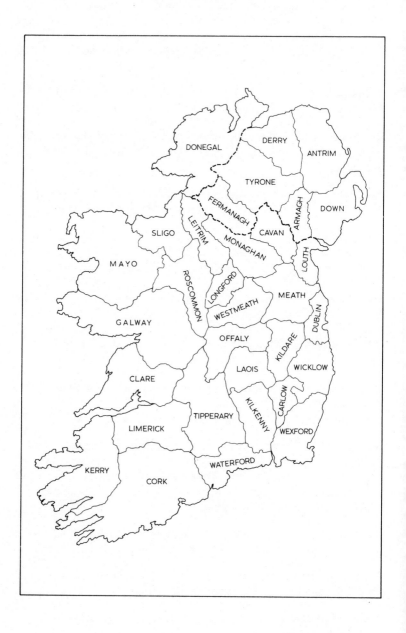

IRELAND

ANTRIM

Ballymoney William Hunter, author of the hymn 'Joyfully, Joyfully Onward I Move', was born here on 26 May 1811 and died in Alliance, Ohio, in 1877.

Richard Mant, author of the hymn 'Bright the Vision That Delighted', which was published when he was Bishop of Down and Connor, died here on 2 November 1848.

Belfast Howard Ferguson, composer and music scholar, was born at Shimna, Deramore Park, on 21 October 1908. He moved later to 42 Windsor Park.

James Galway, virtuoso flautist, spent his childhood at 17 Carnalea Street, having been born on 8 December 1939 in a nearby house that was destroyed during World War II.

Heather Harper, soprano singer, soloist in the first performance of Britten's *War Requiem*, was born here on 8 May 1930.

Hamilton Harty, composer and conductor, was organist of St Barnabas's Church 1895–6.

Herbert Hughes, composer, editor and folk-song collector, was born here on 16 March 1882 and died in Brighton on 1 May 1937.

Franz Liszt played at a concert in the Music Hall on 15 January 1841. He stayed the night at the Donegal Arms.

Kenneth Montgomery, conductor, was born on 28 October 1943 in Eglantine Avenue. He spent most of his childhood at 28 Wandsworth Parade.

Niccolò Paganini gave recitals in the Assembly Rooms on 8 and 10 October, and in the Theatre on 11 October 1831.

Archibald Potter, composer, conductor and writer on music, was born here on 22 September 1918.

John Philip Sousa conducted his band at two concerts in Ulster Hall on 16 February 1911. He stayed at the Grand Central Hotel.

Arthur Sullivan, composer and conductor, stayed with Robert Dunville at Richmond Lodge, Holywood Road, during the summer of 1864. His first ideas for the *Irish Symphony* came to him on a trip back from Holywood 'through the wind and rain on an open jaunting car'.

Cushendall Charles Villiers Stanford's song-cycle *Cushendall* was based on poems by John Stevenson and published in 1910. One of his greatest songs, *The Fairy Lough*, a setting of a poem by Moira O'Neill and published in 1901, refers to nearby Loughareema.

Lisburn Andrew Ashe, esteemed flautist, who played in Haydn's London concerts, was born here in 1759 and died in Dublin in 1838.

Portballintrae Hamilton Harty, composer and conductor, spent the summer of 1936 here, finding inspiration for his tone poem *The Children of Lir* during a walk to Runkerry.

ARMAGH

Armagh Edward Bunting, folk-song collector, was born here in February 1773 and died on 21 December 1843 at 45 Upper Baggot Street, Dublin.

Charles Wood, composer, was born at 11 Vicar's Hill on 15 June 1866.

Lurgan Annie Patterson, writer on music, folk-song collector and composer, was born here on 27 October 1868.

George William Russell, poet, essayist, painter and author of the hymn 'When the Unquiet Hours Depart', was born in William Street on 10 April 1867 and died in Bournemouth on 17 July 1935.

Portadown David Frederick Ruddell Wilson, composer of the hymn tune *Drumcondra*, sung to 'O Holy Spirit, God', was born here on 7 January 1871 and died in Dublin on 24 November 1957.

CARLOW

Carlow Franz Liszt, travelling from Kilkenny to Dublin, had luncheon here on 3 January 1841.

Niccolò Paganini gave a recital here on 19 September 1831.

Leighlinbridge John Tyndall, scientist and authority on acoustics, was born here on 2 August 1820 and died in Hindhead, Surrey, on 4 December 1893.

CAVAN

Cavan Percy French was residing here when he wrote the words and composed the music of *Phil the Fluther's Ball* in 1889. A return visit inspired *Come Back, Paddy Reilly, to Ballyjamesduff* in 1912.

Killinkere Myles O'Reilly, composer of *King James's March to Irland*, which is now better known as *Lochaber No More*, was born here in about 1635.

CLARE

Ennis Harriet Smithson, actress, wife of Berlioz and inspiration for the *Fantastic Symphony*, was born here in 1800 and died in Montmartre, Paris, on 3 March 1854. She was buried initially in the Cimetière St Vincent, but in 1864 her body was moved to the Cimetière Montmartre, ultimately next to her husband.

CORK

Bandon William Vipond Barry, composer, pianist, organist and pupil of Liszt, was born here in March 1827 and died in Port of Spain, Trinidad, on 13 March 1872.

Nicholas Brady, who was born here on 25 October 1659 and died in Richmond, London, on 20 May 1726, wrote the verses of 'Ode on St Cecilia's Day' for Purcell in 1692 and, with Nahum Tate, the hymn 'Through All the Changing Scenes of Life'.

Blackrock Frederick Lacy, composer and educationist, was born here on 27 March 1862 and died in Cork on 31 August 1935.

Cobh Eyre Massey Shaw, Chief of London's Fire Brigade, who was immortalized in Sullivan's *Iolanthe*, was born in Ballymore in 1830.

Cork Arnold Bax, composer and Master of the King's and Queen's Music, died on 3 October 1953 at Glen House, Ballyvolane. He is buried in St Finbarr's Cemetery. He was a guest at Glen House of Aloys Fleischmann, composer, conductor and educationist, who was born in Munich in 1910.

Philip Cogan, composer and organist, among whose pupils were

Thomas Moore and Michael Kelly, was born here in 1748 and died in Dublin on 3 February 1833.

John Cummins, author of the hymn 'Jesus, Lord of Life and Glory', was born here on 5 May 1795 and died in Buckland, Surrey, on 23 November 1867.

Franz Liszt stayed at the Imperial Clarence Hotel 28 December 1840–1 January 1841. At a concert in the hotel on 28 December he played a *Lucia di Lammermoor* transcription, his transcription of the overture to *William Tell* and the *Grand Galop chromatique*. On 29 December he visited Cobh, where he had a lunch of oysters and turkey at the Navy Hotel. At a concert in the Imperial Clarence on 30 December he extemporized on Lover's *Rory O'More* and Moore's *The Last Rose of Summer* and played a *Norma* transcription. On 31 December he visited the cemetery and lunatic asylum in company with other musicians. On 1 January, he played in a third concert here.

Havelock Nelson, conductor, composer and pianist, was born here on 25 May 1917.

Niccolò Paganini gave recitals here on 23, 27 and 29 September and 1 October 1831.

Annie Patterson, writer on music, folk-song collector and composer, died here on 16 January 1934. She resided at 43 South Mall and, formerly, at Janemount Sunday's Well.

John Philip Sousa conducted his band at two concerts in the Assembly Rooms on 13 February 1911. He stayed the night at the Imperial Hotel.

Fermoy Franz Liszt, travelling from Kilkenny to Cork, had supper at The Queen's Arms on 27 December 1840. Returning to Kilkenny, he had supper again here on 1 January 1841.

Old Head of Kinsale O'Brien Butler, composer of *Muirgheis*, the first opera in Gaelic, staged in Dublin on 7 December 1903, was born in 1870 and died on 7 May 1915 when the Cunard liner *Lusitania* was torpedoed and sunk by a German submarine off Old Head of Kinsale.

DONEGAL

Conwal Stopford Brooke, author of the hymns 'It Fell upon a Summer Day', 'Let the Whole Creation Cry' and 'When the Lord of Love Was Here', was born here on 14 November 1832.

Glencolumbkille Arnold Bax, composer and Master of the King's and Queen's Music, frequently stayed here. The Fourth Symphony, in particular, is associated with Glencolumbkille. In his autobiography *Farewell, My Youth* Bax wrote: 'I like to fancy that on my deathbed my last vision in this life will be the scene from my window on the upper floor at Glencolumcille, of the still, brooding, dove-grey mystery of the Atlantic at twilight.'

Letterkenny Jean Glover, author of 'O'er the Muir amang the Heather' and wayward beauty, who, according to Burns, 'visited most of the correction-houses in the West', died here in 1801.

DOWN

Ballee Alessia Faussett, author of the hymns 'Be with Us All for Evermore' and 'O Lamb of God, That Tak'st Away', was born at Ballee Rectory on 8 January 1841 and died in Drogheda, Louth, on 30 September 1902.

Comber Herbert Kennedy Andrews, composer, organist and writer on music, was born here on 10 August 1904.

Donaghadee Franz Liszt spent his last night in Ireland, 16 January 1841, here before embarking for Scotland.

Dromore Thomas Percy, poet and antiquary, author of the song 'O Nanny, Wilt Thou Go With Me?', died here in 1811. He is buried in the cathedral.

Hillsborough Hamilton Harty, composer and conductor, was born in Main Street on 4 December 1879 and spent his childhood in the Organist's House, Ballynahinch Street. From February 1894 until November 1895 he was organist at Magheragall, 4 miles north of Hillsborough. His ashes are interred in the churchyard at Hillsborough.

Holywood Kathleen Schlesinger, music scholar, was born here on 27 June 1862 and died in London on 16 April 1953.
    Emma Toke, author of the hymns 'Glory to Thee, O Lord', 'O Lord, Thou Knowest All the Snares' and 'Thou Art Gone Up On High', was born here on 9 August 1812.

Newry Franz Liszt, travelling from Dublin to Belfast, spent the night of 14 January 1841 here.

Seapatrick Joseph Medlicott Scriven, author of the hymn 'What a Friend We Have in Jesus', was born here on 10 September 1819 and died in Bewdley, Ontario, on 10 August 1886.

DUBLIN

Dublin Cecil Frances Alexander, hymn writer, was born at 25 Eccles Street in 1818.

Michael Balfe, composer of the opera *The Bohemian Girl* (which includes the aria *I Dreamt that I Dwelt in Marble Halls*), the songs *Killarney* and *Come into the Garden, Maud* and the aria *The Light of Other Days* from the opera *The Maid of Artois*, was born at 10 Balfe Street (demolished), formerly Pitt Street, on 15 May 1808. He resided here until 1818. He was at 2 Hamilton's Row 1818–23, where he wrote his first important song, *The Lover's Mistake*, initially entitled *Young Fanny*.

Thomas Bateson, composer, was born in about 1570 and died here in 1630.

Brian Boydell, composer, conductor and educationist, was born here on 17 March 1917. He spent his earliest years at Temple House, Temple Road, Rathmines.

Charles Thomas Carter, composer of *O Nanny, Wilt Thou Go With Me?*, was born here in about 1735 and died in London on 12 October 1804.

Pietro Castucci, violinist, was born in Rome in 1679 and died here on 29 February 1752.

Thomas Cooke, composer, tenor singer, conductor and violinist, was born here in 1782 and died at his home in Great Portland Street, London, on 26 February 1848. He is buried in Kensal Green Cemetery. Among his best known songs is *Hey for the Life of a Soldier*.

Edward Denny, author of the hymns 'What Grace, O Lord, and Beauty Shone' and 'Light of the Lonely Pilgrim's Heart', was born here on 2 October 1796 and died in London on 13 June 1889.

Michèle Esposito, founder and conductor of the Dublin Orchestral Society, pianist and composer, who was born in Castellammare di Stabia, Italy, on 29 September 1855 and died in Florence on 26 November 1929, lived in Dublin for forty years. He resided at St Ronan's, Sandford Road.

John Farmer, composer of the madrigals *Fair Nymph, I Heard One Telling* and *Fair Phyllis I Saw*, was organist of Christ Church Cathedral around 1600.

John Field, composer, pianist, pupil of Clementi, teacher of Glinka, was born in Golden Lane in July 1782. He was residing with his parents in Camden Street at the time of their departure for Bath in the summer of 1793. Never returning to Ireland, he died in Moscow on 23 January 1837. He is buried in the Vedensky Cemetery.

Francesco Geminiani, composer and violinist, who was born in Lucca, Italy, in December 1687, came to Dublin in 1733. He resided for six years in Spring Gardens before leaving for London. He returned to Ireland in 1759 and died in College Green on 17 September 1762. He is buried in St Andrew's. It is said that his death was precipitated by the theft of one of his manuscripts.

Tommaso Giordani, composer, was born in Naples in about 1730 and died in Dublin in February 1806.

Alfred Percival Graves, folk-song collector, lyricist, who wrote 'Father O'Flynn' and whose verses were set by Stanford, Parry, Charles Wood and Mackenzie, was born here on 22 July 1846 and died in Harlech, Gwynned, on 27 December 1931.

Charles Graves, writer on music and author of biographies of Parry and Grove, was born here on 15 December 1856 and died in Carlisle, Cumbria, on 17 April 1944.

George Frideric Handel, at the invitation of the Duke of Devonshire, Lord Lieutenant of Ireland, arrived in Dublin on 18 November 1741. Reporting this event, Faulkner's *Dublin Journal* described him as 'a Gentleman universally known by his excellent Compositions in all Kinds of Musick'. The composer's intention was to give a series of concerts during the winter and return to London in the spring, but he eventually stayed until 13 August 1742. During his nine months' visit, he rented a house in Abbey Street. The first of the concerts, which were presented in Neale's Musick Hall in Fishamble Street, took place on 23 December. The other five concerts in the series were held on 13, 20 and 27 January, and 3 and 10 February. These excited immense enthusiasm, much in excess of anything Handel had recently experienced in London, and he therefore embarked on a second series, the concerts being given on 17 February, 2, 17, 24 and 31 March, and 7 April. By now he seemed to have been sufficiently happy with his singers' and orchestra's capabilities to bring forward the new work that had lain for four months in his house in Abbey Street. Accordingly, the following advertisement appeared on 27 March in the *Dublin Journal*.

'For Relief of the Prisoners in the several Gaols, and for the support of Mercer's Hospital in Stephen's Street, and of the Charitable Infirmary on the Inns Quay, on Monday the 12th of April, will be performed at the Musick Hall in Fishamble Street, *Mr. Handel's new Grand Oratorio, call'd the* MESSIAH, in which Gentlemen of the Choirs of both Cathedrals will assist, with some Concertoes on the Organ, by Mr. Handel.'

The six choristers from St Patrick's appeared by permission of their Dean, Jonathan Swift, who, at one stage, decided that none of his flock should take part 'as songsters, fiddlers, pipers, trumpeters, drummers, drum-majors, or in any sonal quality'. Handel is known to have called upon him and may have persuaded him to change his mind; when he was announced, Swift is said to have exclaimed: 'Oh! A *German*, and a genius! A prodigy! Admit him.'

The public rehearsal of *Messiah* on 9 April produced an over-whelming effect. The *Dublin News-Letter* declared that, 'in the opinion of the best Judges', the work 'far surpasses anything of that Nature, which has been performed in this or any other Kingdom'. The demand for tickets for the première, put back a day to 13 April, was so great that 700 tickets, instead of the usual 600, were sold; ladies were asked to come without their hoops, and the men without their swords. The performance, which began at midday, exceeded all expectation. 'Words are wanting to express the exquisite Delight it afforded to the admiring crouded Audience,' wrote the *Dublin Journal*. Handel could well have considered making his departure after this triumph, but he was clearly enjoying his stay. On 25 May he gave a further concert and on 3 June directed a second performance of *Messiah*. This concluded his music-making, but he remained for another two months in the city that had treated him so cordially. He is said to have spent many evenings at Clontarf Castle and to have visited Cork. On 12 August he appears to have seen Garrick in *Hamlet* at the Smock Alley Theatre.

He was often at his most ebullient in Dublin. It was at one of these concerts that the violinist Matthew Dubourg suddenly embarked upon a vast cadenza, roaming nomadically through distant keys, until, like Odysseus returning to Ithaka, he at last alighted on familiar ground. 'You are welcome home, Mr Dubourg!' roared Handel, to the delight of orchestra, singers, audience and perhaps even passers-by in Fishamble Street.

Felicia Hemans, whose poetry inspired songs by Gounod, Tchaikovsky and others, died at 21 Dawson Street on 16 May 1835. She is buried in St Ann's Church.

Although he was born in London and spent most of his life in England, Arnold Bax made frequent trips to Ireland, where he found inspiration for a number of his most memorable works. He died during a visit to Cork in 1953 and is buried there, in St Finbarr's Cemetery. A year earlier, he had written, 'I have known Ireland intimately for forty-five years and love her better than any land "beneath the visiting moon".' (*Bassano & Vandyk Studios*)

In the music hall that formerly stood behind this entrance in Fishamble Street, Dublin, George Frideric Handel directed the world première of *Messiah* on 13 April 1742. The oratorio was immediately acclaimed; it 'Transports the Ear, and ravishes the Heart', wrote Laurence Whyte. Eleven months later, the work received its first performance in London, exciting much less enthusiasm. 'What the English like', Handel once warned Gluck, 'is something they can beat time to, something that hits them on the drum of the ear.' (*Bord Fáilte Photo*)

The birthplace of Charles Villiers Stanford in Dublin. 'It was in Herbert Street (No 2) I was born, and all around were names of Herbert history: Wilton, Mount Merrion, Sidney and many more. . . . Dublin, as I woke to it, was a city of glaring contrasts. Grandeur and squalor lived next door to each other, squalor sometimes under the roof of grandeur. . . . Beauty was everywhere, dirt was everywhere too, trying its best to conceal it.' (*Bord Fáilte Photo*)

Victor Herbert, composer, conductor and cellist, was born here on 1 February 1859.

Katharine Hinkson, author of the hymn 'I Would Choose To Be a Doorkeeper', was born here on 23 January 1861 and died in Wimbledon, London, on 2 April 1931.

Leonard Hirsch, violinist, was born here on 19 December 1902.

Ethel Hobday, pianist, was born here on 28 November 1872.

Francis Ireland, composer, was born in Dublin on 13 August 1721 and died here in 1780.

Robert Irwin, bass singer, was born here on 20 September 1905.

John Jebb, writer on Church music, was born here in 1805 and died in Peterstow, Hereford and Worcester, on 8 January 1886.

William Henry Kearns, conductor, violinist and composer, was born here in 1794 and died in London on 28 December 1846.

Michael Kelly, tenor singer, actor and composer, the first Don Basilio and Don Curzio in *La nozze di Figaro*, friend of Mozart and Sheridan, was born in Mary Street on 25 December 1762.

Charles B. Lawlor, composer of *The Sidewalks of New York, Daisy McIntyre* and *The Irish Jubilee*, was born here in 1852 and died in New York in 1925.

Samuel Lee, violinist, music publisher and conductor, died here on 21 February 1776. Handel used him as a copyist in Dublin 1741–2.

Joseph Sheridan Le Fanu, poet and novelist, whose 'Shamus O'Brien' and 'Phaudrig Crohoore' inspired two of Stanford's finest works, was born at what is now St Mary's Chest Hospital on 23 August 1814 and died at his home, 70 Merrion Square, on 7 February 1873.

Richard Levey, composer, conductor and teacher, whose pupils included Robert Stewart and Stanford, was born in Dublin on 25 October 1811 and died here on 28 June 1899.

William Levey, composer, conductor and son of Richard Levey, was born here on 25 April 1837 and died in London on 18 August 1894.

Franz Liszt stayed at Morrison's Leinster Hotel, in Dawson Street, 17–26 December 1840, playing in three concerts at the Rotunda. On the 17th he saw Charles Kean, the son of Edmund Kean, in *Macbeth*. On 18 December he performed Weber's *Konzertstück* and his own transcription of the overture to *William Tell*; on 21 December a *Lucia di Lammermoor* transcription and the *Grand Galop chromatique*; on 23 December the *Hexaméron* and extemporizations on John Orlando Parry's *Wanted, a Governess*, an Irish folk-song and the Russian national anthem, combining all three melodies in an astonishing finale. On the 24th he had dinner with Lord Morpeth.

After a trip to Cork, he was again at Morrison's Leinster Hotel 4–8 January 1841. On the 4th he went to *Fra Diavolo* at the Theatre Royal. On the 6th he visited Trinity College, seeing its library and museum. On the 7th he played the *Grand Galop chromatique* at a concert in the Rotunda, and later in the day, again in the Rotunda, performed a Beethoven violin sonata with Joseph Rudersdorff.

After a trip to Limerick, he once more stayed at Morrison's, 12–14 January, playing in further concerts at the Rotunda on the 12th and 13th.

Samuel Lover, composer, painter and author, was born at 60 Grafton Street on 24 February 1797. Among his best known songs are *Angel's Whisper*, *The Letter*, *What Will You Do, Love?*, *The Fairy Tempter* and *Rory O'More*.

William Ludwig, baritone singer, was born here in July 1847 and died in London on 25 December 1923.

Barton M'Guckin, tenor singer, was born here on 28 July 1852 and died in Stoke Poges, Buckinghamshire, on 17 April 1913.

Thomas Moore, poet and songwriter, author of 'Believe Me, If All Those Endearing Young Charms', 'Erin, the Tear and the Smile in Thine Eyes', 'Go Where Glory Waits Thee', 'The Harp That Once through Tara's Halls', 'And Doth Not a Meeting Like This Make Amends', 'Come, Rest in This Bosom, My Own Stricken Deer', 'The Minstrel Boy to the War Is Gone', ''Tis the Last Rose of Summer', 'Oft, in the Stilly Night' and the 'Canadian Boat Song', was born on 28 May 1779 in a house that stood where 12 Aungier Street is now sited. His verses inspired works by Bantock, Berlioz, Havergal Brian, Cornelius, Hindemith, Ireland, Mackenzie, Mendelssohn, Parry, Rubinstein, Schumann, Spontini, Stanford, Warlock and Weber.

Stanley Murphy, author of the song 'Put on Your Old Grey Bonnet', was born here in 1875 and died in New York in 1919.

John Neale, music publisher, impresario and musical instrument manufacturer, died here in 1734. His son William, who carried on the family business, died here on 18 December 1769.

Vincent O'Brien, organist and composer, was born in Dublin in May 1870 and died here on 21 June 1948.

Robert O'Dwyer, composer and conductor, was born in Bristol on 27 January 1862 and died in Dublin on 6 January 1949.

Sydney Owenson, later Lady Morgan, novelist and composer, was born here in about 1783 and died in London on 14 April 1859. She is buried in Brompton Cemetery.

Niccolò Paganini arrived here on 29 August 1831 and stayed at Willis's Hotel in Westmoreland Street. He took part in concerts on 31

August and on 1, 3, 6, 10, 13, 15 and 17 September, the last six being in the Theatre Royal. He gave a farewell concert in the Rotunda on 7 October.

Annie Patterson, writer on music, folk-song collector and composer, resided at 11 Clare Street during the 1890s.

George Petrie, notable folk-song collector, was born in Dublin in 1789 and died here on 17 January 1866.

Thomas Pinto, violinist and conductor, was born in 1714 and died here in 1783.

Sergey Rakhmaninov took part in a concert here on 26 April 1938.

Frederick Ranalow, baritone singer, was born here on 7 November 1873 and died in London on 8 December 1953.

Joseph Robinson, baritone singer, conductor and composer, was born in Dublin on 20 August 1816 and died here on 23 August 1898.

William Rooke, violinist and composer, was born here on 29 September 1794 and died in Fulham, London, on 14 October 1847. He is buried in Brompton Cemetery.

Daniel Roseingrave, organist and composer, was born in about 1650 and died here in May 1727. He resided in Golden Lane and is buried at St Bride's. He was organist of both Christ Church Cathedral and St Patrick's Cathedral from 1698 until his death.

Ralph Roseingrave, organist, composer and son of Daniel Roseingrave, was born in Salisbury, Wiltshire, in about 1695 and died in Dublin in 1747. He is buried at St Patrick's Cathedral. He succeeded his father as organist of both St Patrick's and Christ Church Cathedral in 1727, holding these posts until his death.

George Bernard Shaw, dramatist, novelist and music critic, whose plays inspired music by Auric, Blitzstein, Honegger and most notably Straus's *Der Tapfere Soldat* and Frederick Loewe's *My Fair Lady*, was born on 26 July 1856 at 33 Synge Street.

Richard Brinsley Sheridan, dramatist, whose plays inspired works by Arne, Samuel Barber, Dussek, Roberto Gerhard, Giordani, Kabalevsky, Klenau, Prokofiev and Stanford, was born at 12 Upper Dorset Street, Dublin, on 30 October 1751 and died at 17 Savile Row, Mayfair, London, on 7 July 1816. He resided during his final years at 14 Savile Row and is buried in Westminster Abbey.

Dmitri Shostakovich received an honorary doctorate at Trinity College in July 1972. He stayed at the Royal Hibernian Hotel.

John Philip Sousa conducted his band at concerts in the Theatre Royal and Rotunda on 5 February 1903. He gave two further concerts, at the Rathmines Rink, on 15 February 1911. He stayed at the Shelbourne Hotel.

Charles Villiers Stanford, composer, conductor, celebrated teacher, pianist, organist and writer on music, was born at 2 Herbert Street on 30 September 1852.

Walter Starkie, literary scholar, writer and music scholar, was born here on 9 August 1894.

John Stevenson, composer, was born in Crane Lane, off Dame Street, in November 1761. He later resided in Lower Mount Street.

Robert Stewart, composer, organist and conductor, was born at 6 Balfe Street on 16 December 1825. He later resided at 61 Baggot Street, 17 Upper Merrion Street and 18 Merrion Row. He died at 40 Upper Fitzwilliam Street on 24 March 1894, and is buried in Mount Jerome Cemetery.

Johann Strauss senior led his orchestra in concerts at the Rotunda on 15 and 17 August 1838, and at the Theatre Royal on 16 and 18 August.

Igor Stravinsky was here 2–9 June 1963. Among the places he visited were Trinity College Library, Howth Castle, Joyce's martello tower at Sandycove and the National Museum.

Nahum Tate, poet and dramatist, was born here in 1652. He became Poet Laureate in 1692 and died in Southwark, London, on 12 August 1715, after taking refuge in the Mint when pursued by his creditors. He wrote the libretto of Purcell's *Dido and Aeneas*, performed in London in December 1689, the Christmas carol 'While Shepherds Watched Their Flocks by Night' and the hymns 'As Pants the Hart for Cooling Streams' and, with Nicholas Brady, 'Through All the Changing Scenes of Life'.

Michael Tippett received an honorary doctorate at Trinity College in December 1964.

Richard Chenevix Trench, theologian, author and poet, many of whose verses have been set as hymns, was born in North Frederick Street on 9 September 1807 and died in London on 28 March 1886.

Pietro Urbani, singer, music publisher, composer and friend of Robert Burns, was born in Milan in 1749 and died at his home in South Cumberland Street, Dublin, in December 1816.

Ralph Vaughan Williams received an honorary doctorate at Trinity College in 1939.

Gerard Victory, composer, was born on 24 December 1921 at 3 Sussex Road. His earliest years were spent in Victoria Street. He resided at 11 High Street (demolished) 1924–34. He was at 30 Rathfarnham Road, Terenure, 1934–48. He resided at 155 Weirview Drive, Stillorgan, 1953–64, and he then moved to 29 Lawnswood Park, Stillorgan, where *Jonathan Swift* and other notable works were written.

Joseph Wade, composer and conductor, was born here in 1801 and died on 15 July 1845 at 350 The Strand, London.

William Walton received an honorary doctorate at Trinity College in 1948.

Thomas Wharton, author of 'Lillibulero', resided here, as Lord Lieutenant of Ireland, 1709–10. He was accompanied to Dublin by Joseph Addison, man of letters, author of the hymn 'The Spacious Firmament on High', who was his Chief Secretary.

Harold White, bass singer, organist and composer, was born here on 12 January 1872.

Oscar Wilde, dramatist, poet and novelist, whose writings inspired works by Bantock, Butterworth, Castelnuovo-Tedesco, Glazunov, Griffes, Ibert, Elisabeth Lutyens, Mossolov, Richard Strauss, Tcherepnin, Vassilenko and Zemlinsky, was born on 16 October 1854 at 21 Westland Row. Shortly afterwards his family moved to 1 Merrion Square. He died on 30 November 1900 in Paris and is buried in the cemetery of Père Lachaise.

Peg Woffington, actress and singer, the subject of Charles Reade's novel, was born here in 1718 and died in 1760.

Richard Woodward, composer and organist, was born in Dublin in 1744 and died here on 22 November 1777. He is buried in Christ Church Cathedral.

William Butler Yeats, poet and dramatist, whose writings inspired works by Bantock, Samuel Barber, Berkeley, Havergal Brian, Frank Bridge, Elgar, Gurney, Patrick Hadley, Lou Harrison, Ireland, Loeffler, Maconchy, Swain and Warlock, was born at 5 Sandymount Avenue on 13 June 1865. He later resided at 82 Merrion Square and 42 Fitzwilliam Square, and died at his home, Riversdale, Rathfarnham, on 28 January 1939. He is buried in Drumcliff, Sligo.

Dundrum Charles Manners, bass singer and opera impresario, was born in London on 27 December 1857 and died in Dundrum on 3 May 1935 at The Hermitage.

Fanny Moody, soprano singer, opera impresario and wife of Charles Manners, died here on 21 July 1945.

Dun Laoghaire Edward Burroughs, author of the hymn 'Lord God, from Whom All Life', was born here on 1 October 1882 and died in Ripon, North Yorkshire, on 13 August 1934.

Cecilia Caddell, author of the hymn 'It Is Finished! He Hath Seen', was born in 1813 and died here on 11 September 1877.

Jimmy Glover, conductor and composer, was born here on 18 June 1861 and died in Hastings on 8 September 1931.

Thomas Roseingrave, organist, composer and son of Daniel Roseingrave, was born in Winchester in 1690 and died in Dun Laoghaire on 23 June 1766. He is buried at St Patrick's in the same grave as his brother Ralph.

Monkstown Malcolm Arnold, composer, resided during the middle of the 1970s at Meadowcroft, The Hill.

Rathmines George Torrance, organist and composer, was born here in 1835 and died in Kilkenny on 20 August 1907.

Richmond Michael Arne, son of Thomas Arne and composer of *The Lass with the Delicate Air, Sweet Poll of Plymouth,* and *The Highland Laddie,* was born in London in about 1740 and died in Lambeth on 14 January 1786. He resided in Richmond, Dublin, in 1777, when, foreshadowing the extramusical experiments of Elgar, he engaged in chemical research that failed to produce gold, but reduced him to bankruptcy, thus repeating his equally fruitless and ruinous attempt ten years earlier to discover the philosopher's stone in his laboratory in Chelsea, London.

Skerries Percy French wrote 'The Mountains of Mourne' here in the summer of 1896, inspired by the view northwards from the nearby cliffs. A monument in Newcastle, Down, some 45 miles away, commemorates the event.

FERMANAGH

Enniskillen Joan Trimble, pianist and composer, was born here on 18 June 1915.

Valerie Trimble, pianist and cellist, sister of Joan Trimble, was born here on 20 August 1917 and died on 16 November 1980. Arthur Benjamin wrote *Jamaican Rumba* as a piano duet for them in 1949.

GALWAY

Ballygar Patrick S. Gilmore, composer and bandmaster, was born here on 25 December 1829 and died in St Louis, Missouri, on 24 September 1892. His most famous work, *When Johnny Comes Marching Home,* was written in 1863.

Galway Emily Anderson, music scholar and translator, was born here on 17 March 1891.

James Power, music publisher, at whose suggestion Thomas Moore produced his *Irish Melodies*, was born here in 1766 and died in London on 26 August 1836.

Leenaun William How, author of many familiar hymns, including 'For All the Saints, Who from Their Labours Rest', died at Dhulough Lodge on 10 August 1897.

KERRY

Kenmare Ernest Moeran, composer, drew inspiration from the Kerry countryside and often stayed here, when he resided at The Lodge. He died here on 1 December 1950, his body being discovered in the River Kenmare.

Killarney Niccolò Paganini visited the Lakes of Killarney on 28 September 1831.

Tralee Arthur O'Leary, composer and pianist, was born here on 15 March 1834.

KILDARE

Kilcullen Franz Liszt, travelling from Dublin to Kilkenny, had luncheon here on 26 December 1840.

Kildare Charles Ancliffe, composer of the waltz *Nights of Gladness*, was born here in 1880 and died in 1952.

Monasterevin Franz Liszt, travelling from Dublin to Limerick, had luncheon at Fleming's Hotel on 8 January 1841. Returning from Limerick on 12 January, he again had luncheon here.

John McCormack, tenor singer, resided for many years in Moore Abbey, now a Sisters of Charity hospital.

Naas Franz Liszt, travelling from Kilkenny to Dublin, had tea here on the afternoon of 3 January 1841.

KILKENNY

Kilkenny James Theobald Bagot Butler, composer, was born here on 24 August 1852 and died in Bournemouth on 16 June 1929.

Franz Liszt, travelling from Dublin to Cork, stayed at the Hibernian Hotel on the night of 26 December 1840. Returning to Dublin, he again stayed here on the night of 2 January 1841.

Niccolò Paganini gave a recital here in the Tholsel on 20 September 1831.

LAOIS

Stradbally Thomas Kelly, author of the hymns 'We Sing the Praise of Him Who Died' and 'The Head That Once Was Crowned With Thorns', was born here on 13 July 1769 and died in Dublin on 14 May 1855.

LEITRIM

Mohill Turlough O'Carolan, renowned harpist and composer, resided here for much of his life.

LIMERICK

Ballyorgan Patrick Weston Joyce, folk-song collector, was born here in 1827.

Limerick Michael Balfe, composer, conducted his opera *Diadeste* in the Old Theatre at the Quay in 1839. The building was so dilapidated and the evening so wet that the audience kept up their umbrellas throughout the performance.

Catherine Hayes, soprano singer, was born here on 25 October 1825 and died in London on 11 August 1861.

Franz Liszt stayed at the Royal Mail Hotel 9–12 January 1841. On the 9th he played at a concert in Swinburne's Great Rooms and had dinner at the home of the Police General, Mr Vaux, with whom he again dined on the 10th. On the 11th he took part in a second concert in Swinburne's Great Rooms.

Joseph O'Mara, tenor singer, was born here on 16 July 1866 and died on 5 August 1927.

George Alexander Osborne, pianist and composer, friend of Berlioz and Chopin, was born here on 24 September 1806 and died in London on 16 November 1893.

Niccolò Paganini gave recitals in Swinburne's Great Rooms on 3 and 5 October 1831. During the first of these, part of the floor collapsed, and several of the audience fell into the room below. Nobody was badly hurt, and, after the injured had been treated, Paganini, who had been extremely close to the disaster area, continued his programme.

John Philip Sousa conducted his band at two concerts in the Theatre Royal on 14 February 1911. He stayed the night at Cruise's Royal Hotel.

Rathkeale Robert Quaile, composer, was born here on 22 March 1867 and died in Mallow, Cork, on 26 July 1927.

LONDONDERRY

Craiggore Denis Hempson, blind bard and harpist, who lived in three centuries, was born here in 1695 and died in Magilligan in 1807.

Londonderry Cecil Frances Alexander, hymn writer, lived in the Bishop's Palace from 1867 until her death here on 12 October 1895. She wrote 'I Bind Unto Myself Today' in 1889.

John Monsell, author of the hymns 'O Worship the Lord in the Beauty of Holiness' and 'Fight the Good Fight with All Thy Might', was born at St Columb's on 2 March 1811.

John Philip Sousa conducted his band at a concert in St Columb's Hall on 17 February 1911.

Magherafelt Charles Dent Bell, author of the hymn 'Be with Us, Gracious Lord, To-day', was born here on 10 February 1818 and died in Westminster, London, on 11 November 1898.

Portstewart Edward Hay, composer and organist, died here on 10 September 1943.

LOUTH

Drogheda Franz Liszt, travelling from Dublin to Belfast, had afternoon tea here on 14 January 1841.

MAYO

Castlebar Margaret Sheridan, soprano singer, was born here on 15 October 1889 and died in Dublin on 16 April 1958.

MEATH

Aclare Richard Singleton, author of the hymns 'The Cross Upraised on Calvary's Height' and 'When Fairest Eve in Eden Rose', was born here on 9 October 1810 and died in York on 7 February 1881.

Ceanannus Mor (Kells) John Stevenson, composer, died at Headfort House on 14 September 1833. He is buried in the Lambart vault of St Mary's Church, Painstown, near Beau Park.

Dangan Garrett Colley Wellesley, Earl of Mornington, composer, music scholar, father of the Duke of Wellington, was born at Dangan Castle on 19 July 1735 and died in London on 22 May 1781. His son's defeat of the French at Vittoria in June 1813 occasioned Beethoven's *Battle Symphony*.

Nobber Turlough O'Carolan, renowned harpist and composer of *Bridget Cruise, Liquor of Life, O'Rourke's Noble Feast, Planxty Jones* (now better known as *Bumper Squire Jones*), *Savourna Deelish* and possibly *The Star Spangled Banner*, was born in Newtown in 1670.

MONAGHAN

Derrylusk Richard Pockrich, virtuoso on the musical glasses, inventor, agrologist and propounder of the theory of blood transfusion, was born here in about 1690 and died in a fire at the Royal Exchange, London, in 1759.

Newbliss Tyrone Guthrie, theatre and opera director, died at his home, Annagh-ma-Kerrig, Doohat, on 15 May 1971.

OFFALY

Birr Henry George Farmer, music scholar, was born here on 17 January 1882 and died in Glasgow on 30 December 1965.

Clonmacnoise Igor Stravinsky visited the ruins in early June 1963, having come by car from Dublin via Athlone. He also went to Clonony and returned to the capital via Kildare.

Cornolore James Molloy, composer of *Love's Old Sweet Song, Darby and Joan,* and *The Kerry Dance,* was born here in 1837 and died in Henley-on-Thames in 1909.

ROSCOMMON

Ballyfarnon Turlough O'Carolan, renowned harpist and composer, died at Alderford House on 25 March 1738, having resided during his final years in Keadow. He is buried in Kilronan Church. His harp is exhibited in Clonalis House, Castlerea.

Cloonkeen Percy French, author of 'The Mountains of Mourne' and composer and author of *Abdulla Bulbul Ameer, Phil the Fluther's Ball* and *Come Back, Paddy Reilly, to Ballyjamesduff,* was born at Cloonyquin House (demolished) on 1 May 1854.

TIPPERARY

Caher Allan Foley, bass singer, was born here on 7 August 1835 and died in Southport, Merseyside, on 20 October 1899.

Clonmel Franz Liszt, travelling from Kilkenny to Cork, had luncheon in the Commercial Room on 27 December 1840. He returned on 2 January 1841, intending to take part in a concert in the Court House, but not a single ticket had been sold. He therefore invited a few music lovers to his hotel, where he and the other members of his concert party went through their entire programme. He used the modest hotel piano: 'So funny to see Liszt firing away at Guillaume Tell on this little Instrument,' wrote John Orlando Parry, 'but it stood his powerful hand capitally.'

While in the town of Laurence Sterne's birth, the composer may have visited the home of his friend Lady Blessington, one of the most beautiful women of her day. A secluded stretch of the River Suir at Clonmel is known as 'Lady Blessington's Bath', where she used to bathe.

Maud MacCarthy, violinist, wife of John Foulds, was born here on 4 July 1884.

Niccolò Paganini gave a recital here on 21 September 1831.

Henry Tull Rhoades, author of the hymn 'Thou, Whose Unseen Servants Stand', was born here on 17 May 1837 and died in Rugby, Warwickshire, on 8 June 1922.

Roscrea Franz Liszt, travelling from Dublin to Limerick, had supper here on 8 January 1841. Returning from Limerick, he had breakfast here on 12 January.

Thurles William Vincent Wallace was organist of the Roman Catholic cathedral in 1830.

TYRONE

Castlederg Cecil Frances Alexander, hymn writer, lived at Derg Lodge, Trienamongan, 1850–5, during which time she wrote 'The Eternal Gates Lift Up Their Heads', 'Jesus Calls Us; o'er the Tumult' and 'The Roseate Hues of Early Dawn'.

Strabane Cecil Frances Alexander, hymn writer, lived at Milltown House, which has since become a school, 1833–50, during which time she wrote 'There Is a Green Hill Far Away', 'Once in Royal David's City', 'All Things Bright and Beautiful', 'Do No Sinful Action' and 'We Are But Little Children Weak'. She lived at Camus Rectory, 3 miles south of Strabane, 1860–7.

WATERFORD

Lismore William Henry Gratton Flood, writer on music, was born here on 1 November 1859.

Waterford George Caldbeck, composer of the hymn tune *Pax Tecum*, often sung to 'Peace, Perfect Peace, in This Dark World of Sin?', was born here in 1852.

Charles Clagget, violinist and inventor of musical instruments, was born here in 1740 and died in about 1795. His improvements to the harpsichord and piano won the regard of Haydn. He invented a double guitar of eighteen strings. His 'chromatic trumpet and french horn' anticipated by some twenty-five years the perfecting of the valve action for brass instruments.

Niccolò Paganini gave a recital in the Assembly Rooms on 22 September 1831.

William Vincent Wallace, composer of the operas *Maritana* and *Lurline*, freebooter, world traveller, absconder, bigamist, friend of Rossini and Berlioz, was born here on 11 March 1812 and died in the Château de Haget, near Tarbes, France, on 12 October 1865. He is buried in Kensal Green Cemetery, London.

WESTMEATH

Athlone John McCormack, tenor singer, was born in Bawn, off Mardyke Street, on 14 June 1884 and died in Dublin on 16 September 1945.

Collinstown Denis Ap Ivor, composer, was born here on 14 April 1916.

Mullingar Wellington Guernsey, poet and composer, was born here on 8 June 1817 and died in London on 13 November 1885.

WEXFORD

Enniscorthy William Henry Gratton Flood, writer on music, died on 6 August 1928. He resided here at Rosemount.

Taghmon Francis Henry Lyte, author of the hymn 'Abide with Me', was curate here in 1816. He stayed with the Hore family at Pole Hore in 1820 and visited his dying friend William Augustus Le Hunte.

Wexford Thomas Moore, poet and songwriter, stayed in the Cornmarket in 1851. A plaque marks his place of residence.

WICKLOW

Avoca Thomas Moore, poet and songwriter, is said to have written 'The Meeting of the Waters' in the Vale of Avoca, at the confluence of the Avonmore and Avonbeg, near Lion Bridge. A monument marks the precise spot.

Bray Harry Plunket Greene, bass-baritone singer, biographer of

Stanford and soloist in the first performances of Stanford's *Songs of the Sea* and *Songs of the Fleet* and Elgar's *The Dream of Gerontius*, was born at Old Connaught House on 24 June 1865.

Hamilton Harty, composer and conductor, was organist of Christ Church 1896–1901.

Enniskerry Ina Boyle, composer of the hymn tune *Enniskerry*, sung to 'Service and Strength, God's Angels and Archangels', was born here in 1889.

Caroline Oliphant, Baroness Nairne, author of numerous well-known Scottish songs, resided here 1831–4.

Hollybrook Robin Adair, immortalized by the verses of his wife, Lady Caroline Keppel, was born here in about 1735.

GREATER LONDON

Acton Myles Birket Foster, organist, composer and writer on music, was born in London on 29 November 1851 and died here on 18 December 1922. He resided at 14 Woodstock Road.

Kate Moss, soprano singer and composer of *The Floral Dance*, who was born in London in 1881, resided during the 1930s at 18 Churchfield Road East.

Ivor Novello, composer, dramatist, singer and actor, having somewhat naïvely committed an offence against the Motor Vehicles Order of 1942, resided 16 May–12 June 1944 in Cell 242, B Hall, Wormwood Scrubs Prison, where he helped design a new theatre stage and conducted the prison choir and orchestra.

Michael Tippett, composer, upholding his pacificist beliefs, resided here as Prisoner 5832, during June, July and August 1943, also taking on the duties of conductor. Ralph Vaughan Williams spoke on Tippett's behalf during the trial in Oxted, Surrey.

Barnes Arthur Bliss, composer and Master of the Queen's Music, was born in Queen's Ride on 2 August 1891.

Gustav Holst, composer, resided at 10 Barnes Terrace 1908–13, during which time he wrote the *Beni Mora Suite* and *St Paul's Suite*. Ralph Vaughan Williams was a frequent visitor here. He came to see the Boat Race from the verandah on 2 April 1909.

Malcolm Williamson, composer, pianist, organist and Master of the Queen's Music, who was born in Sydney, Australia, on 21 November 1931, resided at 32 Hertford Avenue during the 1970s.

Battersea Noël Coward, dramatist, actor, writer, composer, director and singer, resided at 70 Prince of Wales Mansions 1908–13.

Bayswater Benjamin Britten, composer, resided in 1930 at 51 Princes Square.

Edward Dannreuther, pianist and writer on music, who was born in Strasbourg, France, on 4 November 1844 and died in Hastings, East Sussex, on 12 February 1905, resided at 12 Orme Square (demolished) during the 1870s and '80s. He gave the first British performances of Liszt's Second Piano Concerto, Grieg's Piano Concerto and Tchaikovsky's First Piano Concerto.

Richard and Cosima Wagner stayed with him 1 May–4 June 1877. Wagner and Hans Richter shared the conducting of eight concerts of the composer's music that took place at the Albert Hall on 7, 9, 12, 14, 16, 19, 28 and 29 May. Undertaken to repair the desperate financial situation at Bayreuth after the previous year's inaugural *Ring* cycles, the concerts were a commercial failure. 'All is lost save honour!' were Wagner's parting words to English admirers, as the boat-train pulled out of Victoria on 4 June.

Hubert Parry was a visitor on 2 and 5 May. His diary for 5 May records that Wagner 'was in great fettle, and talked to an open-mouthed group in brilliant fashion'. Cosima's diary states: 'R. annoyed at the visitors.' On 17 May, the guests included Parry and George Eliot, to whom Wagner read his recently completed *Parsifal* libretto. 'A day to have lived for,' noted Parry, who again called at Orme Square on 20 and 23 May. He was among those who saluted the Master at Victoria.

The Wagners went to a performance of *Richard III* on 10 May, to the Cannon Street Hotel for Wagner's sixty-fourth birthday party on 22 May and, on 25 May, to a fish dinner at Greenwich. Cosima's diary records: 'Return home by steamer . . . R. says, "This is Alberich's dream come true—Nibelheim, world dominion, activity, work, everywhere the oppressive feeling of steam and fog."' On 26 May they visited the Tower of London. On 2 June they attended the Caxton Quatercentennial service at Westminster Abbey, hearing Mendelssohn's Second Symphony, written for the Gutenberg Quatercentennial celebrations in Leipzig in 1840—'as much out of place' in Westminster Abbey, wrote Cosima, 'as all the monuments'. Their last full day included a trip to Hampton Court and Richmond.

Prosper Sainton, solo violinist to Queen Victoria, resided at 71 Gloucester Terrace (then 71 Gloucester Place) from the 1870s until his death here on 17 October 1890.

Charlotte Sainton-Dalby, wife of Prosper Sainton, contralto singer and composer, to whom Mendelssohn dedicated his *Six Songs*, Op 57, was born in London on 17 May 1821 and died at 71 Gloucester Terrace on 18 February 1885.

Richard and Cosima Wagner dined with them here on 6 May 1877.

Edith Sitwell, poet, resided 1914–32 at 22 Pembridge Mansions, Moscow Road, where *Façade* was written in 1921. William Walton was a visitor here.

Beckenham Arthur Hinton, composer, was born here on 20 November 1869 and died in Rottingdean, East Sussex, on 11 August 1941.

Alexander Hyatt King, librarian and writer on music, was born here on 18 July 1911.

Belgravia Henry Fothergill Chorley, music critic, man of letters, librettist and friend of Dickens, resided at 15 West Eaton Place from 1852 until his death here on 16 February 1872. He is buried in Brompton Cemetery.

Dickens, Nathaniel Hawthorne, Arthur Sullivan, Pauline Viardot and Michael Costa visited him here.

Michael Costa, conductor and composer, resided for most of the 1850s at 7 Eccleston Square. He moved to 59 Eccleston Square in 1858 and remained there until his death in Hove, East Sussex, in 1884.

Richard Wagner visited him at 7 Eccleston Square in March 1855.

Arthur Sullivan and Charles Villiers Stanford visited him at 59 Eccleston Square.

Noël Coward, dramatist, actor, writer, composer, director and singer, resided intermittently at 17 Gerald Road 1931–55.

Nicholas Danby, organist, was born in Chester Square on 19 July 1935.

Judy Garland, popular singer, died at 4 Cadogan Lane on 22 June 1969.

William Schwenck Gilbert, librettist, poet, cartoonist and dramatist, resided, when in London, at 4 Grosvenor Crescent, during the early 1900s and at 90 Eaton Square 1906–11.

Adelaide Kemble, soprano singer and novelist, resided at 99 Eaton Place during the 1840s.

Frédéric Chopin gave his first public piano recital in Britain here on 23 June 1848. 'I had a select audience of 150 at one guinea, as I did not want to crowd the rooms. All the tickets were sold the day beforehand.' The impresario Willert Beale recalled: 'In a drawing-room he was to all a delight to hear, but in a larger space, before a more numerous audience, it gave more pain than pleasure. His appearance was so attenuated and his touch so enfeebled by long suffering.'

Charles Lockhart was born in London in 1745 and died in Lambeth on 9 February 1815. He was organist at the Lock Hospital, Hyde Park

Corner, in 1769, when he composed the hymn tune *Carlisle*, sung to both 'Breathe on Me, Breath of God' and 'Teach Me, My God and King'.

Mrs Mary Ronalds, who was Arthur Sullivan's closest friend over the last twenty years of his life, resided at 7 Cadogan Place during that period. Henry Wood, a frequent visitor, wrote: 'At her house . . . every artist of the day was to be seen; indeed, it was a *rendezvous* for musicians of every nationality.' She herself was an excellent singer and, for one of the first records to be made in Britain, sang *The Lost Chord*, the original manuscript of which was buried with her in Brompton Cemetery in 1916.

William Walton, composer, resided intermittently, from the late 1930s to 1948, at 56A South Eaton Place. *Scapino* was completed here on 28 December 1940. He stayed, 1948–59, when on infrequent visits to London from Ischia, Italy, at Lowndes Cottage, Lyall Mews.

Bethnal Green Charles Craig, tenor singer, was born in Mansfield Street on 3 December 1919.

Bexley Joseph Warren, pianist, organist and writer on music, was born in London on 20 March 1804 and died in Bexley on 8 March 1881.

Blackheath Walter Willson Cobbett, patron of music and lexicographer, was born here on 11 July 1847 and died on 22 January 1937 in London, where he resided at 34 Avenue Road, Regent's Park.

Alan Dickinson, writer on music, was born here on 9 July 1899.

Charles Gounod stayed at 15 Morden Road during the last two weeks of September 1870. He was here again 27 May–8 June 1874.

Boyd Neel, conductor, was born here on 19 July 1905.

Niccolò Paganini gave a recital here on 25 April 1834.

Bloomsbury Désirée Artôt stayed at 21 Beaumont Place in June 1859.

John Barbirolli, conductor, was born on 2 December 1899 at 12 Southampton Row. He resided later at 37 Drury Lane, 17 Granville Street, 46 Marchmont Street and 2 Woburn Court.

William Sterndale Bennett, composer, pianist and conductor, resided on the first floor of Portland Chambers, 75 (later 93) Great Titchfield Street 1838–42; at 42 (later 92) Upper Charlotte Street (between Tottenham Street and Howland Street) 1842–5; and at 15 (later 19) Russell Place (now Fitzroy Street) 1845–59.

Mendelssohn visited him at Portland Chambers in September 1840, at Upper Charlotte Street in June and July 1842, and at Russell Place in August 1846 and May 1847.

Ferdinand David visited him at Portland Chambers.

Spohr, Moscheles, Thalberg, Ernst, Hallé, and Dreyschock visited him at Upper Charlotte Street.

Clara Schumann stayed at Russell Place in April 1856.

Arthur Sullivan came to dinner at Russell Place on several occasions in 1858.

Enrico Bevignani, conductor of the first performances in London of *Aida* (1876), *La Gioconda* (1883) and *Pagliacci* (1893), who was born in Naples on 29 September 1841 and died there on 29 August 1903, resided at 25 Upper Bedford Place (demolished; see p 56) during the 1880s.

Charles Gounod stayed at Tavistock House (demolished), once the home of Charles Dickens, 19 June 1871–27 May 1874. His hostess was the singer Georgina Weldon, with whom he shared a tumultuous, if virtuous, relationship that at times included their wrestling on the floor for possession of a score that he threatened to burn, his purchase of a revolver and his nocturnal ramblings in his nightshirt when he would emit unearthly cries. The most popular work to emerge from this boisterous sojourn was *Funeral March of a Marionette*, parodying the ungainly critic Chorley.

Constant Lambert, composer, conductor and writer on music, resided during the early 1930s at 15 Percy Street, previously occupied by Charles Laughton and Elsa Lanchester.

Elisabeth Lutyens, composer, daughter of Edwin Lutyens, wife of the distinguished conductor and champion of new music Edward Clark, was born at 29 Bloomsbury Square on 9 July 1906.

Alexander Mackenzie, composer and conductor, died in London on 28 April 1935. Eric Coates, who had been his pupil at the Royal Academy of Music, used to visit him at his home, 20 Taviton Street.

Gustav Mahler was in London, on his only trip to the British Isles, 26 May–23 July 1892. He conducted eighteen performances of opera, including two cycles of *The Ring, Tristan and Isolde, Tannhäuser* and *Fidelio*. He stayed initially in Keyser's Royal Hotel (demolished), 69 Torrington Square, and then moved to rooms at 22 Alfred Place (demolished). Prior to his visit, he made a determined effort to learn English, giving particular attention to words and expressions that could be useful in the theatres, Covent Garden and Drury Lane, at which he was to conduct. As a result, he impressed everybody by his command of the language; 'his efforts to speak English, even with those who spoke German fluently,' observed Herman Klein, 'were untiring as well as amusing, though they tended to prolong conversation.' Klein found him 'extraordinarily modest for a musician of his rare gifts and established reputation. He would never consent to talk about himself or his compositions. Indeed the latter might have been non-existent for all that one ever heard about them.'

Paul Dukas was in England at the time and recalled: 'One of the most wonderful musical memories of my life is of a performance of *Fidelio* in London, in the course of which he [Mahler] conducted the *Leonora* Overture No 3, interpreting Beethoven's genius so marvellously that I had the feeling of being present at the original production of this sublime work.'

Lionel Monckton, composer of *The Arcadians* and other operettas, husband of glamorous 'Gaiety Girl' Gertie Millar, was born in London on 18 December 1861 and died here on 15 February 1924. He resided at 69 Russell Square.

Edgar Allan Poe, man of letters, whose writings inspired works by Holbrooke, Ireland, Miaskovsky, Rakhmaninov, Schmitt and Tcherepnin, resided at 47 Southampton Row during 1815.

Christina Rossetti, poet, resided at 30 Torrington Square from 1876 until her death on 29 December 1894. Here she wrote the carol 'Love Came Down at Christmas', published in 1885. 'In the Bleak Mid-Winter' was written at her previous home, 56 Euston Square. Her poems have inspired works by Mackenzie, Parry, Elgar, Vaughan Williams, Ireland, Maconchy and Milhaud.

Johann Peter Salomon, violinist, conductor, impresario and composer, who was responsible for bringing Haydn to London and for commissioning his last twelve symphonies, was born in Bonn, in the same house as Beethoven, in January 1745 and died at his home, 70 Newman Street, London, on 28 November 1815. He is buried in Westminster Abbey.

George Smart, composer, conductor and organist, died at his home, 12 Bedford Square, on 23 February 1867. Arthur Sullivan visited him here. He is buried in Kensal Green Cemetery.

Richard and Cosima Wagner were guests of Maximilian Schlesinger at 25 Upper Bedford Place (later 25 Bedford Way, demolished during World War II) on 4 May, 27 May and 2 June 1877. At dinner on 4 May they met Robert Browning.

Brixton Frederick Bevan, composer of the songs *The Flight of Ages* and *The Admiral's Broom*, who was born in London on 3 July 1856 and died in Adelaide, Australia, in 1935, resided at 21 Bonham Road during the 1890s.

William Havergal Brian, composer, resided at 63 Stockwell Park Road during January and February 1914.

Camden Town John Baptiste Calkin, composer of the hymn tune *St John Baptist*, sung to 'Lift Up Your Heads, Ye Gates of Brass', was organist of St Thomas's 1870–84. He was born in London on 16 March 1827 and died here on 15 May 1905.

Edward Holmes, writer and organist, friend of Keats, Shelley, Lamb, Berlioz, Mendelssohn and Liszt, distinguished biographer of Mozart, and described by Leigh Hunt as 'the best musical critic which this nation has produced', was born in 1797 and died on 28 August 1859 at 65 Albert Street.

Cheam William Rockstro, pianist, writer on music and pupil of Mendelssohn, was born here on 5 January 1823 and died in London on 2 July 1895.

Chelsea Richard Addinsell, composer, was born in London on 13 January 1904 and died on 14 November 1977. He resided at 1 Carlyle Mansions, Cheyne Walk. His distinguished film music includes scores for *Goodbye, Mr Chips, Blithe Spirit, The Prince and the Showgirl, The Waltz of the Toreadors* and most notably, in 1941, *Dangerous Moonlight*, which introduced his *Warsaw Concerto*, played by Louis Kentner with the London Symphony Orchestra conducted by Muir Mathieson.

Thomas Attwood, composer, organist, pupil of Mozart, friend of Mendelssohn, died at 17 Cheyne Walk on 24 March 1838. He is buried in St Paul's.

Béla Bartók was a frequent visitor in March 1922, and May and November 1923 to the home of the violinist Adila Fachiri at 10 Netherton Grove.

Leoš Janáček came to her home on 1 May 1926 for a rehearsal of his Violin Sonata.

Thomas Carlyle, man of letters, resided at 24 Cheyne Row from 1834 until his death in 1881.

Frédéric Chopin visited him here in the summer of 1848. Jane Welsh Carlyle wrote to her friend Jane Stirling: 'Oh, how I wish he understood English! How I wish I could open my heart to him!'

Jelly d'Arányi, violinist, resided at 18 Elm Park Gardens during the 1920s.

Béla Bartók frequently visited her in March 1922. At a concert in the Aeolian Hall on 24 March they gave the world première of his First Violin Sonata. On 7 May 1923 they gave the world première of his Second Violin Sonata at a concert in Queen's Square. He returned to London in November 1923 to take part in further concerts, and again in October 1927 to broadcast the first British performance of his First Piano Concerto. On 6 January 1930, with Joseph Szigeti, he broadcast the British première of his Second Rhapsody and on 14 February 1930 played the First Piano Concerto at the Queen's Hall with Henry Wood.

At the end of his 1923 visit he took home a large quantity of bananas, since he had a particular love of them, and they were scarce in Hungary.

Edward Elgar, composer and Master of the King's Music, frequently visited Alice Stuart-Wortley, daughter of Millais, at her home at 7 Cheyne Walk. Hers is believed to be 'the soul' enshrined in Elgar's Violin Concerto.

Gabriel Fauré stayed in March 1908 with John Singer Sargent at 31 Tite Street, which Whistler had owned in the early 1880s.

Percy Grainger frequently called at 31 Tite Street and met Fauré for the first time during the latter's visit. '*Il a beaucoup de flamme*,' Fauré told Sargent, after looking through some of Grainger's compositions. It is believed that Grainger also met Delius for the first time here, in April 1907.

Percy Grainger resided briefly around 1902 at 26 Coulson Street. He was at 63 Oakley Street in 1903; at 14 Upper Cheyne Row 1905–7; and at 31A King's Road 1908–14.

John Ireland, composer, made 14 Gunter Grove his London residence 1908–53. He was organist of St Luke's, Chelsea, 1904–26, during which time he composed the hymn tune *Love Unknown*, sung to 'My Song Is Love Unknown'.

Henry Lahee, composer of the hymn tune *Nativity*, sung to 'O for a Thousand Tongues To Sing', was born in Cheyne Walk on 11 April 1826 and died in Croydon on 29 April 1912.

Constant Lambert, composer, conductor and writer on music, spent most of his childhood at 25 Glebe Place. Some years later in 1926–7, he was at 59 Oakley Street, where he wrote *The Rio Grande*.

Basil Nevison, cellist, characterized in the twelfth variation of the *Enigma Variations*, resided at 3 Tedworth Square. Edward Elgar and

John Ireland first met here.

James Robinson Planché, librettist of *Oberon*, was born in London on 27 February 1796 and died at his home, 10 St Leonard's Terrace, on 29 May 1880.

Dante Gabriel Rossetti, poet and painter, who was born in Hallam Street, St Marylebone, on 12 May 1828 and died at the bungalow 'Westcliff', Birchington, Kent, on 9 April 1882 and whose verses inspired works by Bantock, Bax, Debussy, Elgar, Ireland and Vaughan Williams, resided at 16 Cheyne Walk from 1862 until shortly before his death.

Percy Grainger had his first sexual experience in this house in 1902 with its occupant, his patron Mrs Lowrey. He was 20, and she was somewhat older. Other visitors included Roger Quilter and Cyril Scott.

Osbert Sitwell, man of letters, compiler of the text of William Walton's *Belshazzar's Feast*, author of the text of Elisabeth Lutyens's *Winter the Huntsman*, who was born at 3 Arlington Street, St James's, on 6 December 1892 and died at Castello di Montegufoni, Montagnana, Italy, on 4 May 1969, resided intermittently at 2 Carlyle Square 1919–63.

Sacheverell Sitwell, man of letters, writer on music, librettist of Lord Berners's ballet *The Triumphs of Neptune*, author of the text of Constant Lambert's *The Rio Grande*, who was born at Wood End, Scarborough, on 15 November 1897, resided here intermittently 1919–25.

William Walton, composer, resided here intermittently 1919–32. Works associated with this period include *Façade*, first performed on 24 January 1922 at 2 Carlyle Square, with Edith Sitwell as reciter and Walton conducting, *Portsmouth Point, Siesta*, the *Sinfonia Concertante*, dedicated to the three Sitwells, the Viola Concerto and *Belshazzar's Feast*.

George Gershwin, Constant Lambert, Peter Warlock and writers such as Aldous Huxley and T. S. Eliot were visitors here.

Arthur Sullivan, composer and conductor, boarded, during his years as a chorister of the Chapel Royal, with Thomas Helmore at 6 Cheyne Walk.

Karol Szymanowski first visited London in June and July 1914, staying initially in Belsize Park and thereafter at 19 Edith Grove, the home of Paul and Muriel Draper.

Igor Stravinsky came to dinner at 19 Edith Grove while Szymanowski was here. Others who were guests during his stay include Eugène Ysaye, Pau Casals, Artur Rubinstein and Fyodor Shalyapin.

Ralph Vaughan Williams, composer, resided at 13 Cheyne Walk (demolished) 1905–29. Works dating from this period include his arrangement of the melody for 'He Who Would Valiant Be', the *English Folk Songs Suite, Fantasia on a Theme by Tallis, Flos campi, Hugh the Drover*, the hymn tunes *Down Ampney*, sung to 'Come Down, O Love Divine' and *Sine nomine*, sung to 'For All the Saints Who from Their Labours Rest', *The Lark Ascending, Old King Cole, O Clap Your Hands, Five Mystical Songs, The Wasps, Three Preludes on Welsh Hymn Tunes, Fantasia on Christmas Carols, Salve festa dies, Sir John in Love* and Symphonies Nos 1, 2 and 3.

Maurice Ravel, with whom Vaughan Williams had studied in Paris in 1908, stayed with him in Cheyne Walk in April 1909. After his visit, Ravel wrote to Adeline Vaughan Williams: 'Here I am, once again a Parisian; but a Parisian homesick for London. I have never previously really missed another country.' During his stay, a chamber concert was given, on 26 April at the Bechstein Hall, comprising his own works and those of Florent Schmitt, who was also in London. Ravel was again Vaughan Williams's guest in 1911.

Gustav Holst, Ivor Gurney, George Butterworth, Arthur Bliss and Isadora Duncan were among other visitors here.

Peter Warlock, composer and writer on music, resided at 14 Whiteheads Grove in 1916. During 1923 he was at 125 Cheyne Walk. He died in a gas-filled room at 12A Tite Street on 17 December 1930.

Chingford Barry Rose, organist, conductor and composer, was born here in 1934.

Kaikhosru Shapurji Sorabji, composer, pianist and writer on music, was born here on 14 August 1892.

Chislehurst Rollo Myers, writer on music, was born here on 23 January 1892.

Józef Poniatowski, Prince of Monte Rotondo, composer, was born in Rome on 20 February 1816 and died in Chislehurst, on 8 July 1873, where he resided.

Arthur Sullivan, composer and conductor, was a frequent visitor to Camden Place, Camden Park, the home of Empress Eugénie of France during the 1870s.

Chiswick Frank Bridge, composer and conductor, was living at 23 Foster Road during the period in which he wrote his tone poem *Summer, Lament* for strings and the songs *Love Went A-Riding, So Perverse* and *Go Not, Happy Day.*

The City Thomas Attwood, composer, organist, pupil of Mozart, friend of Mendelssohn, was organist of St Paul's from 1796 until his death in 1838. Mendelssohn frequently went with him to St Paul's, playing the organ here on 10 June 1832, 23 June 1833 and 10 September 1837. On one of these occasions, when he was playing at the end of the afternoon service, the congregation made no attempt to leave, and the vergers took the unusual step of stopping the working of the bellows, much to Mendelssohn's surprise and annoyance.

François Barthélémon, violinist and composer of the hymn tune *Morning Hymn*, sung to 'Awake, My Soul, and with the Sun', was born in Bordeaux, France, on 27 July 1741 and died at his home, 23 Hatfield Street, Blackfriars, on 23 July 1808.

Adrian Batten, composer and organist, was organist of St Paul's from about 1624 until his death, which probably took place in 1637.

William Boyce, composer and organist, was organist of St Michael's, Cornhill, 1736–68.

Anton Bruckner, making his only trip to Britain, stayed at Seyd's German Guesthouse, 39 Finsbury Square, from 29 July to the end of August 1871. Representing Austria, he took part in a series of recitals, in the Albert Hall, inaugurating the new organ. Camille Saint-Saëns had been chosen for France. Bruckner's six recitals were so well received that he was invited to give a further four performances at the Crystal Palace, where, on 19 August, he played to an audience of 70,000. 'Tremendous applause, always unending. Requests for encores . . . Heaps of compliments,' he wrote to a friend. 'Everywhere my name appears in letters bigger than myself!' His joy at this success prompted him to start work on his Second Symphony while he was here.

Thomas Campion, poet and composer, died here on 1 March 1620. He is buried in St Dunstan-in-the-West, Fleet Street. His poems have been set to music by Parry, Stanford, Vaughan Williams, Ireland, Bax and Rubbra.

Jeremiah Clarke, organist and composer, was born in about 1674 and died in the precincts of St Paul's, where he was master of the choristers, on 1 December 1707, after shooting himself. *The Prince of Denmark's March*, better known as *Trumpet Voluntary*, was published as a keyboard piece in 1700. It may have been first performed in an instrumental version as an entr'acte that Clarke supplied for the production of

Motteux's *The Island Princess*, staged in London in 1699. He also composed the hymn tunes *St Magnus (Nottingham)*, sung to 'The Head That Once Was Crowned With Thorns', and *Brockham*, sung to 'The Heavens Declare Thy Glory, Lord'.

John Dunstable, composer, died in London on 24 December 1453. He is buried in St Stephen's Walbrook, near the Mansion House.

Giles Farnaby, composer, was born in about 1565 and died here in November 1640. He was married in St Helen's, Bishopsgate, on 28 May 1587 and appears to have resided in that parish. During the 1630s he lived in Grub Street. His death is recorded in the register of St Giles's, Cripplegate.

Maurice Greene, composer of the anthem *Lord, Let Me Know My End* and Master of the King's Music, was organist of St Dunstan-in-the-West 1716–18 and he then became organist of St Paul's. He was born in London in 1695 and died here on 1 December 1755. He was buried at St Olave's, Jewry, in Ironmonger Lane. This church was pulled down in 1888, and on 18 May of that year Greene's remains were taken to St Paul's, where they lie next to those of Boyce.

Felix Mendelssohn played the organ at Christ Church, Newgate Street, on 12 September 1837, 30 September 1840 and 16 June 1842. On the first occasion, Samuel Wesley also played. The building was gutted in 1941.

Thomas Morley, composer and organist, was born in 1557 and died in London in October 1602. He was organist, it is presumed, of St Giles's, Cripplegate, in 1590 and of St Paul's in 1591.

Elizabeth Mounsey, organist and composer, who was born in London on 8 October 1819 and died here on 3 October 1905, resided at 58 Brunswick Place for eighty-three years. From 1834, at the age of 14, to 1882, she was organist of St Peter's, Cornhill, where Mendelssohn played the organ on 30 September 1840 and 12 June 1842. The manual is preserved in the vestry.

John Newton, author of the hymns 'Glorious Things of Thee Are Spoken', 'Amazing Grace' and 'How Sweet the Name of Jesus Sounds', was born in London on 24 July 1725. He was rector of St Mary Woolnoth, in King William Street—the temporal nonconformity of which church was noted by T. S. Eliot in 'The Waste Land'—from 1780 until his death on 21 December 1807.

Thomas Ravenscroft, composer and music editor, who was born in about 1590 and died in about 1633, was, in his youth, a chorister at St Paul's.

John Redford, composer, organist, dramatist and poet, who died in London in 1547, was a vicar-choral of St Paul's and, for the last dozen years of his life, Master of the Choristers and presumably organist of the cathedral.

Philip Rosseter, composer and lutenist, was born in 1568 and died in London on 5 May 1623. He is buried in St Dunstan-in-the-West.

Musicians buried in St Paul's include Thomas Arne, William Boyce, Thomas Attwood, Arthur Sullivan and Hubert Parry.

Clapham Edvard Grieg stayed at 47 North Side, the home of the publisher John Augener, in May 1888, during his first visit to London, and again in February and March 1889 and October, November and December 1897. His début before a British audience took place on 3 May 1888. 'When I showed myself at the orchestra doorway, the whole of the vast St James's Hall, completely full, broke into an uproar, so intense and so continuous (I think for over three minutes) that I didn't know what to do . . . Is it not wonderful, and in a foreign land?' Frederick Delius, then 26, was at this concert and, on the following day, he had dinner with Grieg at the Hotel Metropole in Northumberland Avenue. When, shortly afterwards, Grieg met Delius's father, he persuaded him that Delius's future lay in music and that his allowance, which the father had threatened to withdraw, should be continued.

George Grove, lexicographer, writer on music, educationist, engineer, music administrator, geographer, Bible scholar, friend of Brunel, Brahms, Sullivan, Tennyson, Browning and Gladstone, was born at Thurlow Terrace on 13 August 1820. Thurlow Terrace was a large bungalow with about six acres of grounds situated where Wandsworth Road Station now stands.

Coulsdon Irene Richards, violinist, was born here on 10 January 1911.

Covent Garden Thomas Arne, composer, was born at 34 King Street on 12 March 1710. He died at his home in Bow Street on 5 March 1778. He is buried in St Paul's.

Domenico Dragonetti, celebrated double-bass player, resided during the 1790s at 29 Suffolk Street.

Wolfgang Amadeus Mozart, together with his father, mother and sister, lodged with a barber, John Couzin, at 19 Cecil Court (demolished) 24 April–6 August 1764. They spent their first night in London, 23 April, at The White Bear (demolished) in Piccadilly. Leopold Mozart wrote to a friend: 'In London everybody seems to me to be in fancy dress; and you cannot imagine what my wife and my little girl look like in English hats and I and our big [aged 8] Wolfgang in English clothes.' In a further letter, he observed, '. . . in England there is a kind of native complaint, which is called a *"cold"*. That is why you hardly ever see people wearing summer clothes. They all wear cloth garments. This so-called *"cold"*, in the case of people who are not constitutionally sound, becomes so dangerous that in many instances it develops into a *"consumption"*, as they call it here . . . and the wisest course for such people to adopt is to leave England and cross the sea; and many examples can be found of people recovering their health on leaving this country. I caught this *"cold"* . . .'

Cricklewood Manuel Garcia, tenor singer, inventor of the laryngoscope, teacher of Jenny Lind, was born in Madrid on 17 March 1805 and died in London on 1 July 1906. He resided at Mon Abri, Cricklewood. He was the brother of Malibran and Pauline Viardot. He first visited London in 1816.

Crofton Park Robert Simpson, composer, administrator, writer on music and doughty polemicist, spent most of his childhood at 21 Manwood Road.

Croydon Henry Balfour, organist and conductor, was born in London on 28 October 1859 and died in Croydon on 27 December 1946. He resided at 13 Elmwood Road.

Samuel Coleridge-Taylor, composer and conductor, resided from about 1880 to 1894 in Waddon New Road. He resided in Holmesdale Road, Selhurst, 1894–6. In 1896 he moved to 9 Fernham Road, Thornton Heath, where he worked on *Hiawatha's Wedding Feast*, which was completed at his next address, 21 Saxon Road, Selhurst. Following his marriage at the end of 1899, he resided briefly in St James's Road, then at 30 Dagnall Park, Selhurst, and in 1902, at 11 Dagmar Road, Selhurst. In 1903 he moved to 10 Upper Grove, South Norwood and in 1907 to Hill Crest, London Road, Norbury. In 1910 he took up residence in Aldwick, St Leonard's Road, Waddon, where he died on 1 September 1912. He is buried in Bandon Hill Cemetery, Croydon.

Avril Coleridge-Taylor, conductor and composer, was born at 10 Upper Grove, South Norwood, on 8 March 1903.

Norman Demuth, composer, leading writer on French music and author of *A Manual of Street Fighting*, produced for the Army, was born in South Croydon on 15 July 1898 and died in Chichester, West Sussex, in 1968.

Hubert Foss, writer on music, was born here on 2 May 1899 and died in London on 27 May 1953.

Joseph Holbrooke, composer and pianist, was born here on 5 July 1878 and died in London on 5 August 1958.

Franz Liszt, travelling from Chelmsford to Brighton, had supper here on 24 September 1840.

William Henry Reed, violinist, conductor, composer and close friend and biographer of Elgar, spent the latter part of his life at Froom, 33 Chatsworth Road. Edward Elgar stayed with him here in May and June 1933.

Stanley Roper, organist and composer, was born here on 23 December 1878 and died in London on 19 November 1953.

William Shakespeare, tenor singer, pianist and distinguished teacher of singing, was born here on 16 June 1849.

George Robertson Sinclair, organist and conductor, the aquatic adventures of whose dog Dan are imperishably portrayed in Elgar's *Enigma Variations*, was born here on 28 October 1863 and died in Birmingham on 7 February 1917.

John Philip Sousa conducted his band at a concert here on 11 February 1905.

Crystal Palace William Havergal Brian, composer, resided at 1 Jasper Road 1929–34, and at 10A Lunham Road 1934–8.

Henry Littleton, music publisher, who was born on 7 January 1823 and died here on 11 May 1888, resided for the last seven years of his life at Westwood House (demolished), near Westwood Hill.

Antonín Dvořák stayed here in September 1884 and in April and May 1885. On 24 April 1885 he wrote to a friend in Czechoslovakia: 'The weather has been lovely so far, but a change has set in, and I'm afraid it will last for a while, as so often happens in England. The hawthorns and the trees in the gardens—all in the loveliest flower. Roses, violets to be seen everywhere. Here, everything is at least a month earlier.'

Franz Liszt stayed with Littleton 3–20 April 1886. Littleton's son Alfred, together with a small party of Liszt's friends and admirers, travelled to Calais to accompany the composer across to Dover. By permission of the Chairman of the London, Chatham and Dover Railway, the boat-train stopped at Penge instead of going straight through to Victoria. More admirers had gathered at the station, where Liszt was welcomed with a speech in Hungarian and a bouquet. A reception then took place at Westwood House, with some three hundred people present. The composer was thereafter daily lionized by London society. Although in his seventy-fifth year, he generously agreed to attend innumerable concerts, recitals, receptions and other functions; he went to Marlborough House to dine with the Prince of Wales and to Windsor to play for the Queen. It is hardly surprising that at one concert he fell asleep during a performance of his oratorio *St Elizabeth*. He played the piano sparingly, and once, at Westwood House, a telephone was secretly placed under the piano, so that members of the Littleton family who lived nearby could hear him. It is interesting to recall, in this respect, that thirty years earlier Hans Christian Andersen had envisaged the eventual possibility of being able to listen in Copenhagen to Liszt playing the piano in Weimar; he also predicted that Americans would one day 'come flying on wings of steam' to see Europe's 'ancient monuments and crumbling ruins'.

Liszt's day of release, on 20 April, began with a speech and bouquet at Herne Hill Station. At Dover, he received a speech from the mayor and a bouquet from the mayor's daughter. Alfred Littleton and his brother Augustus took their leave of him at Calais. 'In Liszt we have lost the greatest musician of our time,' said the *Monthly Musical Record*, following the composer's death three months after his visit. 'We are glad to think that he did not feel any ill effects from the exciting and busy time he spent in London in the spring.'

Denmark Hill Felix Mendelssohn stayed with his wife's relations the Beneckes in Denmark Hill during June and July 1842. Here he composed his *Song without Words* No 3, subtitled *Spring Song*, on 1 June. The site of the Beneckes' house is now a part of Ruskin Park.

Richard Wagner visited the Beneckes in the summer of 1855. 'The good people did not know what to do with me, apart from congratulating me on the excellence of my Mendelssohn performances [he conducted at the Philharmonic Society concerts the *Scottish Symphony*, *Italian Symphony*, Violin Concerto, *Fingal's Cave* and the overture to *A Midsummer Night's Dream*], and rewarding me with descriptions of the generous character of the deceased.'

Hector Berlioz visited the Beneckes on 24 June 1855. 'I am back from my rural excursion,' he wrote to Liszt a day later. 'Klindworth was there, he played a delightfully sad piece of yours; then we sang, he, the two daughters of the house, a young German painter, and I, some five-part songs of Purcell that these ladies seem to know like their Bible; Klindworth and I were less charmed. The others lapped it up like consecrated milk. Anyhow, there is musical feeling at the bottom of these English natures, but it is a conservative feeling, above all religious, and the reverse of impassioned. Wagner did for himself in the eyes of the London public by appearing to set small store by Mendelssohn. And Mendelssohn, for a good many people, is Handel and a half!!! . . .

Wagner is wrong in not considering the puritan Mendelssohn to be a richly endowed personality. When a master is a master, and when that master has honoured and respected art always and everywhere, one must honour and respect him, too, whatever divergence there may be between the line you follow and the line he has followed.'

Wagner's lack of regard for Mendelssohn, to which Berlioz alludes, was most noticeably manifested when, on 16 April 1855 at a Philharmonic Society concert, he put on a pair of gloves to conduct the *Italian Symphony*—'a very bad symphony'. However, one critic declared that the work, on this occasion, 'went better than we have yet heard it'.

Deptford Fritz Hart, composer, novelist and conductor of the Honolulu Symphony Orchestra, was born here on 11 February 1874 and died in Honolulu on 9 July 1949.

Dulwich William Havergal Brian, composer, resided February 1914–January 1916 at 13 Wykeham Mansions in Rosendale Road, 62 Rosendale Road, 18 Wykeham Mansions and 17 Wykeham Mansions. He returned here in 1927, residing for two years at 16 Wykeham Mansions. He resided at 35 South Croxted Road 1938–40.

Alan Bush, composer, was born at Bridge House, Lordship Lane, on 22 December 1900.

Ann Storace, soprano singer, was born in London in 1766 and died here on 24 August 1817. She is buried at St Mary's, Lambeth. On 1 May 1786 in Vienna she created the role of Susanna in the première of *The Marriage of Figaro*. She has a further link with Mozart, for the scena and aria *Ch'io mi scordi di te*, K505, was written for her, bearing in its dedication the date 26 December 1786. Some fifteen years later she had a son by John Braham. Her brother Stephen, composer and artist, who was born in London on 4 January 1763 and died there on 19 March 1796, was also a close friend of Mozart.

Ealing Peter Racine Fricker, composer, resided at 42 Colebrook Avenue 1932–8.

Tony Hewitt-Jones, composer and conductor, was born here on 27 January 1926.

Gustav Holst, composer, died on 25 May 1934 in the nursing home at Beaufort House. His ashes are buried in Chichester Cathedral.

Herbert Oakeley, organist, music scholar and composer, was born in Ealing Vicarage on 22 July 1830.

Eastcote Michael Tippett, composer, who was born in London on 2 January 1905, spent his first few months in Eastcote.

East Finchley Charles Groves, conductor, was born at 55 Park Hall Road on 10 March 1915 and spent his early childhood at 30 Queens Avenue, Whetstone.

East Sheen David Fanshawe, composer, explorer, conductor, music scholar and writer, resided 1971–7 at 6 Avenue Gardens, where he composed *African Sanctus, Salaams, Requiem for the Children of Aberfan, Arabian Fantasy, Fantasy on Dover Castle* and music for the television programmes *When the Boat Comes In* and *Requiem for a Village*. In 1977 he moved to St David's, 8 Firs Avenue, where he wrote the scores for *Flambards, Tarka the Otter* and *The Good Companions* and began research into music of the South Pacific.

Edgware George Frideric Handel was composer in residence to Baron Chandos at Canons Park (demolished) 1717–19. *Haman and Mordecai*, later to be reworked as *Esther*, and *Acis and Galatea* were presented for the first time here. The *Chandos Anthems* were also composed during this period and may have been first performed in St Lawrence's, Whitchurch, where Handel is thought often to have played the organ. William Powell, the fabled 'harmonious blacksmith' was a resident of Whitchurch. He is remembered through Powell Close, opposite Handel Close, off Canons Drive. One of the fireplaces from Canons Park was acquired by The Chandos Arms in Edgware. John Christopher Pepusch, who arranged the music for *The Beggar's Opera*, was director of music here 1712–32.

Eltham John Hunt, pianist, was born here on 15 February 1905.

Enfield Vernon Handley, conductor, was born here on 11 November 1930.

John Hollingsworth, conductor, was born here on 20 March 1916.

Finchley William Alwyn, composer, resided at 45 Milholm 1929–45. He was at 8 North Square 1945–60, where he wrote his Symphonies Nos 1–4, *The Magic Island*, Harp Concerto, *Autumn Legend, Elizabethan Dances, Derby Day* and scores for the films *Odd Man Out, Fallen Idol, The Mudlark, Shake Hands with the Devil*, and many others.

David Bedford, composer of *Instructions for Angels, The Odyssey, The Rime of the Ancient Mariner, Star's End, The Tentacles of the Dark*

This cartoon of Franz Liszt, warts and all, appeared in *Vanity Fair* on 15 May 1886, a month after he had visited London for the last time. He was then seventy-four and had been an abbé for twenty years. His interpretation of his religious role was characteristically distinctive, eschewing both the tonsure and celibacy

(*above left*) Gustav Holst's home in Barnes from 1908 to 1913. His music room was on the top floor, overlooking the Thames. Ralph Vaughan Williams often visited him here, and the two composers watched the University Boat Race from the verandah in April 1909 (*Jane Jacomb-Hood*); (*above right*) the patio of 8 Halliford Street, Islington, where Benjamin Britten resided whenever he was in London during the last six years of his life. The music studio, in the centre, was specially built for him, and here he composed some of *Death in Venice*. Because he was too weak, after an operation, to go to Buckingham Palace to receive his peerage, he was invested in this house, on 8 July 1976. Dmitri Shostakovich visited him here (*Jack Phipps*); (*below*) Charles Villiers Stanford's spacious house in Holland Street, Kensington, where he lived for almost twenty years. Many of his students, who included Ralph Vaughan Williams, Gustav Holst, John Ireland, Herbert Howells and Leopold Stokowski, visited him here. Among his foreign guests were Piotr Tchaikovsky and Camille Saint-Saëns (*Author*)

Nebula and *The Song of the White Horse*, was born at 41 Litchfield Way on 4 August 1937.

Henry Bishop, composer and conductor, who was born in London on 18 November 1786 and died here on 30 April 1855, is buried in St Marylebone Cemetery. His song *Home! Sweet Home!* comes from the opera *Clari or The Maid of Milan*, first performed on 8 May 1823 in London.

Warwick Braithwaite, conductor, was born in Dunedin, New Zealand, on 9 January 1896 and died in London on 18 January 1971. He resided at 23 Linden Lea.

Eric Coates, composer, resided 1924–30 at 7 Willifield Way, where he wrote *The Selfish Giant, The Three Bears, Four Ways* and *Cinderella*, and the songs *I Heard You Singing, Bird Songs at Eventide* and *I Pitch My Lonely Caravan*.

Harold Darke, organist, conductor and composer, was born in London on 29 October 1888 and died here in 1976. He resided at 24 Widecombe Way.

Peter Racine Fricker, composer, resided during the late 1940s at 224 Ballards Lane, where he wrote his Wind Quintet, First String Quartet and First Symphony. He was at 53 Avondale Road 1950–64. Works written here include the Second and Third Symphonies, Piano Concerto, Viola Concerto, *The Vision of Judgement* and the Pastorale for organ.

Edmund Rubbra, composer, resided at The Little House, Hillcrest Avenue, during the late 1920s and early '30s.

Forest Gate Gladys Ripley, contralto singer, was born here on 9 July 1908 and died in Chichester, West Sussex, on 21 December 1955.

Fulham Elizabeth Billington, soprano singer, pupil of J. C. Bach and composer, who was born in London in about 1765 and died in Venice on 25 August 1818, resided for a time at a cottage in Fulham, where she was visited by her admirer the Prince of Wales, later George IV.

Constant Lambert, composer, conductor and writer on music, was born at St Clement's Nursing Home, Fulham Palace Road, on 23 August 1905.

Lucia Vestris, celebrated contralto singer, actress and beauty, who created the role of Fatima in Weber's *Oberon* at Covent Garden on 12 April 1826, was born in London in 1797 and died here on 8 August 1856.

Golders Green Geoffrey Bush, composer, moved to 43 Corringham

Road at the end of the 1950s. Many of his best known works were written here.

Bernard van Dieren, composer and writer, who was born in Rotterdam on 27 December 1884 and died in London on 24 April 1936, resided towards the end of his life at 35A St George's Road.

Nikolay Medtner, composer, was born in Moscow on 5 January 1880 and died in London on 13 November 1951. He resided at 69 Wentworth Road.

Goodmayes Eda Kersey, violinist, was born here on 15 May 1904 and died in Ilkley, West Yorkshire, on 13 July 1944.

Greenford Peter Racine Fricker, composer, resided at 196A Mansell Road 1938–40.

Greenwich Lavinia Fenton, soprano singer, who played Polly Peachum in the first performance of *The Beggar's Opera* on 29 January 1728 in London, was born in London in 1708 and died at West Combe Park on 24 January 1760. She is buried in Greenwich Church.

Alfonso Ferrabosco, violist, singer and composer, was born in Greenwich in about 1575 and died here in March 1628.

Henry VIII, uxoricidal monarch and composer, was born here on 28 June 1491 and died in Windsor on 28 January 1547.

Jacob Kirkman, celebrated harpsichord manufacturer, was born in Bischwiller, France, in 1710 and died in Greenwich in 1792. He resided at Crooms Hill. Around 1770, when the guitar began to become popular, Kirkman purchased several of these instruments and, by giving them to street singers and other members of the lower classes, averted a potential threat to the thriving London harpsichord industry, but with unfortunate far-reaching consequences.

Nicholas Lanier, composer and painter, was born in 1588 and was the first Master of the King's Music, from 1626 until his death here in February 1666.

William Newark, composer, was born in about 1450 and died here in November 1509. He is buried in Greenwich Church.

John Relfe, composer, whose pupils included Robert Browning, was born here in 1763 and died in London in about 1837.

Elizabeth Stirling, organist and composer, was born here on 26 February 1819 and died in London on 25 March 1895.

Thomas Tallis, composer and organist, was born in about 1505 and died here on 23 November 1585. He is buried in St Alphege's. His final years are thought to have been spent in Greenwich.

Hackney Marie Lloyd, popular singer, resided for several years at 55 Graham Road.

Hammersmith Frederic Austin, baritone singer and composer, was born in London on 30 March 1872 and died here on 10 April 1952. He resided at 174 Latymer Court.

Francesco Bianchi, opera composer, was born in Cremona, Italy, in 1752 and committed suicide at his home in Hammersmith on 27 November 1810.

Gustav Holst, composer, resided at 162 Shepherd's Bush Road 1901–3. He was at 10 Luxemburg Gardens 1913–15. From 1905 until the year of his death, 1934, he was Director of Music at St Paul's Girls' School, Brook Green; most of his works from this period were written out here in the sound-proof music room.

James Henry Leigh Hunt, poet, dramatist, novelist and opera critic, was born in Southgate in 1784 and died at his home, 16 Rowan Road, on 28 August 1859.

August Johannes Jaeger, music publisher, was residing at 16 Margravine Gardens at the time Elgar's *Enigma Variations* immortalized him as 'Nimrod'.

Hampstead Emily Anderson, music scholar and translator, died on 26 October 1962. She resided at 4 Ellerdale Court, Ellerdale Road.

Joanna Baillie, poet and dramatist, author of the songs 'Woo'd and Married and A'' and 'Poverty Parts Good Companie', died at her home, Bolton House, Windmill Hill, on 23 February 1851. She is buried in Hampstead Cemetery.

Arnold Bax, composer and Master of the King's and Queen's Music, spent much of his youth at Ivybank (demolished), Haverstock Hill. From the time of World War I until 1941 he was at 155 Fellows Road, where most of his major works were written.

Arthur Benjamin, pianist, conductor and composer of *Jamaican Rumba*, was born in Sydney, Australia, on 18 September 1893 and died in London on 10 April 1960. He resided at 15 Ranulf Road.

Arthur Bliss, composer and Master of the Queen's Music, resided at 1 East Heath Road 1929–39, during which period he wrote the symphony *Morning Heroes*, music for the film *Things To Come* and the ballet *Checkmate*. William Walton was a visitor here.

John Blockley, composer of *The Arab's Farewell to His Steed* and *Jessie's Dream* (to lines by the poet Benjamin Britten), was born in London in 1800 and died at his home, 6 Upper Park Road, on 24 December 1882.

York Bowen, composer and pianist, was born in London on 22 February 1884 and died on 23 November 1961. He resided at 25 Langland Gardens.

Benjamin Britten, composer, resided at 559 Finchley Road during the latter part of the 1930s, at the time he wrote *Variations on a Theme of Frank Bridge.*

Clara Butt, contralto singer, resided at 7 Harley Road 1901–29.

Francis Chagrin, composer and conductor, was born in Bucharest on 15 November 1905 and died in Hampstead on 10 November 1972. He resided at 48 Fellows Road.

Eric Coates, composer, resided 1913–15 at Douglas Mansions, West End Lane. He was at 22 Rosslyn Hill 1923–4. He occupied Acrise Cottage, Christchurch Hill, 1941–3.

Benjamin Dale, composer, was born in Crouch Hill on 17 July 1885 and died in Hampstead on 30 July 1943. He resided at 17c Abbey Road.

Henry Walford Davies, composer, educationist, organist, and Master of the King's Music, was residing at 21 Fawley Road during the early 1900s and at 32 West Heath Drive when he wrote the *Royal Air Force March Past* in 1919.

Sibelius came to dinner with him in West Heath Drive in September 1912, when he remarked: 'Haydn builds up his harmony from the bass with the melody as its crown. I think of my melody first and of the harmony as depending from it.'

Mary Davies, mezzo-soprano singer, was born in London on 27 February 1855 and died here on 22 June 1930. She resided at 11 Provost Road.

Frederick Delius, composer, resided in Belsize Park Gardens from October 1918 until the spring of 1919. In February and March 1921 he was again in Hampstead, where he worked on his Cello Concerto.

Norman Del Mar, conductor and writer on music, was born on 31 July 1919 at 12 Kidderpore Gardens, where he spent all his childhood.

Thomas Dunhill, composer and writer, was born in Hampstead on 1 February 1877 and died in Scunthorpe, Humberside, on 13 March 1946. During his final years he resided at 27 Platt's Lane.

Edward Elgar, composer and Master of the King's Music, resided, January 1912–October 1921, at Severn House, 42 Netherhall Gardens (demolished), where he wrote *Falstaff.*

Among those who visited him here were Alexander Ziloti, who

conducted the first Russian performance of the *Enigma Variations*, Paderewski, Heifetz, to whom the composer dedicated one of his violin pieces, John Ireland and Arthur Bliss.

Howard Ferguson, composer and music scholar, resided during the 1930s at 8 East Heath Road, where he wrote his First Violin Sonata, and at 51 Willoughby Road, where he began his Piano Sonata. He was at 106 Wildwood Road 1938–72, where he completed the Piano Sonata and composed the Second Violin Sonata, *Discovery* and *The Dream of the Rood*.

Gerald Finzi, composer, resided intermittently at 30 Downshire Hill during the mid-1930s.

Percy French, composer and author of *Abdulla Bulbul Ameer, Phil the Fluther's Ball* and *Come Back, Paddy Reilly, to Ballyjamesduff* and author of 'The Mountains of Mourne', resided at 27 Clifton Hill for the last fifteen years of his life. He died in Formby, Merseyside, on 24 January 1920.

Elena Gerhardt, mezzo-soprano singer, was born in Leipzig on 11 November 1883 and died in London on 11 January 1961. She resided at 53 Redington Road.

Wilfred Josephs, composer, resided here during the 1960s and '70s, at 14 Nassington Road, 19 Tanza Road and 50 Downshire Hill.

Hamish MacCunn, composer and conductor, died in London on 2 August 1916. He resided at 6 Abbey Mansions, Abbey Road and, formerly, at 21 Albion Road.

Heinrich Marschner, composer of the operas *Hans Heiling* and *Der Vampyr*, visited London in July 1857. Sterndale Bennett took him to 'The Spaniards'. The two composers are linked through Schumann's *Études symphoniques*, which quotes the chorus *Du Stolzes England* from Marschner's *Der Templer und die Jüdin* and is dedicated to Sterndale Bennett.

Tobias Matthay, celebrated piano teacher, resided at 21 Arkwright Road during the early years of this century.

Ernest John Moeran, composer, resided at 55 Belsize Lane during his final years.

Franz Reizenstein, composer and pianist, was born in Nürnberg, West Germany, on 7 June 1911 and died in London on 15 October 1968. He resided at 34 Hollycroft Avenue.

Cecil Sharp, outstanding and influential collector of folk-music, was born in Denmark Hill on 22 November 1859 and died at his home, 4 Maresfield Gardens, Hampstead, on 23 June 1924.

Martin Shaw, composer and organist, resided at 32 Stanley Gardens at the time of World War I.

Antoinette Sterling, contralto singer, was born in Sterlingville, New York, on 23 January 1850 and died in London on 9 January 1904. She resided at 70 Belsize Park Gardens.

Phyllis Tate, composer, moved to 12 Heath Hurst Road in 1955. Works written here include *The Lodger, Dark Pilgrimage, Gravestones, Serenade to Christmas* and *The Rainbow and the Cuckoo*.

Arthur Goring Thomas, composer, died at West Hampstead Station on 20 March 1892, having thrown himself under a train. He is buried in Finchley Cemetery.

Dimitri Tiomkin, composer, who was born in Leningrad in 1899, died at his home, Three Oaks, Courtenay Avenue, on 11 November 1979. He won Academy Awards for his scores for *High Noon, The High and the Mighty* and *The Old Man and the Sea* and for the song *Do Not Forsake Me, Oh My Darlin'* from *High Noon*. Among more than a hundred scores that he composed for films were also those for *The Guns of Navarone, Gunfight at OK Corral, Giant, The Alamo, Lost Horizon* and *The Fall of the Roman Empire*.

August Wilhelmj, virtuoso violinist, who led the violins at the first Bayreuth Festival in 1876, was born in Usingen, West Germany, on 21 September 1845 and died at his home, 54 Priory Road, Hampstead, on 22 January 1908. His Bach transcription, *Air for the G String*, was published in 1871.

Henry Wood, celebrated conductor, resided at 4 Elsworthy Road 1902–37.

Camille Saint-Saëns visited him here in 1902. When Mrs Wood apologized because the drawing-room curtains were at the cleaners, Saint-Saëns, according to Wood, 'dashed to the piano and proceeded to improvize a free *fantasia* to express the horror of his feelings at being asked into a drawing-room without curtains'.

Max Reger came for luncheon in 1907, drinking four whiskies and twenty bottles of beer.

Jean Sibelius visited in 1909.

Frederick Delius stayed here throughout September 1918. 'I can't bear the ticking of a clock', he told Wood, and every clock in the house was left to unwind into silence during that month.

Leoš Janáček visited in 1926.

Béla Bartók visited in 1930.

Michael Zacharewitsch, violinist, who at the age of 12 performed Tchaikovsky's Violin Concerto in Odessa, with the composer conducting, was born in Ostrów Wielkopolski, Poland, on 26 August 1878 and died in London on 20 December 1953. He resided at 118 Greencroft Gardens.

Hampton John Beard, tenor singer, much admired by Handel, was born in about 1717 and died here on 5 February 1791.

Julian Bream, notable guitarist, was born in Battersea on 15 July 1933 and spent his childhood at 25 Cleveland Road, Hampton.

David Garrick, actor, dramatist and author of 'Heart of Oak', who was born in Hereford on 19 February 1717, resided at Hampton House, Hampton Court Road, from 1745 until his death on 20 January 1779.

Harefield William Schwenck Gilbert, librettist, poet, cartoonist and dramatist, resided intermittently at Breakspears, a country house, 1883–90.

Harlington William Byrd, composer, resided here 1577–93.

Harrow-on-the-Hill Harrison Birtwistle, composer, resided at 44A High Street during the 1960s and early '70s. Works written during this period include *The Visions of Francesco Petrarca, Tragoedia, Punch and Judy, Verses for Ensembles, Nomos, The Fields of Sorrow* and *The Triumph of Time*.

William Havergal Brian, composer, resided at 25 Southway 1940–58 —the longest time he ever spent at any of his addresses. During this period he wrote his Symphonies Nos 6–12.

Bayan Northcott, music critic and writer on music, was born here on 24 April 1940.

Richard Redhead, composer and organist, was born here on 1 March 1820. His best known hymn tunes are No 76, sung to 'Rock of Ages, Cleft for Me', and No 46, sung to 'Bright the Vision That Delighted'.

Igor Stravinsky visited the painter and poet David Jones at 2 Northwick Park Road on 1 June 1963.

Harrow Weald William Schwenck Gilbert, librettist, poet, cartoonist and dramatist, resided at Grim's Dyke, now a hotel, Old Redding, from 1890 until 29 May 1911, when he died while saving a girl from drowning in his lake. At Grim's Dyke he wrote *Utopia Limited* and *The Grand Duke*. He was cremated at Golders Green; his ashes are interred in Great Stanmore Churchyard.

Hendon Henry Sutherland Edwards, writer on music, was born here on 5 September 1829 and died in London on 21 January 1906.

William Shakespeare, tenor singer, pianist and distinguished teacher of singing, died in London on 1 November 1931. He resided at 11 Heather Gardens.

Highgate Ian Wallace, bass singer, noted for his buffo roles, was born in London on 10 July 1919 and spent his childhood here. He later resided at 8A Denewood Road.

Holborn George Thalben-Ball, organist and composer, who was born in Sydney, Australia, on 18 June 1896, was organist of Temple Church 1923–81.

Leonard Borwick, pianist and pupil of Clara Schumann, was born in Walthamstow on 26 February 1868 and died at Le Mans, France, on 15 September 1925. He resided at 14 Brunswick Square, Holborn.

Henry Carey, composer, poet and dramatist, who was probably born in Yorkshire in about 1687, hung himself in his home in Dorrington Street, Holborn, on 4 October 1743. He wrote the words of 'Sally in Our Alley', published in 1726. It is unlikely that he composed, as has been suggested, *God Save the King*.

Samuel Coleridge-Taylor, composer and conductor, was born at 15 Theobald's Road on 15 August 1875.

Henry Walford Davies, organist, educationist, Master of the King's Music and composer of the *Royal Air Force March Past* and *Solemn Melody*, was organist of Temple Church 1898–1923.

John Dowland, lutenist, singer and composer, who was born in 1563 and died in January 1626, resided in Fetter Lane during the first decade of the seventeenth century.

Edward John Hopkins, who was born in Westminster on 30 June 1818 and died in Camden Town on 4 February 1901, was organist of the Temple Church 1843–98, during which time he composed the hymn tunes *St Hugh*, sung to 'Lord, Teach Us How To Pray Aright', *Creation*, sung to 'The Spacious Firmament On High', and *Ellers*, sung to 'Saviour Again to Thy Dear Name We Raise'.

Constant Lambert, composer, conductor and writer on music, resided 1927–9 at 189 High Holborn.

Daniel Purcell, composer, organist and brother of Henry Purcell, was born in The Great Almonry, in about 1660 and, from 1713 until his death on 12 December 1717, was organist of St Andrew's, Holborn Circus.

John Stanley, blind organist, composer, and Master of the King's

Music, who was born in London on 17 January 1713, was organist of Temple Church from 1734 until his death in London on 19 May 1786.

Samuel Webbe the elder, who was born in London in 1740 and composed many fine glees and familiar hymn tunes, including *Melcombe*, sung to 'New Every Morning Is the Love', and *Veni, Sancte Spiritus*, sung to 'Come, Thou Holy Spirit, Come', died at Gray's Inn on 25 May 1816.

Holloway Ethel Smyth, composer and author, spent two months in Holloway Prison in 1912 after throwing a stone, in support of the Suffragette Movement, through a window of the house of the Secretary of State for the Colonies, Lewis Harcourt.

Ilford John Alldis, conductor, was born here on 10 August 1929.

Phyllis Sellick, pianist, wife of Cyril Smith, was born at Newbury Park on 16 June 1911.

Islington Jonathan Battishill, composer of the song *Kate of Aberdeen* and the anthem *O Lord, Look Down from Heaven*, was born in London in May 1738 and died here on 10 December 1801.

Benjamin Britten, composer, made 99 Offord Road his London residence 1965–70. He used 8 Halliford Street when he was in the capital 1970–6.

Dmitri Shostakovich visited him at the latter address.

Henry John Gauntlett was organist of Union Chapel 1852–61. During this period he published his hymn tunes *St Fulbert*, sung to 'Ye Choirs of New Jerusalem', *University College*, sung to 'Oft in Danger, Oft in Woe' and *Irby*, sung to 'Once in Royal David's City'. He died in Kensington on 21 February 1876.

Kensal Green Musicians buried in Kensal Green Cemetery include Lucia Vestris, Julius Benedict, John Goss, William Wallace, Michael Balfe, Cipriani Potter, George Smart, Michael Costa, John Hullah, William Horsley, John Braham, Therese Tietjens, Samuel Lover, William Cusins, Mendelssohn's friend Carl Klingemann, Catherine Hayes, Ferdinand Praeger and John Barbirolli.

Kensington Emma Albani, soprano singer, was born in Chambly, near Montreal, on 1 November 1847 and died on 3 April 1930 in London, where she resided at 61 Tregunter Road. She had earlier resided at 16 The Boltons.

Fernández Arbós, conductor, violinist, composer and orchestrator of extracts from Albéniz's *Iberia*, who was born in Madrid on 24 December 1863 and died in San Sebastián on 2 June 1939, resided for several years at 13 Clareville Grove.

John Barry, composer, resided intermittently at 137 Coleherne Court at the time he received two Hollywood Academy Awards, in 1966, for his film music for *Born Free* and an Academy Award again, in 1968, for his score for *The Lion in Winter*.

Béla Bartók stayed with Duncan Wilson at 7 Sydney Place in November 1933. On 8 November in the Queen's Hall, he and Adrian Boult gave the first British performance of his Second Piano Concerto. His next appearance in London was in January 1936, when he met Paul Hindemith. He was again here in January 1938. He returned in June of that year to play, together with his wife, the British première of the Sonata for Two Pianos and Percussion.

Anthony Bernard, conductor, pianist and composer, was born in London on 25 January 1891 and died here on 6 April 1963. He resided at 6 Emperor's Gate.

Arthur Bliss, composer and Master of the Queen's Music, resided at 21 Holland Park 1896–1923, during which time he wrote the *Colour Symphony*. He resided at 15 Cottesmore Gardens 1948–55, when he wrote the ballet *Adam Zero*.

Eric Blom, music scholar, was born in Berne on 20 August 1888 and died on 11 April 1959 in London, where he resided at 10 Alma Terrace, Allen Street.

William Boyce, organist, composer, and Master of the King's Music, was probably born in London in about 1710 and died here on 7 February 1779. His song *Heart of Oak* comes from the pantomime *Harlequin's Invasion or A Christmas Gambol*, first performed on 31 December 1759 in London. He is buried in St Paul's.

Frank Bridge, composer and conductor, resided intermittently at 4 Bedford Gardens during the last decade of his life.

Benjamin Britten, composer, resided at 173 Cromwell Road during the early 1930s, at the time the *Simple Symphony, Hymn to the Virgin* and *Rejoice in the Lamb* were written. His London residence 1948–53 was at 22 Melbury Road.

Olivia Buckley, pianist, organist, harpist, composer and the daughter of Dussek, was born in London on 29 September 1801 and was organist of Kensington Parish Church from 1840 until her death here in 1847. Her father lived in London 1789–1801, marrying the singer Sophia Corri in 1792.

Albert Chevalier, actor, popular entertainer and songwriter, best known for *Knocked 'Em in the Old Kent Road* and *My Old Dutch*, was born at 17 St Ann's Villas on 21 March 1861 and died on 10 July 1923.

Muzio Clementi, composer, pianist, teacher of John Field, resided at 128 Kensington Church Street 1819–23.

William Horsley, organist and composer, who was born in London on 15 November 1774, bought 128 Kensington Church Street from Clementi in 1823 and died here on 12 June 1858. He is buried in Kensal Green Cemetery. His daughter Mary married Isambard Kingdom Brunel.

Felix Mendelssohn was a frequent guest of the Horsleys 1829–47. Ignaz Moscheles, Ludwig Spohr and John Orlando Parry were also visitors.

Arnold Cooke, composer, resided at 50 Adam and Eve Mews from after World War II to 1963. Works written here include the First Symphony, Oboe Concerto, Concerto for Strings and the opera *Mary Barton*.

Edward Elgar, composer and Master of the King's Music, resided at 3 Marloes Road during the summer of 1889. From March 1890 to June 1891 he was at 51 Avonmore Road, where he wrote *Froissart*.

Michael Flanders, lyricist and actor, was born in London on 1 March 1922 and died on 14 April 1975. He resided at 1A Scarsdale Villas during the 1950s. Most of the songs from *At the Drop of a Hat*, presented at the New Lindsey Theatre, Notting Hill Gate, on 31 December 1956, were written here, and much of Donald Swann's music was composed here.

William Schwenck Gilbert, librettist, poet, cartoonist and dramatist, resided at 24 The Boltons 1870–83, during which time he wrote *Thespis, Trial by Jury, The Sorcerer, HMS Pinafore, The Pirates of Penzance, Patience* and *Iolanthe*, and prepared the text of *The Martyr of Antioch*. He was at 39 Harrington Gardens 1883–90, where he wrote *Princess Ida, The Mikado, Ruddigore, The Yeoman of the Guard* and *The Gondoliers*. During the late 1890s he resided, when in London, at 27 Prince's Gardens.

Percy Grainger resided at 31 Gordon Place for several months in 1901. In 1907 he was at 5 Harrington Road.

Harry Plunket Greene, bass-baritone singer, biographer of Stanford and soloist in the first performances of Stanford's *Songs of the Sea* and *Songs of the Fleet* and Elgar's *The Dream of Gerontius*, died on 19 August 1936. He resided at 65 Holland Park Road. He had earlier been at 34 Kensington Square, where Hubert Parry, who was his father-in-law, and Charles Villiers Stanford often visited him.

Clement Harris, composer, pianist and pupil of Clara Schumann, was born in Wimbledon on 8 July 1871 and died, fighting for Greece, in the

Battle of Pentepagadia on 23 April 1897. He resided latterly at 19 Collingham Gardens, Kensington.

George Henschel, conductor, baritone singer and composer, resided at 45 Bedford Gardens throughout the 1890s. Piotr Tchaikovsky and Arrigo Boito visited him here in June 1893.

Ferdinand Hiller stayed at 46 Prince's Gate in June 1873.

Alfred Hipkins, authority on musical instruments, was born in London on 17 June 1826 and died here on 3 June 1903. He resided at 100 Warwick Gardens. During his visit to London in 1848, Chopin usually liked to have his piano tuned by Hipkins, then 22 and an employee of Broadwood.

Francis Hueffer, writer on music, was born in Münster on 22 May 1843 and died on 19 January 1889 in London, where he resided at 72 Elsham Road.

Joseph Joachim stayed at 25 Phillimore Gardens in February 1873 and at 13 Airlie Gardens in March 1886.

Wilhelm Kuhe, conductor, pianist and composer, was born in Prague on 10 December 1823 and died in London on 8 October 1912. He resided at 5 Cathcart Road.

Constant Lambert, composer, conductor and writer on music, resided at 42 Peel Street 1929−31 and again during World War II.

Liza Lehmann, composer and soprano singer, spent her childhood at 1 South Villas, Campden Hill. Jenny Lind visited this house in the 1860s, when Lehmann sang for her.

Jenny Lind, celebrated soprano singer, who was born in Stockholm on 6 October 1820, visited London for the first time in April 1847. She stayed in Eccleston Street, Victoria, and then moved to Clairville Cottage (demolished), the site of which is now in Brechin Place, where she remained until October 1847. She was again at Clairville Cottage April 1848−March 1849. Around the end of 1855 she was briefly at Laurel House, High Street, Putney. In 1858 she resided at Roehampton Lodge, Roehampton, and, in the following year, moved to Argyle Lodge, Parkside, Wimbledon. She was at Oak Lea, Victoria Road, Wimbledon Park, 1864−74. At the beginning of 1875 she stayed for a short time at 11 Cleveland Road, Barnes, before going to 1 Moreton Gardens (now 189 Old Brompton Road), where she remained until her death in Little Malvern on 2 November 1887.

Otto Goldschmidt, composer, conductor, pianist, pupil of Mendelssohn and husband of Jenny Lind, was born in Hamburg on 21 August 1829 and died at 1 Moreton Gardens, Kensington, on 24 February 1907.

Franz Liszt was the guest of honour at a luncheon given by Theodore

Duka on 12 April 1886 in his home at 55 Nevern Square.

Andrew Lloyd Webber, composer, was born on 22 March 1948 at the Westminster Hospital and spent his childhood at 10 Harrington Court.

Julian Lloyd Webber, cellist, was born in Kensington on 14 April 1951 and also spent his childhood at 10 Harrington Court.

Stéphane Mallarmé, poet, whose 'L'Après-midi d'un faune' and other verses inspired works by Debussy, Hindemith, Milhaud and Ravel, stayed at 6 Brompton Square in 1862 and 1863. He was married in Brompton Oratory on 10 August 1863.

Frank Merrick, composer and pianist, resided at 53A Tregunter Road during the 1930s.

Henry Newbolt, poet, whose verses are immortalized in Stanford's *Songs of the Sea* and *Songs of the Fleet*, died at his home, 29 Campden Hill Road, on 19 April 1938. He is buried at the Island Church, Orchardleigh, near Frome, Somerset.

Norman O'Neill, composer and conductor, was born at 16 Young Street on 14 March 1875. Thackeray resided here 1846–53, writing during that time *Vanity Fair, The History of Pendennis* and *The History of Henry Esmond, Esq.* From 1904 until his death on 3 March 1934, O'Neill was at 4 Pembroke Villas.

Frederick Delius was a frequent visitor to 4 Pembroke Villas during his trips to London, first coming in 1907. He stayed with O'Neill in June 1909, at the time Beecham conducted the première of *A Mass of Life*, and also in June 1914. He visited again in 1915, 1916 and 1917. He stayed for a fortnight in February 1920. The *Dance Rhapsody* No 2 is dedicated to O'Neill.

Other visitors to 4 Pembroke Villas include Gustav Holst, Percy Grainger and Cyril Scott.

Hubert Parry, composer, resided from 1886 until the year of his death, in 1918, at 17 Kensington Square, where he wrote the *Symphonic Variations*, the anthem *I Was Glad, Jerusalem, Songs of Farewell*, the Newfoundland national anthem and the hymn tunes *Repton*, sung to 'Dear Lord and Father of Mankind', *England*, sung to 'Hark What a Sound, and Too Divine for Hearing' and *Laudate Dominum*, usually sung to 'O Praise Ye the Lord'.

Maurice Ravel initially visited and subsequently stayed at 14 Holland Park, the home of the singer Louise Alvar-Harding, in June 1922, April 1923, April 1924, October 1928, January 1929 and February 1932. During his 1924 visit he completed the *Tzigane*, which received its world première at an all-Ravel concert in London on 26 April. *The Times* said of the concert: 'To hear a whole programme of Ravel's works is like watching some midget pygmy doing clever but very small things within a limited scope. Moreover, the almost reptilian cold-bloodedness . . . is almost repulsive when heard in bulk; even its beauties are like the markings on snakes and lizards.' During his last visit he conducted the first British performance of the Piano Concerto in G Major at the Queen's Hall on 25 February 1932. Lennox Berkeley often called upon Ravel here, acting as his guide in London.

Malcolm Sargent, conductor, resided at 12 Wetherby Place during the 1930s. Arthur Schnabel rented this house 1933–4 while Sargent was convalescing, for some time in Switzerland, after a serious illness. Sargent died on 3 October 1967 at his home, 9 Albert Hall Mansions, where he spent the last twenty years of his life.

Clara Schumann stayed at 14 Hyde Park Gate in 1870 and 1871 and at 42 Hyde Park Gate in 1888.

Julian Slade, composer, was born in Eccleston Square on 28 May 1930 and spent his childhood at 49 Tregunter Road.

Jan Smeterlin resided at 7 St Mary Abbot's Place during the 1930s. Karol Szymanowski stayed with him here in October and November 1934, taking part in a broadcast performance of his *Symphonie concertante* on 27 October.

William Barclay Squire, music scholar, was born in London on 16 October 1855 and died in Kensington on 13 January 1927. He resided at 16 Albert Place.

Charles Villiers Stanford, composer, conductor, celebrated teacher, pianist, organist and writer on music, resided at 50 Holland Street 1892–1916, during which period he composed the Fifth and Sixth Symphonies, the Second Piano Concerto, the first four *Irish Rhapsodies, Songs of the Sea, Songs of the Fleet, Phaudrig Crohoore*, the opera *Shamus O'Brien* and the song cycles *Songs of Erin, Cushendall* and *A Sheaf of Songs from Leinster.*

Piotr Tchaikovsky, Camille Saint-Saëns, Max Bruch and Arrigo Boito visited him here on the evening of 9 June 1893. Stanford thought that Tchaikovsky looked like an ambassador and Bruch 'like a storekeeper from the Middle West'.

Arthur Sullivan, composer and conductor, was organist of St Peter's, Cranley Gardens, 1867–72.

Maggie Teyte, soprano singer, resided in 1914, during the time of her liaison with Thomas Beecham, at 8A Kensington Palace Gardens.

Albert Visetti, conductor, composer and teacher, was born in Salona, Italy, on 13 May 1846 and died in London on 10 July 1928. During the 1890s, he resided at 14 Trebovir Road. Arrigo Boito stayed with him in June 1893, and on 8 June a party was given in his honour. Among the guests were Sullivan, Tchaikovsky and Saint-Saëns.

Maude Valérie White, composer of the songs *Absent yet Present, To Althea from Prison, The Devout Lover* and *So We'll Go No More A-Roving*, was born in Dieppe, France, on 23 June 1855 and died in London on 2 November 1937. She resided at 40 Pelham Court, Fulham Road.

Kentish Town Phyllis Tate, composer, resided at 7 Alma Street during the 1940s and early '50s, writing here the Saxophone Concerto, Sonata for Clarinet and Cello and *Nocturne for Four Voices*.

Kew Peter Racine Fricker, composer, resided August 1925–August 1932 at 25 West Park Avenue.

Sidney Jones, composer of *The Geisha*, produced in London on 25 April 1896, was born in London on 17 June 1861 and died here on 29 January 1946.

Alec Rowley, composer of the song *Sacramento*, was born in London on 13 March 1892 and died during a game of tennis on 10 January 1958. He resided at 19 Ennerdale Road.

Kilburn Edward German, composer, resided at 13 Kilburn Priory during the early 1890s, writing during this period the incidental music to *Henry VIII* and *Romeo and Juliet*, the *Gipsy Suite* and the *Norwich Symphony*.

Mathilde Marchesi, mezzo-soprano singer and teacher of Calvé, Eames, Sanderson, Nevada and Melba, was born in Frankfurt-am-Main on 24 March 1821 and died at 16 Greville Place, the home of her daughter Blanche, on 18 November 1913.

Kingston-upon-Thames Derek Bourgeois, composer, was born here on 16 October 1941.

John Eccles, composer and Master of the Queen's and King's Music, was born in London in 1668 and died here on 12 January 1735.

Hugo Rignold, conductor, was born here on 15 May 1905.

Knightsbridge Isaac Albéniz resided at 16 Michael's Grove, now part of Egerton Terrace, during the early 1890s.

Marie Collier, soprano singer, was born in Ballarat, Australia, on 16

April 1927 and fell to her death from a window in Leicester Square on 8 December 1971. She resided at 6 Cadogan Lane, Knightsbridge.

Gerald Finzi, composer, resided at 21 Caroline Street, now 21 Caroline Terrace, 1926–33. *A Young Man's Exhortation* was written during this period.

Catherine Stephens, soprano singer, was born in London on 18 September 1794 and died at her home, 9 Belgrave Square, on 22 February 1882.

Ladbroke Grove Granville Bantock, composer and conductor, was born in Westbourne Park Road on 7 August 1868.

Howard Ferguson, composer and music scholar, was residing at 12 Clarendon Road when he wrote *The Twa Corbies* and *Five Irish Folk Tunes*.

Thea Musgrave, composer, resided at 80 Ladbroke Road 1956–70. Works written during this period include *Triptych for Tenor and Orchestra, The Phoenix and the Turtle, The Five Ages of Man, The Decision, Nocturnes and Arias*, Concerto for Orchestra, Clarinet Concerto and *Beauty and the Beast*.

Cyril Scott, composer, pianist and poet, resided at 37 Ladbroke Grove during the 1930s.

Lambeth Charlotte Brent, soprano singer, who took part in first performances of works by Handel and Arne, died at 6 Vauxhall Walk on 10 April 1802.

Charles Chaplin, actor, director, dramatist and composer of theme music for such films as *City Lights, Modern Times* and, most notably, *Limelight*, was born in East Lane, Walworth, on 16 April 1889. He moved later to West Square, St George's Road, Lambeth, to 3 Pownall Terrace, Kennington Road, and to 287 Kennington Road. He died in Switzerland on Christmas Day 1977.

Arthur Sullivan, composer and conductor, was born at 8 Bolwell Street (demolished) on 13 May 1842.

Ralph Vaughan Williams, composer, resided at 2 St Barnabas Villas, South Lambeth Road, 1895–6. At the time he was organist at St Barnabas's Church.

Leyton John Lill, pianist, was born on 17 March 1944 at Forest Gate Hospital and spent his childhood in Buckland Road, Leyton.

Maida Vale Frederic Cowen, conductor, and composer of the *Scandinavian Symphony* and *The Language of Flowers*, was born in

W.S. Gilbert possessed a remarkable visual imagination and was a gifted draughtsman. He directed his operettas, often planning the sets and costumes, and illustrated *The Bab Ballads*. His house in Harrington Gardens, Kensington, where he lived during the 1880s, was built to his own design and is now highly prized as an exuberant example of Victorian architecture (*London County Council; Hesketh Pearson Estate*)

(*above left*) George Frideric Handel lived at 25 Brook Street, London, for more than thirty years, dying there on 14 April 1759. The top floor was added at a later date. Many of his most famous works were composed in this building, notably *Messiah* (*Greater London Council*); (*above right*) the Eccentric Club, Ryder Street, St James's. This was formerly the Dieudonné Hotel, and Piotr Tchaikovsky stayed here during his last three visits to London, in 1888, '89 and '93. It was within easy reach of St James's Hall, where the Philharmonic Society concerts used to be given and which has since been replaced by the Piccadilly Hotel. The Dieudonné's foremost attraction was its cuisine, which Whistler much esteemed (*Author*); (*below*) Hector Berlioz lodged at 58 Queen Anne Street, St Marylebone, in 1851, when he represented France on the musical jury at the Great Exhibition. He had the unenviable task of judging thousands of instruments from all over the world, most of which, he wrote, could be classified under a heading of 'pots, pans and penny whistles'. After a peaceful early-morning walk through Hyde Park, where he observed 'cows lying in the thick grass', the noise of the instruments had a curious effect on him: 'the desire to sleep became irresistible' (*Author*)

Kingston, Jamaica, on 29 January 1852 and died in London on 6 October 1935. He resided at 105 Maida Vale.

Edward German, composer, died in London on 11 November 1936. He resided at 5 Biddulph Road.

Mayfair Vincenzo Bellini stayed at 3 Old Burlington Street (demolished) from about 26 April to 15 August 1833. On 29 April he attended a performance of *La Cenerèntola* at the King's Theatre; also in the audience were Mendelssohn, Paganini, Hummel and Malibran. He and Paganini were among those present at the world première of the *Italian Symphony* in the Hanover Square Rooms on 13 May. During his visit *La Sonnambula* was staged at Drury Lane and *Il Pirata* at the King's Theatre. *Norma* received its first British presentation at the King's Theatre on 20 June, and *I Capuleti ed i Montecchi* in the same theatre on 20 July. On 16 May Bellini wrote: 'I find myself in the midst of a world of beautiful women, truly, of celestial beauties; but I indulge in nothing but sentiment, and that's little for somebody who has to leave the country in two months; and so I put more value upon friendship than upon love, so as not to run the risk of acquiring a wife.'

William Blake lived on the first floor at 17 South Molton Street 1803–21. In 1820 he began work on the water-colour illustrations that inspired Vaughan Williams's ballet *Job*, first performed on 5 July 1931.

Edward Bulwer-Lytton, novelist, dramatist and poet, wrote his novel *Rienzi, or the Last of the Tribunes*, on which Wagner based his opera, at 36 Hertford Street in 1834.

Frédéric Chopin stayed at 48 Dover Street (demolished) 24 April–5 August 1848. He went to the opera to hear Jenny Lind and saw Queen Victoria there, 'but what impressed me even more was Wellington, sitting beneath the royal box like an old monarchical watch-dog in his kennel, beneath his mistress'. He went to a Philharmonic Society concert; this English orchestra, he wrote to a friend, 'like their roast beef or turtle soup, is strong and efficient, but nothing more'. He played at the Duchess of Sutherland's, when the Queen, Prince Albert and Wellington were all present, and received 20 guineas. One of the Rothschilds advised him to ask for less in future if he wanted to have sufficient engagements. 'I gather from this that they are not so open-handed here and that money is tight everywhere.' On 7 July he gave a recital at Lord Falmouth's in St James's Square. He took pupils, one of whom 'has already left for the country, leaving nine lessons unpaid'. He met Walter Scott, Charles Dickens and Lady Byron—'I can well understand why she bored Byron.'

To his family in Warsaw, he wrote: 'If only London were not so black, and the people so heavy and dull, and if only there were no fogs or smells of soot, I might have learnt English by now. But these English are so different to the French, to whom I've become attached as if they were my own people; they consider everything in terms of money; they like art only because it's a *luxury*. They're kindhearted souls, but so eccentric that I can easily believe that if I remained here I'd become solidified or turn into a machine. If I were younger, perhaps I'd let myself become a machine and give concerts all over the place and play the most awful rubbish (anything for some money!). But it's hard at this stage to start turning oneself into a machine.'

Eric Coates, composer, resided at 39 Hill Street 1949–53.

Johann Baptist Cramer, pianist, composer and music publisher, much admired by Beethoven, was born in Mannheim on 24 February 1771 and died on 16 April 1858 in London. His publishing business was situated initially at 120 New Bond Street and then at 201 Regent Street.

Gabriel Fauré stayed with Earl de Grey at 12 Bruton Street when he came to London to take part in the first British concert devoted entirely to his works. This was held at St James's Hall on 10 December 1896. 'It must be confessed,' said *The Musical Times*, 'that the effect of an entire programme by a composer possessed of great talent, but not of genius, was rather monotonous.' Giacomo Puccini was often a guest at 12 Bruton Street during the summer of 1900.

George Gershwin made his first visit to London during the early months of 1923, when he composed *The Rainbow*, which received its world première at the Empire Theatre on 3 April of that year. On the day after his arrival, he wrote to his brother Ira, 'the rain is coming down in the manner we've heard about for years . . . The English are the politest people I've yet met. Even the taxi drivers are polite. How different from the Yellow Cabs of New York.' He returned in the summer of the following year, staying at 10 Berkeley Street, where he wrote *Primrose*, introduced at the Winter Garden on 11 September 1924. This work, published by Chappell, was his first musical comedy to be printed. He told his friends the Paleys on 8 July, 'The weather has been great—for London. It has been very cool.' He was beginning to acquire a taste for golf: 'I believe I shall [take] it up professionally. That's a good way to knock off some heiress.' He was again in London during the late spring and early summer of 1925, starting work on the Concerto in F. His fourth visit, when he resided in Pall Mall, from

January to April 1926, was occasioned by the British première of *Lady, Be Good*. His final trip to London, lasting about a week, took place in March 1928.

George Frideric Handel settled in London after making his second trip to England during the autumn of 1712, when he was 27. After residing briefly in the City, he accepted an invitation from the Earl of Burlington and moved to Burlington House, where he occupied rooms at the back of the building, from which he could view open country. He remained until 1717 and wrote part of the *Water Music* here. Through Burlington, a patron of the arts and later an influential architect, he met Pope, Gay and other writers with whom he was later to collaborate.

In about 1721, after his years at Canons Park, in Edgware, he settled at 25 Brook Street, where he died on 14 April 1759. The top floor of this building was added by a later tenant. Handel paid rent of £20 a year for 25 Brook Street; the annual rates were about 3s 6d. The majority of those works by which he is best known were written here, including *Zadok the Priest, Alcina, Semele, Israel in Egypt, Judas Maccabeus, Belshazzar, Messiah,* the Organ Concertos and the *Royal Fireworks Music.* In his later years he lived here in great comfort and possessed two Rembrandts. He left £17,500, which for those times, compares favourably with the fortunes bequeathed by Verdi and Richard Strauss.

Christoph Gluck, who was in London from the autumn of 1745 to the summer of 1746, visited him here. They took part in a concert on 25 March 1746.

Charles Ives visited London in 1924, 1932, '33, '34, and '38. In August 1924, he stayed at St James's Palace Hotel and made trips to Oxford, Stratford-upon-Avon and Winchester. Thereafter, he stayed at 18 Half Moon Street. In June and July 1932, he went to Durham and the Lake District; in June 1933, to Exeter, Bath and Wells.

Jerome Kern, George Gershwin, Ira Gershwin and Vincent Youmans were guests at a reception on 20 March 1928 at 52 Maddox Street.

Aram Khachaturian stayed at the Dorchester Hotel 16–30 January 1977.

Franz Liszt was the guest of honour at a luncheon given by Baroness Burdett-Coutts on 13 April 1886 in her home at 1 Stratton Street.

Giacomo Meyerbeer stayed at the York Hotel, Albermarle Street, in May 1862, when his *Ouverture en forme de marche* was performed at the opening of the International Exhibition.

John Mason Neale, author of many well-known hymns, was born in Conduit Street on 24 January 1818.

Frederick Gore Ouseley, music scholar and composer, was born in Grosvenor Square on 12 August 1825.

Giacomo Puccini was a visitor to 1 Seamore Place, the home of Alfred de Rothschild, during the summer of 1900. He was a frequent visitor, between 1912 and 1920, to 41 South Street, the home of Sybil Seligman, who was possibly the greatest love of his life.

Sergey Rakhmaninov made fifteen visits to London, giving his first concert here on 19 April 1899 and his last on 11 March 1939. He frequently stayed at the Piccadilly Hotel, which stands on the site once occupied by St James's Hall, where Saint-Saëns, Dvořák, Tchaikovsky, Grieg and other composers often conducted their works.

Gioachino Rossini stayed at 90 Regent Street 13 December 1823–26 July 1824 on his only trip to Britain. The Channel crossing made him so ill and nervous that he spent a week in bed after his arrival. The purpose of his visit was simply to make money, by accompanying his wife Isabella Colbran at private engagements, giving a few lessons and conducting eight of his operas. By the time he returned to Paris these activities had gained him the incredible sum of 175,000 francs, which supported him for the remaining forty-four years of his life. 'I never made enough from my art to be able to save anything, except for my stay in England,' he told Ferdinand Hiller. 'And in London I earnt money not as a composer, but as an accompanist . . . I charged the rather high fee of £50 for our participation in musical soirées; we took part in about 60 of them, and that, after all, was worth the bother. By the way, in London, musicians will do anything and everything to make money. I saw the oddest things there . . .' But, in addition, 'I received attentions that it would be difficult to parallel anywhere else.' The only composition to emerge from this visit was the cantata *Il pianto delle muse in morte di Lord Byron*, occasioned by the poet's death in Missolonghi, Greece, on 19 April 1824; it was performed in London on 9 July. A more important work that received its world première in London, on 5 June 1919, was *La Boutique fantasque*, with which Rossini would no doubt have been delighted.

Edgar Speyer, businessman and patron of music and painting, who was born in Frankfurt-am-Main on 7 September 1862 and died in London on 16 February 1932, resided for many years at 46 Grosvenor Street, now the Japanese Embassy. His wife was the violinist Leonora Stosch.

Edvard Grieg stayed with them during May 1906, spending much of the time sitting in the hall, attired in hat and overcoat, disinclined to converse with anybody. He first met 'the wonderful Percy Grainger' here and was captivated by him, noting in his diary on 24 May that he loved him 'almost as if he were a young woman'. Grainger was a frequent visitor to the Speyers' house during the early 1900s.

Richard Strauss, who dedicated *Salome* to Speyer, stayed at 46 Grosvenor Street in 1902, 1903, 1904, 1910 and 1914. At dinner here on 11 April 1910 Edward Elgar and Percy Grainger were among the other guests. A year later Strauss became the first German to conduct Grainger's works in Germany. Henry Wood had dinner here in 1903 when Strauss was staying. He later recalled that the composer of *Schlagobers* had been particularly delighted with the delicious dessert: 'This is well orchestrated,' he told his hostess.

Claude Debussy stayed with the Speyers in January 1908 and July 1914. He, too, during his 1908 visit became acquainted here with Percy Grainger, who described him as 'a little spitting animal'. According to Grainger, when they were invited to move into another room for tea, Debussy said: 'No, I won't eat with anybody. Bring my tea in here, so I can eat alone.'

Gabriel Fauré visited the Speyers in March 1908.

Edward Elgar and Charles Villiers Stanford came here on several occasions.

Karol Szymanowski visited London for the second time in November and December 1920, staying at 3 Cork Street, where Artur Rubinstein was also residing at that time. Despite his dislike of the fog and 'that grim Victoria Station', he told friends in Poland that he preferred London to Paris. In November 1934, he gave a private recital at 66 Grosvenor Street, the home of Victor Cazalet, to whom he dedicated his Two Mazurkas, Op 62.

Richard Tauber, tenor singer, was born in Linz on 16 May 1892 and died in London on 8 January 1948. He resided at the Grosvenor House Hotel.

Henri Vieuxtemps stayed at 4 Maddox Street in March 1846 and at 137 Regent Street in March 1864.

Charles Widor stayed at 6 Hamilton Place in April 1888 and March 1890.

Muswell Hill Jennifer Bate, distinguished organist, was born in London on 11 November 1944 and spent her childhood and succeeding years at 35 Collingwood Avenue.

August Johannes Jaeger, music publisher and 'Nimrod' ('Jäger' = 'Hunter'>'Nimrod') of the *Enigma Variations*, who was born in Düsseldorf on 18 March 1860, resided at 37 Curzon Road from June

1902 until his death here on 18 May 1909. Edward Elgar visited him here.

Nicholas Maw, composer, resided during the early 1960s at 19 Farrer Road, where he wrote *Scenes and Arias* and *One-Man Show*.

Robert Simpson, composer, administrator, writer on music and doughty polemicist, resided at 18 Grand Avenue 1949–61.

New Malden Harold Bauer, celebrated pianist, was born here on 28 April 1873 and died in Miami on 12 March 1951.

Norwood Thomas Attwood, organist, composer, conductor and pupil of Mozart, was born in London on 23 November 1765 and resided in Beulah Hill South, near the junction with Hermitage Road, May 1821–December 1834.

Felix Mendelssohn, recovering from a severe leg injury sustained after being thrown out of a cabriolet and crushed beneath it, stayed with him from 13 November 1829 for about four or five days. 'This is Norwood, famous for good air, for it lies on a hill as high as the cross on St Paul's—so say the Londoners—and I'm sitting late at night in my own little room, with the wind howling wildly outside my window, while the chimney fire burns very quietly. I've had a walk of two miles today, and the air has really had a very beneficial effect on me . . .' The composer's friend Carl Klingemann came to visit him and found him not walking, but in a cart drawn by a beautiful white donkey. 'In the said vehicle sat Felix; the donkey trotted briskly along the road; several dogs frisked about the conveyance . . .' As they proceeded up the road they were joined by other acquaintances; thus 'a caravan, consisting of one lady, four young men, the vehicle with the milk-white donkey and three dogs, moved placidly up the hill and into the village—a glorious subject for artists, a subject that would have made an immortal work.' Mendelssohn again stayed with Attwood in May 1832.

August Manns, conductor, noted for his championing of new music, was born near Szczecin, Poland, on 12 March 1825 and died in London on 1 March 1907. He resided at Gleadale, Harold Hill. He conducted at the Crystal Palace the British premières of works by every major contemporary composer, ranging from Schumann's Fourth Symphony, on 15 March 1856, to Richard Strauss's *Also Sprach Zarathustra*, on 6 March 1897.

Notting Hill Frank Merrick, composer and pianist, resided at 5 Horbury Crescent during the 1960s, then moved to 16 Horbury Crescent. He died on 19 February 1981.

Eugène Oudin, baritone singer, was born in New York on 24 February 1858 and died in London on 4 November 1894. He resided at 31 Linden Gardens.

Charles Steggall, organist and composer, was born in London on 3 June 1826 and died in London on 7 June 1905. He resided at 8 Horbury Crescent.

Orpington Gioachino Rossini's *Il Signor Bruschino* received its British première here on 14 July 1960.

Osterley Ernest John Moeran, composer, was born here on 31 December 1894.

Paddington Walter Bache, pianist, resided during the 1880s at 17 Eastbourne Terrace. Franz Liszt visited him here on 6 April 1886.

Béla Bartók and the violinist Jelly d'Arányi took part in a private recital at 18 Hyde Park Terrace on 14 March 1922. They played the First Violin Sonata, ten days before its public world première in the Aeolian Hall. Igor Stravinsky was apparently among the small audience. Hyde Park Terrace is now a part of Bayswater Road.

William Sterndale Bennett, composer, pianist and conductor, resided at 50 (later 47) Inverness Terrace 1859–65 and at 38 Queensborough Terrace 1865–73. In 1866 he acquired 18 Porchester Terrace, backing on to 38 Queensborough Terrace and tended to reside more at this latter address 1871–3. Joachim visited Sterndale Bennett at Porchester Terrace.

Clara Novello resided at 18 Porchester Terrace in the 1850s.

Matthew Dubourg, violinist, who was leader of the orchestra for the first performance of Handel's *Messiah*, was born in London in 1703 and died here on 3 July 1767. He is buried in Paddington Churchyard.

Hamilton Harty, composer and conductor, was organist of All Saints Church, Norfolk Square, in 1901, and was dismissed from this position at the end of his first week.

Arthur Hervey, writer on music and composer, was born in Paris on 26 January 1855 and died in London on 10 March 1922. He resided at 1 Norfolk Crescent.

Wilfred Josephs composed his *Requiem* at 17 Aubrey House, 7 Maida Avenue.

Liza Lehmann, composer and soprano singer, was born at 139 Westbourne Terrace on 11 July 1862. At the time of her death in Pinner on 19 September 1918, she resided at 40 Warwick Avenue.

Arthur Sullivan was often at 139 Westbourne Terrace in the early 1860s. Other visitors included Charles Dickens, Robert Browning,

Holman Hunt, Wilkie Collins, H. F. Chorley and Eduard Hanslick.

Blanche Marchesi, soprano singer, was born in Paris on 4 April 1863 and died in London on 15 December 1940. She resided at 76 Lancaster Gate.

Cipriani Potter, composer, pianist and conductor, was born in London on 2 October 1792 and died here on 28 September 1871. He resided at 3 Craven Hill. He was acquainted with Beethoven, whose First, Third and Fourth Piano Concertos he played for the first time in Britain. On 7 July 1871, when he was 78, he took part in the first British performance of Brahms's *Requiem*, given at 35 Wimpole Street, the home of Kate Loder, who, with Potter, provided the piano accompaniment. On 28 May 1855 Wagner conducted Potter's Symphony in G minor at a Philharmonic Society concert. In 1826 Potter produced his piano work *The Enigma, Variations in the Style of Five Eminent Masters.*

Landon Ronald, conductor and composer of *Down in the Forest* and *Believe Me If All Those Endearing Young Charms,* was born in London on 7 June 1873. At the time of World War I he resided at 118 Westbourne Terrace. He later resided at 34 Warwick Avenue and died here on 14 August 1938.

Henry Russell, pupil of Rossini, father of Landon Ronald and composer of *Oh, Woodman, Spare That Tree, The Wreck of the Hesperus, Cheer, Boys, Cheer!* and *A Life on the Ocean Wave,* died on 8 December 1900. He resided at 18 Howley Place.

Charles Salaman, pianist, conductor and composer, was born in London on 3 March 1814 and died here on 23 June 1901. He resided at 24 Sutherland Avenue.

Cyril Scott, composer, pianist, and poet, resided at 24 Newton Road during World War I.

Petts Wood Heddle Nash, tenor singer, born in London in 1896, died here on 14 August 1961. He resided at 49 Towncourt Crescent.

Purley Ronald Binge composed *Elizabethan Serenade* in 1952 at his home, 18 Smitham Bottom Lane.

Putney Ralph Hill, writer on music, was born in Watford, on 8 October 1900 and died in London on 20 October 1950. He resided at 39 Hazelwell Road.

Regent's Park Benjamin Britten, composer, made 5 Chester Gate his London residence 1953–8.

Edward Elgar, composer and Master of the King's Music, stayed at 8 Gloucester Terrace on visits to London in 1901 and 1902.

Constant Lambert, composer, conductor and writer on music, resided at 197 Albany Street from 1948 until his death in 1951. Alan Rawsthorne and William Walton visited him here.

Alexander Mackenzie, composer and conductor, resided for more than twenty years at 15 Regent's Park Road. Piotr Tchaikovsky visited him here on 1 June 1893.

Ignaz Moscheles, pianist, composer and conductor, resided at 3 Chester Place from the autumn of 1830 to the autumn of 1846. Felix Mendelssohn was a frequent guest between 1832 and 1846. Henry Litolff came for lessons 1831–4. Niccolò Paganini visited in May 1831. Mendelssohn and Giacomo Meyerbeer came to dinner on 25 April 1832. Malibran and Sigismond Thalberg came to dinner on 12 June 1836. On 2 May 1836 Ole Bull visited. Carl Czerny was a guest in May 1837. Franz Liszt visited in 1840 and 1841. Joseph Joachim came in 1844. The first rehearsal of *Elijah* took place here on 10 August 1846.

Ralph Vaughan Williams, composer, resided at 10 Hanover Terrace from 1953 until his death here on 26 August 1958. Works dating from this period include the Violin Sonata, *Hodie, The England of Elizabeth, A Vision of Aeroplanes, Epithalamion,* Variations for Brass Band, *Ten Blake Songs, Three Vocalises, Four Last Songs,* the Bass Tuba Concerto and Symphonies Nos 8 and 9.

Visitors here included Percy Grainger, Arthur Bliss, Herbert Howells, Arthur Benjamin, Gerald Finzi, Patrick Hadley, Elizabeth Maconchy, Grace Williams, Ross Lee Finney, Andrzej Panufnik, Leopold Stokowski, Adrian Boult, John Barbirolli and Eugene Goossens.

Henry Wood, celebrated conductor, resided at 63 Harley House, Marylebone Road, from 1942 until his death on 19 August 1944.

Richmond Malcolm Arnold, composer, resided at 19 Denbigh Gardens during the early 1960s.

Johann Christian Bach resided here from the summer of 1777 to the spring of 1779.

Gustav Holst, composer, resided at 31 Grena Road 1904–7 and at 23 Grena Road 1907–8. While at the earlier address he wrote the carol *In the Bleak Midwinter.*

Franz Liszt stayed here during the summer of 1840.

Niccolò Paganini gave a recital in the King's Theatre on 26 April 1834.

Johann Strauss senior led his orchestra in a concert at the Castle Hotel on 30 May 1849.

St James's Thomas Attwood, organist, composer, pupil of Mozart and friend of Mendelssohn, was organist of the Chapel Royal from 1836 until his death in 1838.

Michael Balfe, composer, wrote most of his opera *The Bohemian Girl* at 19 Piccadilly (demolished).

John Blow, organist, composer, teacher of Purcell, was an organist of the Chapel Royal from 1676 until his death in 1708.

William Boyce, composer and organist, was organist of the Chapel Royal from 1758 until his death in 1779.

John Bull, composer, organist and virginalist, was an organist of the Chapel Royal 1591–1613.

William Byrd, composer, was an organist of the Chapel Royal from 1572 until his death in 1623.

Frédéric Chopin stayed at 4 St James's Place 31 October–23 November 1848. Returning from three months in Scotland, he at once became extremely ill and remained so until his departure for Paris. On 16 November he made the last public appearance of his life when he played at a concert and ball held at the Guildhall in aid of Polish refugees. 'I simply cannot breathe here; the climate is inconceivable for people in my state', he wrote to a friend. 'We light the candles at 2 o'clock.' As his train left 'this hellish London' on the 23rd he had a seizure, but was sufficiently recovered to take a meal at Folkestone before crossing to Boulogne. He died in Paris on 17 October of the following year.

Jeremiah Clarke, organist and composer of the *Trumpet Voluntary*, was an organist of the Chapel Royal from 1704 until his death in 1707.

William Croft, composer and organist, was an organist of the Chapel Royal from 1704 until his death in 1727.

Lorenzo da Ponte, librettist of *La nozze di Figaro, Don Giovanni* and *Così fan tutte*, ran a bookshop at 5 Pall Mall from about 1799 to 7 April 1805, when he left for the USA. During that period Michael Kelly, the first Don Basilio in *La nozze di Figaro*, had a bookshop a few doors away in Pall Mall. For a time, da Ponte was in partnership with Jan Dussek. Da Ponte decided to become a bookseller while taking refuge in a bookshop to avoid a bull that was running along The Strand.

Richard Rodgers and Lorenz Hart stayed at 29 St James's Street during the spring of 1927, working on the revue *One Dam Thing After Another*. The words and music of *My Heart Stood Still* were written here. The revue received its world première at the London Pavilion on

19 May 1927. The Prince of Wales was in the audience, which delighted Rodgers 'because I was sure that the resulting publicity would be of tremendous box-office value'. C. B. Cochran, the producer, feared, however, that the Prince's presence might prove disastrous, 'since, given the choice, Britons much preferred spending an evening watching royalty than what occurred on stage. As the show progressed, it looked as if C.B. was absolutely right. No matter what was happening in the revue, everyone was staring at the royal box, as if to await a signal indicating when to laugh and when to applaud . . . they reacted in all the wrong places.'

Thomas D'Urfey, poet, dramatist and musician, died in London on 26 February 1723. He is buried in St James's Church, Piccadilly.

Edward Elgar, composer and Master of the King's Music, resided intermittently, between 1921 and 1923, at 37 St James's Place. John Ireland visited him here.

Orlando Gibbons, composer and organist, was an organist of the Chapel Royal from 1605 until his death in 1625.

Joseph Haydn resided at 1 Bury Street (demolished) from the beginning of February 1794 to 15 August 1795. He was thus only a few minutes' walk away from Rebecca Schroeter, who was at 6 James Street, off Buckingham Gate; the composer told his biographer Albert Dies that she was 'a beautiful and amiable woman whom I might very easily have married if I had then been free'. According to Dies, Haydn 'generally dined with her when he was invited nowhere else'.

During this second stay in England he directed the world premières of the following of his symphonies: No 99 on 10 February 1794; No 101 on 3 March 1794; No 100 on 31 March 1794; No 102 on 2 February 1795; No 103 on 2 March 1795; No 104 on 4 May 1795. Nos 99, 100 and 101 were given at the Hanover Square Rooms; Nos 102, 103 and 104, at the King's Theatre, Haymarket. All these works were performed from manuscript and, apart from No 99, were written in London. At the première of No 102 on 2 February 1795 a chandelier is said to have fallen into the middle of the auditorium during the symphony's finale. Not a single member of the audience was injured. There were cries of 'Miracle! Miracle!' By some obscure process the title *Miracle Symphony* soon afterwards attached itself to No 96, remaining with that work since then. When Dies questioned Haydn about the crashing chandelier, he replied, 'I know nothing about it.'

He was a witness to the marriage of Gaetano Bartolozzi and Therese Jansen at St James's, Piccadilly, on 16 May 1795.

Henry Lawes, composer, was an organist of the Chapel Royal from 1660 until his death in 1662.

Franz Liszt had dinner with the Prince of Wales and Princess Alexandra at Marlborough House on 11 April 1886.

Carl Nielsen had tea here with Alexandra, then Queen Mother, on 29 June 1923, having conducted a concert of his works on the 28th. She, being Danish, was one of the few people in London with whom he could adequately communicate. He had studied a primer, *English in a Hundred Hours*, prior to his arrival in the capital, but was unable to find the hundred hours necessary for its completion. He later said he had mastered only two words: 'Ivory', the sound of which particularly delighted him, and 'Yes'. Having forgotten to pack a dark suit, he had to borrow one at the last moment for his audience with Queen Alexandra. The trousers unfortunately turned out to be too small, and he was quite unable to do up the top button. He adjusted to his dilemma with easy grace by holding his left hand across his midriff while greeting and conversing with the Queen. When, alas, they were joined by the Empress Dagmar of Russia and he was required to escort both ladies to the tea-table, one on either arm, his predicament became acute. However, the walk across the room was safely negotiated, the composer desperately holding in his breath and stomach, lest other buttons follow the example of the first.

Jules Massenet stayed at the Cavendish Hotel, Jermyn Street, when he came to London for the world première of *La Navarraise* at Covent Garden on 20 June 1894.

Felix Mendelssohn stayed at 35 Bury Street (demolished) from the second week of September to 29 November 1829. He is known to have played the organ at St James's, Piccadilly, possibly in September 1840.

Giacomo Meyerbeer stayed at the Waterloo Hotel, Jermyn Street, in May 1832, while supervising the British première of *Robert le diable*. 'The climate doesn't agree with my stomach,' he wrote to his wife. Moreover 'in this famously clean and comfortable London I have been so badly lodged, so dirtily and uncomfortably, that in three days I've twice changed hotels . . . the cooking doesn't suit me, and neither does the beer.'

Thomas Morley, composer and organist, was a Gentleman of the Chapel Royal from 1592 until his death in October 1602.

William Mundy, composer of the anthem *O Lord, the Maker of All Things*, who was born in about 1529, was a Gentleman of the Chapel Royal from February 1564 until his death in, it is supposed, 1591.

Henry Purcell, composer, was an organist of the Chapel Royal from 1682 until his death in 1695.

Richard Pygott, composer, was born in about 1485 and was a Gentleman of the Chapel Royal from 1524 until his death in Greenwich in 1552.

Alan Rawsthorne, composer, resided at 4 St James's Place during the late 1940s. Chopin had stayed here in 1848.

John Shepherd, composer, born about 1520, was a Gentleman of the Chapel Royal from 1552 until his death in about 1563.

George Smart, composer, conductor and organist, was organist of the Chapel Royal from 1822 until his death in 1867.

Leopold Stokowski, conductor, was organist of St James's, Piccadilly, from 1903 until his departure for the USA in August 1905.

Arthur Sullivan, composer and conductor, was a chorister of the Chapel Royal during the early 1850s.

Thomas Tallis, composer and organist, was a Gentleman of the Chapel Royal from about 1545 until his death in 1585.

Piotr Tchaikovsky stayed at the Dieudonné Hotel, now the Eccentric Club, in Ryder Street 19–24 March 1888, 9–12 April 1889 and 29 May–14 June 1893. His only other trip to London had taken place in August 1861, when he spent practically all the time sightseeing. In a letter of 10 August 1861 he told his father that London 'makes a gloomy impression on the soul. You never see the sun, and it rains at every step.' But, four days later, he was able to write that he had nevertheless enjoyed his visit. 'I very much like their food. The dishes are simple—plain, even—but filling and tasty.' This strongly contrasts with Verdi's dislike of English food, which, in 1847, he considered to be 'full of drugs and pepper'. During his first stay at the Dieudonné Tchaikovsky conducted the British première of the *Serenade for Strings*, and, in the following year, that of the First Suite. In 1893 he conducted the first performance in Britain of the Fourth Symphony. On 11 April 1889 he wrote to his nephew: 'Last year I enjoyed the fog daily, but I never dreamt of the sort of thing we had today. When I went to rehearsal this morning, it was rather foggy, the way it often is in Petersburg. But when, at midday, I left St James's Hall with Sapellnikov and went into the street, it was blackest night—as dark as a moonless autumn night at home.' He had much better weather in June 1893 and was able to spend more time sightseeing. 'Paris is a mere village compared to London,' he told his brother Modest. 'Walking in Regent Street and Hyde Park, one sees so many carriages, so much splendid and luxurious equipment, that the eye is fairly dazzled.'

Max Bruch and Anton Rubinstein also used to stay at the Dieudonné.

Sigismond Thalberg stayed at the Brunswick Hotel, Jermyn Street, in March 1848.

Thomas Tomkins, composer and organist, pupil of William Byrd, was an organist of the Chapel Royal from 1621 until his death in 1656.

St John's Wood John Francis Barnett, composer, was born in London on 16 October 1837 and died in London on 24 November 1916. He resided at 56 Acacia Road, having resided earlier at 28 Carlton Hill.

William Sterndale Bennett, composer, pianist and conductor, resided at 66 St John's Wood Road (demolished) until his death here on 1 February 1875. Hans von Bülow and Charles Hallé visited him here. Bennett is buried in Westminster Abbey.

Arthur Bliss, composer and Master of the Queen's Music, resided at 8 The Lane, Marlborough Place, from 1955 until his death here on 27 March 1975. Dmitri Shostakovich visited him here in August 1962.

Benjamin Britten, composer, resided at 45A St John's Wood High Street 1943–6. His London residence 1958–65 was at 59 Marlborough Place, and he was staying here when he first met Shostakovich during the Russian composer's visit to London in 1962.

Max Bruch stayed at 20 Avenue Road in June 1893.

Eric Coates, composer, resided 1921–3 at 18 Cavendish Avenue, where he wrote the overture *The Merrymakers*.

Frederick Corder, composer, author, pupil of Hiller, teacher of Bantock and Bax, was born in London on 26 January 1852 and died here on 21 August 1932. For several years he lived at 9 Carlton Hill.

Frederic Cowen, composer of the *Scandinavian Symphony* and *The Language of Flowers* and conductor, resided for many years at 73 Hamilton Terrace and later at 54 Hamilton Terrace.

Tchaikovsky visited him at 73 Hamilton Terrace in June 1893.

Luigi Denza, composer, was born in Castellammare di Stabia, Italy, on 24 February 1846 and died on 26 January 1922 in London, where he resided at 9 Clifton Hill. His song *Funiculì-Funiculà* was written in 1880, a year after his arrival in London. During the early 1900s he resided at 16 Abercorn Place.

Giacomo Puccini was a frequent visitor to 16 Abercorn Place.

Gervaise de Peyer, virtuoso clarinettist, was born in London on 11 April 1926. He spent his childhood in Marlborough Place.

Kathleen Ferrier, contralto singer, was residing at 40 Hamilton Terrace at the time of her death on 8 October 1953 in hospital. She had previously lived at Frognal Mansions, 97 Frognal, Hampstead.

Gerald Finzi, composer, was born at 53 Hamilton Terrace on 14 July 1901.

Edward German, composer, resided at 5 Hall Road 1896–1921. During this period he wrote the operettas *Merrie England* and *Tom*

Jones, the orchestral work *Welsh Rhapsody* and the incidental music for *As You Like It, Much Ado About Nothing* and *Nell Gwyn.*

Eugene Goossens, conductor and composer, was born in London on 26 May 1893 and died in Hillingdon on 13 June 1962. He resided at 76 Hamilton Terrace, St John's Wood.

Charles Gounod stayed at 62 Avenue Road while supervising the first British production of *Faust,* staged at Her Majesty's Theatre on 11 June 1863.

Hamilton Harty, composer and conductor, was residing at 10 Grove End Road at the time of World War I. He was at 1 Norfolk Road from 1933 until shortly before his death in 1941.

Victor Hely-Hutchinson, composer of *A Carol Symphony,* was born in Cape Town, South Africa, on 26 December 1901 and died in London on 11 March 1947. He resided at 26 Queen's Grove.

Myra Hess, pianist, was born in London on 25 February 1890 and died on 25 November 1965 at her home, 23 Cavendish Close.

Albert Ketèlbey was residing at 57 Springfield Road at the time he composed *In a Monastery Garden* in 1915.

George Macfarren, composer and music scholar, died at his home, 7 Hamilton Terrace, on 31 October 1887. He is buried in Hampstead Cemetery.

Herbert Murrill, composer, was born in London on 11 May 1909 and died in London on 25 July 1952. He resided at 16 Cavendish Avenue.

Alfredo Piatti, generally recognized as the nineteenth century's greatest cellist, resided for many years at 15 Northwick Terrace.

Roger Quilter, composer, died in London on 21 September 1953. He resided at 23 Acacia Road.

Karl Rankl, conductor and composer, was born in Gaden, Austria, on 1 October 1898 and died in London on 6 September 1968. He resided at 25 Acacia Road.

Charles Santley, renowned baritone singer, for whom Gounod inserted *Avant de quitter ces lieux* in the second act of *Faust* when the opera was first performed in London, died at his home, 13 Blenheim Road, on 22 September 1922. He resided formerly at 67 Carlton Hill.

Humphrey Searle, composer, pupil of Webern and writer on music, notably on Liszt, moved to 44 Ordnance Hill in the late 1940s. The majority of those works by which he is known, including the Symphonies Nos 1–5, have been written here.

Jack Strachey, composer, who was born in Chelsea on 25 September 1894, was residing at 61 Clifton Hill when he wrote the song *These Foolish Things* in 1935. He died on 27 May 1972.

Piotr Tchaikovsky came to dinner with Lawrence Alma-Tadema at

17 (now 44) Grove End Road in June 1893. Other visitors to this house include Camille Saint-Saëns, Arrigo Boito, Max Bruch, Clara Schumann, Pablo Sarasate, Joseph Joachim, Anton Rubinstein and Nellie Melba.

Giuseppe Verdi was first in London from the middle of June to the end of July 1847, when he completed and conducted *I Masnadieri*, commissioned by Her Majesty's Theatre. He afterwards wrote to a friend: 'Though I found the London climate horrifying, nevertheless I was extremely delighted with the city. No, it's not a city, it's a world. There's nowhere else that compares with it for size, richness, the beauty of the streets, the cleanliness of the houses. You stand amazed and feel very humble when, in the midst of all this splendour, you gaze upon the Bank of England and the Docks. Who could resist such a people?' He made short business trips to the capital in 1854, 1855 and 1856. His next extended visit was April–June 1862 for the world première of his cantata *Inno delle nazioni*, written for that year's International Exhibition. He stayed at 43 Alpha Road (demolished to make way for Marylebone Station). By now he was sufficiently famous to be inundated by 'requests for autographs from all quarters, in a very odd and totally English manner. In other countries, people who want autographs either get themselves introduced or else have their album presented by a friend. Over here, nothing of the sort: I get letters through the post, and inside is a stamped envelope addressed to the person for whom I'm meant to be signing the autograph. Who the hell they are, I've not the slightest idea.' He made another brief business trip in June 1874 and went to the Handel Festival at the Crystal Palace, where he heard a choir of 3,500. He was unimpressed: this was 'nothing more than a gigantic confidence trick'. His final visit was to conduct the British première of his *Requiem* at the Albert Hall on 15 May 1875.

George Weldon, conductor, died on 16 August 1963. He resided at 37 St John's Wood Road.

St Marylebone Michael Balfe, composer, resided at 12 Seymour Street during the 1850s and early '60s.

Granville Bantock, composer and conductor, resided at 12 Granville Place from about 1880 to 1897.

John Barbirolli, conductor, was in his flat, at 45 Huntsworth Mews, when he suffered the heart attack that ended his life on 29 July 1970.

Julius Benedict, pupil of Weber, composer of the opera *The Lily of Killarney* and conductor, born in Stuttgart on 27 November 1804, died at 2 Manchester Square on 5 June 1885. Giacomo Meyerbeer, Hector Berlioz, Charles Gounod and Camille Saint-Saëns visited him here.

Francesco Berger, composer, pianist and administrator, who was born in London on 10 June 1834 and died in London on 26 April 1933, resided for more than forty years at 6 York Street. As Secretary to the Philharmonic Society he commissioned Dvořák's Seventh Symphony and Saint-Saëns's Third Symphony.

Piotr Tchaikovsky had dinner with him here on 21 March 1888. Berger wrote in his memoirs: 'Like most foreigners, Tschaikowsky was fond of English food, cooked English fashion, so our dinner consisted mainly of such . . . His conversation, carried on in French and German (for I do not speak Russian), was easy without being brilliant, and in all he said there was apparent the modest, gentle spirit which was so characteristic of the man. I noticed on this and other occasions that he never spoke of "politics", and if in the course of conversation that topic cropped up, he would remark that "Music and Art generally were fit matters for Musicians to discuss—not politics."'

Oscar Beringer, pianist and composer, pupil of Moscheles and Tausig, soloist on 14 October 1882 in the first London performance of Brahms's Second Piano Concerto, was born in Furtwangen, Germany, on 14 July 1844 and died in London on 21 February 1922. He resided during the 1880s and '90s at 12 Hinde Street.

Beringer gave the British première of Dvořák's Piano Concerto at the Crystal Palace on 13 October 1883, and the Czech stayed with him at Hinde Street 8–26 March 1884. Beringer relates that Dvořák 'used frequently to get up at six o'clock in the morning and go out for a stroll'. During the course of one of these lengthy perambulations the composer found himself outside the Athenaeum and, taking it for a café, went in, sat down, ordered coffee and was shortly afterwards ejected.

On subsequent of his nine trips to London, Dvořák conducted the world première of his Seventh Symphony at St James's Hall on 22 April 1885 and the world première of his Cello Concerto at the Queen's Hall on 19 March 1896.

Hector Berlioz stayed May–July 1848 at 26 Osnaburgh Street (demolished), where Heine had visited in 1827. He was at 27 (now 58) Queen Anne Street 10 May–28 July 1851; at 10 Old Cavendish Street (demolished) 4 March–21 June 1852; at 17 Old Cavendish Street (demolished) 10 May–9 July 1853, where Ferdinand Hiller called upon him on 26 June. During his final trip to London, 8 June–7 July 1855, he lodged at 13 Margaret Street (demolished). It was during the 1851 visit that he wrote his famous description of the London Season: 'But after the French Season, "The London Season! The London Season!"

is the cry of every Italian, French, Belgian, German, Bohemian, Hungarian, Swedish and English singer; virtuosos from all nations repeat it with fervour while setting foot on the steamboat, just as the soldiers of Aeneas, when they boarded their ships, shouted "Italiam! Italiam!" In no other country in the world is so much music consumed in a season as in London. Thanks to this immense consumption, all artists with genuine talent, after a few months spent in becoming known, are assured of work there. Once they are known and have been taken up, they are expected to return every year; it is assumed they will reappear, like the pigeons in North America. And never, to the very end of their lives, have they been known to fail the expectations of the English public, that model of fidelity, which is ever ready to welcome, applaud and admire them, "without perceiving the irreparable ravages of the years." One must have witnessed the rush and tumult in the lives of favourite performers in London to have any idea of what it can be like.'

As a conductor, Berlioz was always enthusiastically received; his compositions were less cordially treated. 'Berlioz, musically speaking,' declared the *Dramatic and Musical Review*, 'is a lunatic; a classical composer only in Paris, the great city of quacks. His music is simply and undisguisedly nonsense. He is a kind of orchestral Liszt, than which I could name nothing more intensely disagreeable.'

Henry Bishop, composer of *Home, Sweet Home*, resided at 15 Margaret Street in 1835.

Luigi Cherubini stayed at 10 Charles Street, now part of George Street, from the beginning of March to the beginning of June 1815. The house in which he resided was next to the Roman Catholic church, Spanish Place, where he went to Mass. The Symphony in D Major was composed here and received its first performance on 1 May in the Argyll Rooms, Regent Street. Parted from his wife during the three months in London, he assured her, 'I'm being as good as gold.' The word 'gold' was relevant to his visit; he returned to Paris better off by £200, a large sum in those days.

Frédéric Chopin stayed at 10 Bentinck Street 20–4 April 1848, at the start of the second of his two visits to the British Isles. His earlier stay, lasting a fortnight, had been in July 1837.

Eric Coates, composer, resided 1915–21 at Berners Street Mansions, Berners Street, where he wrote *Wood Nymphs* and *Summer Days*. He was at 176 Chiltern Court, Baker Street 1930–9, where he wrote *From Meadow to Mayfair, London Suite, London Again Suite, London Bridge, The Three Men* and *Saxo-Rhapsody*. He was at 130 Berkeley Court

1939–41, where the march *Calling All Workers* was composed. He resided at 53 Berkeley Court 1943–9. He occupied 2 Mansfield Street 1953–7, where he wrote *The Dambusters*.

Harriet Cohen, pianist, who was born in London on 2 December 1901 and died here on 13 November 1967, resided 1923–34 at 13 Wyndham Place. Visitors to this address include Edward Elgar, Ralph Vaughan Williams, Gustav Holst, Arnold Bax, William Walton, Constant Lambert, George Gershwin, Anton Webern, Adrian Boult, George Bernard Shaw, Arnold Bennett, H. G. Wells, W. Somerset Maugham and H. E. Bates.

William Cusins, organist, pianist, conductor and composer, was born in London on 14 October 1833 and was Master of the Queen's Music from 1870 until his death in Remonchamps, Belgium, on 31 August 1893. For some years he lived at 33 Nottingham Place.

Peter Maxwell Davies, composer, resided intermittently at 26 Fitzroy Square 1969–73. Works largely completed here include *Bell Tower* and incidental music and realizations for the film *The Boyfriend*.

James William Davison, music critic, resided during the 1850s at 30 Percy Street. Hector Berlioz was a frequent visitor here. *Le Corsaire*, published in 1855, is dedicated to Davison.

André de Chénier, poet and subject of Umberto Giordano's opera, resided at 31 Portman Square 1787–90 while working as secretary to the French ambassador.

Frederick Delius, composer, stayed at the Langham Hotel, now the property of the BBC, Langham Place, for three weeks in August 1929.

Edward Elgar, composer and Master of the King's Music, resided at 58 New Cavendish Street during the early part of 1910 and at 75 Gloucester Place during the latter half of 1911. Part of the Violin Concerto was composed in New Cavendish Street.

Eduard Hanslick, whose Jewish blood incited Wagner to ridicule him as Beckmesser in *Die Meistersinger*, first visited London in 1862. He met Arthur Sullivan at Jenny Lind's home, Argyle Lodge, Parkside, Wimbledon, and Charles Dickens and Wilkie Collins at 139 Westbourne Terrace, the home of Frederick Lehmann; he also visited Oxford and went to the Derby. The second of his two trips took place in June 1886, when he stayed at 17 Lower Seymour Street, now part of Seymour Street. During the following August he published in Vienna's *Neue Freie Presse* a lengthy report on London musical life. He was less than complimentary. Of a Philharmonic Society concert in St James's Hall on 2 June, he wrote that Mozart's Symphony No 40 'plodded along, for better or worse, badly played, without feeling or elegance'. The fault lay with the conductor, Arthur Sullivan, 'who never lifted his eyes from the score, as if he were reading it for the first time'. *The Musical Times*, however, felt that the performance displayed 'the powers of the orchestra and the masterly conductorship of Sir Arthur Sullivan to the utmost advantage'. (Two years later, Grieg and Tchaikovsky declared the orchestra to be the finest they had ever conducted.) Hanslick also went to *The Mikado*. 'Sir Arthur Sullivan's music is not notable for its originality or for any traces of genius, but it has valuable attributes . . . Sullivan has accomplished something, if in a secondary genre, that no Englishman has hitherto accomplished: to be melodious and amusing for an entire evening!'

Henri Herz stayed at 22 Great Marlborough Street during the summer of 1832.

Johann Nepomuk Hummel had dinner on 16 May 1830 with the pianist Lucy Anderson at her home, 2 New Cavendish Street. She was Queen Victoria's piano teacher.

Leoš Janáček, on his sole visit to the British Isles, stayed at the Langham Hotel 29 April–7 May 1926. On 30 April a reception was given for him at Claridge's. On 2 May he visited Henry Wood at Chorley Wood and attended a reception at the Czech Embassy. On 3 May he took a ride on the underground and did some sightseeing. He also went to the zoo, where he watched a walrus for twenty minutes and spent half an hour observing the monkeys, noting down their different calls. Extending this practice to humans, he noted down the speech patterns of the page-boy at the Langham. The word 'yes' particularly interested him during his stay; he put twenty versions of it into his notebook. On 4 May there was a reception for him at London University. Meanwhile, the General Strike had begun, but the Czech ambassador saved him any inconvenience by driving him to various functions. On 5 May Janáček wrote to a friend: 'Should I continue to live as I do now, I would certainly be dead within a month. Nothing but parties, food and sailing around in cars all day long. There's a strike here. The Londoners almost went without milk this morning.' A concert of his works was given on 6 April at the Wigmore Hall; because of the strike, Leon Goossens had to set out from his home three hours before the concert began. Instead of returning immediately to Prague, the composer stopped at Flushing for two days to recuperate.

Louis Jullien, conductor and impresario, resided 1847–8 at 76 (now 27 and rebuilt) Harley Street.

Hector Berlioz, on his first trip to the British Isles, stayed with Jullien 5 November 1847–20 April 1848, at which time the house was seized for the Queen's taxes, because of Jullien's bankruptcy. Berlioz returned to Paris, having conducted for Jullien at Drury Lane, with only a single month's salary. During his visit he caught the *grippe*, which was followed by bronchitis.

Karl Klindworth resided at 9 Manchester Street during the mid-1850s. Richard Wagner may have visited him here in 1855. Klindworth, he wrote in his autobiography, 'became a faithful and intimate friend, not only during my stay in London, but ever afterwards. Young as he was, the short time he had spent in London had sufficed to give him an opinion of English musical life, the justice of which I was soon compelled to admit, terrible though it was.'

Constant Lambert, composer, conductor and writer on music, died at the London Clinic, Devonshire Place, on 21 August 1951. His ashes are interred in Brompton Cemetery.

Henry Litolff, composer, pianist and music publisher, who was born in London on 6 February 1818 and died in Bois-le-Combes, France, on 6 August 1891, stayed at 36 Clipstone Street around Christmas 1840.

Eric Maschwitz, lyric writer, whose successes included the musical comedies *Balalaika, Carissima* and *Love from Judy* and the songs 'A Nightingale Sang in Berkeley Square' and 'These Foolish Things', was born in Birmingham on 10 June 1901 and died in Ascot on 27 October 1969. He resided at 8 Queen Anne's Street, London.

Nellie Melba, soprano singer, resided at 30 Great Cumberland Place during the first decade of the twentieth century. Percy Grainger visited her here.

Felix Mendelssohn stayed at 103 Great Portland Street (demolished), on the corner of Riding House Street, from 21 April to about 20 July 1829, from 23 April to about 22 June 1832, from 25 April to about 17 May 1833 and from 5 June to 25 August 1833. His landlord, Heinke, was a German ironmonger and locksmith who had assisted in opening the locked door to Weber's room on the morning after his death. On 14 May 1832 Mendelssohn was present when Thomas Attwood conducted the world première of *Fingal's Cave* at the King's Theatre, Covent Garden. On 13 May 1833 the composer conducted the world première of his *Italian Symphony* at the Hanover Square Rooms.

Mrs Heinke was an excellent cook. The dishes that she most frequently prepared were mutton chops and bread-and-butter pudding. Mendelssohn particularly relished the latter, often asking for some to be left for him as a nightcap after a concert.

Following his first trip to London, Mendelssohn wrote: 'That smoky nest is fated to be forever my favourite city; my heart swells when I think of it.'

Bernhard Molique stayed at 21 Old Cavendish Street in 1848.

Ignaz Moscheles, pianist, composer and conductor, who was born in

Prague on 30 May 1794 and died in Leipzig on 10 March 1870, resided at 77 Norton Street, now 77 Bolsover Street, London, from the autumn of 1825 to the autumn of 1830. Carl Maria von Weber visited him here in 1826; Heinrich Heine in 1827; Felix Mendelssohn in 1829.

Vincent Novello, music publisher, organist, pianist, conductor and composer, was born at 240 Oxford Street on 6 September 1781 and died in Nice on 9 August 1861.

George Alexander Osborne, composer and pianist, resided during the 1850s at 33 Devonshire Street. Hector Berlioz was a frequent visitor here.

Adelaide Procter, poet, who was born in 1825 and died in 1864, resided at 38 Harley Street at the time she wrote 'A Lost Chord', set to music by Arthur Sullivan in 1877 as *The Lost Chord*.

Roger Quilter, composer, resided at 7 Montagu Street from the time of World War I through the 1920s and '30s.

Ignazio Raimondi, composer and violinist, was born in Naples in about 1737 and died at his home, 74 Great Portland Street, London, on 14 January 1813.

Alberto Randegger, conductor and composer, who was born on 13 April 1832 in Trieste, Italy, and died in London on 18 December 1911, resided during the 1880s at 17 Duke Street. His final address was 5 Nottingham Place.

Richard Redhead was organist of Old Margaret Chapel (now All Saint's Church), Margaret Street, Cavendish Square, 1839–64. In 1853 were published his hymn tunes No 46, sung to 'Bright the Vision That Delighted', and No 76, sung to 'Rock of Ages, Cleft for Me'.

Richard Rodgers and Lorenz Hart stayed at 11 York Terrace during the summer of 1930, working on *Ever Green*.

Prosper Sainton, violinist, who was born in Toulouse on 5 June 1813, resided at 8 Hinde Street (demolished and rebuilt) during the 1850s and '60s.

Hector Berlioz and Richard Wagner were fellow dinner guests on more than one occasion during June 1855. In his autobiography, Wagner writes: 'I was now brought face to face with this strangely gifted person, tormented and even blunted as he then was. When I saw him, a man considerably my senior [Berlioz was 51; Wagner was 42], coming here merely in the hope of earning a few guineas, I could deem myself perfectly happy and almost floating on air by contrast; for my own coming had been motivated rather by a desire for distraction, a craving for outward inspiration. His whole being expressed weariness and despair, and I was suddenly seized with deep sympathy for this man whose talent so far surpassed that of his rivals—for this was as clear as daylight to me. Berlioz seemed to be pleasantly affected by the attitude of gay spontaneity that I adopted with him.' Berlioz wrote to a friend: 'Wagner embraces me fervently, weeps, stamps his feet. Scarcely has he left [London], when "The Musical World" publishes the passages in his book [*Opera and Drama*] in which he knocks me about in the most comical and witty fashion.'

Camille Saint-Saëns made numerous trips to London. His most notable visit, when he stayed at 49 George Street, was to conduct the world première of his Third Symphony at St James's Hall on 19 May 1886.

Johann Peter Salomon, violinist, conductor, impresario and composer, who commissioned from Haydn the twelve *London* (or *Salomon*) *Symphonies*, who was born in Bonn, in the same house in which Beethoven was born, in January 1745, died at his home, 70 Newman Street, on 28 November 1815. He is buried in Westminster Abbey.

Francesco Schira, conductor and composer, was born in Malta on 21 August 1809 and died in London on 15 October 1883. He resided at 60 Welbeck Street.

William Shakespeare, tenor singer, pianist and distinguished teacher of singing, resided, around 1900, at 14 Mansfield Street. Fritz Kreisler visited him here.

Jean Sibelius, who came to London in 1905, 1908, 1909, 1912 and 1921, stayed at the Langham Hotel during his last two visits. In 1909 he boarded in a house near Campden Hill, where he completed his String Quartet; during this visit, he made the acquaintance of Claude Debussy. 'I liked England very much,' he said some years later. 'It was an indescribable joy to me to see ancient, special culture at every step based on respect for the power of traditions, which appealed to me very strongly. I immediately discovered the error in the very general impression current at that time that Englishmen have no natural talent for music. On the contrary, they are very capable musicians, although in their splendid isolation they do not trouble to advertise themselves.' His only complaint was that, when he was composing the String Quartet, the room below was occupied by a woman who, wishing to express artistic empathy, often applied herself to the *Moonlight Sonata* on a piano somewhat impaired by the passing of the years.

Alexander Skryabin stayed at the Welbeck Palace Hotel 11–30 March 1914. On 14 March he took part in performances conducted by Henry Wood of *Prometheus* and the Piano Concerto in the Queen's

Hall. On 20 and 26 March he gave recitals of his piano music at Bechstein Hall, across the road from his hotel. On about 13 March he contracted the lip infection that was to end his life a year later. This caused him considerable discomfort and embarrassment during his visit. 'I had to appear before the English public for the first time with a swollen lip!' he wrote to Tatyana Schloezer. Henry Wood later recalled that 'he looked far from well and seemed to be a mass of nerves'. His misery was aggravated by 'a mountain of letters asking for my autograph . . . Tillett tells me I must comply with Londoner's requests for these, and it will take me all of 3 hours to be their victim. Where am I to find the time? I saw London in all its magnificence today for the first time. It was the first good day . . . I went around in a taxi.'

George Smart, composer of the hymn tune *Wiltshire*, sung to 'Through All the Changing Scenes of Life', conductor and organist, resided at 91 Great Portland Street (demolished) from August 1801 until a few months before his death in Bedford Square on 23 February 1867.

Carl Maria von Weber stayed with him from 5 March 1826 until his death here during the early hours of 5 June 1826. Although desperately ill with consumption, he had agreed to come to London to conduct the world première of *Oberon*, which was commissioned by the impresario Charles Kemble. In Paris, shortly before his trip, Weber called on Rossini, who, seeing his pathetic condition, pleaded with him not to go. He was determined, however, for his family's sake, to reap the large rewards that lay in store for him in London. He completed the score of the opera at 91 Great Portland Street, finishing the overture on 9 April. Three days later he conducted the first performance at Covent Garden. During the next two months he accepted a number of other conducting engagements. Meanwhile, his health, further undermined by the English climate, continued to deteriorate. On 18 April in a letter to his wife, he said there was 'such a dark yellow fog that one can hardly exist in the room without a light. The sun has no rays and is like a red point in the sky; it's quite terrible.' His final letters speak of how joyfully he looks forward to his imminent return to Dresden, but the increasingly shaky handwriting betrays his ebbing strength. His departure was planned for 6 June, and when his bedroom on the second floor was broken into on 5 June and he was seen to be dead, they found all his clothes and possessions in neat piles, ready to be packed for the journey. In a dresser drawer was £782 6s that he had earned in London. He was buried on 21 June in the Catholic chapel in Moorfields. His body was disinterred in October 1844 and reburied on 15 December 1844 in

Dresden. The Catholic chapel, at Finsbury Circus, is now the Church of St Mary.

Richard Wagner, on his first visit to London, in August 1839, came and stood outside 91 Great Portland Street.

Ludwig Spohr stayed at 1A Devonshire Street March–August 1820 on the first of his six visits to London. He came to England again in 1839, 1843, 1847, 1852 and 1853. Neglected nowadays, he was then regarded as one of the greatest composers. When, in 1885, the Mikado sang of 'Bach interwoven with Spohr and Beethoven', audiences would not have been surprised by such a juxtaposition. The overture to *Jessonda* was performed twenty-four times at Philharmonic Society concerts between 1826 and 1885. During the same period the overture to *The Marriage of Figaro* was programmed on only ten occasions. So fervently was he admired that he could go nowhere in London without being besieged by autograph hunters. Departing from London by steamer in the summer of 1843, he wearily remarked: 'There can hardly be a music lover in England who doesn't now have my autograph.' No sooner had he spoken, however, than a rowing-boat pulled alongside, and several people jumped on board laden with their own and friends' albums. The signing recommenced, the boat rowing beside the steamer until, with Gravesend in sight, and the albums all inscribed, it swung back up-river.

Several of Spohr's works received their world premières in London. These include the Fourth Symphony on 23 February 1835; the Fifth Symphony on 9 March 1840; the Sixth Symphony on 6 April 1840; and the Eighth Symphony on 1 May 1848.

Spohr's very first day in London began unfortunately. Wishing to make a good impression, he attired himself in 'a bright red Turkish shawl-pattern waistcoat' and set out from Devonshire Street to meet the directors of the Philharmonic Society. This garment, 'which was considered on the Continent to be a most elegant article and of the newest fashion', would have been particularly striking, for he was a man of heroic build. Yet, 'scarcely had I appeared in the street', than he was subjected to the derision of passers-by. Matters became worse as his journey proceeded; angry words, that he could not understand, were shouted, and people began to tag along behind him continuously mouthing abuse. On reaching his destination and escaping his pursuers, he was informed that George III had recently died. He immediately took a cab back to his lodgings, exchanged his red waistcoat for a black one and made a fresh start.

Charles Villiers Stanford, composer, conductor, celebrated teacher, pianist, organist and writer on music, resided at 9 Lower Berkeley Street, now the site of Lloyd's Bank, Fitzhardinge Street, from 1916 until his death here on 29 March 1924. He is buried in Westminster Abbey.

Leopold Stokowski, conductor, was born in Marylebone Street on 18 April 1882.

Karol Szymanowski stayed at 107 Gloucester Place in April 1921.

John Thomas, harpist to Queen Victoria, conductor and composer, died in London on 19 March 1913. He resided during his later years at 53 Welbeck Street.

Paolo Tosti, composer and singing teacher to the royal family, who was born in Ortona sul Mare, Italy, on 9 April 1846 and died in Rome on 2 December 1916, resided during the last twenty years of his life at 12 Mandeville Place. Giacomo Puccini was often a guest here.

Pauline Viardot stayed at 30 Devonshire Street from the autumn of 1870 to the summer of 1871. Charles Gounod, Camille Saint-Saëns and Ivan Turgenev were visitors here, often taking part in charades with the Viardot family.

Giovanni Viotti, composer and violinist, was born in Fontanetto Po, Italy, on 12 May 1755 and died at 5 Berkeley Street, Portman Square, on 3 March 1824.

Richard Wagner stayed at 65 Balcombe Street (then 31 Milton Street), the home of Ferdinand Praeger, on the night of 4 March 1855. From there, he moved to 22 Portland Terrace (demolished), near the North Gate of Regent's Park, remaining at that address until 26 June 1855, when he returned to Zurich. He liked watching the sheep in Regent's Park, feeding the ducks, and going to the zoo. He conducted eight Philharmonic Society concerts. 'On various occasions I also visited some not uninteresting theatres in London, strictly avoiding opera houses, of course'—his own operas were not yet being played in London. He attended a number of oratorio performances. 'It was here that I came to understand the true spirit of English musical culture, which is bound up with the spirit of English Protestantism. This accounts for the fact that an oratorio attracts the public far more than an opera. A further advantage is secured by the feeling among the audience that an evening spent in listening to an oratorio may be regarded as a sort of service, and is almost as good as going to church. Everybody holds a Handel piano score in the same way that one holds a prayerbook in church. These scores are sold at the box-office in shilling editions and are followed most diligently—out of anxiety, it seemed to me, not to miss certain points solemnly enjoyed by the whole audience. For instance, at the beginning of the *Hallelujah Chorus* it is considered proper for everybody to rise from his seat. This movement, which probably originated in an expression of enthusiasm, is now carried out at every performance of *Messiah* with painful precision.'

His recollections of this visit to London became 'merged in the all-absorbing memory of almost uninterrupted ill-health, caused primarily, no doubt, by the state of the London climate at that season of the year, which is notorious throughout the world. I had a perpetual cold, and I therefore followed the advice of my friends to take a heavy English diet by way of resisting the effects of the air, but this did not improve matters in the slightest.' It made work almost impossible, and the orchestrating of *Die Walküre* was limited to a few hundred pages during his stay of three and a half months. 'In absolute despair I plunged into Dante, making for the first time a serious effort to read him. The "Inferno", indeed, became a never-to-be-forgotten reality in the London atmosphere.'

Ferdinand Praeger should not be confused with Professor Praeger of Hamm, who, in the 1850s, translated Wagner into Turkish.

Wagner visited George Critchett, the celebrated opthalmologist, at 21 Harley Street in May 1877 and was pleased to find a bust of himself in the waiting-room. Critchett had some new spectacles made for him, and these were sent in June to Ems, where Wagner was recovering from his final trip to London by taking the waters. The composer broke one of the pairs of spectacles on the same day they arrived.

Charles Wesley, hymn writer, who died in London on 29 March 1788, his son Charles, organist and composer, who died in London on 23 May 1834, and his son Samuel, composer and organist, who died in London on 11 October 1837, are buried in the cemetery of Old St Marylebone Church.

Henry Wood, celebrated conductor, was born at 318 Oxford Street on 3 March 1869. He resided at 49 Hallam Street 1937–9.

Sergey Rakhmaninov visited him at 49 Hallam Street in October 1938.

Agnes Zimmermann, pianist and composer, was born in Cologne on 5 July 1847 and died in London on 14 November 1925. She resided at 16 Devonshire Street and, formerly, at 13 Portman Square. She gave the British première on 7 December 1872 at the Crystal Palace of Beethoven's Violin Concerto transcribed as a piano concerto.

St Pancras Frederick Crouch, composer and conductor, was born in

Warren Street on 31 July 1808 and died in Portland, Maine, on 18 August 1896, having invented the engraving process of zincography, composed the song *Kathleen Mavourneen* and fought for the Confederate Army in the American Civil War.

Karl Marx, economist and political philosopher, whose writings have inspired or dictated numerous musical works, was born in Trier, West Germany, on 5 May 1818 and died at his home, 41 Maitland Park Road, on 14 March 1883. He is buried in Highgate Cemetery. He earlier resided at 28 Dean Street, Soho, and at 46 Grafton Terrace.

Henry Smart, composer, who was born in London on 26 October 1813, was organist of St Pancras Church, Euston Road, from 1864 until his death at his home in King Henry's Road, Hampstead, on 6 July 1879, during which time he published the hymn tunes *Regent Square*, sung to both 'Jesus Came—the Heavens Adoring' and 'Light's Abode, Celestial Salem'; *Heathlands*, sung to 'God of Mercy, God of Grace'; *Rex Gloriae*, sung to 'See the Conqueror Mounts in Triumph'; and *Everton*, often sung to 'Alleluia! Alleluia! Hearts to Heaven and Voices Raise'. He also composed the songs *The Lady of the Lea* and *Only a Rose*. He is buried in Hampstead Cemetery, Finchley Road.

Samuel Webbe senior, composer and organist, was born in 1740 and died in his chambers at Gray's Inn on 25 May 1816. He is buried in St Pancras Cemetery.

Shortlands John Veale, composer, pupil of Roy Harris, was born here on 15 June 1922.

Soho Johann Christian Bach, who was born in Leipzig on 5 September 1735 and died in London on 1 January 1782, resided mostly in Soho during the last twenty years of his life. At first lodging in Jermyn Street, he soon moved to Meard Street, where Mozart visited him in 1764 and 1765. He was later in Carlisle Street and Queen Street, Golden Square. He occupied 80 Newman Street from 1774.

Theresa Cornelys, singer and entrepreneuse, who was born in Venice in 1723 and died in the Fleet Prison, London, on 19 August 1797, acquired in 1760 Carlisle House, which stood on the corner of Sutton Row and was pulled down in about 1800. J. C. Bach and Carl Friedrich Abel took part in some of the concerts given here. Mrs Cornelys also provided other entertainments and in February 1771 was arraigned for keeping 'a common disorderly house'.

She led a varied life. At 17, she was residing with a Venetian senator of 76. Not long afterwards, she met Casanova and bore him a daughter.

Her marriage to the dancer Angelo Pompeati was terminated when he disembowelled himself. She first sang in London in 1746. In 1748 and 49, she appeared in Hamburg and Copenhagen in operas conducted by Gluck. After associations with the Margrave of Bayreuth and Prince Charles Alexander of Lorraine, she supposedly married again, although her husband was never seen in London. At the end of her life she opened a breakfast bar in Knightsbridge, selling asses' milk. Too far ahead of its time, this venture precipitated her terminal bankruptcy and incarceration.

William Croft was organist of St Anne's Church, Soho, 1700–12. He was organist of Westminster Abbey and composer to the Chapel Royal from 1708 until his death in 1727. His *Burial Service* is widely used. His hymn tune *St Anne*, published in 1708 and sung to 'O God, Our Help in Ages Past', ranks among the world's greatest melodies. It is highly probable that he also composed *Hanover*, which is sung to 'O Worship the King All Glorious Above'.

Richard D'Oyly Carte, impresario, whose name will be forever linked with the operettas of Gilbert and Sullivan, was born in Greek Street on 3 May 1844.

Domenico Dragonetti, double-bass player and composer, was born in Venice on 7 April 1763 and died on 16 April 1846 in London, where he resided in Leicester Square.

Jan Ladislav Dussek resided for several years during the 1790s at 67 and 68 Dean Street.

Michael Festing, violinist and composer, who was possibly born in Germany in 1680, died on 24 July 1752 in London, where he resided in Warwick Street.

Noel Gay, composer of *The Lambeth Walk, The King's Horses* and *Run, Rabbit, Run,*, was organist of St Anne's during World War I. He died in London on 4 March 1954.

Handel, Mozart, Haydn, Clementi, Hummel, Mendelssohn, Liszt and Chopin were among the visitors to Broadwood's offices at 33 Great Pulteney Street, which were situated here 1742–1904. The building has since been demolished.

Johann Nepomuk Hummel stayed at 33 Golden Square during the summer of 1833.

Franz Liszt was 12 years old when, accompanied by his father, he made his first trip to England in the summer of 1824, remaining until the early months of the following year. He gave his first concert in London on 21 June 1824. During this visit he composed the opera *Don Sanche*, produced in Paris on 17 October 1825; the overture to the opera appears to have been first performed in Manchester on 20 June 1825, when he took part in a concert there at the time of his second trip. He and his father lodged in Frith Street for most of the 1825 visit, during which he played for George IV at Windsor. He also went to dinner with Charles Salaman, who recalled: 'He was a very charmingly natural and unaffected boy, and I have never forgotten his joyful exclamation, "Oh! gooseberry pie!" when his favourite dish was put upon the table.' Father and son returned in the summer of 1827, the young man performing a Hummel concerto at a Philharmonic Society concert on 21 May. He made further visits in 1840 and 1841, during which he gave a recital in Buckingham Palace, stayed for a while in Richmond, went to Ascot and toured the British Isles. He was often at Gore House, demolished to make way for the Royal Albert Hall, where he was a guest of Lady Blessington, who once remarked: 'What a pity to put such a handsome man to a piano!'

Wolfgang Amadeus Mozart, together with his father, mother and sister, lodged with Thomas Williamson, a corset-maker, at 20 Frith Street (demolished) from about 25 September 1764 to 24 July 1765. The *Public Advertiser* of 11 March 1765 states: 'For the Benefit of Master MOZART, of eight Years, and Miss MOZART, of Twelve Years of Age, prodigies of Nature, before their Departure from England, which will be in six Weeks Time. THERE will be performed at the End of this Month, or the Beginning of April next, a Concert of Vocal and Instrumental MUSIC. Tickets at Half a Guinea Each. To be had of Mr. Mozart, at Mr. Williamson's in Thrift-street [now Frith Street], Soho; where those Ladies and Gentlemen, who will honour him with their Company from Twelve to Three in the Afternoon, any Day in the Week, except Tuesday and Friday, may, by taking each a Ticket, gratify their Curiosity and not only hear this young Music Master and his Sister perform in private; but likewise try his surprising musical capacity, by giving him any Thing to play at Sight, or any Music without Bass, which he will write upon the Spot, without recurring to his Harpsichord.'

Niccolò Paganini began his first visit to London on 14 May 1831, when he stayed at the Hotel Sablionière et Provence (demolished) in Leicester Square. He left for Dublin towards the end of August. His concerts in London during June, July and August were among the most sensational ever given in the British Isles; the receipts amounted to over £10,000. Musicians were staggered by his violin playing. 'They could not sleep at night for thinking of him,' wrote Leigh Hunt, for whom a typical reaction was the 'O Christ!' murmured by somebody standing near him at one of the concerts. Mary Shelley told her friend Mrs

Gisborne that Paganini 'threw me into hysterics. I delight in him more than I can express—his wild ethereal figure, rapt look—and the sounds he draws from his violin are all superhuman.' So intense was the interest in him that 'I can never step outdoors,' he wrote to Luigi Germi, 'without being mobbed by people who, not content with following and jostling me, actually get in front of me and prevent my moving in any direction, address me in English—of which I don't know a word—and even feel me, as if to determine whether I'm flesh and blood. And not just the ordinary people, but even the upper classes.' He made further visits to London in November 1831 and February 1832. In July and August 1832 he stayed in a house near the edge of Regent's Park. He was again here April–August 1833. On 14 May 1833 he and Mendelssohn took part in the world première of the Trio Concertante for Viola, Guitar and Cello, with Paganini playing the viola and Mendelssohn performing the guitar part on the piano; the cellist was Robert Lindley. His final visit was in the spring and summer of 1834, which lasted until 21 June. His love affair with Charlotte Watson, whom he met in London in June 1831, when she was 16 and he was 48, did not survive his departure in 1834.

Johann Peter Salomon, violinist, conductor, impresario and composer, who commissioned from Haydn the twelve *London* (or *Salomon*) *Symphonies*, was residing at 18 Great Pulteney Street (demolished) at the time Haydn made his London debut in 1791.

Joseph Haydn resided with Salomon at 18 Great Pulteney Street from the beginning of January 1791 to the beginning of July 1792. In a notebook entry for 5 December 1791 he wrote: 'The fog was so thick that one could have spread it on bread. I had to light the lights at 11a.m. so I could write.' During this stay, the composer directed the world premières, at Hanover Square Rooms, of the following of his symphonies: Nos 95 and 96 in the spring of 1791; No 93 on 17 February 1792; No 98 on 2 March 1792; No 94 on 23 March 1792; No 97 on 3 May 1792. All these works were written in London and performed from manuscript.

Wilhelmine Schröder-Devrient stayed at 23 Golden Square in June 1832.

George Smart, composer, conductor and organist, was born in Argyll Street on 10 May 1776.

Johann Strauss senior stayed at the Hotel du Commerce, now Manzi's Restaurant, Leicester Street, from the middle of April 1838 to 10 June 1838. He had booked rooms in another hotel, at 5 Fleet Street, but finding it unsatisfactory, had soon left, whereupon the proprietor took him to court. The judge ordered Strauss to pay the proprietor £29; costs were £140. Meanwhile, all the composer's money had been stolen, and he was threatened with debtors' prison. However, the publisher Robert Cocks came to his rescue, discharging his debts.

Strauss led his orchestra at more than sixty concerts and balls while he was in London, introducing during that time his waltz *Homage to Queen Victoria of Great Britain* at Buckingham Palace on 10 May 1838, seven weeks before the coronation, the *Musical Telegraph* and *Mosaic Waltz*. Two years later he wrote his *Myrthen Waltz* to celebrate the marriage of Victoria and Albert. He was in London again, at the Hotel Versailles (demolished), 2 Leicester Place, 22 April–10 July 1849, a few months before his death. Works stemming from this visit are the *Frederika Polka, March of the Royal Horseguards, Almack's Quadrille, Alice Polka* and *Exeter Polka*, presented at the Exeter Hall.

Johann Strauss junior made one visit to London, 15 August–26 October 1867, when he conducted at sixty-three concerts in the Royal Opera House, Covent Garden. Works composed for these concerts include the waltz *Remembrances of Covent Garden*, the *Festival Quadrille* and the *Potpourri Quadrille*.

Eduard Strauss came to London in the summer of 1885 and again in 1895 and 1897. On 9 June 1885 he conducted the Strauss orchestra at a concert in the Albert Hall, the idea of which might have astonished his father, Johann senior.

Richard Strauss frequently dined at the Venezia Restaurant in Great Chapel Street during his final visit to London in 1947.

Richard Wagner stayed at The King's Arms (demolished) in Old Compton Street 13–20 August 1839. He had been recommended to try The Hoop and Horseshoe (demolished) in Queen Street, next to The Mint, but found the area so distasteful that he left 'with all possible haste'. During this first trip to London he visited the Houses of Parliament, where he listened to Lord Melbourne and the Duke of Wellington make speeches. On the last day before leaving he, his wife Minna and their dog Robber 'shuddered through a ghastly London Sunday, and wound up with a train trip (our very first) to Gravesend Park'.

Southwark Henry John Gauntlett was organist of St Olave's at the time Mendelssohn chose him to play the organ part in the first performance of *Elijah* on 26 August 1846 in Birmingham.

John James, composer and organist, was organist of St Olave's in the 1730s. He died in 1745.

Carl Maria von Weber died in this house, since demolished, in Great Portland Street, London, on 5 June 1826. He had been lodging there, as the guest of the composer and conductor George Smart, since the first week in March, while completing *Oberon*, which received its world première at Covent Garden on 12 April. The overture to the opera was written in the front room on the second floor (*Greater London Council*)

As far as can be determined, the only London house in which Wagner stayed that has neither been demolished nor rebuilt is 65 Balcombe Street, where he spent the night of 4 March 1855. The address was formerly 31 Milton Street (*Stewart Spencer*)

This photograph of Richard Wagner was taken by Elliott & Fry on 24 May 1877, during the composer's final visit to London. He had celebrated his sixty-fourth birthday two days earlier. A flattering water-colour portrait of him by Hubert Herkomer, also executed at that time, disappeared in 1945; Wagner said of it, 'Yes, I like to look like that!' (*Bassano & Vandyk Studios*)

Wolfgang Amadeus Mozart, with his mother, father and sister, lodged at 180 Ebury Street, London, during the summer of 1764, when he was eight years old. His first two symphonies were written here. This was his only visit to Britain (*Greater London Council*)

180

Francis Pott, author of several well-known hymns, was born here on 29 December 1832.

Donald Swann, composer and entertainer, spent most of his childhood at 92 Walworth Road.

Stepney James Edmeston, author of the hymn 'Lead Us, Heavenly Father, Lead Us', was born in Wapping on 10 September 1791 and died in Homerton on 7 January 1867.

Stoke Newington Daniel Auber came to London at the age of 20, in 1802, to acquire commercial knowledge and improve his English. He stayed for almost a year and a half and, on returning to France, abandoned his business career to devote himself to music. When Dickens met him in Paris in 1855 Auber told him he had lived in 'Stock Noonton' and that his English was all forgotten.

William Dalrymple Maclagan, born in Edinburgh on 18 June 1826, was vicar of St Mary's 1869–75. His hymn tune *Newington* is sung to 'Thine for Ever! God of Love'. He died in Kensington on 19 September 1910.

William Henry Monk, composer and organist, was born in London on 16 March 1823 and died here on 1 March 1889. His great hymn tune *Eventide*, sung to 'Abide with Me', was composed here and published in 1861. Among his other hymn tunes are *Merton*, sung to 'Hark! A Thrilling Voice is Sounding', and *St Ethelwald*, often sung to 'Soldiers of Christ, Arise'. He was organist of St Matthias's Church for many years.

Isaac Watts, author of numerous familiar hymns, was educated 1690–4 at the Nonconformist Academy, where Daniel Defoe had been a student twenty years earlier. He lived in the home of Sir John Hartopp, as tutor to his son, 1696–1702. In 1698 he became an assistant minister and, in 1702, pastor of the Independent Church in Newington. He lived with the Abney family in Cheshunt 1712–35. The final years of his life were spent largely in Newington, where he died on 25 November 1748.

The Strand Claude Debussy, on the first of his seven visits to London, stayed at the Hotel Cecil, in The Strand, in July 1902. 'Would you believe it to be impossible to procure a decent cup of tea?' he wrote to his wife. 'Oh for my Rue Cardinet and my dear wife who, among other gifts, can make tea. In England there are no such women. Their women, with complexions like uncooked ham and primitive animal-like gestures, are for the Horse Guards. Well, certain journeys are necessary, if only to learn that one would do better to stay at home.' In May 1903 he returned to report on *The Ring* at Covent Garden and again stayed at the Hotel Cecil. As 'a reward for good behaviour' in sitting through *The Ring* he went to the Empire Music Hall, which he much enjoyed. In July 1904 he came to London for a single day to see Sarah Bernhardt as Pelléas and Mrs Patrick Campbell as Mélisande in Maeterlinck's play.

His first visit as a conductor was in January 1908, when he directed performances of *L'Après-midi d'un faune* and *La Mer*. He conducted at a second concert in February 1909 and, being inexperienced with the baton, entirely lost his way in *Fêtes*. However, despite the fact that he had stopped conducting, the orchestra, superbly rehearsed by Henry Wood, played the work through to its conclusion, and to such good effect that it was encored. Later in the evening a reception was given for him at the Aeolian Hall. Arnold Bax met him there and found him somewhat oriental in appearance. 'Never shall I forget the impression made upon me by that thick-set clumsy figure, the huge greenish, almost Moorish face beneath the dense thicket of black hair, and the obscure dreaming eyes that seemed to be peering through me at some object behind my back.'

In May 1909 Debussy was once more in London, to supervise the British première of *Pelléas et Mélisande*. His final visit was in 1914, when he took part in a chamber concert on 17 July at the home of Edgar Speyer.

Manuel de Falla spent a good deal of time with Dyagilev at the Savoy on his visit to London to supervise the world première of *The Three-Cornered Hat* on 22 July 1919 at the Alhambra Theatre. *The Miller's Dance* was written at the last moment in London, after Dyagilev had requested a further solo number for Leonide Massine.

Richard D'Oyly Carte, impresario, died at his home, 4 Adelphi Terrace, on 3 April 1901. He is buried at St Andrew's Church, Fairlight, East Sussex.

Antonín Dvořák stayed at the Charing Cross Hotel 12–13 June 1891.

John Field, composer, pianist, pupil of Clementi and teacher of Glinka, resided at 6 Beaufort Buildings in the Strand during his stay in London from September 1831 until the latter part of 1832. He had previously resided in London 1793–1802.

Benjamin Franklin, statesman, writer, scientist, inventor, composer and perfecter of the armonica, was born in Boston, Massachusetts, on 17 January 1706 and died in Philadelphia on 17 April 1790. He lived in London for about seventeen years between 1724 and 1775, residing, on separate occasions during the 1750s, '60s and '70s at 36 Craven Street.

It was here that, in 1761, he made his improvements to the armonica, for which Mozart composed his Armonica Quintet, K617, thirty years later.

William Schwenck Gilbert, librettist, poet, cartoonist and dramatist, was born at 17 Southampton Street on 18 November 1836.

Heinrich Heine, poet, whose verses inspired songs by Balakirev, Borodin, Brahms, Frank Bridge, Franz, Grieg, Griffes, Holst, Liszt, Loewe, MacDowell, Mackenzie, Mendelssohn, Mussorgsky, Rakhmaninov, Rimsky-Korsakov, Schubert, Schumann, Stanford, Richard Strauss, Tchaikovsky, Wagner and Wolf, resided during 1827 at 32 Craven Street.

Matthew Locke, composer, died in London in August 1677 and is thought to have been buried in the Queen's Chapel of the Savoy, Savoy Hill.

George Macfarren, composer and music scholar, was born at 24 Villiers Street on 2 March 1813.

Nellie Melba frequently resided at the Savoy Hotel from around 1890 to the time of World War I.

Ivor Novello, composer, dramatist, singer and actor, resided in a flat on the top floor of 11 Aldwych from 1913 until his death here on 6 March 1951. Among the first works he wrote here, in 1914, was *Keep the Home Fires Burning*.

Bessie Palmer, contralto singer, was born at 9 Fountain Court on 9 August 1831 and died in London on 1 September 1910.

Sergey Prokofiev first came to London during the summer of 1914 to see the Dyagilev Ballet Company at Drury Lane. His next visit, when he stayed at the Savoy Hotel, was to conduct the British première of *Chout* at the Prince's Theatre on 9 June 1921; among the audience were Igor Stravinsky and Manuel de Falla. Two days later, at the Prince's, he conducted the first performance in Britain of the *Classical Symphony*. He was here again in 1922, introducing the Third Piano Concerto at the Queen's Hall on 24 April. On 10 March 1923 he played the First Piano Concerto at the Queen's Hall. He returned to London for the British première of *Le Pas d'acier* at the Prince's on 4 July 1927, following this with premières of the Third Piano Sonata and Second Piano Concerto on 5 and 9 December of that year. In June 1932 he was here to record the Third Piano Concerto. He made two trips in 1934, introducing the Fifth Piano Concerto, with Bruno Walter, on 31 January and the Third Symphony on 19 October. His final appearance in London was in January 1938, when he conducted the British première of the Second Violin Concerto on the 26th.

'The London musical world is more conservative than the Parisian,' he once wrote, 'the British are slow to accept anything new, but, once they have accepted it, they are less apt to change their minds so quickly.' Their wealth was also noted; at the première of *Le Pas d'acier*, 'the flashing of diamonds hurt one's eyes'. The critics were less to his taste. 'The English are supposed to be very polite, but that certainly does not apply to their music critics. English music critics are the most impolite in the world, with the possible exception of the Americans.' In those days, however, music critics had to cover a rather wide range of artistic activities, and the impoliteness unfortunately often stemmed from ignorance; Ernest Newman of *The Sunday Times*, for instance, was under the impression that a ballet score was composed after the choreography had been completed.

Giacomo Puccini made many trips to London, almost all of which were connected with the British premières of his operas. He first came in 1894 for the première of *Manon Lescaut* on 14 May at Covent Garden; his last visit was to supervise *Il Trittico*, staged at Covent Garden on 18 June 1920. From 1900, at the time of the *Tosca* première, he always stayed at the Savoy Hotel. He grew to like London more and more, finding it 'hardly beautiful, but fascinating'. He enjoyed its 'immense movement, infernal, indescribable; Paris is nothing compared to it. The language impossible, the women most beautiful, splendid theatres and entertainments in profusion.' It was during the *Tosca* visit that he saw David Belasco's *Madam Butterfly* at the Duke of York's Theatre and immediately decided to turn the play into an opera. The exclusiveness of the Savoy greatly appealed to him; he derived much pleasure from finding himself, during the summer of 1911, sitting next to Marconi in the hotel barber shop. London's magnificent stores were another source of delight, and he often bought suits in Savile Row. His passion for ties found fulfilment in the Burlington Arcade, where, one June afternoon in 1919, he purchased Old Etonian and Old Harrovian ties and other assorted emblems of privilege. At lunch in the Savoy Grill on the following day, he suavely sported the tie of the Rifle Brigade.

Richard Strauss stayed at the Savoy Hotel in January 1920.

Igor Stravinsky came to London more than twenty times. His first visit was connected with the British première of *The Firebird* at Covent Garden on 18 June 1912, and his last was to conduct *The Firebird Suite* in the Royal Festival Hall on 14 September 1965. During the late 1920s and early '30s his trips to London were so frequent that he kept a flat in Albemarle Street. In 1912 he stayed at the Savoy Hotel, which he used

on many other occasions, although in July 1914 he was at the Hotel
Cecil, in August 1957 at the Dorchester, and in November 1959 at the
Ritz (where Eric Coates had lunch with Maurice Ravel in the early
'30s). During Stravinsky's first stay in London, Dyagilev, who was also
at the Savoy, took him to *Iolanthe*, which was playing in the theatre next
door. 'After this initiation,' Stravinsky recalled in 1968, 'whenever I
returned to London I would visit the Savoy Theatre. I believe I heard
all the operas except *The Grand Duke* and *Utopia Limited*.' The hotel
was to bring him another pleasant introduction, for, on 8 December
1956 in the Savoy Grill, he met T. S. Eliot for the first time. London
became one of his favourite cities, particularly in early summer, 'with
its green lawns, the beautiful trees in the parks, the river on its outskirts
gay with numberless boats, and everywhere the frank good humour of
healthy athletic youth'. He also thought highly of English musicians. 'It
is alleged that they are not musical; but this is contrary to my
experience. I have nothing but praise for their ability, precision, and
honest, conscientious work, as shown in all my dealings with them, and
I have always been struck by the sincere and spontaneous enthusiasm
which characterizes them in spite of inept prejudice to the contrary
prevalent in other countries.'

Those of his works that received world premières in London include
the suite from *L'Histoire du soldat*, *Ragtime* and *Symphonies of Wind
Instruments*.

Peter Warlock, composer and writer on music, was born in the Savoy
Hotel on 30 October 1894. Synecdochically inverted snobbery infects
his claim that he was born on the Embankment.

Anton Webern stayed at the Strand Palace Hotel 28 November–5
December 1929, on the first of his six trips to London; each of the visits
was made, at the instigation of Edward Clark, to conduct BBC concerts.
On 2 December 1929 he conducted the British première of his *Five
Pieces*, Op 10. While in the capital he saw his first talking film, which
he 'liked very much!' He was again in London 6–10 May 1931,
conducting, on the 8th, British premières of his *Five Movements*, Op 5,
and Schoenberg's *Accompaniment to a Film Scene*. He was next here
17–24 April 1933. On the 21st he gave the first British performance of
Berg's Chamber Concerto. He was delighted with the results of his
second concert, on the 23rd, and wrote to Schoenberg: '*The orchestra is
really splendid*. How they played Mahler's Fourth! There was at times
an absolutely fabulous sound, really and truly quite ideal.' On this visit
he went to the British Museum and saw the Parthenon frieze, standing
in front of it for an hour and a half. 'It's an indescribable miracle,' he
wrote to a friend. 'What a conception. Here is the most exact counter-

part to our method of composition: always the same thing in a thousand forms. Overwhelming.' His fourth trip was in the following year, when he conducted a concert on 25 April. Exactly a year later, on 25 April 1935, he directed the British premières of his *Six Pieces*, Op 6, and the *Passacaglia*. On his final visit, in May 1936, he stayed at the Bentinck Hotel. He conducted the British première of Berg's Violin Concerto on 1 May, and, two days later, performed Bruckner's Seventh Symphony.

Thomas Weelkes, composer and organist, who died on 30 November 1623, was buried on 1 December of that year in St Bride's Church, near Ludgate Circus. Samuel Richardson is also buried here.

Streatham Arnold Bax, composer and Master of the King's and Queen's Music, was born at Heath Villa, Angles Road, on 8 November 1883.

Clifford Bax, brother of Arnold Bax, man of letters, author of the hymn 'Turn Back, O Man, Forswear Thy Foolish Ways', was born here on 13 July 1886 and died on 18 November 1962. He resided at F2 Albany, Mayfair.

Benno Hollander, violinist, composer and pupil of Saint-Saëns, was born in Amsterdam on 8 June 1853 and died in London on 27 December 1942. For some years he resided at 23 Westwell Road.

Ian Parrott, composer, educationist and writer on music, was born here on 5 March 1916.

Surbiton Maria Caradori-Allan, soprano singer, who took part in the first British performance of Beethoven's Ninth Symphony, was born in Milan in 1800 and died in Surbiton on 15 October 1865.

Sutton Geoffrey Bush, composer, who was born in Willesden Hospital on 23 March 1920, spent his childhood at 102 Benhill Avenue.

Noël Coward, dramatist, actor, writer, composer, director and singer, resided at Helston, Lenham Road, 1905–8.

John Henry Maunder, organist, conductor and composer of the cantata *Olivet to Calvary*, who was born in Chelsea in 1858 and died in 1920, was organist of Christ Church around the turn of the century.

William Whittemore, author of the hymns 'I Want To Be Like Jesus' and 'We Won't Give Up the Bible', was born on 18 September 1820 and died here on 27 July 1894.

Sydenham George Grove, lexicographer, writer on music, educationist, engineer, music administrator, geographer, Bible scholar, friend of Brunel, Brahms, Sullivan, Tennyson, Browning and

Gladstone, resided at 1 Church Meadow (demolished) 1852–60. He then moved to Grove House, Sydenham, where he died on 28 May 1900. He is buried at Ladywell Cemetery, Lewisham.

Teddington Noël Coward, dramatist, actor, writer, composer, director and singer, was born at Helmsdale, Waldegrave Road, on 16 December 1899 and died at Firefly Hill, Jamaica, on 26 March 1973.

Thornton Heath Edward Elgar, composer and Master of the King's Music, resided at Oaklands, Fountain Road, from the autumn of 1889 to March 1890.

Tooting Peter Katin, pianist, was born at 3 Ramsdale Road on 14 November 1930.

Harry Lauder, comedian, singer and composer of *I Love a Lassie* and *Roamin' in the Gloamin'*, resided at 46 Longley Road 1903–11.

Twickenham John Hawkins, music historian, who was born in London on 30 March 1719 and died there on 21 May 1789, resided in Twickenham during the 1760s.

Victoria Lucy Broadwood, eminent folk-song collector, who died in London on 22 August 1929, resided during the early part of the century at 84 Carlisle Mansions, Victoria Street.

Percy Buck, music scholar, was born in London on 25 March 1871 and, at the time of his death, on 3 October 1947, resided at 78 Buckingham Gate.

Henry Fothergill Chorley, music critic, man of letters, librettist and friend of Dickens, resided at 15 Victoria Square 1841–51. Felix Mendelssohn visited him here. Hector Berlioz came to dinner in November 1847. Frédéric Chopin was a guest in 1848.

Noël Coward, dramatist, actor, writer, composer, director and singer, resided intermittently at 111 Ebury Street from 1917 to the early 1930s.

Frederick Delius, composer, although residing in France for the last forty years of his life, maintained an address in London, 8A Hobart Place, that he occasionally used on visits to England.

Edward Elgar, composer and Master of the King's Music, stayed at 12 Gillingham Street during visits to London in the mid-1880s.

Felix Mendelssohn stayed with his friend Carl Klingemann and his wife at 4 Hobart Place, opposite St Peter's Church, 27 August–13 September 1837; in September and early October 1840; 10 May–10 July 1844; 17–23 August 1846; and April–May 1847, during his tenth and last visit to Britain.

Wolfgang Amadeus Mozart, together with his father, mother and sister, lodged at 180 Ebury Street from 6 August to about 25 September 1764. Here, at the age of 8, he wrote his first two symphonies, K16 and K19. Ebury Street was in those days on the edge of the countryside surrounding London. Indeed, in one letter from Ebury Street, Leopold Mozart gave his address as 'Chelsea near London'. Unwell at this time, he says in another letter, 'I am now in a spot outside the town, where I have been carried in a sedan chair, in order to get more appetite and fresh strength from the good air. It has one of the most beautiful views in the world. Wherever I turn my eyes, I see gardens and in the distance the finest castles; and the house in which I am living has a lovely garden.'

Vic Oliver, actor, writer, comedian, conductor, violinist, pianist, pupil of Mahler, son-in-law of Winston Churchill, was born in Vienna on 8 July 1898 and died in Johannesburg on 15 August 1964. He resided at 66 Westminster Gardens.

Sergey Prokofiev, alighting at Victoria Station at approximately 8.25 on the evening of 3 March 1923, was met by Henry Wood, who, for the purpose of identifying himself, wore, pinned across his chest, the score of the Russian composer's First Piano Concerto.

Anton Rubinstein was a frequent guest during the 1870s at 9 Victoria Square, the home of John Ella. On one visit he met Robert Browning here.

Eyre Massey Shaw, Chief of the Metropolitan Fire Brigade 1861–91 and immortalized in *Iolanthe*, died on 25 August 1908. He resided at 114 Belgrave Road and is buried in Fireman's Corner, Highgate Cemetery.

Arthur Sullivan, composer and conductor, was the organist of St Michael's, Chester Square, 1861–7. He resided at 47 Claverton Terrace (demolished) 1864–71, during which time he wrote the *Irish Symphony*, the overtures *In Memoriam, Marmion* and *Di Ballo*, incidental music to *The Merchant of Venice, Cox and Box* and *Thespis*. He was at 8 Albert Mansions, Victoria Street (demolished), and 9 Albert Mansions (demolished) 1871–81, when he wrote *The Lost Chord*, incidental music to *Henry VIII, The Martyr of Antioch, Trial by Jury, The Sorcerer, HMS Pinafore, The Pirates of Penzance* and *Patience*. He resided at 1 Queen's Mansions, Victoria Street (demolished), from 1881 until his death here on 22 November 1900. Works composed during this final period include *Iolanthe, Princess Ida, The Mikado, The Golden Legend, Ruddigore, The Yeomen of the Guard*, incidental music to *Macbeth, The Gondoliers, Ivanhoe, Utopia Limited, The Grand Duke, The Rose of Persia* and *Victoria and Merrie England*. He is buried in St Paul's Cathedral.

Wallington Ernest Austin, composer, was born in London on 31 December 1874 and died here on 24 July 1947. He resided at The Sheiling, St George's Road.

Wandsworth Frederick Wiseman, composer of the hymn tunes *Abney, All Hallows, Bocking, Christina, Colvend, Dallas, Fons Amoris, Medak, God of My Life, Lovest Thou Me* and *Wonderful Love,* died here on 16 January 1944. He resided at 33 Routh Road.

Wanstead John Sanders, organist and composer, was born here on 26 November 1933.

Waterloo Felix Mendelssohn played the organ at St John's, Waterloo Road, one Sunday morning around 1840. His friend John Horsley recalled: 'We were taken straight to the organ-loft, where the sight of the gaping congregation and the drawn curtains, exposing him and us to the public gaze, ruffled the usually seraphic temper of Mendelssohn, and "slewing" himself across the organ-bench, after a few preliminary words with the organist, he dashed into an extempore of the most startlingly magnificent kind, thundering forth in music his perturbed spirit. Finally quieting down, he played the introduction of one of Bach's most superb fugues, at the close of which he darted up from his seat, seized his hat, which he jammed down on his head, and made his escape, evidently much annoyed.'

Watford Gerald Moore, unexcelled accompanist, was born here on 30 July 1899.
   Ralph Vaughan Williams was billeted at 76 Cassio Road during the spring of 1915.

Wembley May Brahe, composer of *Bless This House,* who was born in Melbourne, Australia, resided at 55 Barn Hill during the 1930s.
   Stanley Sadie, writer on music and editor, was born here on 30 October 1930.
   John Tavener, composer, was born in London on 28 January 1944 and spent his childhood here.

Westminster John Blow, organist, composer, teacher of Purcell, was organist of Westminster Abbey 1669–80 and, following Purcell's death, again from 1695 until his own death in 1708.
   William Croft, composer and organist, was organist of Westminster Abbey from 1708 until his death in 1727.

Thomas Ford, composer and lutenist, was born in about 1580 and died here in November 1648. He is buried in St Margaret's.

Orlando Gibbons, composer and organist, was organist of Westminster Abbey from 1623 until his death in 1625.

Thomas Greatorex, composer and organist, was organist of Westminster Abbey 1819–31. The Prince of Wales, later George IV, once said to him: 'My father is rex, but you are a greater rex.'

John Hilton the younger, composer, was born in 1599 and died in London in March 1657. He is buried in St Margaret's.

John Hingston, composer of *Fantasia for Cornet, Trombone and Organ* and organist to Oliver Cromwell, died here in December 1683. He is buried in St Margaret's.

Craig Sellar Lang, composer and educationist, was born in Hastings, New Zealand, in 1891 and died in 1972. He resided at 3M Artillery Mansions, Westminster.

Henry Lawes, composer, died at his home in Dean's Yard on 21 October 1662, and is buried in Westminster Abbey. Until shortly beforehand he resided in The Great Almonry, which ran west between present-day Victoria Street and Orchard Street; his house in this street would have been approximately where the Board of Trade is now situated.

George Frederick Pinto, violinist and composer, was born in London on 25 September 1786 and died here on 23 March 1806. He is buried in St Margaret's.

Walter Porter, composer and tenor singer, was born in about 1595 and died in London. He was buried on 30 November 1659 in St Margaret's.

Henry Purcell, composer, seems likely to have been born in The Great Almonry during the autumn of 1659, his parents' house being next to that in which Henry Lawes was then residing. After his father's death in 1664, his mother moved to Tothill Street, presumably taking her six children. Following his marriage, Purcell took up residence in 1682 in St Ann's Lane. In 1684 he moved to Bowling Alley East and in 1692 to Marsham Street, where he died on 21 November 1695. He is buried in Westminster Abbey, of which he had been organist since 1680.

Frank Schuster, patron of music, who was born in 1852 and died on 26 December 1927, resided for many years at 22 Old Queen Street.

Edward Elgar often visited him here. 'He was always the most loving, strongest and wisest friend man ever had,' Elgar wrote after Schuster's death. Schuster, in turn, held the composer in strong affection and left him £7,000. Elgar and Richard Strauss were dinner guests here on 18 December 1904.

Gabriel Fauré stayed with Schuster on more than one occasion during his eight visits to England. His earliest trip to London was in May 1882, when he went to the British première of *The Ring*. He next came in 1894 and again in 1896, when, on 1 May in St James's Hall, he took part in the first performance in Britain of his First Piano Quartet. He stayed at 22 Queen Street in April 1898, when Mrs Patrick Campbell read him extracts from *Pelléas et Mélisande*, persuading him to write incidental music for the play; he also met Elgar here during this visit. He returned in June 1898 and, on the 21st, conducted the world première of his *Pelléas* score at The Prince of Wales Theatre. He was again in London in 1908, accompanying Susan Metcalfe in performances of his songs at a concert in Buckingham Palace on 23 March. His final visit was in June 1914, when he met Adrian Boult at Schuster's and attended three concerts, at the Aeolian Hall, in which his complete works for piano were played by Robert Lortat.

Ralph Vaughan Williams, composer, resided briefly in Smith Square in 1895. In 1898 he was at 16 North Street and 5 Cowley Street. He resided at 10 Barton Street 1899–1905, when he completed *Linden Lea* and *In the Fen Country*.

Robert White, composer, the date and place of whose birth remain unknown, was buried in St Margaret's on 11 November 1574.

John Wilson, composer, lutenist and singer, was born on 5 April 1595 and died in his home at the Horseferry, Westminster, on 22 February 1674. He is buried in Westminster Abbey.

Musicians buried in Westminster Abbey include Orlando Gibbons, Pelham Humfrey, Henry Lawes, John Blow, Henry Purcell, William Croft, George Frideric Handel, Charles Burney, Johann Peter Salomon, William Shield, Muzio Clementi, Thomas Greatorex, William Sterndale Bennett, Charles Villiers Stanford and Ralph Vaughan Williams.

West Wickham Alan Ridout, composer, was born here on 9 December 1934.

Wimbledon Inglis Gundry, composer, writer on music and novelist, was born here on 8 May 1905.

Wood Green Peter Racine Fricker, composer, was born at 12 Forfar Road on 5 September 1920.

Woolwich Sims Reeves, celebrated tenor singer, who sang with Jenny Lind, Clara Novello, Adelina Patti and Christine Nilsson, was born at the Royal Artillery Barracks on 26 September 1818 and died in Worthing, West Sussex, on 25 October 1900.

Ladislas Zavertal, distinguished conductor of the Royal Artillery Band 1881–1906 and composer, who was born in Milan on 29 September 1849 and died in Cadenabbia on 29 January 1942, resided in Plumstead during his period at the depot in Woolwich.

Antonín Dvořák visited him at 5 Adelaide Terrace, Herbert Road, on 9 and 12 March 1884 and on the 12th attended a concert, at the Royal Artillery Theatre, Woolwich, in which Zavertal conducted the overture *My Home* and the *Slavonic Dance* No 4. Zavertal showed him round the Artillery Museum, where Dvořák noticed a pair of old parchmentless drums lying forlornly in a corner. 'Poor dumb things', he said.

By the following year, Zavertal had moved to Bonnie Blink, Eglinton Road. Dvořák visited here on 26 April 1885, smashing a cup and overturning a table.

THE MIDLANDS

DERBYSHIRE

Bakewell Ole Bull stayed with the Duke of Devonshire at Chatsworth House in 1836.

Belper Samuel Harrison, tenor singer, was born here on 8 September 1760 and died in London on 25 June 1812.

Buxton Niccolò Paganini gave a recital in the Theatre Royal on 24 August 1833.

John Philip Sousa conducted his band at concerts here on 22 and 23 February 1905.

Tom Wotton, writer on music and bassoonist, was born here on 15 January 1862 and died in Patcham, East Sussex, on 2 January 1939.

Chesterfield Paul Patterson, composer, was born here on 15 June 1947.

Chinley Ralph Harrison, composer of the hymn tune *Warrington*, often sung to 'Jesus, Where'er Thy People Meet', was born here on 10 September 1748.

Derby Alfred Barker, violinist, conductor and composer, was born here on 30 November 1895.

Ronald Binge, composer, was born here on 15 July 1910.

Ralph Downes, organist and conductor, was born here on 16 August 1904.

Edwin Hatch, author of the hymn 'Breathe on Me, Breath of God', was born here on 4 September 1835.

Franz Liszt played at a concert in The King's Head on 10 September 1840.

John Philip Sousa conducted his band at two concerts in the Drill Hall on 27 January 1911. He stayed the night at the Royal Hotel.

Johann Strauss senior led his orchestra in concerts here on 9 October and 28 November 1838. By the time of the second concert, the composer, who had by now endured almost eight months of British weather, was so unwell that he went to a local doctor, who gave him a dose of opium. This failed to arrest his illness.

Hulland John Storer, organist and composer, was born here on 18 May 1858 and died in Berwick-upon-Tweed, Northumberland, on 1 May 1930.

North Wingfield Thomas Greatorex, organist and composer, was born here on 5 October 1758 and died in Hampton, London, on 18 July 1831.

Wilderslowe Francis Davenport, composer, was born here on 9 April 1847 and died in Scarborough, North Yorkshire, on 1 April 1925.

HEREFORD AND WORCESTER

Astley William Havergal, hymn writer and composer of the hymn tune *Franconia*, sung to 'Blest Are the Pure in Heart', was vicar here in the 1830s. He was born in Chipping Wycombe, Buckinghamshire, on 18 January 1793 and died in Royal Leamington Spa, Warwickshire, on 19 April 1870.

His daughter, Frances Havergal, author of hymns that include 'Take My Life and Let It Be' and 'Jesus, Master, Whose I Am', was born here on 14 December 1836 and died at Oystermouth, West Glamorgan, on 3 June 1879.

William Havergal Brian adopted his middle name in 1899, possibly after coming across the works of William Havergal.

Barnt Green Granville Bantock, composer and conductor, spent the last year of his life at Sherriff Cottage, 36 Bittel Road. He died in London on 16 October 1946.

Broadway Edward Elgar, composer and Master of the King's Music and John McCormack, tenor singer, were guests of Mary Anderson de Navarro at Court Farm on 18 July 1932.

Maude Valérie White, composer of the songs *Absent yet Present, To Althea from Prison, The Devout Lover* and *So We'll Go No More A-Roving*, resided at Bell Farm 1896–1901.

Brockhampton (near Ross-on-Wye) Edward Elgar, composer and

Master of the King's Music, used to stay with Lieutenant-Colonel Arthur Foster at Brockhampton Court.

Bromsgrove Rosemary Hughes, writer on music, was born here on 26 November 1911.

Drayton William Felton, organist and composer of *Felton's Gavotte*, also known as *Farewell, Manchester*, was born in Drayton in 1715 and died in Hereford on 6 December 1769.

Evesham Muzio Clementi, composer and pianist, was born in Rome on 23 January 1752 and died at Elm Lodge on 10 March 1832. He is buried in Westminster Abbey.

John Field, pupil of Clementi, composer, pianist, teacher of Glinka, called upon him here shortly before Clementi's death.

Eric Coates, composer, wrote the second and third movements of *The Three Elizabeths* at the Northwick Arms in 1944. Initially he worked every morning in the hotel lounge and, later, until opening time, in the greater seclusion of the bar-room.

Fockbury Alfred Edward Housman, poet, whose verses inspired works by Samuel Barber, Bax, Butterworth, Gurney, Ireland, Elisabeth Lutyens, Moeran and Vaughan Williams, was born in Valley House, now Housemans, on 26 March 1859 and died in Cambridge on 30 April 1936.

Great Malvern Edward Elgar, composer and Master of the King's Music, resided at Forli, 37 Alexandra Road, June 1891–March 1899. Charles Villiers Stanford, who stayed at Tintern House, Abbey Road, in September 1896, called several times on Elgar at Forli. During this period, Elgar wrote the Serenade in E minor, *Bavarian Dances, Chanson de matin* and *Chanson de nuit, Imperial March* and *Enigma Variations*. He made use of a summer cottage, Birchwood Lodge, Storridge, 1898–1904, where he wrote part of *The Dream of Gerontius* and *Sea Pictures* and where Arnold Bax visited him in 1901. In March 1899 he moved from Alexandra Road to Craeg Lea, 86 Wells Road, Malvern Wells, where he worked on *The Dream of Gerontius* and also wrote *Cockaigne, In the South* and the *Pomp and Circumstance Marches* Nos 1 and 2. During the summer of 1904 he moved to Hereford. He is buried at St Wulstan's, Little Malvern.

Isabel Fitton, portrayed in the sixth variation of the *Enigma Variations*, resided at Fairlea, 83 Graham Road. Elgar visited her here.

Arthur Troyte Griffith, commemorated in the seventh variation of the *Enigma Variations*, resided in rooms above the Priory Gateway. Elgar frequently visited him here.

John Philip Sousa conducted his band at a concert in the Assembly Rooms on 26 January 1911.

Great Witley Walter Parratt, organist, composer, educationist and Master of the Queen's and King's Music, was organist of Great Witley Church 1861–8.

Hereford John Bull, composer, organist and virginalist, who was born in about 1562 and died in Antwerp in March 1628, was organist of Hereford Cathedral 1582–91.

Edward Elgar, composer and Master of the King's Music, resided at Plas Gwyn, 27 Hampton Park Road, Hereford, from July 1904 to the end of 1911, during which period he wrote *Pomp and Circumstance Marches* Nos 3 and 4, *Introduction and Allegro, Wand of Youth Suites* Nos 1 and 2, *Elegy for Strings*, the Violin Concerto and Symphonies Nos 1 and 2. His assays in chemical research were conducted in an outhouse that he called 'The Ark'.

Percy Hull, organist and conductor, was born here on 27 October 1878 and died on 31 August 1968. He resided at Vaga House, Lynch Road, Farnham.

Frederick Gore Ouseley, music scholar and composer, died here on 6 April 1889. He is buried at St Michael's, Tenbury Wells.

George Robertson Sinclair, organist and conductor, resided from 1889 until his death in Birmingham on 7 February 1917 at 20 Church Street. His dog Dan, immortalized in the eleventh variation of the *Enigma Variations*, died here on 1 July 1903; he was buried 'under the big apple tree'. Dan's grave, marked by a tombstone, now lies next to a telegraph pole in the grounds of 102 East Street, backing on to 20 Church Street. The apple tree no longer exists. Sinclair's visitors' book, containing many references made by Elgar to Dan, is housed at St Michael's, Tenbury Wells.

Samuel Sebastian Wesley, composer and organist, was organist of the cathedral 1832–5.

Kempsey Walter Haynes, organist and composer, was born here on 21 November 1859 and died in London on 4 February 1900.

Kidderminster Thomas Helmore, composer of the hymn tune *Veni Emmanuel*, sung to 'O Come, O Come, Emmanuel', was born here on 7 May 1811 and died in London on 6 July 1890.

Edward Elgar and his wife stand in front of Birchwood Lodge, Birchwood, near Malvern. They used this house as a summer retreat between 1898 and 1904. The full score of *The Dream of Gerontius* was completed here in August 1900 (*Elgar's Birthplace Museum*)

The birthplace of Edward Elgar at Broadheath, near Worcester. The house is now a museum, within which are stored a wealth of manuscripts, scores, photographs and mementos. Few museums match its sense of intimacy or benefit so strongly from the atmosphere of the surrounding countryside (*Elgar's Birthplace Museum*)

Edward Elgar can be seen, somewhat faintly, on the verandah outside his study at Plas Gwyn, his home in Hereford from 1904 to 1911. Works written here include *Introduction and Allegro*, both the symphonies, the Violin Concerto and *Pomp and Circumstance Marches* Nos 3 and 4 (*Elgar's Birthplace Museum*)

The tomb of Dan the bulldog near the cathedral in Hereford. His aquatic adventures in the River Wye have become part of our heritage through the eleventh of the *Enigma Variations*. Dan lived with G.R. Sinclair, organist of the cathedral, on whom Elgar often called, writing in the visitors' book themes depicting Dan's various moods. Several of these themes later went into the composer's works, notably at the beginning of *In the South*, which originally portrayed 'Dan triumphant (after a fight)'. Dan died on 1 July 1903. 'He has out-soared the shadow of our night.' (*Miss T.P. Holland, Vivian's Studio*)

Ledbury Henry Scott Holland, author of the hymn 'Judge Eternal, Throned in Splendour', was born in Underdown on 27 January 1847.

John Masefield, poet and novelist, whose verses inspired works by Lord Berners, Gurney, Holst, Ireland, Walton and Warlock, was born at The Knapp on 1 June 1878 and died on 12 May 1967.

Leigh Winifred and Florence Norbury, who are portrayed in the eighth variation of the *Enigma Variations*, lived at Sherridge, the character of which house presides over the variation.

Edward Elgar visited them here.

Little Malvern Jenny Lind, celebrated soprano singer, spent the last summers of her life at her country home, Wynd's Point, near the Herefordshire Beacon, where she died on 2 November 1887. She is buried in the cemetery in Wilton Road, Great Malvern.

Madresfield Lady Mary Lygon, who is said to be enshrined in the thirteenth variation of the *Enigma Variations*, resided at the time of the work's composition in 1898 at Madresfield Court, where Edward Elgar used to visit.

Malvern Wells Béla Bartók gave a recital in the hall of the Abbey School on 4 May 1923.

Martin Hussingtree Thomas Tomkins, composer and organist, pupil of William Byrd, died here in June 1656. He resided in the Manor House.

Monkland Henry Baker, who was born in London on 27 May 1821, was vicar of Monkland from 1851 until his death here on 12 February 1877, during which period he wrote the hymns 'O Praise Ye the Lord!' and 'The King of Love My Shepherd Is'.

Pershore Joseph Haydn is traditionally thought to have visited Mrs Hodges, 'the most beautiful woman I ever saw in my life', at her country home, Amory Court. There is no evidence that he met her outside London. It is said that he called upon her whenever he stayed with Clementi at Evesham. Haydn was in England 1791–5; as far as can be determined, Clementi did not move to Evesham until 1831.

Ross-on-Wye William Henry Squire, cellist and composer of *The Harbour Lights* and *Three for Jack*, was born here on 8 August 1871 and died on 17 March 1963. He resided at 28 Queen's Grove, St John's Wood, London.

Stoke Prior (near Bromsgrove) Edward Elgar, composer and Master of the King's Music, used to stay with his sister Polly Grafton at her home, The Elms, a black and white farmhouse above the Stoke Works, where she lived 1883–1920.

Stourport-on-Severn Julius Harrison, composer and conductor, was born here on 26 March 1885 and died on 5 April 1963. He resided at The Greenwood, Ox Lane, Harpenden, Hertfordshire.

Easthope Martini, composer of the song *Come to the Fair*, was born here in 1882 and died in London in 1925.

Weobley The tune of the carol *Joseph and Mary* was collected here by Vaughan Williams.

Worcester Ivor Atkins, organist, composer and friend of Elgar, died here on 26 November 1953.

Edgar Cook, organist and composer, born here on 18 March 1880.

Antonín Dvořák stayed here 6–12 September 1884. On 11 September he conducted his *Stabat Mater* in the cathedral and, in the evening, his Sixth Symphony in the Shire Hall. Elgar was among the first violins in the performance of the symphony and wrote to a friend: 'I wish you could hear Dvorak's music. It is simply ravishing, so tuneful & clever & the orchestration is wonderful; no matter how few instruments he uses it never sounds thin. I cannot describe it; it must be heard.' Both works were rapturously received. *The Musical Times* felt that this enthusiasm demonstrated to the composer that 'the English people are ever ready to recognize, and give a welcome to, the highest representative men in art, whatever may be the country of their birth'. The citizens of Worcester left Dvořák in no doubt about their admiration. 'Everywhere I appear, whether in the street or at home or even when I go into a shop to buy something, people crowd round me and ask for my autograph. There are pictures of me in all the booksellers', and people buy them only to have some memento.' And there were additional pleasures, for the Dean of Worcester presented him 'to all the élite of beautiful ladies'.

Edward Elgar, composer and Master of the King's Music, was born at The Firs, Lower Broadheath, now the Elgar Birthplace Museum, on 2 June 1857. Two years later, his family moved to 1 Edgar Street, Worcester, and in 1866 to 10 High Street (demolished). During the early 1880s he lived with his sister Polly and her husband at Loretto

Villa, now 12 Chestnut Walk, and from 1883 with his sister Lucy and her husband at The Elms, 4 Field Terrace, Bath Road. At the time of his marriage, in 1889, he moved to London. He resided at Napleton Grange, Kempsey, 1923–7, and then for a few months at Battenhall Manor (demolished), Worcester. In 1929 he purchased Marl Bank (demolished), Rainbow Hill, where he wrote the *Pomp and Circumstance March* No 5, the *Nursery Suite* and the *Severn Suite*; he died here on 23 February 1934. The Elgar Birthplace Museum is open every day except Wednesdays, 1.30–6.30pm in the summer, and 1.30–4.30pm in the winter.

Nathaniel Giles, composer and organist, who was probably born in Worcester in about 1558, was organist of Worcester Cathedral 1581–5.

George Marson, organist and composer, was born here in about 1573 and died in Canterbury on 3 February 1632.

Nathaniel Pattrick, composer and organist, died here in March 1595.

John Philip Sousa conducted his band at a concert in the Public Hall on 26 January 1911. He stayed the night at the Star Hotel.

Johann Strauss senior led his orchestra at a concert in the Shire Hall on 5 October 1838.

Thomas Tomkins, composer and organist, pupil of William Byrd, was organist of Worcester Cathedral from about 1596 to 1646.

LEICESTERSHIRE

Ashby de la Zouch Reginald Jacques, conductor, organist and educationist, was born here on 13 January 1894 and died on 2 June 1969. He resided at Manna Wood Farm, Stackyard Green, Monks Eleigh, Suffolk.

Brooksby Thomas Vautor, composer of the madrigal *Sweet Suffolk Owl*, resided here in the house of his patron Sir George Villiers around 1600.

Cotesbach John Marriott, author of the hymn 'Thou, Whose Almighty Word', was born here in 1780 and died in London on 31 March 1825.

Empingham George Frideric Handel was a guest of the Gainsborough family at Exton Park.

Hugglescote Thomas Hemsley, baritone singer, was born here on 12 April 1927.

Leicester John Ella, composer, music critic and concert promoter, was born here on 19 December 1802 and died on 2 October 1888 in London, where he resided at 9 Victoria Square, Victoria.

George Enescu conducted a concert here on 20 September 1947.

William Gardiner, composer and stocking manufacturer, was born in Leicester on 15 March 1770 and died here on 16 November 1853. On 10 August 1804 he dispatched to Haydn in Vienna six pairs of cotton stockings, 'For the many hours of delight which your musical compositions have afforded me.' Into the stockings were woven themes from Haydn's works, including the *Emperor's Hymn* and the *Andante* from the *Surprise Symphony*.

He is notable, also, for his early championship of Beethoven. He was responsible for Beethoven's String Trio, Op 3, being played—from manuscript (it was not published until 1797)—in Leicester in 1794; he took the viola part himself. This appears to be the first performance of any Beethoven work in the British Isles; indeed, it was among the first performances of Beethoven anywhere outside Bonn.

Franz Liszt played at a concert in the Mechanics' Institute on 9 September 1840.

Niccolò Paganini gave a recital in the New Rooms on 18 October 1833.

John Philip Sousa conducted his band at a concert here on 15 February 1905.

Johann Strauss senior led his orchestra at a concert in the Wellington Rooms on 8 October 1838. He returned on 29 November and stayed at the White Lion, and gave his last concert of the 1838 tour in the Wellington Rooms on 30 November. He was now so ill that he could not take part in the second half of the concert. On the following day he immediately set out for Dover. He collapsed at Calais, but, after several days' rest, was able to continue his journey to Vienna.

Market Harborough Franz Liszt took part in a concert here on 9 September 1840, playing to an audience of forty people.

Melton Mowbray Malcolm Sargent, conductor, took up his first musical appointment here in 1914 as organist of the parish church and resigned from this position in 1924. He resided in Park Road.

Newton Burgoland John Compton, notable organ builder, was born here on 20 June 1874 and died in London on 6 April 1957.

Shackerstone Charles Jennens (1700–73), compiler of the text of *Messiah*, resided at Gopsall Hall (demolished) during the last forty years of his life.

George Frideric Handel stayed with him here on a number of occasions. His hymn tune *Gopsal* is sung to 'Rejoice! The Lord Is King'.

Smeeton Westerby Frederick Iliffe, organist, conductor and composer, was born here on 21 February 1847 and died on 2 February 1928. He resided at 18 Warnborough Road, Oxford.

Uppingham Ferdinand David visited Uppingham School in August 1868 immediately prior to the appointment of his son Paul as music master.

Whitwick Anne Macnaghten, violinist, was born here on 9 August 1908.

WEST MIDLANDS

Bilston Henry Newbolt, poet, whose verses are immortalized in Stanford's *Songs of the Sea* and *Songs of the Fleet*, was born here on 6 June 1862.

Birmingham Francis Edward Bache, pianist and composer, was born in Birmingham on 14 September 1833 and died here on 24 August 1858. His brother Walter, pianist and pupil of Liszt, was born here on 19 June 1842 and died in London on 26 March 1888.

Granville Bantock, composer and conductor, resided 1900–7 at Strathfield (demolished), King's Norton, at The Jungle (demolished), Northfield, and at Hazelwood (demolished), Coppice Road, Moseley. In 1907 he moved to Broad Meadow (demolished), Lifford Lane, King's Norton, and in 1913 to Ferndell (demolished), Elvetham Road, Edgbaston. From 1919 to the mid-1920s he resided at Tir-Nan-Og (demolished), Wheeley's Road, Edgbaston, and then at Metchley Lodge, Metchley Lane, Harborne, until 1934.

Jean Sibelius, who dedicated his Third Symphony to Bantock, stayed with him at Hazelwood in December 1905. Rosa Newmarch met him here. 'I remember that with his hair the colour of oats in sunshine, his ice-blue eyes, his well set-up figure, neat and admirably tailored, he presented a complete contrast to the unkempt *musikant*, with whom one associated the apparition of a genius.' He again stayed with Bantock, at Broad Meadow, when he came to conduct the British première of his Fourth Symphony in the Town Hall on 1 October 1912. Frederick Delius attended the rehearsal, remarking: 'Damn it, this is not conventional music.' Sibelius visited Bantock for a third time, at Tir-Nan-Og, when he conducted at another concert in the Town Hall on 20 February 1921. Myrrha Bantock, then a schoolgirl, later recalled: 'I must admit that I found him rather terrifying. He radiated force and power; without knowing why, you felt awed in his presence.'

Gustav Holst also visited Bantock at Tir-Nan-Og.

William Havergal Brian, composer, resided January 1916–May 1919 at 15 Ellesmere Road, Alum Rock; 97 Edwards Road, Erdington, and 27 Beaufort Road, Edgbaston.

Ferruccio Busoni gave concerts here in 1902 and 1905.

Edward Caswall, author of several familiar hymns, entered the Oratory of St Philip Neri in 1850 and died here on 2 January 1878. During this time he wrote 'Bethlehem, of Noblest Cities', 'Jesu, the Very Thought of Thee' and 'When Morning Gilds the Sky'.

Hamilton Clarke, composer and conductor, was born here on 25 January 1840.

John Copley, opera producer, was born here on 12 June 1933.

William Fenney, composer, was born here on 21 May 1891 and died in Epsom, Surrey, in 1957.

Niels Gade conducted the world première of his *Psyche* in the Town Hall on 31 August 1882.

Charles Gounod conducted the world première of his *Rédemption* in the Town Hall on 30 August 1882. His *Mors et Vita*, conducted by Hans Richter, received its first performance on 26 August 1885 in the Town Hall.

Sydney Grew, writer on music, was born in Birmingham on 31 August 1879 and died here on 24 December 1946.

Barnabas Gunn, organist and composer, was born in about 1680, possibly in Birmingham, and died here on 6 February 1753.

Charles Swinnerton Heap, conductor and composer, was born in Birmingham on 10 April 1847 and died here on 11 June 1900. He resided at 22 Clarendon Road.

Ferdinand Hiller came here for the world première of his cantata *Nala and Damayanti* in the Town Hall on 1 September 1870.

Dorothy Howell, pianist and composer, was born here on 25 February 1898.

Gervase Hughes, composer, conductor and writer on music, was born here on 1 September 1905.

George Hope Johnstone, businessman and patron of music, who, as Chairman of the Birmingham Musical Festival, commissioned Elgar's *The Dream of Gerontius, The Apostles* and *The Kingdom*, resided 1886–1906 at Headingly, Hampstead Hill, Handsworth.

Edvard Grieg stayed with him during the last week of August 1888, conducting his overture *In Autumn* on the 29th, and the *Holberg Suite* on the 30th, in the Town Hall. George Grove was present at the performance of *In Autumn*. 'A very interesting thing was Grieg's overture last night and his conducting of it. How he managed to inspire the band as he did and get such nervous thrilling bursts and such charming sentiment out of them I don't know.' Frederick Bridge recalled: 'Extremely fastidious, and demanding the most minute attention to the nuances in his music, he kept the band hard at it for a very long time' during rehearsals, becoming 'a complete wreck from his exertions.' A fellow guest at Johnstone's was the pianist Adelina de Lara, who later wrote of Grieg: 'I can see him now as he sat at the piano in a worn velvet coat which he loved. He had dreamy grey eyes and his manner was gentle and very quiet. He was a most beautiful pianist . . . He could never leave the piano for long, but would sit for hours, extemporizing or playing through a song or some other work of his own . . . for he loved his own music quite openly.' He returned to Birmingham on 26 November 1897, when he took part in a concert in the Town Hall.

Antonín Dvořák stayed with Johnstone 5–9 October 1891. On 9 October he conducted the world première of his *Requiem* in the Town Hall. Again a guest at Headingly, Adelina de Lara found Dvořák 'very different from any musician I had ever met. My first impression was that he was "a jolly good fellow" and at the same time rather quaint. His face was broad, his eyes very bright above a squat nose and a beard which he wore trimmed very close. With his dark velvet coat he wore a huge silk bow, which seemed out of keeping with the rest of his appearance. He would stroll about with his hands in his pockets, and you could always tell where he was, for he would whistle or hum as he walked. The son of a butcher who lived near Prague, he would make a point of driving in the carriage and pair with my friend, our host's daughter, to buy good sharp knives in Birmingham for his father. Butchering and music did not seem to go together, but he was a dutiful son and took obvious pride in his father's work.'

During Dvořák's stay in Birmingham, Johnstone gave a large luncheon party that was somewhat marred by rain. The downpour did nothing to dampen the composer's spirits; it would be good for his

[handwritten margin note: No. He stayed at Edgbaston with the Harding family]

potatoes back home, he said.

Albert Ketèlbey, composer of *In a Monastery Garden, In a Persian Market, Bells across the Meadows, In the Mystic Land of Egypt* and *In a Chinese Temple Garden*, was born here on 4 August 1875.

Franz Liszt played at a concert in the Old Royal Hotel (demolished) on 26 November 1840 and, according to one of his travelling companions, John Orlando Parry, 'broke three strings on one note'. He had dinner at Dea's Royal Hotel and afterwards felt unwell.

Charles Lunn, notable writer on the art of singing, was born here on 5 January 1838 and died in London on 28 February 1906.

Felix Mendelssohn took part in the 1837 festival concerts held in the Town Hall. On 19 September he played the organ, extemporizing on themes from Handel and Mozart, and conducted his overture to *A Midsummer Night's Dream*; on 20 September he conducted *St Paul*; on 21 September he was the soloist in the world première of his Second Piano Concerto; on 22 September he performed Bach's *St Anne* Prelude and Fugue on the organ. He also took part in the 1840 festival, staying, together with Ignaz Moscheles, at the home of Joseph Moore in The Crescent. On 22 September he played the organ; on 23 September he conducted the world's second performance of his Second Symphony and afterwards played the organ and, later in the day, was soloist in his First Piano Concerto; on 24 September he played the organ. He came to Birmingham again for the 1846 festival and conducted the world première of *Elijah* on 26 August; he had dinner with Sterndale Bennett and other friends on 25 August at the Woolpack Inn. He once more stayed with Joseph Moore. His final visit was to conduct *Elijah* in the Town Hall on 27 April 1847.

David Munrow, conductor, music scholar and composer, was born here on 12 August 1942.

John Henry Newman lived at the Oratory of St Philip Neri in Edgbaston for almost forty years and died here on 11 August 1890. During that time he wrote 'The Dream of Gerontius', published in 1866, on which Elgar's oratorio is based and from which comes the hymn 'Praise to the Holiest in the Height', set by Dykes to the hymn tune *Gerontius*. His other great hymn, 'Lead Kindly Light, Amid the Encircling Gloom', set by Dykes to the tune *Lux Benigna*, was written on 16 June 1833, while the cargo vessel in which he was travelling from Palermo to Marseille lay becalmed in the Strait of Bonifacio, between Corsica and Sardinia.

Elgar's *The Dream of Gerontius*, conducted by Hans Richter, was given its first performance on 3 October 1900 in the Town Hall.

Niccolò Paganini gave concerts in the Theatre Royal on 1, 2, 3, 22,

Wynd's Point, Jenny Lind's home in Malvern, where she died in November 1887. She did much to extend and improve the house, which has magnificent views to the east. The entrance, shown here, was designed by her and is in the traditional Swedish style, with the supporting posts retaining their bark (*Miss T.P. Holland, Vivian's Studio*)

Craeg Lea, Malvern Wells, where Edward Elgar lived from 1899 to 1904, stands in a commanding position on the edge of the Malvern Hills. 'I get a wonderful view of the surrounding country', he wrote. He worked in the upstairs room whose corner occupies the centre of the photograph; from here, he could see as far as Pershore and Tewkesbury. In this room, he composed *The Dream of Gerontius, Cockaigne, Pomp and Circumstance Marches* Nos 1 and 2 and *In the South* (*Miss T.P. Holland, Vivian's Studio*)

Eric Coates (*Archives Department, Chappell International*)

Eric Coates was born in this house in Watnall Road, Hucknall, near Nottingham, in August 1886. His childhood was spent here, before he went to the Royal Academy of Music. Thereafter, he lived mostly in London and West Sussex (*Margaret M. Clarke, The Studio, Bulwell*)

Maurice Ravel in his academic robes at Oxford on 23 October 1928, when he was made an honorary Doctor of Music. The degree ceremony was followed by a concert of his works in the Town Hall, during which he conducted the *Introduction and Allegro*. His acceptance of the original offer of the doctorate could not necessarily have been predicted, since, eight years earlier, he had refused the Legion of Honour (*Courtesy of Charles Harding*)

Birmingham Town Hall has played an important part in the history of music in Britain. Mendelssohn conducted the world première of *Elijah* there in 1846, and *The Dream of Gerontius* received its first performance in 1900. Gounod, Saint-Saëns and Dvořák also wrote works expressly for the Birmingham Musical Festivals. Many other famous composers have appeared at the Town Hall, including Sibelius.

23 and 24 February 1832 and on 23, 24 and 25 July and 21 October 1833.

William Pole, civil engineer of international eminence, music scholar and authority on whist, was born here on 22 April 1814 and died in London on 30 December 1900. He resided at 9 Stanhope Place, Paddington, London.

Brian Priestman, conductor, was born at 161 Woodlands Park Road, Birmingham 30, on 10 February 1927 and spent most of his childhood at 144 Heath Road.

Priscilla German Reed, actress, contralto singer and wife of Thomas German Reed, was born here on 1 January 1818 and died in Bexleyheath, London, on 18 March 1895.

Camille Saint-Saëns conducted the world première of his cantata *La Lyre et la harpe* in the Town Hall on 28 August 1879. Shortly afterwards he wrote in a French newspaper: 'I wish people who describe the English as unmusical could hear the Birmingham singers. This wonderful choir has everything: intonation, perfect timing and rhythm, finely shaded expression and a lovely sound. If people who sing like this are not musical, well, they certainly perform as if they were the finest musicians in the world.'

Clement Scholefield, composer of the hymn tune *St Clement*, sung to 'The Day Thou Gavest, Lord, Is Ended', was born in Edgbaston on 22 June 1839.

John Philip Sousa conducted his band at a concert here on 20 February 1905. He gave a further concert, in the Town Hall, on 25 January 1911. He stayed the night at the Grand Hotel.

William Stockley, conductor and organist, resided at 29 Calthorpe Road during the 1890s.

Stephen Stratton, music critic and writer on music, who was born in London on 19 December 1840 and died in Birmingham on 25 June 1906, resided during the 1880s at Park House, Monument Road.

Antonín Dvořák stayed with him here 20–4 October 1886. On 21 October he conducted his Sixth Symphony in the Town Hall. Edward Elgar was among the first violins. During this visit to Birmingham, Dvořák took a trip to Stratford-upon-Avon.

He had earlier been in Birmingham in August 1885, when, on the 27th, he conducted *The Spectre's Bride* in the Town Hall. 'I'm here in this immense industrial city,' he wrote to a friend, 'where they make excellent knives, scissors, springs, files and goodness knows what else, and, besides these, music too. And how well! It's terrifying how much the people here manage to achieve!'

Johann Strauss senior stayed at the White Horse Hotel 30 July–3

August 1838 and led his orchestra at a concert in the Town Hall on 31 July. He gave a second concert in the Town Hall on 27 August 1838.

Franklin Taylor, pianist, was born here on 5 February 1843 and died in London on 19 March 1919.

Coventry Brian Ferneyhough, composer, was born here on 16 January 1943.

Franz Liszt took part in a concert here on 7 September 1840, playing to an audience of thirty people.

Denis Matthews, pianist and music scholar, was born here on 27 February 1919.

Joseph Vernon, tenor singer and composer, was born here in about 1738 and died in London on 19 March 1782.

Dudley Frederick Torrington, conductor and organist, was born here on 20 October 1837 and died in Toronto on 20 November 1917.

Oldbury Frederick Bridge, composer, organist of Westminster Abbey, conductor and writer on music, was born here on 5 December 1844 and died in London on 18 March 1924.

Cyril Christopher, composer and organist, was born here on 23 June 1897.

Olton Leslie Huggins, composer of the hymn tune *Stowe*, sung to 'Say Not the Struggle Naught Availeth', was born here in 1896.

Tipton Horace Nicholl, organist and composer, was born here on 17 March 1848 and died in New York on 10 March 1922.

Walsall John Darwall was vicar of Walsall Parish Church from 1769 until his death on 18 December 1789, during which time he published the hymn tune *Darwall's 148th*, sung to 'Ye Holy Angels Bright'.

John Philip Sousa conducted his band at a concert here on 17 February 1905.

Wednesbury Morgan Kingston, tenor singer, was born here on 16 March 1881.

West Bromwich Jack Judge, composer of the song *It's a Long, Long Way to Tipperary*, was born in 1878 and died here on 28 July 1938.

Wolverhampton Christopher Dearnley, organist and composer, was born here on 11 February 1930.

Franz Liszt played at a concert here on 27 November 1840.

John Philip Sousa conducted his band at a concert here on 16 February 1905.

Maggie Teyte, soprano singer, was born here on 17 April 1888.

NORTHAMPTONSHIRE

Aldwinkle John Dryden, poet and dramatist, whose verses have been set to music by Blow, Boyce, Mackenzie, Wellesz and notably by Purcell, in *King Arthur* and *The Indian Queen*, and by Handel, in *Alexander's Feast* and *Ode for St Cecilia's Day*, was born in the Old Rectory on 9 August 1631 and died in London on 1 May 1700.

Ashby St Ledgers William Walton, composer, spent much time here, from the mid-1930s to 1948, at the home of Lady Alice Wimborne. Works written during this period include the Violin Concerto, *Crown Imperial* and the film music for *Henry V* and *Hamlet*.

Clipston Thomas Jarman, composer of the hymn tune *Lyngham*, was born in Clipston in 1776 and died here in 1861.

Gayton Henry Montagu Butler, author of the hymn '"Lift Up Your Hearts!" We Lift Them, Lord, to Thee', was born at Gayton Rectory on 2 July 1833.

Great Billing Gervase Elwes, tenor singer, was born on 15 November 1866 at Billing Hall, which was also his home in his final years. On 12 January 1921, while on a concert tour in Massachusetts, he was struck by a train and killed.

Kettering GUS (Footwear) Band, dating from 1961, was originally Munn & Felton's Works Band, which was formed here in 1933. It won the National Championship two years later.

John Philip Sousa conducted his band at a concert here on 14 February 1905.

King's Cliffe John Fane, Lord Burghersh, eleventh Earl of Westmorland, founder of the Royal Academy of Music and composer , to whom Rossini dedicated his five string quartets, was born on 3 February 1784 and died at his home, Apethorpe Hall, on 16 October 1859.

Lowick William Jones, composer of the hymn tune *St Stephen*, often sung to 'The Lord Will Come and Not Be Slow', was born here on 30 July 1726.

Morton Pinkney Samuel Gilkes, violin maker, was born here in 1787 and died in 1827.

Northampton William Alwyn, composer, was born at 54 Kettering Road on 7 November 1905.

Malcolm Arnold, composer, was born here on 21 October 1921.

Philip Doddridge, author of several favourite hymns, who was born in London on 26 June 1702 and died in Lisbon on 26 October 1751, was pastor of the Castle Hill Meetinghouse Church from 1730 until his death. His hymn 'Hark the Glad Sound! The Saviour Comes' was completed here on 28 December 1735.

Franz Liszt played at a concert here on 8 September 1840.

Colin Mason, music critic, was born here on 26 January 1924.

Edmund Rubbra, composer, was born in Cambridge Street on 23 May 1901 and spent most of his childhood at 4 Balfour Road.

John Philip Sousa conducted his band at a concert here on 13 February 1905. He gave a further concert, in the Corn Exchange on 23 January 1911. He stayed the night at the George Hotel.

Harry Waldo Warner, viola player and composer, was born here on 4 January 1874 and died in London on 1 June 1945.

Oundle Ebenezer Prout, music scholar and composer, was born here on 1 March 1835 and died in London on 5 December 1909. He resided at 246 Richmond Road, Hackney, London.

Rushden Thomas Britton, the 'musical small-coal man', patron of music, who was among the first to organize public concerts, was born here on 14 January 1644 and died in London, after being terrified by a ventriloquist, on 27 September 1714. He is buried in St James's, Clerkenwell, London.

Towcester William Walton, composer, was a frequent guest during the 1930s at Weston Hall, the home of Sacheverell Sitwell. Much of *Belshazzar's Feast* and the First Symphony were written here.

NOTTINGHAMSHIRE

Beeston Dan Godfrey senior, bandmaster and composer, was born in London on 4 September 1831 and died in Beeston on 30 June 1903.

Gedling Malcolm Binns, pianist, was born at Kenya, Arnold Lane, on 29 January 1936.

Hucknall Eric Coates, composer, was born at Tenter Hill, Watnall Road, on 27 August 1886. He lived here until 1906.

George Gordon, Lord Byron, poet and dramatist, who was born in London on 22 January 1788 and died in Missolonghi, Greece, on 19 April 1824, is buried in Hucknall, save for his heart, which remains in Missolonghi. He resided intermittently for many years at nearby Newstead Abbey. Among the works inspired by his writings are Berlioz's *Harold in Italy* and *Le Corsair*, Schumann's *Manfred*, Tchaikovsky's *Manfred* and compositions by Balakirev, Bantock, Havergal Brian, Donizetti, Elgar, Glière, Gounod, Mackenzie, Mendelssohn, Mussorgsky, Parry, Rimsky-Korsakov, Rossini, Schoenberg, Stanford, Verdi and Grace Williams.

Mansfield Walter Greatorex, composer of the hymn tune *Woodlands*, sung to '"Lift Up Your Hearts!" We Lift Them, Lord, to Thee', was born here on 30 March 1877 and died in Bournemouth on 29 December 1949.

Franz Liszt took part in a concert in the Town Hall on 11 September 1840, playing before an audience of thirty people.

John Ogdon, pianist, was born here on 27 January 1937.

Mansfield Woodhouse Frederick Sharp, baritone singer, was born here on 19 October 1911.

Newark-on-Trent John Blow, organist and composer, teacher of Purcell, was born here in February 1649 and died in London on 1 October 1708. He is buried in Westminster Abbey. It has been claimed by certain music historians that Blow was not born in Newark, but in North Collingham.

Archie Camden, bassoonist, was born here on 9 March 1888 and died in Wheathampstead, Hertfordshire, in 1979.

Franz Liszt played at a concert here and stayed the night on 11 September 1840.

Newstead Franz Liszt visited Newstead Abbey on 11 September 1840.

Nottingham Ferruccio Busoni played at a concert here on 28 November 1899.

George Enescu conducted a concert here on 19 May 1948.

Christopher Hogwood, conductor and keyboard player, was born here on 10 September 1941.

John Horton, noted authority on Grieg, was born here on 22 October 1905.

Franz Liszt played at a concert here on 10 September 1840.

Niccolò Paganini gave concerts in the Theatre Royal on 30 and 31 August 1833.

Robert Radford, bass singer, was born here on 13 May 1874 and died in London on 3 March 1933.

John Philip Sousa conducted his band at a concert here on 21 February 1905. He gave two further concerts, in the Mechanics' Large Hall, on 28 January 1911. He stayed the night at the Victoria Station Hotel.

Johann Strauss senior led his orchestra at a concert in the Exchange Room on 10 October 1838. He stayed at the Crown Inn.

Edmund Turpin, organist, editor and composer, was born here on 4 May 1835 and died in London on 25 October 1907. He resided at 18 The Avenue, Willesden, London.

Eric Warr, conductor, was born here on 4 May 1905.

Henry Kirke White, author of the hymns 'Oft in Danger, Oft in Woe' and 'When Marshalled on the Nightly Plain', was born in Exchange Alley on 21 March 1785. A plaque in Cheapside commemorates him.

Sherwood Constance Shacklock, mezzo-soprano singer, was born here on 16 April 1913.

Southwell Herbert Irons was organist of Southwell Minster 1857–72, during which period he composed the hymn tune *Southwell*, sung to 'Jerusalem, My Happy Home'. From 1876 until his death in Nottingham on 29 June 1905, he was organist of St Andrew's, Nottingham.

Reginald Spofforth, composer, was born here in 1770 and died in London on 8 September 1827.

OXFORDSHIRE

Abingdon George Frideric Handel stayed here on 5 July 1733.

Banbury John Ireland, composer, resided here December 1940–April 1942. During this time he wrote *Sarnia, Three Pastels* and *Epic March*.

Boars Hill Lennox Berkeley, composer, was born here on 12 May 1903 and spent his childhood at 304 Woodstock Road, Oxford.

Robert Bridges, poet, author of the hymns 'Love of Love, and Light of Light' and 'Rejoice, O Land, in God Thy Might', whose verses inspired works by Frank Bridge, Finzi, Gurney, Holst, Moeran, Parry, Stanford and Vaughan Williams, died at his home, Chilswell, on 21 April 1930. He is buried in Yattendon, Berkshire, where he had resided at the Manor House 1882–1904.

Brightwell William Hine, composer and organist, was born here in 1687 and died in Gloucester on 28 August 1730.

Ewelme Margaret Ritchie, soprano singer, died here on 7 February 1969. She resided at The Garden House.

Faringdon Gerald Hugh Tyrwhitt-Wilson, Lord Berners, composer, painter and novelist, lived at Faringdon House from 1931 until his death in 1950. He had a suitably bizarre folly erected on the top of nearby Faringdon Hill.

Igor Stravinsky stayed with him on a number of occasions during the 1920s and '30s and 'slept in a crystal bed, walked in deep meadows, rode roan horses, and sat by brick fireplaces in Hepplewhite chairs. Faringdon's atmosphere was not exclusively traditional, however. Meals were served in which all the food was of one colour pedigree; i.e., if Lord Berners' mood was pink, lunch might consist of beet soup, lobster, tomatoes, strawberries. And outside, a flock of pink pigeons might fly overhead, for Lord Berners' pigeons were sprayed with (harmless) cosmetic dyes.'

William Walton, Constant Lambert and Salvador Dali are among others to have stayed at Faringdon House.

Garsington Peter Warlock, composer and writer on music, was a guest at the Manor House, the home of Lady Ottoline Morrell, in 1916 at the same time as D. H. Lawrence. Others who came here include William Walton, Aldous Huxley, Lytton Strachey, Katherine Mansfield, Siegfried Sassoon, Rupert Brooke and T. S. Eliot.

Great Milton Matthew Wilkins, composer of the hymn tune *Stroudwater*, often sung to 'When Christ Had Shown God's Dawning Reign', was born in Great Milton in 1704 and died here in August 1772.

Great Tew Richard Goodson, organist and composer, was born in 1655 and died here on 13 January 1718.

Henley-on-Thames John Hobbs, tenor singer and composer, was born here on 1 August 1799 and died in Croydon, London, on 12 January 1877.

Ipsden Charles Reade, novelist, dramatist and authority on Cremona violins, was born here on 8 June 1814 and died in London on 11 April 1884.

Kidlington Alexander Reinagle, composer of the hymn tune *St Peter*, sung to 'How Sweet the Name of Jesus Sounds', died here on 6 April 1877.

North Stoke Clara Butt, contralto singer, who gave the first performance of Elgar's *Sea Pictures* at Norwich on 5 October 1899, died at Brooke Lodge on 23 January 1936.

Robert Kennerley Rumford, baritone singer and husband of Clara Butt, was born in London on 2 September 1870 and died at Brooke Lodge on 9 March 1957.

Oxford Hugh Allen, teacher, conductor and composer, died in the Acland Home on 20 February 1946, having been knocked down by a motor-cyclist near the Martyrs' Memorial three days earlier.

William Crotch, organist, pianist, painter and composer of the *Westminster Chimes*, was organist of St John's College 1797–1807.

Jacqueline du Pré, distinguished cellist and wife of the conductor and pianist Daniel Barenboim, was born in Beechcroft Road at 11am on 26 January 1945.

Gerald Finzi, composer, died here on 27 September 1956.

John Eliot Gardiner, conductor, organist and educationist, was born here on 6 December 1928.

Orlando Gibbons, composer and organist, was born here in 1583.

Alexander Glazunov received an honorary doctorate in June 1907.

Edvard Grieg received an honorary doctorate on 22 May 1906.

George Frideric Handel directed performances of *Esther* in the

Sheldonian Theatre on 5 and 7 July 1733. On 8 July the *Utrecht Te Deum and Jubilate* and two coronation anthems were sung in St Mary's Church. On 10 July, in the Sheldonian Theatre, he led the world première of *Athalia*; a second performance was given on the following day. At 9am on 11 July *Acis and Galatea* was presented in Christ Church Hall. On 12 July *Deborah* was performed in the Sheldonian Theatre. The *Norwich Gazette* reported: 'It is computed that the famous Mr Handell cleared by his Musick at Oxford upwards of £2,000.' During this profitable visit, the composer declined the offer of an honorary doctorate.

Edwin Hatch was Vice-Principal of St Mary's Hall in 1878, when his hymn 'Breathe on Me, Breath of God' was published. He died at Headington on 10 November 1889.

Joseph Haydn conducted his works in concerts in the Sheldonian Theatre on 6, 7 and 8 July 1791. On 8 July he received the honorary degree of Doctor of Music. A notebook entry records: 'In connection with my doctor's degree at Oxfortt, I had to pay 1½ guineas to have the bells rung and ½ a guinea for the robes. The trip cost 6 guineas.' The robes consisted of a white silk gown with sleeves of red silk and a small black silk hat. 'I looked quite funny,' Haydn told his biographer Albert Dies, 'and the worst of it was that I had to go about the streets in this masquerade . . . Still, I owe much, if not everything, in England to this doctorate. Through it, I became acquainted with the most important people, and it gained me entry to the greatest houses.'

Paul Hindemith received an honorary doctorate in July 1954.

Henry Scott Holland, author of the hymn 'Judge Eternal, Throned in Splendour', died here on 17 March 1918.

Frank Howes, writer on music, was born here on 2 April 1891 and died on 28 September 1974. He resided at Newbridge Mill, Standlake, Witney.

Bryan Kelly, composer and conductor, was born here in 1934.

Franz Liszt took part in a concert at The Star and stayed the night there on 24 November 1840.

Robin Milford, composer, was born here on 22 January 1903 and died in Lyme Regis, Dorset, on 29 December 1959.

Hugo Pierson, composer, was born here on 12 April 1815 and died in Leipzig on 28 January 1873. He is buried in Sonning, Berkshire.

Francis Poulenc received an honorary doctorate on 25 June 1958.

Maurice Ravel received an honorary doctorate on 23 October 1928. Afterwards he conducted at a concert of his works in the Town Hall. He was delighted with his pink silk robe, but, wrote Gordon Bryan, 'we had quite a job to adjust its considerable length to his diminutive stature. The quizzical expression on his face while the long Latin oration was read and the anxiety with which he demanded an exact translation at the first opportunity were typical reactions.'

Alexander Reinagle was organist of St Peter's-in-the-East 1822–53, during which time he composed the hymn tune *St Peter*.

Camille Saint-Saëns received an honorary doctorate in June 1907.

Eliza Salmon, soprano singer whose voice and beauty disarmed criticism for two decades, was born here in 1787 and died in abject poverty in London on 5 June 1849.

Humphrey Searle, composer, pupil of Webern and writer on music, notably on Liszt, was born at 29 Banbury Road on 26 August 1915.

Dmitri Shostakovich received an honorary doctorate on 25 June 1958.

Jean Sibelius visited Oxford on 23 and 24 February 1921. He had tea with Hugh Allen in New College and, during his first evening, took a walk round the outside of the college and saw Magdalen Tower 'in the most wonderful moonlight. In this magic light, Oxford reminded me in a strange way of Venice.' He dined, that same evening, in the hall of New College.

John Philip Sousa conducted his band at two concerts in the Town Hall on 1 March 1911. He stayed the night at the Randolph Hotel.

John Stainer, composer of *The Crucifixion*, who was born in London on 6 June 1840 and died in Verona on 31 March 1901, is buried at Holywell Cemetery.

Johann Strauss senior led his orchestra at a concert in the Town Hall on 6 June 1849.

Richard Strauss received an honorary doctorate on 11 June 1914.

Igor Stravinsky had lunch with Isaiah Berlin on 20 October 1961 and 29 May 1963. He conducted the *Symphony of Psalms* here on 29 June 1964.

John Taverner, composer and organist, was organist of Christ Church Cathedral 1526–30.

William Turner, composer, was born here in 1651 and died at his home in Duke Street, Westminster, on 13 January 1740. He is buried in Westminster Abbey.

Ernest Walker, writer on music and composer, was born in Bombay on 15 July 1870 and died in Oxford on 21 February 1949.

William Walond, organist and composer, was born in about 1725 and died here in 1770.

Anthony Wood, music historian, was born in Oxford on 17 December 1632 and died here on 25 November 1695. He resided opposite the gate of Merton College.

Radley George Butterworth, composer, who was born in London on 12 July 1885 and was killed in the Battle of the Somme on 5 August 1916, taught at Radley College 1910–11.

Edwin George Monk, composer of the hymn tune *Angel Voices*, sung to 'Angel Voices, Ever Singing', died here on 3 January 1900.

Sarsden John Wilson, composer, lutenist and singer, resided here during the 1650s.

Stanford-in-the-Vale Christopher Wordsworth, hymn writer, who was born in Lambeth, London, on 30 October 1807 and died on 20 March 1885, was vicar of Stanford-in-the-Vale-cum-Goosey 1850–68, during which time he published the hymns 'Alleluia! Alleluia! Hearts to Heaven and Voices Raise', 'See the Conqueror Mounts in Triumph', 'Hark! The Sound of Holy Voices' and 'Gracious Spirit, Holy Ghost'.

Stanton St John John Milton, composer and father of the poet, was born here in about 1563 and died in London in March 1647. He is buried in St Giles's, Cripplegate, London.

Tetsworth Ralph Vaughan Williams spent the summer of 1922 at Wheatfield, the home of Cordelia Curle.

Wallingford Evelyn Rothwell, oboist and wife of John Barbirolli, was born in 1911 at Elmhurst, Castle Street.

SALOP

Bishop's Castle Robin Legge, music critic, was born here on 28 June 1862 and died in London on 6 April 1933.

Bridgnorth Henry Cope Colles, music scholar, was born here on 20 April 1879 and died in London on 4 March 1943.

Thomas Percy, poet and antiquary, author of the song 'O Nanny, Wilt Thou Go With Me?', was born here in 1729.

Clungunford Elizabeth Maconchy, composer, spent most of World War II at Downton Castle, where she wrote her Fourth String Quartet, Sonata for Violin and Piano, Theme and Variations for Strings, Divertimento for Cello and Piano and *Variations on a Well-Known Theme*.

163

Harley Silas Taylor, historian, composer and customs officer, was born here on 16 July 1624 and died in Harwich, Essex, on 4 November 1678.

Hodnet Reginald Heber, author of numerous memorable and poetic hymns, was vicar here from 1807 until his appointment as Bishop of Calcutta in 1823. 'Brightest and Best of the Sons of the Morning' and 'By Cool Siloam's Shady Rill' are among the earliest of the Hodnet hymns. Those dating from later in this period include 'God That Madest Earth and Heaven', 'The Son of God Goes Forth to War', 'I Praised the Earth, in Beauty Seen', and 'Holy, Holy, Holy! Lord God Almighty!'. The great hymn 'From Greenland's Icy Mountains' was written during a visit to Wrexham, Clwyd, in 1819. 'God Is Gone Up with a Merry Noise', published posthumously, was also probably written at Hodnet.

Ironbridge Lloyd Powell, pianist, was born here on 22 August 1888.
Edward Woof, violinist, was born here on 18 January 1883 and died in London on 31 December 1943.

Ludlow Henry Lawes, composer, was music teacher to the Earl of Bridgewater's family, at Ludlow Castle, during the 1630s.
Milton's masque *Comus*, written at the request of Lawes, who supplied the music and played the part of the Attendant Spirit, was introduced at the castle on Michaelmas Night, 29 September 1634.

Oswestry Henry Walford Davies, composer of the *Royal Air Force March Past* and *Solemn Melody*, organist, educationist and Master of the King's Music, was born in Willow Street on 6 September 1869.

Rowton Richard Baxter, author of the hymns 'He Wants Not Friends That Hath Thy Love' and 'Ye Holy Angels Bright', was born here on 12 November 1615 and died in London on 8 December 1691.

Shrewsbury Hugo Botstiber, music scholar, was born in Vienna on 21 April 1875 and died in Shrewsbury on 15 January 1941.
Charles Burney, music historian, was born here on 7 April 1726 and died in Chelsea, London, on 12 April 1814.
Henry Hiles, composer and organist, was born here on 31 December 1826 and died in Worthing, West Sussex, on 20 October 1904.
William How, author of many fine hymns, was born here on 13 December 1823.
Niccolò Paganini gave a recital in the ballroom of the Lion Hotel on

15 August 1833. Jenny Lind and Charles Dickens also stayed at the hotel. Jenny Lind sang at a concert here on 26 February 1849.

John Philip Sousa conducted his band at a concert here on 25 February 1905.

Stockton Gerald Hugh Tyrwhitt-Wilson, Lord Berners, composer, painter and novelist, was born at Apley Park on 18 September 1883 and died in London on 19 April 1950.

Wellington Henry John Gauntlett, composer and organist, was born here on 9 July 1805. He played the organ at the première of *Elijah* on 26 August 1846 in Birmingham. Mendelssohn wrote of him: 'I know but very few of either his countrymen or mine whose masterly performance on the organ, whose skill in composing and whose perfect knowledge of musical literature of ancient and modern times may be compared to his.'

Whitchurch Edward German, composer, was born here on 17 February 1862.

Whittington William How was rector of Whittington 1851–79, during which time he wrote the hymnic blockbuster 'For All the Saints Who from Their Labours Rest', as well as 'To Thee, Our God, We Fly' and 'Soldiers of the Cross, Arise!'.

STAFFORDSHIRE

Burton-upon-Trent Felix Borowski, writer on music and composer, was born here on 10 March 1872 and died in Chicago on 6 September 1956.

John Philip Sousa conducted his band at a sacred concert in the Opera House on Sunday 29 January 1911.

Cannock Elgar Howarth, composer and conductor, was born here in 1935.

Dresden William Havergal Brian, composer, was born at 35 Ricardo Street on 29 January 1876 and spent most of his childhood at 47 Ricardo Street; neither of these buildings survives. His family moved to 12 Alberta Street, Florence, when he was 10 years old. He later resided at 39 Dunrobin Street, Longton, and at 11 Gordon Street, now

Dominic Street, Hartshill, 1900–9. In 1911 he was at 9 Leyfield Road, Trentham. In 1913 he moved to 50 James Street, Stoke-on-Trent, and departed towards the end of the year, for London. It was while he was at 39 Dunrobin Street that he added the Havergal to his original name, William Brian.

Eccleshall Richard Sampson, composer, was born in about 1475 and died here on 25 September 1554.

Ellastone George Frideric Handel used to stay with the Granville family at Calwich.

Hamstall Ridware Edward Cooper, hymn writer, who was born in London in 1770, was vicar here from 1799 until his death on 26 February 1833, during which time he wrote 'Father of Heaven, Whose Love Profound'.

Hanley Harold Rhodes, organist and composer, was born here on 15 September 1889 and died in London on 27 February 1956.

Haughton John Darwall, composer of the hymn tune *Darwall's 148th*, sung to 'Ye Holy Angels Bright', was born here in January 1731.

Himley Thomas Norris, composer, organist and tenor singer, died at Himley Hall on 3 September 1790.

Ingestre Arthur Sullivan, composer and conductor, stayed at Ingestre Hall in 1873 as the guest of Lady Shrewsbury.

Lichfield John Alcock, organist and composer, was born in London on 11 April 1715 and died here on 23 February 1806.
  Muzio Clementi, composer and pianist, resided at Lincroft House 1830–1.
  Michael East, composer, who was born in about 1580 and died in 1648, was organist of Lichfield Cathedral from about 1618 to 1638.
  Frederick Thurston, clarinettist, for whom works were written by Bax, Finzi, and Bliss, was born here on 21 September 1901 and died in London on 12 December 1953.

Newcastle-under-Lyme Franz Liszt took part in a concert on 28 November 1840 at The Roebuck. He stayed there the night.
  Niccolò Paganini gave recitals on 16 and 17 August 1833 at the Theatre Royal.

Penkridge George Frideric Handel used to stay with Fisher Littleton at Teddesley Hall (partly demolished).

Stafford Niccolò Paganini gave a recital on 3 May 1834 in the Theatre.
John Philip Sousa conducted his band at a concert here on 17 February 1905.

Whitmore Samuel Stone, author of the hymn 'The Church's One Foundation', was born at Whitmore Rectory on 25 April 1839. He died in London on 19 November 1900.

Wootton Jean-Jacques Rousseau, writer and composer, stayed throughout 1776 at Wootton Hall, where he embarked on and completed much of *Les Confessions*.

WARWICKSHIRE

Chilvers Coton George Halford, conductor, was born here on 13 February 1858. During the 1890s he resided at 9 Soho Road, Handsworth, West Midlands.

Dunchurch William Tan'sur, composer, was born here in 1706.

Ettington William Croft, composer and organist, was born here and was baptized on 30 December 1678.

Halford Franz Liszt, travelling from Oxford to Royal Leamington Spa, had luncheon here on 25 November 1840.

Nuneaton John Philip Sousa conducted his band at a concert here on 15 February 1905.

Royal Leamington Spa Franz Liszt took part in a concert at the Crown Hotel on 7 September 1840. He played in a second concert on 25 November 1840 and was amused to note that another Leamington concert-giver announced the intention of performing *William Tell*—the entire opera—on the harp.
Wilfred Mellors, music scholar and composer, was born here on 26 April 1914.
Rosa Newmarch, distinguished writer on Slavonic music, was born here on 18 December 1857 and died in Worthing, West Sussex, on 9 April 1940.

Niccolò Paganini gave recitals in the Royal Assembly Rooms on 10 August and 22 October 1833.

Robert Simpson, composer, administrator, writer on music and doughty polemicist, was born here on 2 March 1921.

John Philip Sousa conducted his band at a concert in the Winter Hall on 23 January 1911.

Johann Strauss senior led his orchestra at a concert in the Theatre Royal on 29 August 1838. He gave another concert in the Assembly Rooms on 4 October 1838, exactly a year after he and the members of his orchestra parted from their families in Vienna to tour Germany, France, Belgium and the British Isles.

Rugby Henry Buckoll was a master at Rugby School from 1826 until his death here on 6 June 1871, during which time he wrote the hymn 'Lord, Dismiss Us with Thy Blessing, Thanks for Mercies Past Receive'.

Stratford-upon-Avon Adelaide Phillipps, contralto singer, was born here on 26 October 1833 and died in Karlovy Vary, Czechoslovakia, on 3 October 1882.

William Shakespeare, dramatist and poet, was born in Henley Street in April 1564 and died at his home, New Place, on 23 April 1616. He is buried in the parish church. His writings have inspired works by Arne, Malcolm Arnold, Balakirev, Balfe, Bantock, Samuel Barber, Beethoven, Bellini, Sterndale Bennett, Berkeley, Berlioz, Bernstein, Bishop, Bliss, Bloch, Boughton, Boyce, Braham, Brahms, Havergal Brian, Frank Bridge, Britten, Bruch, Alan Bush, Geoffrey Bush, Castelnuovo-Tedesco, Chausson, Jeremiah Clarke, Eric Coates, Coleridge-Taylor, Copland, Cornelius, Cowen, Dankworth, Walford Davies, Debussy, Delius, Dieren, Dittersdorf, Dukas, Dussek, Dvořák, Easdale, Elgar, Fauré, Fibich, Finzi, Flotow, Foss, Frankel, Gade, Gatty, German, Godard, Goetz, Goldmark, Gounod, Grieg, Gurney, Halévy, Haydn, Henschel, Holbrooke, Holst, Honegger, Howells, Humperdinck, Ibert, D'Indy, Ireland, Kabalevsky, Ketèlbey, Khachaturian, Kodály, Korngold, Krenek, Kuhlau, Lambert, William Linley, Liszt, Locke, MacCunn, MacDowell, Mackenzie, Maconchy, Malapiero, Frank Martin, Mendelssohn, Milhaud, Moeran, Moniuszko, Morley, Musgrave, Nicolai, Nielsen, O'Neill, Orff, Robin Orr, Parry, Persichetti, Pierné, Pijper, Cole Porter, Prokofiev, Purcell, Quilter, Rawsthorne, Rheinberger, Rietz, Richard Rodgers, Rossini, Rubbra, Rubinstein, Salieri, Satie, Schmitt, Schubert, Schumann, Seiber, Shaporin, Shebalin, Shostakovich, Sibelius, Smetana, Spohr,

Stanford, Stenhammar, Richard Strauss, Stravinsky, Suk, Sullivan, Suppé, Svendsen, Tchaikovsky, Ambroise Thomas, Virgil Thomson, Tippett, Vaughan Williams, Verdi, Volkmann, Wagner, Walton, Warlock, Weber, Weelkes, Wellesz, Widor, Grace Williams, Wirén, Charles Wood and Zandonai.

Jean Sibelius visited here. He also went to the Forest of Arden and Royal Leamington Spa on 16 February 1921.

Johann Strauss senior stayed at the Shakespeare Hotel on 6 and 7 September 1838.

Tiddington Edward Elgar, composer and Master of the King's Music, resided at Tiddington House (demolished) February 1928–December 1929.

Warwick James William Elliott, organist and composer of *Sing a Song of Sixpence, Hey, Diddle Diddle, Humpty Dumpty Sat on a Wall, Jack and Jill Went up the Hill, Little Jack Horner Sat in a Corner, Little Bo-Peep Has Lost Her Sheep* and *See-Saw Margery Daw*, was born here in 1833 and died in 1915.

THE NORTH-EAST

CLEVELAND

Brotton Mary Jarred, contralto singer, was born here on 9 October 1899.

Hartlepool Franklyn Kelsey, bass singer and author, was born here on 28 July 1891 and died in Cardiff on 16 December 1958.

John Philip Sousa conducted his band at concerts in the Town Hall on 19 February 1903.

Lionel Tertis, celebrated viola player, for whom works were composed by Bax, Bliss, Frank Bridge, Cyril Scott and Vaughan Williams, was born here on 29 December 1876 and died on 22 February 1975.

Middlesbrough Florence Easton, soprano singer, was born here on 24 October 1884.

Sergey Rakhmaninov played at a concert in the Town Hall in March 1939.

Cyril Smith, pianist, husband of Phyllis Sellick, was born in Costa Street on 11 August 1909 and died in East Sheen, London, on 1 August 1974.

John Philip Sousa conducted his band at a concert in the Assembly Hall on 24 February 1911, staying the night at the Corporation Hotel.

Normanby Maurice Besly, composer and conductor, was born here on 28 January 1888 and died in Horsham on 20 March 1945.

Stockton-on-Tees Niccolò Paganini gave a recital in the Theatre Royal on 7 October 1833.

Thomas Wright, composer of the hymn tune *Stockton*, often sung to 'O for a Heart To Praise My God', was born here on 18 September 1763 and was organist of Stockton Church 1797–1817. He died on 24 November 1829 in Wycliffe Rectory, Durham. He is notable also as an inventor. In 1795 he manufactured a pocket metronome and published during the same year a keyboard concerto annotated with metronome markings. He was, in addition, a pioneer in piano modification, successfully building an organ attachment. A machine for calculating eclipses and another for raising coal were further valuable products of his fertile imagination.

DURHAM

Darlington Franz Liszt took part in a concert here (during the course of which an inebriate offered him a sovereign to play *Rule, Britannia*) on 27 January 1841. Afterwards he stayed the night in Darlington.

John Philip Sousa conducted his band at a concert in the Town Hall on 24 February 1911.

Durham Philip Armes, composer, organist and first Professor of Music at the university, died here on 10 February 1908.

Algernon Ashton, composer, was born here on 9 December 1859 and died on 10 April 1937 in London, where he resided at 22A Carlton Vale. Although a prolific composer, he devoted much of his energies to writing to the press. More than 2,000 of his letters were published, many of them relating to the disrepair of the graves of famous people.

John Bacchus Dykes was Precentor and Minor Canon of Durham Cathedral 1849–62. During this period he composed the following hymn tunes: *St Oswald*, sung to 'Through the Night of Doubt and Sorrow'; *Horbury*, sung to 'Nearer, My God, to Thee'; *St Aëlred*, sung to 'Fierce Raged the Tempest o'er the Deep'; *Melita*, sung to 'Eternal Father, Strong To Save'; *St Cross*, sung to 'O Come and Mourn with Me Awhile'; *Nicaea*, sung to 'Holy, Holy, Holy! Lord God Almighty!'; *Hollingside*, sung to 'Jesu, Lover of My Soul'. The last of these is named after the cottage in which he lived in Durham. From 1862 until his death in 1876 Dykes was vicar of St Oswald's Church, Durham. Dating from this time are: *Rivaulx*, sung to 'Father of Heaven, Whose Love Profound'; *Dominus regit me*, sung to 'The King of Love My Shepherd Is'; *Lux benigna*, sung to 'Lead, Kindly Light, Amid the Encircling Gloom'; *Gerontius*, sung to 'Praise to the Holiest in the Height'. The last two of these were set to verses by Cardinal Newman, who once remarked, 'Dr Dykes was a great master'. The tune of *Lead, Kindly Light* occurred to Dykes not in Durham, but while he was walking in The Strand in London.

His son John St Oswald Dykes, born in 1863, was a pupil of Raff and Clara Schumann and became a successful pianist and a professor at the Royal College of Music.

Franz Liszt played in a concert at The Theatre on 26 January 1841. He stayed the night at The Waterloo Hotel.

Felix Mendelssohn, travelling to Scotland, stayed here on 24 July 1829.

Niccolò Paganini gave a recital in the Theatre Royal on 5 October 1833.

Stanhope John Russell, conductor, was born here on 2 October 1914.

HUMBERSIDE

Brigg Percy Grainger first visited here in 1905. He stayed at Brigg Manor House and collected the song 'Brigg Fair', which he passed to Delius in April 1907.

Cleethorpes Norma Procter, contralto singer, was born here on 15 February 1928.

Epworth Charles Wesley, one of the world's greatest hymn writers, was born here on 18 December 1707 and spent his childhood in the Old Rectory, Albion Hill, which is open to the public. He died in London on 29 March 1788. Among his best known hymns are 'Lo! He Comes with Clouds Descending', 'Jesu, Lover of My Soul', 'Gentle Jesus, Meek and Mild', 'Christ, the Lord, Is Risen Today', 'Soldiers of Christ, Arise', 'Lift Up Your Heart, Lift Up Your Voice', 'Christ, Whose Glory Fills the Skies', 'Love Divine, All Loves Excelling', 'Let Saints on Earth in Concert Sing', 'Rejoice! The Lord Is King' and the carol 'Hark, the Herald Angels Sing'.

John Wesley, founder of Methodism and brother of Charles Wesley, was born here on 17 June 1703 and died in London on 2 March 1791.

Grimsby Margaret Ritchie, soprano singer, born here on 7 June 1903.

John Philip Sousa conducted his band at a concert in the Town Hall on 28 February 1911.

Kingston-upon-Hull John Bacchus Dykes, one of the world's greatest hymn composers, was born here on 10 March 1823.

Alfred Hollins, blind organist, pianist and pupil of Bülow, was born at 123 Coltman Street on 11 September 1865 and died on 17 May 1942 in Edinburgh, where he resided at 3 Grosvenor Street.

Franz Liszt took part in a concert here on 11 December 1840. He stayed the night at the Kingston Hotel.

William Mason, composer, dramatist, inventor and writer on music, was born here on 12 February 1724 and died in Aston, South Yorkshire, on 5 April 1797.

Niccolò Paganini gave recitals in the Theatre Royal on 13 February 1832 and 10 October 1833.

John Philip Sousa conducted his band at a concert in City Hall on 27 February 1911. He stayed the night at the Royal Station Hotel.

Johann Strauss senior stayed at the Crown Tavern 21–4 October 1838. He led his orchestra at concerts on the 22nd and 23rd. He gave a third concert here on 23 November 1838.

LINCOLNSHIRE

Boston Franz Liszt played at a concert in The Peacock and Royal Hotel on 14 September 1840. He stayed the night there. The site of the hotel, in Market Place, is now occupied by Boots.

John Taverner, composer and organist, spent the latter part of his life in Boston, where he died on 18 October 1545. He is buried beneath the famous St Botolph's Church bell-tower, known as the Boston Stump.

Gainsborough Willoughby Bertie, fourth Earl of Abingdon, music patron and composer, was born here on 16 January 1740 and died at Rycote, Oxfordshire on 26 September 1799.

John Longmire, composer, pianist and biographer of John Ireland, was born here on 19 January 1902.

Grantham Franz Liszt played at a concert here on 15 September 1840.

Nicholas Maw, composer, was born at 40A Watergate (demolished) on 5 November 1935.

John Wills, pianist, was born here on 6 May 1893.

Grimsthorpe Thomas Linley junior, violinist, composer, friend of Mozart and brother-in-law of Sheridan, was drowned here on 5 August 1778, while boating on the estate of the Duke of Ancaster.

Horncastle Franz Liszt played at a concert here on 14 September 1840.

Lincoln William Byrd, composer, was organist of Lincoln Cathedral 1563–72. He is thought to have been born in Lincolnshire in 1543.

Reginald Goodall, conductor, who directed the first performance of *Peter Grimes* on 7 June 1945 at Sadler's Wells and was later acclaimed for his interpretation of Wagner's *The Ring*, was born here on 13 July 1905.

Hubert Gregg wrote and composed his song *I'm Going To Get Lit Up When the Lights Go On in London* at the Old Barracks, Burton Road.

Franz Liszt played at a concert here on 12 September 1840 and remained in the city for the following day.

Neville Marriner, conductor, was born on 15 April 1924 at 26 St Andrew's Drive, where he spent his childhood.

Niccolò Paganini gave a recital here on 15 October 1833.

Steve Race, composer, pianist and popular broadcaster, was born at 6 St Catherines on 1 April 1921. His evergreen song *Nicola* was composed in Room 319, St Katherine's House, Kingsway, London.

John Philip Sousa conducted his band at a concert in New Central Hall on 28 February 1911. He stayed the night at the Great Northern Station Hotel.

James Stimpson, organist, was born here on 29 February 1820 and died in Birmingham on 4 October 1886.

Gilbert Vinter, conductor and composer, was born here in 1909.

Sidney Peine Waddington, composer and conductor, was born here on 23 July 1869 and died in Uplyme, Devon, on 2 June 1953.

Long Sutton Alfred Piccaver, tenor singer, was born here on 25 February 1884 and died in Vienna on 23 September 1958.

North Coates Timothy Matthews was rector here 1859–1907, during which time he wrote the hymn tunes *Margaret*, sung to 'Thou Didst Leave Thy Throne', and *North Coates*, often sung to 'Holy Spirit, Hear Us'.

Scampton Christopher Simpson, composer and viola da gamba player, is thought to have died either here or in London in 1669. His patron Sir John Bolles had residences both in Scampton and in the capital.

Somersby Alfred Tennyson, poet, whose verses inspired works by Bantock, Bax, Sterndale Bennett, Frank Bridge, Britten, Delius, Elgar, Gounod, Holst, Liszt, MacDowell, Mackenzie, Messiaen, Parry, Quilter, Stanford, Richard Strauss, Sullivan and Vaughan Williams, was born in Somersby House on 5 July 1807 and resided here until 1837. He is also the author of the hymn 'Sunset and Evening Star'.

Stamford Franz Liszt played at a concert here on 16 September 1840. Malcolm Sargent, conductor, spent his childhood at 24 Wharf Road.

Tattershall John Taverner, composer and organist, is believed to have been born here in about 1495. The early part of his life was spent here.

NORTHUMBERLAND

Alnwick Franz Liszt, travelling from Edinburgh, spent the night of 24 January 1841 here.

Berwick-upon-Tweed Franz Liszt had supper here on the evening of 24 January 1841.
   Niccolò Paganini gave a recital here on 2 October 1833.
   John Philip Sousa conducted his band at a concert in the Corn Exchange on 16 February 1903.

Ellington Richard Terry, organist, composer and music scholar, was born here on 3 January 1865 and died in London on 18 April 1938. He resided at 87 Prince of Wales' Mansions, Battersea, London.

Hexham Samuel Reay, composer of the hymn tune *Stamford* and organist, was born here on 17 March 1822 and died at Newark-on-Trent, Nottinghamshire, on 21 July 1905.
   Michael Stuart Richards, composer, was born here in 1928.

Rothbury James Allan, celebrated piper, was born here in March 1734 and died in Durham Gaol on 13 November 1810.

Shilbottle John Thirwall, conductor, composer, poet and painter, was born here on 11 January 1809 and died in London on 15 June 1875.

TYNE AND WEAR

Annitsford Owen Brannigan, bass singer, was born here on 10 March 1908 and died in Newcastle-upon-Tyne on 10 May 1973.

Houghton-le-Spring Charles Vincent, composer of the hymn tunes *Ishmael, St Cyril* and *St Dorothea*, was born here on 19 September 1852 and died in Monte Carlo on 23 February 1934.

Newcastle-upon-Tyne Charles Avison, organist and composer, was born in Newcastle-upon-Tyne in 1709 and died here on 10 May 1770. He is buried in the churchyard of St Andrew's. A century later Browning addressed a poem to him, 'Thou, whilom of Newcastle organist!'

Ferruccio Busoni played in concerts on 18 November 1901 and 10 November 1908. 'Life here', he wrote to his wife during his second visit, 'is horrible, grey and joyless.'

Adam Carse, distinguished writer on the orchestra and orchestration, teacher and composer, was born here on 19 May 1878.

Edward Clark, conductor, pupil of Schoenberg, husband of Elisabeth Lutyens and zealous champion of new music, was born here on 10 May 1888 and died in April 1962. He resided at 13 King Henry's Road, Hampstead, London.

George Clinton, clarinettist, who improved the clarinet, was born here on 16 December 1850 and died in London on 24 October 1913.

Marie Hall, violinist and pupil of Elgar, was born here on 8 April 1884 and died in Cheltenham, Gloucestershire, on 11 November 1956. Vaughan Williams's *The Lark Ascending*, of which she gave the first performance, in 1920, is dedicated to her.

Arthur Hedley, leading Chopin scholar, was born here on 12 November 1905.

Thomas Ions, organist, conductor, composer and pupil of Moscheles, was born here on 19 August 1817 and died, while driving home from Gateshead, on 25 September 1857.

Wilfred Josephs, composer, was born here on 24 July 1927. He spent his childhood at 12 Beech Grove Road and 32 Osbaldeston Gardens, Gosforth.

Franz Liszt played at a concert in the Assembly Rooms on 25 January 1841. He stayed the night at The Queen's Head.

Niccolò Paganini gave recitals in the Theatre Royal on 9 and 11 September 1833.

Maurice Ravel took part in a concert here on 20 January 1911.

William Rea, pianist, organist and composer, was born in London on 25 March 1827 and died here on 8 March 1903.

John Ross, organist and composer, was born here on 12 October 1764 and died in Aberdeen on 28 July 1837.

John Philip Sousa conducted his band at concerts in the Town Hall on 16 and 18 February 1903. He gave two further concerts in the Town Hall on 23 February 1911. He stayed at the Central Station Hotel.

Graham Steed, organist, conductor and composer, was born here on 1 March 1913.

On 19 November 1849, John Bacchus Dykes was appointed precentor of Durham Cathedral at £100 a year. On the same day, he decided to buy 'a very pretty little cottage . . . about a mile out of Durham, with a nice little bit of garden and a very fine prospect.' This was Hollingside Cottage, where he lived until September 1853. One of his most celebrated hymn tunes, *Hollingside*, commemorates his stay there. The photograph was taken by the present organist of Durham Cathedral (*Richard Hey Lloyd*)

The drawing of Durham Cathedral was sketched by Felix Mendelssohn on 24 July 1829, during his journey to Scotland. Dykes had a fervent admiration for the German composer and, when he heard of his death, went to the piano and played one of the *Songs without Words*, his eyes overflowing with tears (*The Bodleian Library*)

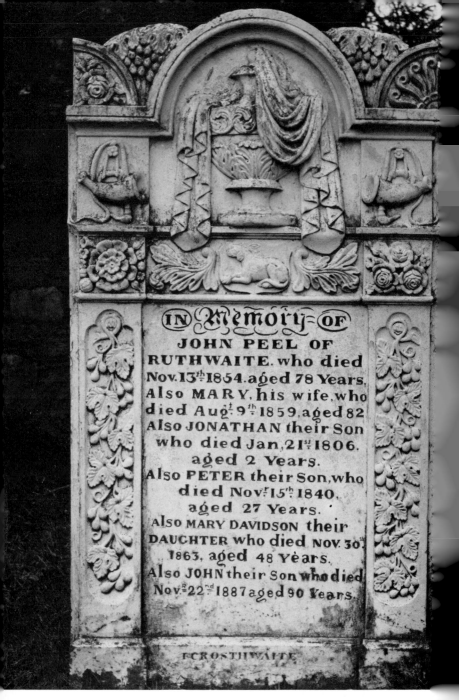

IN Memory OF
JOHN PEEL OF
RUTHWAITE. who died
Nov.13ᵗʰ 1854. aged 78 Years,
Also MARY, his wife, who
died Augᵗ 9ᵗʰ 1859, aged 82
Also JONATHAN their Son
who died Jan, 21ˢᵗ 1806,
aged 2 Years.
Also PETER their Son, who
died Novʳ 15ᵗʰ 1840,
aged 27 Years.
Also MARY DAVIDSON their
DAUGHTER who died Nov. 30ᵗʰ
1863, aged 48 Years,
Also JOHN their Son who died
Novʳ 22ⁿᵈ 1887 aged 90 Years,

CROSTHWAITE

John Peel's tombstone in Caldbeck, Cumbria. John Woodcock Graves, autho[r]
the song that immortalized him, wrote after Peel's death, 'You may know tha[t]
was six feet and more, and of a form and gait quite surprising, but his face and h[...]
were somewhat insignificant. He was of a very limited education beyond hunti[ng]
He was also extremely insensitive, which somebody who goes around bellow[ing]
'View halloo' first thing in the morning is liable to be (*Gordon Wood*)

Johann Strauss senior led his orchestra in concerts here, on 29 October 1838, in the Assembly Rooms, and on 30 October, in the Music Hall. He played at a ball in the Assembly Rooms on 19 November 1838. He stayed at the Royal Exchange Hotel.

William Gillies Whittaker, music scholar and conductor, was born here on 23 July 1876 and died in Orkney on 5 July 1944.

Shiney Row John Birkbeck, composer of the hymn tune *Sacred Rest*, was born here in 1831 and died in 1917.

South Shields Jack Brymer, virtuoso clarinettist, was born here on 27 January 1915.

Sunderland Muriel Foster, mezzo-soprano singer, was born here on 22 November 1877 and died in London on 23 December 1937.

Edward Gregson, composer, notably of brass band music, conductor and pianist, was born here on 23 July 1945.

Franz Liszt played at a concert in the Assembly Rooms on 26 January 1841.

Desmond MacMahon, composer, was born here on 26 July 1898.

John Philip Sousa conducted his band at two concerts in the Victoria Hall on 17 February 1903. He gave two further concerts in the Victoria Hall on 25 February 1911. He stayed the night at the Grand Hotel.

Washington James Sanderson, composer of *Hail to the Chief*, often played to announce the president of the United States, was born here in 1769 and died in London in about 1841.

Whickham William Shield, composer, violinist, Master of the King's Music and pupil of Avison, was born here on 5 March 1748.

NORTH YORKSHIRE

Boroughbridge Franz Liszt, travelling from Darlington to Leeds, had dinner here on 28 January 1841.

Dalton Sabine Baring-Gould was curate of Dalton in 1867, when he wrote the hymn 'Through the Night of Doubt and Sorrow'.

Harrogate Edward Henry Bickersteth, who was born in London on 25 January 1825 and died there on 16 May 1906, wrote the hymn 'Peace,

Perfect Peace, in This Dark World of Sin?' in Harrogate in August 1875.

George Enescu conducted a concert here on 20 May 1948.

Gerald Finzi, composer, resided at Birkholt, 22 Duchy Road, 1914–22.

Niccolò Paganini gave a recital in the ballroom of the Dragon Hotel on 7 September 1833.

Gordon Slater, organist, conductor and composer, was born here on 1 March 1896.

Leyburn Charles Kitson, music scholar, was born here on 13 November 1874 and died in London on 13 May 1944.

Little Ribston Edward Dent, music scholar, was born at Ribston Hall on 16 July 1876 and died on 22 August 1957 in London, where he resided at 17 Cromwell Place.

Malton Francis Jackson, composer and organist, was born here on 2 October 1917.

Masham William Jackson, composer and organist, was born here on 9 January 1815 and died in Bradford on 15 April 1866.

Pickering Arthur Tate, organist, music critic and composer of the songs *Somewhere a Voice Is Calling, A Bachelor Gay* and *The Green Vales of Antrim*, was born here in 1880.

Richmond Franz Liszt played at a concert here on 27 January 1841.

Scarborough Eric Fenby, composer and amanuensis to Delius, was born here on 22 April 1906.

Florence Hooton, cellist, was born here on 8 July 1912.

Edward Naylor, composer of the hymn tune *From Strength to Strength*, sung to 'Soldiers of Christ, Arise', was born here on 9 February 1867 and died in Cambridge on 7 May 1934.

John Philip Sousa conducted his band at a sacred concert in The Olympia on 26 February 1911. He stayed the night at the Royal Hotel.

Settle Edward Elgar, composer and Master of the King's Music, was a frequent guest of Dr Charles William Buck, whose house in the Market Place is now occupied by the National Westminster Bank. Elgar is thought to have written *Salut d'amour* here in August 1888. In 1906 Dr

Buck moved to Cravendale, Belle Hill, Giggleswick, where he died in 1932 and where Elgar also visited him.

Slingsby Edmund Carter, who was born in New Malton on 3 February 1845 and died in Scarborough on 23 May 1923, composed here in 1865 the hymn tune *Slingsby*, sung to 'Day by Day We Magnify Thee'. He also played cricket for Yorkshire.

Tadcaster Charles Hague, violinist and composer, was born here on 4 May 1769 and died in Cambridge on 18 June 1821.

Thirkleby Laura Taylor, composer, was born here in 1819 and died in Coleshill, Buckinghamshire, in 1905.

Topcliffe John Julian, author of the monumental and matchless *Dictionary of Hymnology* and of the hymn 'Father of All, to Thee', was vicar of Topcliffe from 1905 until his death here on 23 January 1913.

York Wystan Hugh Auden, poet, librettist of Stravinsky's *The Rake's Progress* and Henze's *Elegy for Young Lovers*, whose many texts for Benjamin Britten include *Our Hunting Fathers*, *Paul Bunyan*, *Hymn to St Cecilia* and *A Shepherd's Carol*, whose verses have also inspired works by Elisabeth Lutyens, Berio and, notably, Bernstein's symphony *The Age of Anxiety*, was born at 54 Bootham on 21 February 1907 and died in Vienna on 28 September 1973.

Joseph Barnby, organist, conductor and composer of *Sweet and Low*, was born here on 12 August 1838 and died in London on 28 January 1896.

John Barry, composer, was born here in 1933. Among his many successful film scores are those for *Goldfinger* and other James Bond movies, *The Ipcress File*, *Born Free*, *The Quiller Memorandum*, *The Lion in Winter*, *Midnight Cowboy* and *Mary, Queen of Scots*.

Alan Gray, organist and composer, was born here on 23 December 1855 and died in Cambridge on 27 September 1935.

Reginald Kell, clarinettist, was born here on 8 June 1906.

Franz Liszt stayed at The White Swan 12–14 December 1840. He took part in a concert at the Great Rooms in Blackwall Street on the evening of the 14th.

Felix Mendelssohn stayed here on 23 July 1829, on his way to Scotland.

Reginald Morris, composer of the carol tune *Hermitage*, sung to 'Love Came Down at Christmas', was born here on 3 March 1886 and died in London on 14 December 1948.

Niccolò Paganini gave recitals in the Festival Concert Room on 7 and 8 February 1832, and on 12 October 1833.

John Philip Sousa conducted his band at a concert in Exhibition Hall on 27 February 1911.

Johann Strauss senior led his orchestra at a concert here on 20 October 1838. He stayed at The White Swan.

John White, organist, was born here on 8 January 1779 and died in Leeds on 22 August 1831.

Frederick Wiseman, composer of the hymn tunes *Abney, All Hallows, Bocking, Christina, Colvend, Dallas, Fons Amoris, Medak, God of My Life, Lovest Thou Me* and *Wonderful Love*, was born here on 29 January 1858.

SOUTH YORKSHIRE

Barnsley John Casken, composer, was born here on 15 July 1949.

Bradfield Nicholas Gatty, composer and music critic, was born here on 13 September 1874 and died in London on 10 November 1946.

Bramley Walter Midgley, tenor singer, was born here on 13 September 1914.

Broom Hill Dora Bright, composer and pianist, was born here on 16 August 1863 and died in London in December 1951.

Doncaster William Bright, author of the hymns 'And Now the Wants Are Told' and 'At Thy Feet, O Christ, We Lay', was born here on 14 December 1824 and died in Oxford on 6 March 1901.

Francis Linley, blind organist and composer, was born in Doncaster in 1771 and died here on 13 September 1800.

Franz Liszt stayed here on the nights of 6 and 7 December 1840. He took part in a concert at the Mansion House on the 7th.

Edward Miller was organist of Doncaster Parish Church from 1756 until his death here on 12 September 1807. His famous hymn tune *Rockingham*, sung to 'When I Survey the Wondrous Cross', was published in 1790.

Niccolò Paganini gave a recital here on 14 October 1833.

Ecclesfield Alfred Scott-Gatty, composer, writer and Garter Principal

King-of-Arms, was born in Ecclesfield Vicarage on 26 April 1847 and died in London on 18 December 1918. He resided at Wendover Lodge, Welwyn, Hertfordshire.

Grimethorpe Grimethorpe Colliery Institute Band was formed here in 1918.

Hatfield Janet Baker, distinguished mezzo-soprano singer, was born here on 21 August 1933. She spent her childhood at Kingston, Epworth Road.

Hooton Roberts Ralph Vaughan Williams used to stay at the vicarage in the years around 1900. *Linden Lea* was performed for the first time on 4 September 1902 by the Hooton Roberts Musical Union.

Mortomley Douglas Guest, organist, conductor and composer, was born here on 9 May 1916.

Rotherham Robert Lindley, cellist and composer, was born here on 4 March 1776 and died in London on 13 June 1855.

Sheffield Herbert Antcliffe, writer on music, was born here on 30 July 1875.

Denis Arnold, music scholar, was born here on 15 December 1926.

Josephine Barstow, soprano singer, was born here on 27 September 1940.

William Sterndale Bennett, composer, pianist and conductor, was born at 7 (later 21) Howard Street on 13 April 1816, thereafter residing at 46 Norfolk Street, 30 Eyre Street and 31 Eyre Street. In 1859 he stayed at the Victoria Park Hotel (later the Rutledge Medical and Surgical Home) on the corner of Clarkehouse Road and Southbourne Road.

Ferruccio Busoni took part in a concert here on 4 February 1902.

Ernö Dohnányi was the soloist in the world première of his Second Piano Concerto, performed here on 3 December 1947.

John Duarte, composer and writer on music, was born here on 2 October 1919.

Edward Elgar, composer and Master of the King's Music, stayed in October 1902 at Tylecote, Gladstone Road, as the guest of James Dixon.

Arnold Foster, conductor and composer, was born here on 6 December 1898.

Dorothy Lawton, notable music librarian, was born here on 31 July 1881.

Franz Liszt took part in a concert here on 8 December 1840. He stayed at the Pontine Hotel.

James Montgomery, poet and hymn writer, lived in Sheffield from 1792 until his death here on 30 April 1854. During that time he wrote the hymns 'Angels, from the Realms of Glory', 'Songs of Praise the Angels Sang', 'For Ever with the Lord!', 'Lift Up Your Heads, Ye Gates of Brass' and 'Lord, Teach Us How To Pray Aright'.

Niccolò Paganini gave recitals in the Music Hall on 10 and 11 February 1832 and in the Theatre Royal on 29 August 1833.

Janet Patey, contralto singer, was born in London on 1 May 1842 and died in Sheffield on 28 February 1894.

Sergey Rakhmaninov took part in a concert here on 21 October 1936. He performed his Second Piano Concerto, accompanied by Henry Wood, who also conducted the world première of the final version of *The Bells*.

Gilbert Reaney, music scholar, was born here on 11 January 1924.

John Philip Sousa conducted his band at a concert here on 22 February 1905. He gave two further concerts, in the Victoria Hall, on 30 January 1911. He stayed the night at the Grand Hotel.

Johann Strauss senior led his orchestra at concerts in the Theatre Royal on 11, 12 and 13 October 1838. He stayed at the Royal Hotel.

WEST YORKSHIRE

Bardsey William Congreve, dramatist and poet, librettist of Handel's *Semele*, for whose plays *The Old Bachelor* and *The Double Dealer* Purcell wrote incidental music, was born here in February 1670 and died on 19 January 1729. He is buried in Westminster Abbey.

Bradford Ferruccio Busoni played at concerts here on 13 December 1906 and 8 October 1919.

Frederick Delius, composer, was born at 6 Claremont on 29 January 1862.

Hubert Hales, composer, was born here on 29 April 1902.

Sergey Rakhmaninov played at a concert here on 30 January 1914.

John Philip Sousa conducted his band at a concert here on 8 March 1905. He gave two further concerts, in St George's Hall, on 9 February 1911. He stayed at the Victoria Station Hotel.

Johann Strauss senior led his orchestra at a concert in the Exchange

Room on 21 November 1838, and at a concert and ball in the Music Hall on 22 November.

Bramham William Winn, bass singer and composer, was born here on 8 May 1828 and died in London on 4 June 1888.

Brighouse Brighouse and Rastrick Band was formed in 1881.
Susan Sunderland, soprano singer, was born in Brighouse on 30 April 1819 and died here on 6 May 1905.

Calverley Frederick Faber, who was born at Calverley Vicarage on 28 June 1814 and died in London on 26 September 1863, wrote the hymns 'My God, How Wonderful Thou Art', 'O Come and Mourn with Me Awhile', 'There's a Wideness in God's Mercy', 'Hark! Hark! My Soul, Angelic Songs Are Swelling' and 'Most Ancient of All Mysteries'.

Cleckheaton Kathleen Moorhouse, cellist, was born here on 27 January 1900.

Dewsbury Robert Burton, organist and notable chorus master at the Leeds Festival, was born here on 1 September 1820 and died in Harrogate on 2 August 1892.

Fulneck Christian Latrobe, composer of the hymn tune *Fulneck*, sung to 'Far Off We Need Not Rove', was born here on 12 February 1758 and died at Fairfield, near Buxton, Derbyshire, on 6 May 1836.

Girlington John Coates, tenor singer, was born here on 29 June 1865 and died in Northwood, London, on 16 August 1941.

Gomersal Arnold Cooke, composer, was born at Castle House on 4 November 1906. He resided at Springfield 1908–20.
Arnold Goldsbrough, organist and conductor, was born here on 26 October 1892.

Halifax George Dyson, composer, was born here on 28 May 1883 and died on 28 September 1964. He resided at 1 St James's Terrace, Winchester.
Franz Liszt played at a concert in the Oddfellows Hall on 29 January 1841. Afterwards he had dinner at The Swan, where he remained until 2.15am, when he departed for Leeds.
Niccolò Paganini gave a recital in the New Rooms on 9 February 1832.

Herbert Sharpe, pianist and composer, was born here on 1 March 1861 and died in London on 14 October 1925.

John Philip Sousa conducted his band at a concert here on 7 March 1905. He gave a further concert, in the Palace Theatre, on 11 February 1911.

Johann Strauss senior led his orchestra at concerts in the Theatre Royal on 15, 17 and 25 October 1838. He stayed at The Sportsman and later at The Swan.

Harewood George Lascelles, seventh Earl of Harewood, editor, writer on music and administrator, was born at Harewood House on 7 February 1923.

Hebden Bridge Franz Liszt, travelling from York to Manchester, had luncheon, consisting of ham and eggs, at The White Lion on 15 December 1840.

Harry Mortimer, distinguished brass band conductor, was born here on 10 April 1902.

Heckmondwike John Curwen, educationist, publisher and founder of the tonic sol-fa method of teaching, was born here on 14 November 1816 and died in Manchester on 26 May 1880.

Horbury William Baines, composer, was born here on 26 March 1899 and died in York on 6 November 1922.

Sabine Baring-Gould became curate of Horbury at the end of May 1864, remaining here for three years before moving to Dalton. His hymn 'Onward, Christian Soldiers' appeared for the first time on 15 October 1864 in *The Church Times*, entitled 'Hymn for Procession with Cross and Banners'. It was initially performed in Horbury, sung to the principal melody from the slow movement of Haydn's Symphony No 15.

John Bacchus Dykes came here and preached a sermon on 1 June 1859. During his visit he composed the hymn tune *Horbury*, sung to 'Nearer, My God, to Thee'.

Huddersfield Edward Bairstow, organist and composer, was born here on 22 August 1874 and died on 1 May 1946 in York, where he resided at 1 Minster Court.

Arthur Eaglefield Hull, one of the few music critics to attempt suicide, was born in Market Harborough, Leicestershire, on 10 March 1876 and died in London, where he resided at 19 Berners Street, on 4

November 1928. On 18 September of that year he threw himself under a train at Huddersfield Station, following the exposure of inept plagiarism in his book *Music, Classical, Romantic and Modern*, withdrawn by its publishers on 28 August 1928.

Franz Liszt played at a concert in the Philosophical Hall on 5 December 1840. Among the works that he performed was his transcription of Schubert's *Erlkönig*.

Walter Parratt, organist, composer, educationist and Master of the Queen's and King's Music, was born at 6 South Parade on 10 February 1841.

Albert Peace, organist and composer of the hymn tune *St Margaret*, sung to 'O Love That Wilt Not Let Me Go', was born here on 26 January 1844 and died in Liverpool on 14 March 1912.

John Philip Sousa conducted his band at a concert here on 6 March 1905. He gave a further concert, in the Palace Theatre, on 3 February 1911.

Johann Strauss senior stayed at the St George Hotel on visits here in October 1838. He led his orchestra at concerts in the Philosophical Hall on the 18th and 24th.

Herbert Westerby, organist, pianist and writer on music, was born here on 14 June 1865.

Hunslet Herbert Thompson, music critic, was born here on 11 August 1856 and died on 6 May 1945. He resided at 11 Oak Bank, Headingley.

Keighley John Carrodus, violinist, was born in Braithwaite on 20 January 1836 and died in London on 13 July 1895. As leader of the orchestra of the Philharmonic Society of London and of other British orchestras, he played under Verdi, Saint-Saëns, Tchaikovsky, Dvořák, Grieg, Sullivan, Stanford, Parry and other well-known composers.

Leeds Ferruccio Busoni took part in concerts here on 17 November 1908 and 1 October 1920.

Christian Darnton, composer, was born here on 30 October 1905.

Frederick Dawson, pianist, was born here on 16 July 1868 and died at Lymm, Cheshire, in October 1940.

Robert Donnington, music scholar, was born here on 4 May 1907.

Edward Elgar, composer and Master of the King's Music, stayed at the Queen's Hotel during the 1898 music festival.

Gabriel Fauré attended the first British performance of his *La Naissance de Vénus*, conducted by Arthur Sullivan in the Town Hall on 8 October 1898. *The Musical Times* was perplexed 'to understand on what principle' the work had been selected for presentation during that year's festival.

Englebert Humperdinck conducted his *Moorish Rhapsody* in the Town Hall on 8 October 1898.

Frank Kidson, music historian and folk-song collector, was born in Leeds on 15 November 1855 and died here on 7 November 1926.

George Linley, composer and author, was born in Briggate in 1798 and died in London on 10 September 1865.

Franz Liszt played at a concert here on 10 December 1840. He stayed the night at the Scarborough Hotel. He stayed here again on the night of 28 January 1841, travelling from Darlington to Halifax. Returning from Halifax during the early morning of 30 January, he caught the 6.15 train to London.

Niccolò Paganini gave recitals in the Albion Street Music Hall on 17 and 18 January 1832 and 2 September 1833.

Sergey Rakhmaninov took part in concerts here on 12 and 13 October 1910.

Stanford Robinson, conductor and composer, was born here on 5 July 1904.

Percy Scholes, distinguished music scholar and lexicographer, was born here on 24 July 1877 and died in Vevey, Switzerland, on 31 July 1958.

John Philip Sousa conducted his band at two concerts in the Town Hall on 10 February 1911. He stayed at the Queen's Midland Hotel.

Frederick Spark, businessman, editor, publisher, secretary of the Leeds Musical Festival 1877–1907, was born, possibly in Exeter, on 26 February 1831 and died in Leeds on 14 November 1919. He resided during the 1880s and 1890s at 29 Hyde Terrace, now a nurses' home. Among the visitors to his house were Sullivan, Stanford and almost certainly Dvořák, Elgar, Fauré and Humperdinck. Works that received their world premières, conducted by their composers, in Leeds Town Hall include Stanford's *The Revenge* on 14 October 1886; Dvořák's *St Ludmila* on 15 October 1886; Sullivan's *The Golden Legend* on 16 October 1886; Elgar's *Caractacus* on 5 October 1898; Stanford's *Songs of the Sea* on 7 October 1904; Vaughan Williams's *A Sea Symphony* on 12 October 1910; Stanford's *Songs of the Fleet* on 13 October 1910; Elgar's *Falstaff* on 1 October 1913; Holst's *Choral Symphony* (conducted by Albert Coates) on 7 October 1925; and Walton's *Belshazzar's Feast* (conducted by Malcolm Sargent) on 8 October 1931.

Sullivan, who was the festival conductor 1880–98, used often to stay at the Judge's Lodgings, also in Hyde Terrace.

Johann Strauss senior led his orchestra at a concert in the Music Hall on 16 October 1838. He stayed at The Lion Hotel. He gave a second concert in the Music Hall on 19 October and stayed at the Golden Lion Inn. He was at the Albion Hotel 26–8 October; he played at a ball in the Great Assembly Room on the 26th and at a concert in the Theatre Royal on the 27th. He stayed here again on 20 November 1838 when travelling from Newcastle-upon-Tyne to Bradford.

Lidget Green John Fawcett, author of the hymn 'Lord, Dismiss Us with Thy Blessing, Fill Our Hearts with Joy and Peace', was born here on 6 January 1740 and died in Hebden Bridge on 25 July 1817.

Liversedge Leslie Heward, composer and conductor of the City of Birmingham Orchestra, was born at Littletown on 8 December 1897 and died on 3 May 1943 in Birmingham, where he resided at 44 Harborne Road, Edgbaston.

Low Moor Frederic Cliffe, composer, pianist and organist, was born here on 2 May 1857 and died in London on 19 November 1931.

Norland Town Walter Widdop, tenor singer, was born here on 19 April 1892 and died in London on 6 September 1949.

Queensbury The Black Dyke Mills Band originated here and was in existence for forty years before acquiring its famous name in 1855 through the patronage of John Foster, the garment manufacturer and owner of Black Dyke Mills.

Slaithwaite Haydn Wood, composer of *Roses of Picardy*, was born here on 25 March 1882 and died in London on 11 March 1959.

South Elmsall Carlton Main Frickley Colliery Band was formed here in 1897, originally as South Elmsall Village Band.

Sowerby Bridge Norman Cocker, organist and composer, was born here in 1889 and died in 1953.

Stanningley John Varley Roberts, organist and composer, was born here on 25 September 1841 and died in Oxford on 9 February 1920.

Stourton Yorkshire Imperial Metals Band was formed here in July 1936 as Yorkshire Copper Works Band.

Wakefield Rawdon Briggs, violinist and pupil of Joachim, was born here in 1869 and died in Manchester on 20 December 1948.

Noel Gay, composer of the songs *The Lambeth Walk*, *The King's Horses* and *Run, Rabbit, Run*, was born here on 15 July 1898.

Kenneth Leighton, composer, pianist and educationist, was born here on 2 October 1929.

Franz Liszt, travelling from Huddersfield to Doncaster, had luncheon at the Strafford Arms on 6 December 1840. He stayed the night at the hotel on 9 December, taking part in a concert at 8pm. At this time, he was completing his *Reminiscences de Robert le Diable*, which he tried over on the piano at the Strafford Arms.

Johann Strauss senior led his orchestra at a concert in the Music Hall on 24 November 1838.

West Bretton Robena Laidlaw, pianist, to whom Schumann dedicated his *Fantasiestücke*, Op 12, was born here on 30 April 1819 and died in London on 29 May 1901.

Woolley Mary Anne Paton, celebrated soprano singer, died at Bulcliffe Hall, Chapelthorpe, on 21 July 1864.

THE NORTH-WEST

CHESHIRE

Chester Adrian Boult, conductor, was born on 8 April 1889 at 6 Abbot's Road (demolished).

Ferruccio Busoni played in a concert here on 6 November 1903.

George Frideric Handel stayed at The Golden Falcon in Bridge Street, on his way to Dublin, during the second week of November 1741. Charles Burney, then 15, later described this visit. 'I was at the Public School in that city, and very well remember seeing him smoke a pipe, over a dish of coffee, at the Exchange Coffee-houses; for, being extremely anxious to see so extraordinary a man, I watched him narrowly as long as he remained in Chester; which, on account of the wind being unfavourable for his embarking at Parkgate, was several days. During this time, he applied to Mr. Baker, the Organist, my first music-master, to know whether there were any Choirmen in the Cathedral who could sing *at sight*; as he wished to prove some books that had been hastily transcribed, by trying the Choruses which he intended to perform in Ireland. Mr. Baker mentioned some of the most likely singers then in Chester, and, among the rest, a printer of the name of Janson, who had a good base voice, and was one of the best musicians in the Choir . . . A time was fixed for the private rehearsal at the *Golden Falcon*, where Handel was quartered; but alas! on trial of the Chorus in the "Messiah", *And with His stripes we are healed* — poor Janson, after repeated attempts, failed so egregiously, that Handel let loose his great bear upon him; and, after swearing in four or five different languages, cried out, in broken English: "You scoundrel! did not you tell me that you could sing at sight?" "Yes, Sir," says the printer, "and so I can; but not at *first sight*."'

William Lawes, composer, fighting as an officer in the Royalist forces, was killed during the siege of Chester on 24 September 1645.

Miriam Licette, soprano singer, was born here on 9 September 1892.

Franz Liszt stayed at the Royal Hotel on the nights of 29 and 30 November 1840. He took part in a concert there on the 30th. When walking to see the cathedral, he excited astonishment among the citizens of Chester by wearing an enormous Hungarian coat made of many different skins and brightly coloured leathers, with matching cap.

Felix Mendelssohn visited here on the afternoon of 20 August 1829, on his way from Liverpool to Holywell. 'In Chester a bright scene presented itself; the broad town-walls make a promenade round the town, and there I saw a girls' school marching along, whom I followed with my sketch-book. The girls looked very pretty, the distance very blue, the houses and towers in the foreground dark grey; in the evening a gentle rain fell, and when it was dark, we left for Holywell.'

Niccolò Paganini gave a recital in the Theatre Royal on 27 January 1832.

Francis Pilkington, composer, who died in 1638, spent much of his life here, being successively curate of St Bridget's and St Martin's and, later, rector of Aldford.

John Philip Sousa conducted his band at a concert here on 24 February 1905.

Charles Stewart, organist, was born here in 1884 and died in Windsor on 14 November 1932.

Crewe John Ellerton, who was born in London on 16 December 1826, was vicar of Crewe Green 1860–72. Here he wrote the hymns 'Saviour, Again to Thy Dear Name We Raise', in 1866, and 'The Day Thou Gavest, Lord, Is Ended', in 1870.

John Philip Sousa conducted his band at a concert here on 25 February 1905.

Elworth Foden's Motor Works Band was formed here by Edwin Foden in 1902.

Gawsworth Samuel Johnson, composer, was born in 1691 and died here in 1773.

Macclesfield John Philip Sousa conducted his band at a concert here on 23 February 1905.

Malpas Reginald Heber, author of numerous memorable and poetic hymns, was born here on 21 April 1783. He died in India on 3 April 1826.

Nantwich Franz Liszt, travelling from Newcastle-under-Lyme to Chester, had luncheon at The Crown on 29 November 1840.

Neston Thomas Johnson, composer, pianist and writer on music, was born here on 11 March 1908.

Northwich Percy Marshall Young, distinguished and prolific writer on music, composer, conductor and organist, was born here on 17 May 1912.

Warrington Ivor Gurney, composer and poet, recuperating from gassing and shell shock sustained at Ypres, was in the Soldier's Home, Bold Street, when, during June 1918, he first exhibited signs of approaching insanity.

John Philip Sousa conducted his band at a concert here on 4 March 1905 and also in the Palace Theatre, on 6 February 1911.

CUMBRIA

Barrow-in-Furness Ferruccio Busoni gave a concert here on 4 October 1907.

Brampton William Forster, eminent violin maker and music publisher, who printed eighty-three of Haydn's symphonies, was born here on 4 May 1739 and died at 22 York Street, Westminster, London, on 14 December 1808.

Edmund Gibson, writer on music and bishop, was born here in 1669 and died in Bath in 1748.

Bridekirk Jane Euphemia Saxby, author of the hymn 'Show Me the Way, O Lord', was born here on 27 January 1811 and died in Clevedon, Avon, on 25 March 1898.

Caldbeck John Woodcock Graves wrote the words of the song *D'Ye Ken John Peel* here in about 1825. Peel, of whom Graves said, 'He was of a very limited education beyond hunting', was born in Greenrigg in 1776 and died in 1854. The melody of the song was originally known as *Bonnie Annie* or *Cannie Annie*.

Carlisle Joseph Carlyle, author of the hymn 'Lord, When We Bend Before Thy Throne', was born here on 4 June 1758 and died in Newcastle-upon-Tyne on 12 April 1804.

Mandell Creighton, author of the hymn 'O Thou, Who Gavest Power To Love', was born here on 5 July 1843 and died in London on 14 January 1901.

Adelina de Lara, pianist and composer, was born here on 23 January 1872.

Niccolò Paganini gave a recital in the Theatre on 12 September 1833. John Philip Sousa conducted his band at a concert here on 10 March 1905.

Johann Strauss senior led his orchestra at concerts in the Assembly Rooms on 31 October and 16 November 1838. He stayed on both occasions at the Crown Inn.

Dalston Susanna Blamire, author of 'What Ails This Heart o' Mine?' and 'Ye Sall Walk in Silk Attire', was born at Cardew Hall on 12 January 1747 and died in Carlisle on 5 April 1794.

Great Blencow John Troutbeck, music editor and translator, was born here on 12 November 1832 and died in London on 11 October 1899.

Kendal William Smallwood, composer of the hymn tune *Antwerp*, was born in Kendal on 31 December 1831 and died here on 6 August 1897.

John Philip Sousa conducted his band at a concert here on 11 March 1905.

Mary Wakefield, initiator of competitive music festivals, contralto singer and composer, was born in Bank House, Stricklandgate, on 19 August 1853 and died at her home, Nutwood, Yewbarrow, near Grange-over-Sands, on 16 September 1910. She is buried in Crosscrake.

Keswick Frederic Myers, author of the hymn 'Hark What a Sound and Too Divine for Hearing', was born here on 6 March 1843 and died in Rome on 17 January 1901.

Kirkby Lonsdale Humphrey Proctor-Gregg, opera producer, theatrical designer and music scholar, was born here on 31 July 1895 and died on 13 April 1980.

Kirkby Stephen Thomas, first Marquis of Wharton, author of 'Lilliburlero', who was born in 1648 and died in Dover Street, Mayfair, London, on 12 April 1715, resided at Wharton Hall, now a farmhouse.

Windermere Arthur Somervell, composer of the song-cycle *Maud*, was born here on 5 June 1863 and died in London on 2 May 1937. He resided at 105 Clifton Hill, St John's Wood, London.

Giuseppe Verdi visited the Lake District in June 1862.

Wharton Hall, near Kirkby Stephen, Cumbria. This was the family home of Thomas, Lord Wharton, the author of 'Lilliburlero'. He wrote the song in 1687, later boasting that it had 'sung James II out of three kingdoms', which was not far from the truth (*Gordon Wood*)

The Firs at Bowdon in Greater Manchester where Hans Richter lived, 1901 to 1911, while he was conductor of the Hallé Orchestra. Bartók stayed with him in February 1904. Richter much enjoyed his years with the Hallé, writing, 'I shall scarcely be accused of ingratitude or hostility to Manchester if I venture to say that we are not exactly spoilt by sunshine. But as a makeweight for that, the genius of the city has given to the inhabitants a certain warm sensibility to the eloquence of tone. Living in a climate rather unfavourable to the delight of the eye, they seem to be all the more keenly alive to the delight of the ear.' (*Studio Morgan, Altrincham*)

William Walton was born in 1902 in Oldham, where he spent most of his early years. After leaving Oxford, he lived for a time in London, often travelling abroad. He made his home in Switzerland during part of the 1930s and, towards the end of the 1940s, moved permanently to the island of Ischia in the Bay of Naples (*Bassano & Vandyk Studios*)

ISLE OF MAN

Douglas Robert Callin, author of the hymn 'O Lord of Every Lovely Thing', was born here in 1886 and died in Bradford, West Yorkshire, on 11 June 1951.

Hugh Stowell, author of the hymn 'From Every Stormy Wind That Blows', was born here on 3 December 1799 and died in Pendleton, Greater Manchester, on 8 October 1865.

Peel William Henry Gill, who was born in Marsala, Sicily, on 24 October 1839 and died in Angmering, West Sussex, on 27 June 1923, spent most of his life in the Isle of Man. He wrote here the hymn 'Hear Us, O Lord, from Heaven, Thy Dwelling-Place', for which he supplied the tune *Peel Castle*, adapted from a traditional Manx folk-song.

LANCASHIRE

Accrington Harrison Birtwistle, composer, was born here in 1934.

Blackburn Niccolò Paganini gave a recital in the Theatre Royal on 5 September 1833.

John Philip Sousa conducted his band at a concert here on 2 March 1905. He gave a further concert, in the Palace Theatre, on 2 February 1911.

Ronald Stevenson, composer and pianist, was born here on 6 March 1928.

William Wolstenholme, composer and organist, was born here on 24 February 1865 and died in London on 23 July 1931.

Blackpool David Atherton, conductor, was born on 3 January 1944 at 26 Leys Road. He spent his childhood at 35 Mere Road.

John Philip Sousa conducted his band at two concerts in the Winter Gardens on 5 February 1911. He stayed the night at the Metropole Hotel.

Burnley John Philip Sousa conducted his band at a concert in the Mechanics' Institute on 11 February 1911. He stayed the night at the Bull Hotel.

Carnforth John Alexander Fuller-Maitland, music scholar, editor and critic, was born in London on 7 April 1856 and died in Carnforth on 30 March 1936. He resided at Borwick Hall.

Chorley John Philip Sousa conducted his band at a concert in the Town Hall on 8 February 1911.

Thomas Wood, composer and author, was born here on 28 November 1892.

Haslingden Alan Rawsthorne, composer, was born here on 2 May 1905.

Higher Walton Kathleen Ferrier, contralto singer, was born at 1 Bank Terrace on 22 April 1912.

Hoddlesden Edward Harwood, composer of the anthem *Vital Spark of Heavenly Flame*, was born here in 1707 and died in 1787.

Kirkham Frederick Fuller, baritone singer, was born here on 7 November 1908.

Lancaster Niccolò Paganini gave a recital here on 14 September 1833.

John Philip Sousa conducted his band at a concert here on 11 March 1905. He gave a further concert, in the Town Hall, on 1 February 1911. He stayed the night at the County Hotel.

Lytham St Anne's Peter Dickinson, composer and pianist, was born here on 15 November 1934.

Newchurch-in-Rossendale James Whitehead, cellist, was born here on 14 June 1912.

Parbold Hugh Wood, composer, was born here on 27 June 1932.

Preston Arthur Catterall, violinist, was born here in 1884 and died on 28 November 1943 in London. He resided at 35 London Road, Stanmore.

Helen Lemmens-Sherrington, soprano singer, was born here on 4 October 1834 and died in Brussels on 9 May 1906.

Franz Liszt played at a concert here on 2 December 1840.

Niccolò Paganini gave a recital in the Theatre Royal on 27 August 1833.

John Philip Sousa conducted his band at a concert here on 9 March

1905. He gave a further concert, in the Public Hall, on 2 February 1911. He stayed the night at the Park Hotel.

Francis Thompson, poet and author of the hymn 'O World Invisible, We View Thee', was born at 7 Winckley Street on 16 December 1859 and died in London on 18 November 1907. His poems have been set to music by Holst, Bridge, Hindemith and Milhaud.

Rawtenstall Ernest Tomlinson, composer, was born here on 29 May 1927.

Rimington Francis Duckworth, composer of the hymn tune *Rimington*, was born here on Christmas Day 1862 and died in Colne on 16 August 1941.

Wennington John Fawcett, composer of the hymn tunes *Melling*, sung to 'Children of the Heavenly God', and *Relief*, sung to 'O Thou in All Thy Might So Far', was born here, 1½ miles from the town of Melling, on 8 December 1789 and died in Bolton on 26 October 1867. His son John, born in Bolton in 1824, became organist of St John's Church, Farnworth, at the age of eleven and died in Manchester on 1 July 1857.

GREATER MANCHESTER

Ashton-under-Lyne Norman Allin, bass singer, was born here on 19 November 1884 and died in Hereford on 27 October 1973.

Atherton Frank Fletcher, author of the hymn 'O Son of Man, Our Hero Strong and Tender', was born here on 3 May 1870 and died in Hindhead, Surrey, on 17 November 1954.

Bolton Niccolò Paganini gave a recital here on 6 September 1833.

Thomas Pitfield, composer, artist and writer, was born here on 5 April 1903.

John Philip Sousa conducted his band in a concert here on 27 February 1905 and also in the Theatre Royal, on 8 February 1911.

Bowdon Adolph Brodsky, renowned violinist, who gave the world and British premières of Tchaikovsky's Violin Concerto, was born in Taganrog (Chekhov's birthplace), USSR, on 21 March 1851 and died on 22 January 1929 at 3 Laurel Mount, Bowdon, where he had resided for thirty years.

Alexander Ewing, composer of the hymn tune *Ewing*, sung to 'Jerusalem the Golden', resided at 14 Higher Downs 1877–8. Ethel Smyth, his pupil, was a visitor here in July 1877.

John Ireland, composer, was born at Inglewood, St Margaret's Road, on 13 August 1879. Charles Hallé, conductor and pianist, was a visitor to the house.

Egon Petri resided at The Hollies, Richmond Road, 1906–10. Ferrucio Busoni stayed with him at the end of September 1907.

Hans Richter, celebrated conductor, who directed the world premières of such works as *The Ring*, Tchaikovsky's Violin Concerto, Brahms's Third Symphony and *The Dream of Gerontius*, resided 1901–11 at 27 The Firs, while he was conductor of the Hallé Orchestra.

Béla Bartók stayed with Richter 12–19 February 1904. At a concert in the Free Trade Hall on 18 February, Richter conducted the first British performance of the *Kossuth Symphony*, and Bartók played Liszt's *Spanish Rhapsody* and a work by Volkmann. On arriving in Bowdon, the composer wrote to his mother: 'The Richters received me very cordially and have given me a room on the 2nd floor . . . In the afternoon, the weather became very bad indeed — storms of wind and rain — so I haven't been able to see very much of either Manchester or Bowdon. The Richters' home must be a very comfortable place to live in. There's a cheerful blaze in the fireplace (English conservatism).' English trains disappointed him: 'The carriages on the most unimportant branch line in Hungary are better than those here. There's no heating (they merely put a container full of hot water in the carriage) nor head-rests, nor arm-rests; the luggage racks are too narrow. As there are no ashtrays, the floors of the compartments are like that of a pigsty.' Edward Elgar, whose First Symphony received its world première under Richter in the Free Trade Hall on 3 December 1908, was almost certainly a guest here. Another regular visitor was George Bernard Shaw.

Bury Gordon Crosse, composer, was born here on 1 December 1937.

Cheadle Hulme Llewelyn Lloyd, notable writer on acoustic aspects of music, was born here on 20 April 1876 and died in Birmingham on 14 August 1956.

Chorlton-cum-Hardy Michael Kennedy, distinguished biographer of Edward Elgar, Ralph Vaughan Williams and John Barbirolli, was born here on 19 February 1926.

Crumpsall Frédéric Chopin stayed with Salis Schwabe at Crumpsall House (demolished), George Street, from about 27 to 31 August 1848, taking part in a Gentlemen's Concert on 28 August. The *Manchester Guardian* said of the composer: 'He is very spare in frame, and there is an almost painful air of feebleness in his appearance and gait. This vanishes when he seats himself at the instrument, in which he seems for the time perfectly absorbed.' The *Manchester Courier* observed: 'There was a chasteness and purity of style, a correctness of manipulation combined with a brilliance of touch, and delicate sensibility of expression which we never heard excelled.' Jenny Lind stayed at Crumpsall House over Christmas 1848 and in August 1850.

Arthur Jacobs, eminent writer on music, educationist and critic, was born here on 14 June 1922.

Droylsden James Ellor, composer of the hymn tune *Diadem*, was born here in 1819 and died in the USA in 1899.

Egerton James Walch, composer of the hymn tune *Sawley*, was born here on 21 June 1837 and died in Llandudno, Gwynedd, on 30 August 1901.

Fallowfield John Ireland, composer, spent his later childhood at 31 Mauldeth Road.

Edward Isaacs, pianist, conductor and composer, was born in Manchester on 14 July 1881 and died in Fallowfield on 31 July 1953. He resided at 19 Amherst Road.

Heaton Chapel Fairey Aviation Works Band was formed here in August 1937.

Manchester Adolph Brodsky, violinist, was residing at 41 Acomb Street (demolished) when Edvard Grieg stayed with him on the night of 24 November 1897, taking part in a concert that evening at the Free Trade Hall. By postcard from London the composer alerted the Brodskys to his requirements, the first of which was that at 4pm he should have an underdone steak. 'I know this is impudent, and you see for yourself that you should have let us stay in a hotel. But before a concert you *mustn't* be offended if I'm very strict about my food. It's absolutely necessary. The concert is at 7.30 and I must rest beforehand. And there's one more thing you must permit: Bechstein's are sending a pianino; would you please have it put in my room . . . I should be grateful for a fairly warm room.'

Ferruccio Busoni played at concerts in the Free Trade Hall in 1899, 1902, 1904, 1906, 1908, 1909, 1919 and 1922. In November 1904 he wrote to his wife: 'Darkness and frost prevail here, just as they would in a meticulously planned region of Dante's Inferno where travelling virtuosos, who have thrown away the best parts of their lives through greed for fame and money, grind their teeth.' In November 1909 he reported: 'Manchester the same as ever . . . animated by ugly people.'

John Byrom, author of the hymn 'Christians, Awake, Salute the Happy Morn', was born in Manchester on 29 February 1692 and died here on 26 September 1763. His famous hymn was written for his daughter Dolly as a present at Christmas 1749. Byrom was one of the pioneers of modern shorthand, which he taught to the Wesleys. He also wrote the celebrated lines:

> Some say, that Signor Bononcini,
> Compar'd to Handel's a mere ninny;
> Others aver, to him, that Handel
> Is scarcely fit to hold a candle.
> Strange! that such high dispute shou'd be
> 'Twixt Tweedledum and Tweedledee.

Howard Carr, conductor and composer, was born here on 26 December 1880.

Raymond Cohen, violinist, was born here on 27 July 1919.

CWS (Manchester) Band, dating from 1937, was originally CWS Tobacco Factory Band, which was formed here in 1901.

Brian Easdale, composer, was born here on 10 August 1909. His best known film scores include those for *The Red Shoes*, which won him the 1948 Hollywood Academy Award, and *Black Narcissus*.

Gabriel Fauré took part in a chamber concert here on 30 November 1908. The city, he said, was 'black, smoky, foggy and altogether terrible!'

John Field, composer, pianist, pupil of Clementi, teacher of Glinka, took part in two concerts here in July 1832.

John Foulds, composer and conductor, was born here on 2 November 1880 and died in Calcutta on 24 April 1939.

John Gardner, composer, was born here on 2 March 1917.

Anne Gilchrist, authority on folk-song, was born here on 8 December 1863 and died on 24 July 1954.

Charles Hallé, founder and conductor of the Hallé Orchestra, was born in Hagen, West Germany, on 11 April 1819 and died at his home, 36 Greenheys (rebuilt), on 25 October 1895. He formed his famous orchestra in 1857, having settled in Manchester in 1848. His first home was, for a short time, 3 Addison Terrace, Victoria Park.

Ralph Harrison, composer of the hymn tune *Warrington*, often sung to 'Jesus, Where'er Thy People Meet', was minister of the Cross Street Unitarian Chapel from 1777 until his death here on 4 November 1810.

Paul Hindemith conducted his *Nobilissima Visione* and *Symphonic Metamorphoses on Themes of Weber* at the Free Trade Hall on 22 January 1958.

Richard Hoffman, pianist and composer, was born here on 24 May 1831 and died in New York on 17 August 1909.

Johann Nepomuk Hummel took part in concerts here on 5 and 7 July 1830, exciting greater interest and enthusiasm than he ever achieved in London.

Leonard Isaacs, music administrator, was born here on 3 January 1909.

Maurice Johnstone, composer and writer on music, was born here on 28 July 1900 and died in Harpenden, Hertfordshire, in 1976.

Samuel Langford, music critic, was born in Manchester in 1863 and died here on 8 May 1927.

Richard Lewis, notable tenor singer, was born here on 10 May 1914.

Franz Liszt, aged 13, played at concerts in the Theatre Royal on 16 and 20 June 1825. He visited Manchester again in 1840, taking part in a concert at The Atheneum on 4 December and staying the night at the Mosley Arms Hotel. He played in another concert at The Atheneum on 15 December 1840 and once more stayed at the Mosley Arms.

Louise Kirkby Lunn, mezzo-soprano singer, was born here on 8 November 1873 and died in London on 17 February 1930. She resided at 15 Marlborough Road, St John's Wood, London.

James Lyon, composer, was born here on 25 October 1872 and died in Australia on 25 August 1949.

Maria Felicita Malibran, renowned mezzo-contralto singer, was born in Paris on 24 March 1808 and died in the Mosley Arms Hotel at 11.40am on 23 September 1836. She was initially buried in the south aisle of the Collegiate Church of St Mary the Virgin, now the cathedral, but was later reinterred at Laeken, near Brussels, despite a petition signed by 700 prominent Mancunians opposing exhumation.

Felix Mendelssohn visited relations here during June 1842. On 20 April 1847 he conducted *Elijah* in the Free Trade Hall.

Frederic Norton, composer of *Chu Chin Chow*, was born here in 1875.

Nigel Osborne, composer, was born here in 1948.

Franz Paersch, notable horn player, was born in Thalberg, near

Leipzig, on 23 December 1857 and died in Manchester on 30 March 1921.

Niccolò Paganini gave concerts in the Theatre Royal on 12, 13, 14, 19, 20 and 21 January, 18 and 20 February 1832, and on 4 September 1833.

Anna Pollak, mezzo-soprano singer, was born here on 1 May 1915.

Giacomo Puccini came here to supervise the British première of *La Bohème* at the Comedy Theatre on 22 April 1897. His impression of Manchester was 'black smoke, darkness, cold, rain, cotton (but woe betide anybody who doesn't wear wool!) and fog. A veritable Inferno! A terrible place to stay!'

Sergey Rakhmaninov played his Second Piano Concerto at a concert in the Free Trade Hall on 29 January 1914. On 7 March 1935, in the same hall, he gave the first English performance of his *Rhapsody on a Theme of Paganini*.

M. E. Rourke, author of the song 'They Didn't Believe Me', was born here in 1867 and died in 1933.

Jean Sibelius conducted at a concert in the Free Trade Hall in October 1912. He conducted at a second concert on 5 March 1921.

John Philip Sousa conducted his band at concerts here on 28 February and 1 March 1905. He gave two further concerts, in the Free Trade Hall, on 31 January 1911. He stayed at the Midland Hotel.

Johann Strauss senior led his orchestra at concerts in the Theatre Royal on 6, 9, 11, 21 and 25 August 1838.

Richard Strauss conducted at concerts in the Free Trade Hall on 21 January 1922, performing *Till Eulenspiegel* and *Don Juan*, and on 14 November 1926, performing *Don Juan* and an excerpt from *Der Rosenkavalier*.

James Swift, organist, bass singer and composer of *Sailing, Sailing over the Bounding Main*, was born here in 1847 and died in Wallasey, Merseyside, in January 1931.

Joseph Williams, musician and founder of the Amalgamated Musicians' Union, was born here on 10 August 1871 and died in France on 3 August 1929.

Olive Zorian, violinist, was born here on 16 March 1916 and died in London in 1965.

New Moston Arthur Butterworth, composer and conductor, was born here on 4 August 1923.

Oldham John Philip Sousa conducted his band at a concert here on 26 February 1905. He gave two further concerts, in Unity Hall, on 7 February 1911.

Eva Turner, soprano singer, was born here on 10 March 1898.

William Walton, composer, was born on 29 March 1902 at 93 Werneth Hall Road, where he spent his childhood.

— Owen Carley's godfather

Pendlebury Graham Peel, composer of *In Summertime on Bredon*, was born here on 9 August 1877 and died at Marden Ash, Bournemouth, on 16 October 1937.

Rochdale Gracie Fields, popular singer, was born here on 9 January 1898.

Franz Liszt played at a concert here on 3 December 1840.

John Philip Sousa conducted his band at a concert here on 3 March 1905. He gave a further concert, in the Town Hall, on 3 February 1911.

Rusholme Neville Cardus, sportswriter and music critic, was born here on 2 April 1889 and died on 28 February 1975.

Sale William Duncan, composer and writer on music, was born in Sale on 22 April 1866 and died here on 26 June 1920. He resided in Alexandra Road.

Sandy Wilson, composer of *The Boy Friend*, lyric writer and dramatist, was born at Rosegarth, Irlam Road, on 19 May 1924.

Salford John Barbirolli, conductor, resided intermittently at Walton Lodge, New Hall Road, from 1960 until his death in the Middlesex Hospital, London, on 29 July 1970. He had earlier resided at Appleby Lodge, Rusholme. He is buried in Kensal Green Cemetery.

Peter Maxwell Davies, composer, was born on 8 September 1934 at 13 Holly Street.

Niccolò Paganini gave recitals here on 22 and 23 August 1833.

Shaw Norman Walker, bass singer, was born here on 28 November 1907.

Stalybridge Robert Forbes, conductor and pianist, was born here on 7 May 1878 and died on 13 May 1958. He resided at Ballabeg, Winton Road, Bowdon.

Stockport Peter Hope, composer of *The Ring of Kerry Suite*, was born here on 2 November 1930.

Richard Hey Lloyd, conductor, composer and organist, was born here on 25 June 1933.

John Philip Sousa conducted his band at a concert on 3 March 1905.

John Wainwright, composer of the hymn tune *Stockport*, sung to 'Christians, Awake, Salute the Happy Morn', was born in Stockport and baptized on 14 April 1723. His setting of 'Christians, Awake', which Byrom had written at Christmas 1749, was first sung on Christmas Day 1750 at Stockport Parish Church, where Wainwright was organist. He was buried on 28 January 1768 in Stockport Churchyard, but when the church was demolished in 1810, his tombstone disappeared. A century later, it was dug up in a garden in Turncroft Lane.

Wainwright's sons Robert and Richard were also notable musicians. Robert, who was born in Stockport in 1748 and died there on 15 July 1782, succeeded his father as organist of Manchester Cathedral in 1768. In 1875 he was appointed organist of St Peter's Church, Liverpool. He composed the hymn tune *Manchester*. Richard was born in Stockport in 1758 and died in Liverpool on 20 August 1825. He succeeded his brother as organist of Manchester Cathedral in 1775 and as organist of St Peter's Church, Liverpool, in 1782. He composed the hymn tune *Liverpool* and the popular song *Life's a Bumper*. A third brother, William, was a successful bass player. Harriet Wainwright, who is thought to have been the sister of Robert, Richard and William, was a composer and poet.

Stretford Adam Watson, composer of the hymn tune *Wonderful Love*, was born here in 1845 and died at Pinner, London, in 1912.

David Wilde, pianist, was born here on 25 February 1935.

Swinton Peter Maxwell Davies, composer, resided at 13 Wyville Drive 1938–56.

Wardle James Leach, composer and tenor singer, was born here in 1762 and was killed in a stagecoach accident in Blackley on 8 February 1798. He is buried in Rochdale.

Wigan Ernest Bullock, organist and composer, was born here on 15 September 1890 and died in Aylesbury, Buckinghamshire, in 1979.

Wingates Wingates Temperance Band was formed here in 1873.

Withington Carl Fuchs, cellist, was born in Offenbach, West Germany, on 3 June 1865 and died in Withington on 9 June 1951. He resided at 32 Oak Road.

Frank Merrick, composer and pianist, resided at 12 Parsonage Road during World War I.

MERSEYSIDE

Billinge Henry Fothergill Chorley, music critic, man of letters, librettist and friend of Dickens, was born at Blackley Hurst on 15 December 1808.

Birkenhead Richard Austin, conductor, was born here on 26 December 1903.

Winton Dean, music scholar, was born here on 18 March 1916.

Thomas Matthews, violinist, was born here on 9 May 1907.

Cyril Scott, composer, pianist and poet, was born at The Laurels, Oxton, on 27 September 1879 and died in Eastbourne, East Sussex, on 31 December 1970.

George Ratcliffe Woodward, author of 'Ding Dong! Merrily on High', 'Shepherds in the Field Abiding', 'Unto Us Is Born a Son' and 'Past Three o'Clock', was born here on 27 December 1848 and died in London on 3 March 1934.

Blundellsands Adrian Boult, conductor, resided at Brooke House, 1890–1916.

Formby Percy French, composer and author of *Abdulla Bulbul Ameer, Phil the Fluther's Ball* and *Come Back, Paddy Reilly, to Ballyjamesduff* and author of 'The Mountains of Mourne', died here, at the home of his cousin Canon Richardson, on 24 January 1920. He is buried in Formby.

Huyton Thomas Beecham, conductor, impresario and patron of music, resided throughout most of his early years at Ewanville.

John McCabe, composer, pianist and writer on music, was born here on 21 April 1939.

Liscard Granville Bantock, composer and conductor, resided at Holly Mount, 19 Holland Road, 1898–1900.

Edward Elgar stayed with him on 16 July 1899, when Bantock conducted, at New Brighton, the first performance of Elgar's Minuet, Op 21. Other visitors to Holly Mount include Hubert Parry and Charles Villiers Stanford.

Liverpool Béla Bartók took part in a concert here on 30 March 1922.

Marie Brema, mezzo-soprano singer, who sang the part of the Angel in the first performance of *The Dream of Gerontius* on 3 October 1900 in Birmingham, was born here on 28 February 1856 and died in Manchester on 22 March 1925.

Max Bruch was conductor of the Liverpool Philharmonic Society 1880–3. The first public performance of his *Scottish Fantasy* was given on 22 February 1881 in the Philharmonic Hall, with Joseph Joachim as soloist and Bruch conducting the Hallé Orchestra.

Ferruccio Busoni took part in concerts here in 1903, 1920 and 1921.

Arthur Hugh Clough, poet and author of the hymn 'Say Not the Struggle Naught Availeth', was born at 9 Rodney Street on 1 January 1819 and died in Florence on 13 November 1861.

Louis Cohen, violinist and conductor, was born in Liverpool on 17 September 1894 and died here on 25 November 1956.

Nancy Evans, mezzo-soprano singer, who married the librettist Eric Crozier in 1949, was born here on 19 March 1915. She gave the first performance of Britten's *A Charm of Lullabies*, which is dedicated to her, in 1948. She created the role of Nancy in Britten's *Albert Herring*, staged at Glyndebourne in 1947.

George Gershwin came here on 29 March 1926 for the British première of *Lady, Be Good*. The composition of his Concerto in F had been commenced in England during May of the previous year. *Fascinating Rhythm* was also started in this country.

John Liptrot Hatton, composer of the songs *To Anthea*, *The Bells of Shandon*, *Simon the Cellarer*, *Jack o'Lantern* and *Good-Bye, Sweetheart, Good-Bye*, was born here on 12 October 1809 and died in Margate on 20 September 1886.

Felicia Hemans, whose poetry inspired songs by Gounod, Tchaikovsky and others, was born at 118 Duke Street on 25 September 1793.

Johann Nepomuk Hummel took part in a concert here on 8 July 1830.

John Lennon, composer, lyricist, author, singer and actor, was born in the Maternity Hospital, Oxford Street, on 9 October 1940 and was shot to death in New York on 8 December 1980.

Franz Liszt played at a concert in the Theatre Royal on 1 December 1840. He stayed the night at The Feathers, Clayton Square. On 16 December 1840 he had luncheon at The Queen's Arms before embarking for Dublin.

Paul McCartney, composer, lyricist, singer and actor, was born in Walton Hospital on 18 June 1942.

Stewart Macpherson, organist, composer and writer on music, was born here on 29 March 1865 and died in London on 27 May 1941.

Michael Maybrick, baritone singer, composer of *Nancy Lee* and

Mayor of Ryde, Isle of Wight, was born here in 1844 and died on 26 August 1913.

Herman Melville, on whose novella *Billy Budd* Britten's opera is based, twice visited Liverpool, in 1837 and 1856. He resided on the latter occasion at the White Bear Hotel in Dale Street.

Felix Mendelssohn arrived here on the night of 18 August 1829, returning from Scotland. '. . . In the evening a thick fog: the stagecoaches running madly in the darkness. Through the fog we see lamps gleaming along the horizon, the smoke from factories envelops us on all sides, gentlemen on horseback ride past, one coach-horn blows in B flat, another in D, others follow in the distance, and here we are, at Liverpool.' He spent 19 and 20 August in sightseeing, took a boat across the Mersey, briefly boarded the ss *Napoleon*, on which he played the piano, and persuaded a foreman to let him ride under the Mersey along part of the Liverpool–Manchester railway, which was not yet open to the public. 'The speed was fifteen miles an hour; there is no horse, no engine; the carriage goes of its own accord, getting gradually faster, since the track goes almost imperceptibly downhill. We had two lights in front, but the daylight vanished, the draught extinguished the lights, and we were in utter darkness. For the first time in my life I saw *Nothing*. The truck raced on faster and faster, and rattled worse and worse – agony for the nerves! . . . It was bitterly cold. At last the red, warm daylight streamed in at the further end, and, when I alighted, I stood by the harbour. I felt much relieved, and, when on my way back I walked through the market-house, the sight of it quite cheered me up.'

Emma Nevada, formerly Emma Wixon, soprano singer, was born in Alpha, Nevada, on 7 February 1859 and died in Liverpool on 20 June 1940.

Ernest Newman, eminent writer on music, was born here on 30 November 1868.

Niccolò Paganini gave concerts on 9, 10, 11, 23, 24 and 25 January 1832 in the Theatre Royal. He returned to Liverpool in 1833 and gave further concerts on 19 and 20 August and 16 and 18 September. His final visit was in 1834, when he gave recitals on 5 and 6 May, after which he returned to London, abandoning his 'disastrous tour'.

Giacomo Puccini stayed at the Adelphi Hotel 5–7 October 1911. He came to Liverpool for the first English-language performance in Britain of *La Fanciulla del West*, staged on 6 October.

Sergey Rakhmaninov took part in concerts here on 24 October 1911 and 27 January 1914.

Frederick Rimmer, composer and educationist, was born here on 21 February 1914.

Alfred Rodewald, conductor and patron of music, resided at 66 Huskisson Street.

Edward Elgar visited him here. The *Pomp and Circumstance March No 1* is dedicated to Rodewald, who conducted the first performance on 19 October 1901 in Liverpool.

Charles Santley, notable baritone singer, for whom Gounod inserted *Avant de quitter ces lieux* in the second act of *Faust* when the opera was first performed in London, was born here on 28 February 1834.

John Shirley-Quirk, baritone singer, was born at 117 Hall Lane on 28 August 1931. He later resided at 43 Hayes Street and 43 Barford Road, Hunt's Cross.

Jean Sibelius, making his first appearance in the British Isles, conducted at a concert here on 2 December 1905. The works performed were the First Symphony and, according to *The Musical Times,* 'Finlandial'. He took part in another concert here during the autumn of 1912.

John Philip Sousa conducted his band at concerts in the Philharmonic Hall on 6, 7 and 8 January 1905. He gave two further concerts, in the Philharmonic Hall, on 4 February 1911. He stayed the night at the Adelphi Hotel. During the 1905 visit he appears to have conducted *The Diplomat* for the first time.

Johann Strauss senior stayed at the Rainbow Hotel 3–6 August 1838. He led his orchestra at a concert in the Royal Amphitheatre on 4 August. He returned to give further concerts in the same hall on 7, 10, 13, 20, 22 and 24 August.

James Thornton, composer of the song *When You Were Sweet Sixteen*, was born here in 1861 and died in Astoria, New York, in 1938.

John Tobin, conductor and composer, was born here on 25 March 1891.

Jakob Zeugheer, violinist, conductor and composer, was born in Zurich in 1805 and died in Liverpool on 15 June 1865.

Poulton Rita Hunter, celebrated soprano singer, was born on 15 August 1933 at 27 Limekiln Lane, where she spent most of her childhood.

St Helens Thomas Beecham, conductor, impresario and patron of music, was born in Arthur Street on 29 April 1879.

John Philip Sousa conducted his band at a concert in the Town Hall on 6 February 1911.

Saughall Massie Alfred Rodewald, conductor and patron of music, intermittently resided at The Cottage, Saughall Massie.

Edward Elgar stayed with him here in August 1902 and on other occasions.

Southport Anne Howells, mezzo-soprano singer, was born here on 12 January 1941.

John Philip Sousa conducted his band at a concert in the Cambridge Hall on 1 February 1911.

Leslie Stuart, composer of the songs *Lily of Laguna* and *Soldiers of the Queen*, was born here on 15 March 1856 and died in Richmond, London, on 27 March 1928.

Warrington John Hatton, composer of the hymn tune *Duke Street*, sung to 'Fight the Good Fight with All Thy Might', was born in Warrington and lived for many years in Duke Street, Windle, where he died in December 1793, a few months after his tune was published.

West Kirby Adrian Boult, conductor, resided at The Abbey Manor 1916–19.

SCOTLAND

BORDERS

Boleside Walter Scott, novelist, poet and historian, purchased Abbotsford as his country estate in 1811, taking up permanent residence from 1830 until his death in Boleside on 21 September 1832.

Felix Mendelssohn called upon him on 31 July 1829, but found him about to leave on a journey. The visit was accordingly limited, wrote Mendelssohn, to 'half an hour's superficial conversation'.

Cockburnspath John Broadwood, founder of the famous firm of piano makers, was born here in 1732 and died in London in 1812.

Dryburgh Walter Scott, novelist, poet and historian, is buried in Dryburgh Abbey.

Duns Robert Johnson, composer, was born here in about 1490 and died in about 1560.

Ednam Henry Francis Lyte, author of the hymns 'Abide with Me', 'Praise, My Soul, the King of Heaven' and 'God of Mercy, God of Grace', was born here on 1 June 1793.

James Thomson, poet, was born here on 11 September 1700. He wrote the libretto for Thomas Arne's masque *Alfred*, which was first performed on 1 August 1740 and contains the song 'Rule, Britannia'. His poem 'The Seasons', completed in 1730, is the basis of Haydn's oratorio *Die Jahreszeiten*, presented in Vienna on 24 April 1801.

Ettrick James Hogg, the 'Ettrick Shepherd', poet, writer and composer, was born here in November 1770 and died at Altrive Lake, near Mount Benger, on 21 November 1835. He resided for some years at Moss End Farm, now Eldinhope, and at Mountbenger Farm, both nearby. His most celebrated lyrics to be set to music include 'Bonnie Prince Charlie', 'Flora Macdonald's Lament', 'Come o'er the Stream, Charlie' and 'When the Kye Comes Hame'.

Hawick Isobel Baillie, soprano singer, was born here on 9 March 1895.

John McEwen, composer, was born here on 13 April 1868 and died in London on 14 June 1948.

Francis George Scott, composer, was born here on 25 January 1880 and died in Glasgow on 6 November 1958.

Kelso Mary Duncan, author of the hymn 'Jesus, Tender Shepherd, Hear Me', was born here on 26 May 1814.

Lauder William Rogers, musician and English courtier to James III, was hung here on 22 July 1482.

Minto Jane Eliot, author of 'The Flowers of the Forest', was born in Minto House in 1727 and died at Mount Teviot in March 1805.

Mount Benger William Laidlaw, poet, friend of James Hogg, secretary to Walter Scott and author of 'Lucy's Flittin'', was born at Blackhouse in 1780.

Peel Walter Scott, novelist, poet and historian, resided intermittently at Ashiestiel, 1804–12.

Spottiswoode Lady John Douglas Scott, composer of *Annie Laurie*, was born in Spottiswoode in 1810 and died here on 12 March 1900. At the time the song was published, a year before her marriage, she was Alicia Anne Spottiswoode, her maiden name.

Sprouston John Thomson, music scholar and composer, friend of Mendelssohn and Schumann, was born here on 28 October 1805 and died in Edinburgh on 6 May 1841.

Stobo William Moonie, composer and conductor, was born here on 29 May 1883.

CENTRAL

Bridge of Allen Frédéric Chopin stayed with Sir William Stirling-Maxwell at Keir House at the beginning of October 1848.

Dunipace William Cameron, author of the songs 'Meet Me on the Gowan Lea', 'Morag's Faery Glen', 'Sweet Jessie o' the Dell' and 'Bothwell Castle', was born here on 3 December 1801 and died in Glasgow in 1877.

Falkirk John Philip Sousa conducted his band at concerts in the Town Hall on 10 February 1903.

Killin Felix Mendelssohn visited the countryside around here on 5 August 1829. He went to Loch Tay and made a drawing of Ben More.

Kinbuck Walter Chalmers Smith, author of the hymn 'Immortal, Invisible, God Only Wise', died here on 19 September 1908.

Stirling Winifred Christie, pianist and founder of London's Central Music Library, housed in the Buckingham Palace Road Public Library, was born here on 26 February 1882.

Muir Mathieson, conductor particularly associated with films, was born here on 24 January 1911 and died in Oxford on 2 August 1975. He resided at Shogmoor, Frieth, Buckinghamshire. As musical director of various film companies, he was responsible for commissioning scores from Bliss for *Things To Come*, from Walton for *Henry V* and from Britten for *The Young Person's Guide to the Orchestra*.

Edward Platt, composer and horn player, whose brilliant career as an instrumentalist was prematurely terminated by the loss of his teeth, was born on 11 June 1793 and died here on 27 June 1861.

Tillicoultry Wilfred Senior, pianist and conductor, was born here on 20 August 1880.

Tombea Alexander Campbell, organist, composer of *Gloomy Winter's Now Awa'* and long-suffering music teacher of Walter Scott, was born here, beside Loch Lubnaig, on 22 February 1764 and died in Edinburgh on 15 May 1824.

DUMFRIES AND GALLOWAY

Dumfries Robert Burns, poet, died here on 21 July 1796 at his home in Mill Vennel, Burns Street. He is buried in St Michael's Churchyard. Six miles north of here is the farm, Ellisland, at which he resided 1788–91, before moving into Dumfries. A number of his best known songs, including 'A Red, Red Rose' and 'Auld Lang Syne', were written in this farmhouse.

Angus Mackay, piper to Queen Victoria and folk-song collector, was born in about 1813 and drowned near here in the River Nith on 21 March 1859.

John Mayne, author of 'Logan Water', was born here in 1759 and died on 14 March 1836.

Gatehouse-of-Fleet Robert Burns, poet, made up the song 'Scots, Wha Hae' while riding from St Mary's Isle to Gatehouse on 1 August 1793 and is thought to have written it down at the Murray Arms Hotel.

Kirkland Annie Laurie, immortalized through song and legend, was born at Maxwelton at about 6am on 16 December 1682. In later life, she resided at Craigdarroch House; she died and was buried there in 1761. The original verses about her were written by an early lover, William Douglas. These were added to and improved upon by Lady John Douglas Scott at the time she composed the melody of *Annie Laurie* in 1835.

Langholm Arthur Sullivan, composer and conductor, stayed at Grieve's Hotel in 1872.

Newton Stewart William Train, author of 'The Cauld Cauld Winter's Gane, Luve,' was born here on 9 August 1816.

Stranraer Franz Liszt spent the night of 17 January 1841 here, having earlier in the day disembarked from Ireland at Portpatrick. At 5.00am on the following morning, he boarded the *Sir William Wallace* steam packet and sailed for Ayr.

FIFE

Arncroach Thomas Alexander Erskine, sixth Earl of Kelly, composer, violinist and pupil of Johann Stamitz, was born at Kellie Castle on 1 September 1732 and died in Brussels on 9 October 1781.

Colinsburgh Lady Anne Lindsay, poet, was born on 8 December 1750 at Balcarres House, where she wrote 'Auld Robin Gray', and died at her home in Berkeley Square, Mayfair, London, on 6 May 1825.

Arthur Sullivan was a guest at Balcarres House during the 1870s. His song *Sometimes*, published in 1877, is dedicated to Lady Blanche Lindsay.

Crossford Ian Whyte, conductor and composer, was born here on 13 August 1901.

Dunfermline Andrew Carnegie, industrialist and philanthropist, who gave the New World its most famous concert hall, opened in the spring of 1891, was born in Priory Lane on 15 November 1835 and died in New York on 11 August 1919.

Robert Gilfillan, poet, author of the song 'Oh! Why Left I My Hame?', was born here on 7 July 1798 and died in Leith, Lothian, on 4 December 1850.

Dunotter Jessie Seymour Irvine, composer of the hymn tune *Crimond*, sung to 'The Lord's My Shepherd, I'll Not Want', was born here on 26 July 1836.

East Wemyss Jimmy Shand, accordionist, band leader and composer, was born here in 1908.

Inverkeithing Thomas Glen, celebrated bagpipe maker and inventor of the serpentcleides, was born here in 1804 and died in Edinburgh on 12 July 1873.

Kinghorn Patie Birnie, violinist, composer of the song *The Auld Man's Meer's Dead*, was born here in about 1635 and died in about 1710.

Kirkcaldy Janet Frazer, mezzo-soprano singer, was born here on 22 May 1911.

John Philip Sousa conducted his band at concerts in Adam Smith Hall on 11 February 1903.

Ladybank Millar Patrick, music scholar, was born here in 1868 and died in Edinburgh on 2 August 1951.

Limekilns George Thomson, folk-song collector and music editor, who, to his eternal credit, commissioned arrangements from Haydn, Beethoven, Pleyel, Koželuh and Bishop, and texts from Burns and Scott, was born here on 4 March 1757 and died in his home, 1 Vanbrugh Place, Leith, Lothian, on 18 February 1851. He is buried in Kensal Green Cemetery, London, beneath a tombstone bearing an inscription by his grand-daughter's husband, Charles Dickens.

Lochgelly John McQuaid, composer, was born here on 14 March 1909.

St Andrews Mary Maxwèll Campbell, composer of *The March of the*

Cameron Men, was born at Pitlour House in 1812 and died in St Andrews on 15 January 1886.

David Peebles, composer, died here in December 1579.

GRAMPIAN

Aberdeen Ferrucio Busoni played at a concert here on 11 December 1906.

Martin Dalby, composer, was born here on 25 April 1942.

William Dauney, music scholar, was born here on 27 October 1800 and died in Demerara, Guyana, on 28 July 1843.

Finlay Dun, composer and folk-song collector, was born in Aberdeen on 24 February 1795 and died in Edinburgh on 28 November 1853.

Alexander Ewing, composer of the hymn tune *Ewing*, sung to 'Jerusalem the Golden', was born in Old Machar on 3 January 1830. His tune, published in 1853, was written while he was at Marischal College.

Mary Garden, soprano singer, who created the role of Mélisande in Debussy's *Pelléas et Mélisande*, first staged in Paris on 30 April 1902, was born in Aberdeen on 20 February 1874 and died here on 3 January 1967.

John Imlah, poet, author of the songs 'There Lives a Young Lassie Far Down Yon Lang Glen', 'Hey for the Hielan' Heather' and 'Oh! Gin I Were Where Gadie Runs', was born here on 15 November 1799 and died in Jamaica on 9 January 1846.

Jessie Seymour Irvine, composer of the hymn tune *Crimond*, sung to 'The Lord's My Shepherd, I'll Not Want', died here on 2 September 1887.

Percival Kirby, composer and writer on music, was born here on 17 April 1887.

John MacLeod, composer and conductor, was born here on 8 March 1934.

Niccolò Paganini gave recitals here on 11 and 12 November 1831, the first being in the Assembly Rooms and the second in the Theatre.

Walter Chalmers Smith, author of the hymn 'Immortal, Invisible, God Only Wise', was born here on 5 December 1824.

John Philip Sousa conducted his band at two concerts in the Music Hall on 9 February 1903. He gave two further concerts in the Music Hall on 20 February 1911. He stayed the night at the Grand Hotel, which cost him 4s 6d for bed and breakfast.

Henry Watt, authority on the psychology of music, was born here on

15 July 1878 and died in Glasgow on 25 October 1925.

Herbert Wiseman, musical educationist and conductor, was born here on 3 May 1886.

Banchory James Scott Skinner, violinist and composer of *The Bonnie Lass o' Bonaccord, Laird o' Drumblair, Miller o' Hirn* and *Lovat Scouts*, was born here on 5 August 1843 and died in Aberdeen on 17 March 1927.

James Cuthbert Hadden, writer on music, was born here on 9 September 1861 and died on 2 May 1914 in Edinburgh, where he resided at Allermuir, Old Braid Road.

Crimond Jessie Seymour Irvine composed here the hymn tune *Crimond*, sung to 'The Lord's My Shepherd, I'll Not Want'; this was published in 1872.

Fochabers William Marshall, violinist and composer of the strathspeys *The Marquis of Huntly* and *Miss Admiral Gordon*, was born here on 27 December 1748 and died in Dandaleith on 29 May 1833. Burns called him 'the first composer of strathspeys of the age'.

Huntly George MacDonald, author of the hymns 'Our Father, Hear Our Longing Prayer' and 'O Lord of Life, Thy Quickening Voice', was born here on 10 December 1824 and died in Ashtead, Surrey, on 18 September 1905.

Inverey Emma Albani, soprano singer, resided intermittently at Old Mar Lodge during the 1880s and 1890s. Queen Victoria visited her here.

Inverurie William Thom, the 'Bard of Inverurie', author of the songs 'The Mitherless Bairn' and 'They Speak o' Wiles in Woman's Smiles', who was born in Aberdeen in 1789 and died in Dundee on 29 February 1848, resided in North Street 1840–4, the period during which he was at the height of his powers.

Keith William Dempster, composer, was born here in 1808 and died in London on 7 March 1871.

Kincardine O'Neil Peter Milne, violinist and composer, was born here in 1824 and died in Tarland in 1908.

Longside John Skinner, poet, who was born in Birse on 3 October 1721 and died in Aberdeen on 16 June 1807, was pastor of Longside from 1742 until the year of his death. He resided in Linshart and during that period wrote 'Tullochgorum', 'The Ewie wi' the Crookit Horn' and 'John o' Badenyon'. He is buried in Longside.

New Deer Gavin Greig, author, composer and folk-song collector, was born at Parkhill on 10 February 1856 and died at Whitehill on 31 August 1914.

Peterhead Patrick Buchan, author of the song 'Watt o' the Hill', was born here in 1814 and died in 1881.

Pittendreich Clementina Stirling Graham, author of 'The Sailor Boy' and 'Awake, Awake, My Own True Love', was born here on 6 May 1782 and died on 23 August 1877.

Rathen Edvard Grieg's great-grandfather, Alexander Greig, was born in Rathen in 1739. (It is interesting to recall that Erik Satie, christened Eric Alfred Leslie Satie, had a Scottish mother, Jane Leslie Anton. His parents spent their honeymoon in Scotland.)

George Halket, author of the songs 'Logie o' Buchan' and 'Whirry, Whigs, Awa', Man', was born here and died in 1756. The Logie of 'Logie o' Buchan' was in Crimond.

HIGHLAND

Achanalt Charles Villiers Stanford, composer, conductor and writer on music, wrote the song *The Blue Bird* here in August 1911.

Alvie George Henschel, conductor, baritone singer, composer, friend of Brahms and Tchaikovsky, was born in Breslau, Poland, on 18 February 1850 and died in Tullochgrue on 10 September 1934. He had resided since 1901 at Alltnacriche, Alvie.

Ardersier (formerly Campbelltown) Frederick Joseph Ricketts, better known as Kenneth Alford, composed his famous march *Colonel Bogey* in 1913 while stationed at Fort George as bandmaster of the Second Argyll and Sutherland Highlanders. The principal melody came to him when he was playing on the regimental nine-hole golf-course (lapsed) at Fort George. Another golfer had adopted the practice of whistling the notes C and A as a substitute for shouting 'Fore!'. These two notes stuck in Ricketts's mind, and it was not long before he had added to them and created the melody. The other golfer is generally believed to have been Lieutenant-Colonel Edward Maurice Moulton-Barrett.

Rae Robertson, pianist, was born here on 29 November 1893 and died in Los Angeles on 4 November 1956.

Contin William Laidlaw, poet, friend of James Hogg, secretary to Walter Scott and author of 'Lucy's Flittin'', died here in 1845.

Croy Harold Fraser-Simson, composer of the musical comedies *The Maid of the Mountains* and *Toad of Toad Hall* and of the songs *Christopher Robin Is Saying His Prayers* and *They're Changing Guard at Buckingham Palace*, was born in London on 15 August 1878 and died there on 19 January 1944. He resided at Dalcross Castle, near Croy.

Durness Patric M'Donald, folk-song collector, was born at Durness Manse on 22 April 1729 and died in Kilmore, Strathclyde, on 25 September 1824.

Fort William Felix Mendelssohn stayed here on the night of 6 August 1829.

Inverness Robert Grant, author of the hymn 'O Worship the King All Glorious Above', who was born in Bengal in 1779 and died in Dalpoorie, India, on 9 July 1838, came from an old Scottish family and entered Parliament in 1826 as member for Inverness.

Morar Arnold Bax, composer and Master of the King's and Queen's Music, was a frequent visitor between 1928, when he worked on his Third Symphony here, and World War II.

Ruthven James Macpherson, whose poetry inspired works by Bantock, Brahms, Gade, Méhul, Saint-Saëns, Schubert and Shield, was born here in 1736 and died in 1796. His poem 'Fingal' may well have prompted Mendelssohn's visit to Fingal's Cave.

Strath Naver Joseph M'Donald, writer on music and folk-song collector, assisting his brother Patric, was born here on 26 February 1739 and died in India in 1762.

LOTHIAN

Carfrae George Hogarth, writer on music, whose daughter Catherine married Charles Dickens, was born at Carfrae Mill in 1783 and died in London on 12 February 1870.

Crofthead William Findlay, composer of *The Faded Flower Waltz*, *Nebula Waltz* and *Sir Garnet's Hornpipe*, was born in Crofthead on 11 August 1854.

Duddingston Caroline Oliphant, Baroness Nairne, author of numerous well-known songs, resided at Caroline Cottage 1807–30, also residing briefly during this period at Holyrood Palace.

Dunbar Richard Gall, author of the songs 'Scenes of Woe and Scenes of Pleasure', 'My Only Jo and Dearie, O' and 'The Waefu' Heart', was born in Linkhouse in December 1776 and died on 10 May 1801.
    Franz Liszt, travelling from Edinburgh, stopped here for dinner and went to see Dunbar Castle on the evening of 24 January 1841.

Edinburgh William Edmondstone Aytoun, poet, author of 'Annie's Tryste', was born here in 1813 and died in 1865.
    James Ballantine, poet, artist and author of 'Ilka Blade o' Grass', 'Bonnie Bonaly', 'The Nameless Lassie' and 'Castles in the Air', was born in Edinburgh on 11 June 1808 and died here on 18 December 1877.
    Horatius Bonar, author of the hymns 'I Heard the Voice of Jesus Say', 'Thy Way, Not Mine, O Lord' and 'A Few More Years Shall Roll', was born in Edinburgh on 19 December 1808 and died here on 31 July 1889.
    Jane Borthwick, author of the hymn 'Come, Labour On', was born in Edinburgh on 9 April 1813 and died here on 7 September 1897.
    Ferruccio Busoni took part in concerts here in 1899, 1901, 1906, 1919 and 1920.
    Frédéric Chopin stayed at Douglas's Hotel on the nights of 5 and 6 August 1848, having left Euston at 9am on the 5th; the journey via Birmingham and Carlisle took twelve hours. On more than one occasion he stayed for a few days during September and October at 10 Warriston Crescent with Doctor Lyszczyński and his wife. By now he was so weak that Lyszczyński had to carry him upstairs to his room. He was still determined, however, to present a brave front to the world; his hair was curled every day by his servant, and he took the greatest

trouble with his appearance, being always immaculately and fashionably dressed. At 8.30pm on 4 October 1848 he gave a recital at the Hopetoun Rooms, now the hall of the Mary Erskine School, Queen Street. 'Of his execution we need say nothing farther than that it is the most finished we have ever heard,' reported the *Edinburgh Evening Courant*. 'He has neither the ponderosity nor the digital power of a Mendelssohn, a Thalberg, or a Liszt; consequently his execution would appear less effective in a large room; but as a chamber pianist he stands unrivalled. Notwithstanding the amount of musical entertainment already afforded the Edinburgh public this season, the rooms were filled with an audience who, by their judicious and well-timed applause, testified their appreciation of the high talent of Monsieur Chopin.'

Francis Collinson, composer, was born here on 20 January 1898.

Marcus Dods, conductor, was born here on 19 April 1918.

Daniel Dow, music publisher, teacher and composer of the strathspey *Monymusk*, was born in Tayside in 1732 and died in Edinburgh on 20 January 1783.

Isobel Dunlop, composer, was born here on 4 March 1901.

James Geikie, composer of *My Heather Hills* and writer, was born here on 12 January 1811 and died at Ormiston on 14 August 1883. On 16 June 1891, his son Archibald Geikie, the eminent geologist, received an honorary doctorate at Cambridge during the degree ceremony in which Dvořák was granted a similar distinction.

John Glen, music collector, was born in Edinburgh in about 1833 and died here on 29 November 1904.

Niel Gow, son of Nathaniel Gow and grandson of Niel Gow of Strath Braan, composer of *Bonnie Prince Charlie, Cam Ye by Athol* and *Flora Macdonald's Lament*, was born in Edinburgh in about 1795 and died here on 7 November 1823.

George Graham, music scholar and composer, was born in Edinburgh on 29 December 1789 and died here on 12 March 1867.

Cecil Gray, writer on music and composer, was born here on 19 May 1895 and died in Worthing, West Sussex, on 9 September 1951.

Edvard Grieg took part in a concert in the Music Hall on 30 November 1897. Looking forward to this occasion, the August 1897 edition of *Musical Opinion* reminded its readers of Grieg's Scottish ancestry. 'Alexander Greig — the composer's great grandfather, who afterwards changed his name to Grieg — emigrated from Fraserburgh last century. The composer's crest is still that of the Scottish Greigs, with the motto "At spes in fracta". "When I passed through Aberdeen some years ago," said the composer to a Scotch friend in 1894, "I was interested to find from the hotel book that the name is so common. I have various ties in Scotland. I have Scotch friends; my godmother was Scotch — Mrs Stirling; she lived near the town of the same name. I know something of your Scotch writers, too, especially Carlyle. I am fond of reading Carlyle; and I admire Edinburgh — Princes Street, the Gardens, the old town. Ah! they are beautiful!"' He would have come more often to Scotland, he said, 'if it were not for the sea. I am the very worst sailor. Once some years ago I crossed from Bergen to Aberdeen. I shall never forget that night of horrors — never!'

John Gunn, writer on music, was born in Edinburgh in about 1765 and died here in about 1824.

John Hamilton, music collector and poet, who wrote the song *Up in the Morning Early*, was born in 1761 and died here on 23 September 1814.

Hermann von Helmholtz, celebrated acoustical theorist, author of the important work *The Sensation of Tone*, received an honorary doctorate at Edinburgh University in April 1884, in company with Pasteur, De Lesseps, Browning, Charles Hallé and other luminaries.

Joseph Hislop, tenor singer, was born here on 5 April 1884.

Helen Hopekirk, composer and pianist, was born here on 20 May 1856 and died in Cambridge, Massachusetts, on 19 November 1945.

Charles Ives stayed here in July 1932 and June 1938, also visiting Glasgow and the Highlands.

Felix Janiewicz, violinist, was born in Vilnyus, Poland, in 1762 and died here on 21 May 1848.

Frederick Jewson, pianist, composer and sometime Musician in Ordinary to Queen Victoria, was born here on 26 June 1823 and died in London on 28 May 1891.

Johann Lampe, who was born in Saxony in about 1703 and composed a wide range of music, including the hymn tune *Kent*, often sung to 'How Happy Is He Born and Taught', died here on 25 July 1751.

Franz Liszt played at a concert in the Assembly Rooms in George Street on 19 January 1841. He stayed the night at The Royal Hotel (demolished) in Princes Street. After visiting Glasgow on the 20th, he played at a second concert on the 21st, every piece being encored. He had dinner, that evening, at the home of the music publisher Robert Paterson. After a second visit to Glasgow, he took part in a third concert at the Hopetoun Rooms, now the hall of the Mary Erskine School, in Queen Street on the 23rd. He left Edinburgh on 24 January.

James Lockhart, conductor, was born at 64 Marchmont Road on 16 October 1930.

William M'Gibbon, violinist and composer, born in Edinburgh, died here on 3 October 1756. He is buried in Greyfriars' Churchyard.

Alexander McGlashan, violinist and folk-song collector, died here in May 1797. He is buried in Greyfriars' Churchyard.

Alexander Mackenzie, composer and conductor, was born in Nelson Street on 22 August 1847.

Charles Macklean, composer and violinist, died in Edinburgh in about 1772.

Alexander Malcolm, writer on music and mathematician, was born here in 1687.

Felix Mendelssohn stayed here 26 July–1 August 1829. On 30 July he wrote to his family in Berlin: 'In the evening twilight we went today to the palace where Queen Mary lived and loved; a little room is shown there with a winding staircase leading up to the door; up this way they came and found Rizzio in that little room, pulled him out, and, three rooms from there, is a dark corner, where they murdered him. The chapel close to it is now roofless, grass and ivy grow there, and at that broken altar Mary was crowned Queen of Scotland. Everything around is broken and mouldering, and the bright sky shines in. I believe I found today in that old chapel the beginning of my *Scottish Symphony.*' This 'beginning' consists of the opening sixteen bars, which he immediately noted down.

On 29 July he attended the annual competition of Highland pipers at the Theatre Royal. It appears that one of the pipers, who occupied the next room in the hotel where Mendelssohn was staying, spent much of the time practising. Far from being inconvenienced, the composer was so delighted by what he heard that he often went to sit in the piper's room.

Alfred Moffat, composer and music editor, was born here on 4 December 1866 and died in London on 9 June 1950.

Thea Musgrave, composer, was born in 1928 at Bughtlin, Cammo Road, Barnton, where she spent her childhood.

Friedrich Niecks, writer on music, was born in Düsseldorf, West Germany, on 3 February 1845 and died in Edinburgh on 24 June 1924. He resided at 40 George Square.

Niccolò Paganini took part in concerts in the Assembly Rooms in George Street on 20, 22, 25, 27 and 29 October, and 14, 15, 16 and 18 November 1831. The performance on 16 November was a charity concert. He returned in 1833 and gave two further concerts, the first on 27 September in the Hopetoun Rooms and the second on 1 October in the Adelphi Theatre. In 1831 he stayed at Simpson's Hotel.

Euphrosyne Parepa-Rosa, soprano singer, wife of Carl Rosa, was born here on 7 May 1836 and died in London on 21 January 1874.

Mary Anne Paton, celebrated soprano singer, was born here in October 1802. She sang the role of Agatha when *Der Freischütz* was first performed in Britain, on 22 July 1824 and, under Weber's baton, created the role of Reiza in Weber's *Oberon* at Covent Garden on 12 April 1826.

Sergey Rakhmaninov played at a concert here in March 1935.

Allan Ramsay, poet, author of the songs 'Farewell to Lochaber' and 'The Lass o' Patie's Mill', died at his home on Castle Hill on 7 January 1758.

Maurice Ravel took part in concerts here in January 1911 and February 1926.

Davidde Rizzio, bass singer, was born in Turin, Italy, and was stabbed to death in Holyrood Palace on 9 March 1566.

Johann Schetky, cellist, composer and friend of Robert Burns, was born in Darmstadt, West Germany, in 1740 and died here on 29 November 1824. He is buried in Canongate Cemetery.

Walter Scott, novelist, poet and historian, author of the songs 'Pibroch of Donuil Dhu', 'The Bonnets of Bonnie Dundee', 'Hail to the Chief', 'March, March, Ettrick and Teviotdale', 'Jock o' Hazeldean' and many more, was born in College Wynd, near Chambers Street, on 15 August 1771. He resided at 25 George Square 1774–97. Thereafter, he resided at 108 George Street and 10 South Castle Street, and, 1802–26, at 39 Castle Street. Among the works based on his novels and poems are Bellini's *I Puritani*, the overtures *Rob Roy* and *Waverley* by Berlioz, Bizet's *La Jolie Fille de Perth*, Boieldieu's *La Dame blanche*, Donizetti's *Lucia di Lammermoor*, MacCunn's *Jeanie Deans* and the overture *The Land of the Mountain and the Flood*, Marschner's *Der Templer und die Jüdin*, Rossini's *La Donna del Lago*, Schubert's *Ave, Maria*, Sullivan's *Ivanhoe* and various compositions by Auber, Balfe, Bantock, Bishop, Mackenzie, Mendelssohn, Nicolai, Hubert Parry and others.

Scott readily admitted to having no ear for music. 'It is only by long practice', he wrote in his autobiography, 'that I have acquired the power of selecting or distinguishing melodies; and although now few things delight or affect me more than a simple tune sung with feeling, yet I am sensible that even this pitch of musical taste has only been gained by attention and habit, and as it were by my feeling of the words being associated with the tune.'

Dmitri Shostakovich stayed at the George Hotel, George Street, during the course of the 1962 festival. Between 20 August and 8 September, twenty-five of his works were performed, including the

String Quartets Nos 1–8, the Piano Quintet and Symphonies Nos, 4, 6, 8, 9, 10 and 12. Many other distinguished composers have attended the festival. Benjamin Britten was here in 1962 and in other years. Michael Tippett, Pierre Boulez, Leonard Bernstein and Peter Maxwell Davies have been frequent visitors. On 3 September 1949 Ernest Bloch conducted the world première of his *Concerto symphonique*. In 1956 Ernö Dohnanyi played his *Variations on a Nursery Song*. During the following year's festival Francis Poulenc accompanied Pierre Bernac in a song recital. William Walton conducted a concert of his works on 23 August 1959; on 2 September 1960 his Second Symphony received its world première under John Pritchard's direction. On 1 September 1970 Hans Werner Henze conducted the first British performance of his Sixth Symphony. In 1971 Luciano Berio conducted his *Bewegung* and Sinfonia. At the next festival Witold Lutoslawski and Krzystof Penderecki were visitors. Ernst Krenek and Goffredo Petrassi came to conduct their works in 1974. On 6 September 1977 Thea Musgrave conducted the world première of her opera *Mary Queen of Scots*.

Robert Archibald Smith, composer of *Jessie, the Flow'r o' Dunblane* and *Bonnie Mary Hay* and the hymn tune *Selma*, sung to 'Fair Waved the Golden Corn', died here on 3 January 1829. Precentor of St George's for many years, he was buried at St Cuthbert's.

John Philip Sousa conducted his band at concerts in Synod Hall on 13 and 14 February 1903. He gave two further concerts, in Waverley Market Hall, on 22 February 1911. He stayed at Princes Street Station Hotel.

Girolamo Stabilini, violinist, was born in Rome in about 1762 and died in Edinburgh on 13 July 1815. He is buried at St Cuthbert's.

William Stenhouse, writer on music, was born in the Borders in 1773 and died in Edinburgh on 10 November 1827.

Johann Strauss senior stayed at the Turf Hotel 1–7 November 1838; he led his orchestra at concerts in the Assembly Rooms on the 2nd and 6th. He was again at the Turf Hotel 10–14 November, giving a further concert on the 12th and playing at a ball on the 13th.

By the time they reached Edinburgh on 1 November, Strauss and his orchestra, who had not seen Vienna for over a year, had endured seven months of English weather and all were unwell. And now they had to face the Scottish weather. On their arrival at the Turf Hotel, a doctor was immediately called. He treated them with large quantities of hot red wine, nutmeg and ginger. This, coupled with two trips to Glasgow, in unheated carriages that often ploughed to a standstill in axle-deep mud, failed to secure their complete recovery.

Igor Stravinsky stayed here 8–13 September 1959. He did not take part in the festival.

Donald Tovey, music scholar, pianist and composer, whose Cello Concerto was first performed by Pau Casals, died here on 10 July 1940. He resided at 39 Royal Terrace.

Guy Warrack, conductor and composer, was born here on 8 February 1900.

John Wilson, tenor singer, was born here on 25 December 1800 and died in Quebec on 8 July 1849.

Haddington Patrick Douglas-Hamilton, pianist and composer, was born here on 2 August 1950.

Adam Skirving, farmer and poet, who was born in 1719 and died in April 1803, was residing at Garleton when he wrote *Johnnie Cope*. He is buried in Athelstaneford Cemetery.

Lasswade Learmont Drysdale, composer of the overture *Tam o'Shanter*, was born in Edinburgh on 3 October 1866. At the time of his death, on 18 June 1909, he was residing at Christina Bank, Broomieknowe, Lasswade.

Mid Calder Frédéric Chopin stayed with Lord Torphichen at Calder House from 7 August to about 25 August 1848, and visited him again in September and October. 'My health is not really bad, but I'm losing strength, and I'm not yet used to the air here . . . The house I'm staying in is surrounded by a splendid park and century-old trees . . . It's an old manor where John Knox, the Scottish reformer, celebrated Communion for the first time. The walls are eight feet thick — endless corridors, full of ancestral portraits, each blacker and more Scottish-looking than the next. Nothing's missing — there's even a certain "red cap" ghost who puts in an appearance.'

Polbeth Peter M'Leod, folk-song collector and composer of *Oh! Why Left I My Hame?*, *Scotland Yet* and *M'Crimman's Lament*, was born at Polbeth on 8 May 1797 and died in Bonnington on 10 February 1859. He is buried in Rosebank Cemetery.

Portobello Harry Lauder, comedian, singer and composer of the songs *I Love a Lassie* and *Roamin' in the Gloamin'*, was born here on 4 August 1870.

Frederick Simpson, composer of the overture *Robert Bruce*, was born here on 12 December 1856.

ORKNEY

Eday David Skea Allan, composer, was born in Calfsound on 14 March 1840.

Hoy Peter Maxwell Davies, composer, moved here in 1970. Works written here include *Hymn to St Magnus, Stone Litany, Renaissance Scottish Dances, Dark Angels, Ave Maris Stella, The Martyrdom of Saint Magnus, A Mirror of Whitening Light, Salome* and the First and Second Symphonies.

SHETLAND

Unst Bertram Woods, who was born in 1900, composed the hymn tune *Norwick*, sung to 'O Jesus, I Have Promised' and published in 1933, while residing 4 miles south-east of Herma Ness at Norwick. This apparently is the most northerly part of the British Isles in which a popular melody has been written.

STRATHCLYDE

Alloway Robert Burns, poet, was born here on 25 January 1759. Among his songs are 'Auld Lang Syne', 'A Red, Red Rose', 'Comin' thro' the Rye', 'Scots Wha Hae', 'Green Grow the Rashes, O', 'The Banks o' Doon', 'The Birks of Aberfeldie', 'My Love, She's But a Lassie Yet', 'Corn Rigs Are Bonnie', 'Highland Mary', 'Duncan Gray', 'John Anderson My Jo', 'Whistle o'er the Lave o't', 'Of A' the Airts', 'John Barleycorn', 'Up in the Morning Early', 'Ay Waukin, O', 'The Bonny Wee Thing', 'Mary Morison', 'A Highland Lad' and 'Afton Water'. His poetry has inspired works by Malcolm Arnold, Bantock, Bax, Berg, Britten, Robert Franz, Khrennikov, MacDowell, Alexander Mackenzie, Reger, Schumann and Shostakovich.

Arran Albert Peace composed the hymn tune *St Margaret*, sung to 'O Love That Wilt Not Let Me Go', while staying at Brodick Manse in 1884.

Auchinleck Alexander Boswell, son of James Boswell and author of 'Jenny Dang the Weaver', 'Jenny's Bawbee', 'Taste Life's Glad Moments' and 'Goodnight, and Joy Be wi' Ye A'', who was born on 9

Warriston Crescent, Edinburgh. During his visit to Scotland in the summer and autumn of 1848, Frédéric Chopin stayed on more than one occasion with Dr Lyszczyński at 10 Warriston Crescent. The composer, whose health had been rapidly declining, was so weak that he had to be carried upstairs to bed. 'This world seems to slip from me, I forget things, I have no strength', he wrote to a friend (*The Royal Commission on the Ancient & Historical Monuments of Scotland*)

This drawing, entitled 'A View of the Hebrides and Morvern', was sketched by Felix Mendelssohn on 7 August 1829 at Oban. On the same day, he jotted down the opening bars of *Fingal's Cave*. His trip to Staffa was on the following day. The famous theme and the drawing therefore seem to be connected, each expressing 'how extraordinarily the Hebrides affected me'. The buildings on the right of the picture appear to be part of the ruins of Dunollie Castle (*The Bodleian Library*)

Frank Bridge (*Bassano & Vandyk Studios*)

October 1775 and died on 27 March 1822 following a duel with pistols, resided for much of his life in Auchinleck.

Ayr Gavin Gordon, composer and actor, was born here on 24 November 1901.

Franz Liszt disembarked here at about 10am on the morning of 18 January 1841, having sailed from Stranraer in the *Sir William Wallace* steam packet. A great deal of snow had recently fallen, and it was bitterly cold. After taking some nourishment at The King's Arms, he left at 11am in an open third-class train, carrying cattle and pigs, and arrived in Glasgow at 2pm.

Niccolò Paganini gave recitals here in the Theatre on 3 and 4 November 1831.

John Riddell, composer, was born in Ayr on 2 September 1718 and died here on 5 April 1795.

Biggar William Henderson, poet, composer and notable typographer, was born here on 5 August 1831 and died in Ipswich, Suffolk, on 22 May 1891.

Blairmore August Hyllested, pianist and pupil of Liszt, was born in Stockholm on 17 June 1856 and died in Blairmore on 5 April 1946.

Bothwell Joanna Baillie, poet and dramatist, author of the songs 'Woo'd and Married and A'' and 'Poverty Parts Good Companie', was born at Bothwell Manse on 11 September 1762.

Bute John Sterling, author of the hymn 'O Source Divine, and Life of All', was born at Kames Castle on 20 July 1806.

Cathcart Erik Chisholm, composer and conductor, was born here on 4 January 1904.

Dailly Hew Ainslie, author of the songs 'Rover of Lochryan' and 'On wi' the Tartan', was born here on 5 April 1792 and died in Louisville, Kentucky, on 11 March 1878.

Fenwick Hugh Wilson, cobbler and composer of the hymn tune *Martyrdom*, often sung to 'As Pants the Hart for Cooling Streams', was born here in 1766 and died in Duntocher on 14 August 1824. He is buried in Old Kilpatrick Churchyard.

Glasgow Béla Bartók gave a recital here on 10 November 1933.

Robert Bryson, composer, was born here on 31 March 1867.

Ferruccio Busoni played in concerts here in 1899, 1901, 1906, 1919 and 1920. In September 1901, he wrote to his wife: '. . . if destiny, by some devil's trickery, were to force me to live in Glasgow, I would give up music and become an umbrella manufacturer. In the noble heart of Scotland, the occupation of umbrella manufacturer is more profitable, more highly esteemed and, as far as the inhabitants are concerned, more palpably purposeful.' In October 1920, he concluded that many Glaswegians were 'the lowest and rawest of their kind I've ever seen . . . On Saturday evenings, they're let loose and create a vicious tumult.'

Thomas Campbell, poet, author of 'Battle of the Baltic', set by Stanford, and the songs 'Exile of Erin', 'Lord Ullin's Daughter' and 'Ye Mariners of England', was born at 215 High Street on 27 July 1777 and died in London on 15 July 1844. He is buried in Westminster Abbey.

Frédéric Chopin took part in a concert at the Merchants' Hall in Hutcheson Street at 2.30pm on 27 September 1848. The *Glasgow Herald* wrote: 'One thing must have been apparent to every one of the audience, namely, the melancholy and plaintive sentiment which pervaded his music. Indeed, if we would choose to characterise his pieces in three words, we should call them novel, pathetic, and difficult to be understood. M. Chopin is evidently a man of weak constitution, and seems labouring under physical debility and ill health. Perhaps his constitutional delicacy may account for the fact that his musical compositions have all that melancholy sentiment we have spoken of.'

Eugène d'Albert, pianist and composer, whose best known work is probably the opera *Tiefland*, was born at 9 Newton Terrace on 10 April 1864 and died in Riga, Latvia, on 3 March 1932.

James Friskin, pianist and composer, was born here on 3 March 1886.

William Glen, author of 'Wae's Me for Prince Charlie', was born in Glasgow on 14 November 1789 and died here in December 1826.

Iain Hamilton, composer, was born here on 6 June 1922.

Georg Heckman, violinist, was born in Mannheim, West Germany, on 3 November 1848 and died in Glasgow on 29 November 1891.

Charles Hutcheson, composer of the hymn tune *Stracathro*, often sung to 'Jesus, Thine All-Victorious Love', was born in Glasgow in 1792 and died here on 20 January 1860.

Oliver Knussen, composer, was born here on 12 June 1952.

Frederic Lamond, pianist, pupil of Liszt and Bülow, was born here on 28 January 1868 and died in Stirling, Central, on 21 February 1948.

Franz Liszt, travelling from Ayr to Edinburgh, stayed at the George Hotel, George Square, during the afternoon and evening of 18 January 1841. He returned on 20 January and played at a concert. He stayed the night here and left for Edinburgh in the morning. He took part in a second concert, on the 22nd, arriving, according to John Orlando Parry, with 'some very dashing Scotch girls'.

James Loughran, conductor, was born on 30 June 1931 at 138 Garthland Drive, and the family later moved to number 148.

George Matheson, hymn writer, was born here on 27 March 1842 and died at Avenelle, North Berwick, Lothian, on 28 August 1906.

Felix Mendelssohn stayed here on 10 and 14 August 1829. The intervening days were spent in visiting the Trossachs and Loch Lomond. On 15 August he completed his Scottish tour and headed south with his companion Carl Klingemann. On the day of his departure, the composer wrote to his family in Berlin: 'To describe the wretchedness and the comfortless, inhospitable solitude of the country, time and space do not allow; we wandered ten days without meeting a single traveller; what are marked on the map as towns, or at least villages, are a few sheds, huddled together, with one hole for door, window and chimney, for the entrance and exit of men, beasts, light and smoke, in which to all questions you get a dry "No", in which brandy is the only beverage known, without church, without street, without gardens, the rooms pitch black in broad daylight, children and fowls lying in the same straw, many huts without roofs, many unfinished, with crumbling walls, many ruins of burnt houses; and even these inhabited spots are but sparsely scattered over the country. Long before you arrive at a place, you hear it talked of; the rest is heath, with red or brown heather, withered fir stumps and white stones, or black moors where they shoot grouse. Now and then you find beautiful parks, but deserted, and broad lakes, but without boats, the roads a solitude. Imagine, over all this the richly glowing sunlight, painting the heath a thousand divinely warm colours, and then the clouds chasing hither and thither! It is no wonder that the Highlands have been called melancholy. But we two fellows have wandered merrily about them . . . we will not forget it as long as we live.'

William Motherwell, author of 'Jeanie Morrison', which he wrote when he was 14, and 'The Murmur of the Merry Brook', was born at 117 High Street on 13 October 1797 and died in Glasgow on 1 November 1835. He is buried in the Necropolis.

Buxton Orr, composer and conductor, was born here on 18 April 1924.

Niccolò Paganini gave recitals in the Theatre Royal on 13, 14, 15 and

17 October 1831. He returned in 1833 and gave three further concerts here on 23, 26 and 28 September.

William Primrose, viola player, for whom Bartók wrote his Viola Concerto, was born here on 23 August 1903. He gave the first performance of Fricker's Viola Concerto, which he commissioned, on 3 September 1953 in Edinburgh.

John Purser, composer, was born here on 10 February 1942.

Maurice Ravel took part in a concert here in February 1926.

William Reid, author of 'The Lass o' Gowrie' and 'Cauld Kail in Aberdeen', was born in Glasgow on 10 April 1764 and died here on 22 November 1831.

Hugh S. Roberton, choral conductor and composer of *All in the April Evening*, was born in Glasgow on 23 February 1874 and died here on 7 October 1952. He resided at 24 Briar Road.

Richard Rodgers and Lorenz Hart stayed in the Central Hotel at the time of the world première of *Ever Green* at the King's Theatre on 13 October 1930. Rodgers found the train journey from London 'horrendous. It took ten bumpy, sleepless hours to get there.' The Central was 'depressing'. Hart refused to believe that the hotel was right at the station and, instead of allowing a porter to carry his bags into the rear entrance, hailed a taxi. The taxi driver, after attempting to explain the situation, thereby inciting the wrath of the bothered and bewildered lyricist, loaded his luggage and, seconds later, deposited him at the main entrance round the corner.

John Philip Sousa conducted his band during the course of the 1901 Glasgow International Exhibition; the final concert on 4 November was attended by an audience of 152,709. He conducted further concerts, in St Andrew's Hall, on 6 February 1903 and 18 February 1911. On the latter occasion he stayed at the Central Hotel.

Johann Strauss senior led his orchestra at concerts here on 7, 8, 9 and 15 November 1838, and at a ball on 14 November.

Richard Strauss conducted his Serenade in E Flat, *Don Juan* and *Death and Transfiguration* at a concert here on 23 December 1902.

Karol Szymanowski gave a recital here on 31 October 1934.

Ian Whyte, conductor and composer, died here on 27 March 1960. He resided at 72 Clouston Street.

Greenock Jean Adam, the probable author of 'There's Nae Luck About the House', was born in Cartsdyke in 1710 and died in a Glasgow poorhouse on 3 April 1765. She appears to have been residing in Cartsdyke at the time the song was written.

Neil Dougall, composer of the hymn tune *Kilmarnock*, often sung to

'Jesu, the Very Thought of Thee', was born in Greenock on 9 December 1776 and died here on 1 October 1862.

Allan Macbeth, organist, conductor and composer, was born here on 13 March 1856 and died in Glasgow on 25 August 1910.

Hamish MacCunn, composer and conductor, was born here on 22 March 1868.

William Wallace, composer, writer on music, editor, dramatist and ophthalmic surgeon, was born here on 3 July 1860.

Daniel Weir, poet, author of the song 'See the Moon o'er Cloudless Jura', was born here on 31 March 1796 and died on 11 November 1831.

Hamilton Frédéric Chopin stayed with the Duke and Duchess of Hamilton at Hamilton Palace (demolished) at the end of October 1848. By now he had come to realize that, to the British, art meant 'painting, sculpture and architecture. Music is not an art and is not called by that name.' This perception was reinforced one evening when, after he had been playing the piano, a member of the Scottish aristocracy produced a concertina and 'with the utmost gravity, began to perform the most dreadful tunes on it. But what's to be done? Everybody here seems to have a screw loose.' Another titled woman, showing him her album, said: 'I stood beside the Queen while she looked at it.' Another told him she was the thirteenth cousin of Mary Stuart. He was perplexed by what people were wearing; one gentleman, a duke, wore red leather boots, spurs and buckskin trousers, 'with a sort of dressing-gown over the lot'. No woman had yet listened to him playing the piano without commenting, 'Leik water!' Regarding their own efforts at the piano, he observed: 'They all look at their hands and play wrong notes most soulfully. What a rum lot! God help them!'

Innellan George Matheson was minister here 1868–86. He wrote his hymn 'O Love That Wilt Not Let Me Go' one evening in June 1882.

Inverarey William Broomfield, composer of the hymn tunes *St Kilda*, *Shandon* and *Zion*, was born here on 14 October 1826 and died in Aberdeen on 17 October 1888. He is buried in Allanvale Cemetery. There is a monument to his memory in Aberdeen.

Felix Mendelssohn stayed here on the night of 9 August 1829. His companion Carl Klingemann wrote: 'Our host's beautiful daughter in her black curls looked out like a sign over the signboard into the harbour, in which the newest herrings are swimming about all alive at nine o'clock in the morning, and at a quarter past nine are served up fried with the coffee.'

Irvine James Montgomery, author of several well-known hymns, was born here on 4 November 1771.

Johnstone Frédéric Chopin stayed with Mrs Houston at Johnstone Castle from about 3 to about 23 September 1848. 'I am unwell, depressed, and people weary me with their excessive attentions. I can't breathe, I can't work. I feel alone, alone, alone, though I'm surrounded by people . . . They are all cousins here, male and female, all from great families with great names that are unknown on the Continent. The entire conversation is conducted along genealogical lines; it's like the Gospels: such-and-such begat so-and-so, who begat another, who begat yet another, and so on for two pages, until you get to Jesus Christ.'
   Chopin also stayed during September 1848 with Admiral Napier at Milliken House, Milliken Park.

Kilmalcolm Robin Orr composed his Symphony in One Movement at Drumdarach in 1963.

Kilmarnock Jean Glover, author of 'O'er the Muir amang the Heather' and wayward beauty, who, according to Burns, 'visited most of the correction-houses in the West', was born here on 31 October 1758.
   Niccolò Paganini gave a charity concert here on 5 November 1831.

Kilsyth David McCallum, violinist, leader of prominent British orchestras, was born here on 26 March 1897.

Leadhills Allan Ramsay, poet, author of the songs 'Farewell to Lochaber' and 'The Lass o' Patie's Mill', was born here on 15 October 1686.

Lesmahagow Alexander Muir, composer and author of *The Maple Leaf For Ever*, written in 1867, was born here on 5 April 1830 and died in Toronto on 26 June 1906.

Lochwinnoch Robin Orr composed his Second Symphony, *From the Book of Philip Sparrow, Journeys and Places* and the operas *Full Circle* and *Hermiston* at Glenshian, Lochwinnoch, and at St John's College, Cambridge.

Francis Sempill, poet, possible author of the song 'Maggie Lauder', was born at Castle Semple, Beltrees, in 1616 and died in 1682.

Mauchline Robert Burns, poet, resided at Mossgiel from 1784 to 1788, during which time he wrote many of his most popular poems and songs.

Milngavie Walter Taylor, composer and weaver, was born in Milngavie in 1785 and died here in 1847.

Motherwell Alexander Gibson, conductor, was born in the Maternity Hospital on 11 February 1926.

Neilston James Chisholm, pianist and composer of *The Battle of Stirling*, was born here in about 1837 and died in Toronto in December 1877.

Newmilns Andrew Macpherson, tenor singer, was born here in June 1910.

New Stevenston Alexander Gibson, conductor, spent his childhood at Plantation Cottage, 122 Jerviston Street.

Oban Felix Mendelssohn stopped here on 7 August 1829 and made a drawing of the view across Oban Bay. He returned here by boat on the morning of 9 August after his trip to Staffa and Iona.

Paisley Noel Eadie, soprano singer, was born here on 10 December 1901 and died in London on 11 April 1950.

Kenneth McKellar, tenor singer, was born here on 23 June 1927.

Robert Tannahill, author of 'Gloomy Winter's Now Awa'', 'Jessie, the Flower o' Dunblane', 'The Braes o' Gleniffer', 'Thou Bonnie Wood o' Craigielea', 'The Maid of Arranteenie', 'We'll Meet Beside the Dusky Glen' and 'The Braes o' Balquhidder', was born in Castle Street on 3 June 1774 and drowned himself in the stream now known as Tannahill's Pool, near Maxwelton Street, on 17 May 1810. He resided at 11 Queen Street and is buried in Paisley Cemetery.

John Turnbull, composer and writer, was born here on 12 January 1804 and died in Glasgow on 1 November 1844.

Partick William Euing, educationist and music collector, was born here on 20 May 1788 and died in Glasgow on 12 May 1874.

Pollokshaws Robert Dalglish, composer of *Careless of Love* and *Hail, Sweet Spring*, was born in Pollokshaws in July 1806 and died here on 5 August 1875.

Prestwick John Currie, composer, was born here in 1934.

Riccarton John Templeton, one of the greatest of all operatic tenors, was born here on 30 July 1802 and died in Hampton, London, on 2 July 1886.

Staffa Felix Mendelssohn visited Fingal's Cave on 8 August 1829. Inspired by the extraordinary atmosphere of the Inner Hebrides, he had jotted down the initial bars of his famous overture on the day before the trip to Staffa. At that stage he had little idea what the piece was to be called or how the rest of it would go. More than five years passed before he decided to give the work the title by which we know it. The degree to which he enjoyed the voyage to Staffa and Iona is open to doubt, for his companion Carl Klingemann reported that the composer 'is on better terms with the sea as a musician than he is as an individual or a stomach'. The sea was exceedingly rough, and the 5am embarkation from Tobermory must have been an additional discomfort. In a letter of 11 August, written in Glasgow, Mendelssohn commented: 'How much has happened between my last letter and this! The most fearful sickness, Staffa, scenery, travels, people . . .'

Strachur Frédéric Chopin visited Lady Murray at Strachur House in September 1848.

Strathaven Harry Lauder, comedian, singer and composer of the songs *I Love a Lassie* and *Roamin' in the Gloamin'*, died on 26 February 1950. He resided at Lauder Ha.

Tarbolton James Barr, composer of the song *Thou Bonnie Wood o' Craigielea*, perhaps now better known as *Waltzing Matilda*, was born here in 1779 and died in Govan on 24 February 1860.

Tobermory Bobby MacLeod, accordionist, band leader and composer, was born here on 8 May 1925.

Felix Mendelssohn stayed here on the night of 7 August 1829. It appears that the opening of *Fingal's Cave* came to him during his journey from Oban to Tobermory, for he quotes the first twenty bars in a letter dated 7 August — the day before he first saw Fingal's Cave. It should be remembered that the title of the overture was not settled until publication of the full score in April 1835. Mendelssohn considered calling the piece *The Lonely Island, The Isles of Fingal* and *The Hebrides* during the years 1829–35; indeed, the overture initially became known as *The Hebrides*.

Wishaw Frédéric Chopin stayed with Lady Belhaven at Wishaw House in October 1848.

TAYSIDE

Aberfeldy Robert Burns, poet, wrote the song 'The Birks of Aberfeldie' here in September 1787 while standing under the Falls of Moness.

Felix Mendelssohn visited here on 4 August 1829 and made a drawing of the Birks of Aberfeldy.

Auchtergaven Robert Nicoll, poet, and author of the songs 'Bonnie Bessie Lee', 'Ordé Braes' and 'The Bonnie Hieland Hills', was born in Auchtergaven on 7 January 1814 and died on 7 December 1837.

Blair Atholl Felix Mendelssohn visited here on 3 August 1829. 'This is a most dismal, melancholy, rainy day.'

Brechin Robin Orr, composer and educationist, was born at Glebe House, Trinity Road, on 2 June 1909. His childhood was spent at Greensted, Park Road.

Bridge of Balgie James Hogg, poet, writer and composer, wrote the verses of the song 'Come o'er the Stream, Charlie', published in 1831, at Meggernie Castle.

Broom of Dalreoch Caroline Oliphant, Baroness Nairne, author of the songs 'Caller Herrin'', 'The Land o' the Leal', 'The Rowan Tree', 'The Laird o' Cockpen', 'The Hundred Pipers', 'Bonnie Charlie's Now Awa'' and 'Charlie Is My Darling', was born at Gask Auld House on 16 August 1766 and died there on 26 October 1845. She is buried in Gask Chapel. She was married at Gask House on 2 June 1806 and then moved to Duddingston. She returned to reside in Broom of Dalreoch in August 1843 after the death of her husband and son William, her only child. Many of her best known songs were written here. 'The Land o' the Leal' appears to have been produced in Durham.

Cleish Mary Duncan, author of the hymn 'Jesus, Tender Shepherd, Hear Me', died here on 5 January 1840.

Dundee Ferruccio Busoni played at a concert here in November 1903.
David Dorward, composer, was born here on 7 August 1933.
Grainger Kerr, contralto singer, was born here on 12 October 1864 and died in London on 24 February 1955.
Niccolò Paganini gave a matinée concert here on 8 November 1831 at the Caledonian Hall, and a further concert on 9 November.
John Philip Sousa conducted his band at two concerts in Kinnaird's Hall on 12 February 1903. He gave two further concerts in Kinnaird's Hall on 21 February 1911. He stayed the night at the Grand Hotel.

Dunkeld Felix Mendelssohn visited here on 2 August 1829, during which time he made drawings of part of Birnam Wood and Rumbling Bridge.

Forfar James Allan, celebrated violinist, was born in Forfar on 17 October 1800 and died here on 18 August 1877.
Archibald Allen, composer of *Miss Gray of Carse*, was born in Forfar in about 1794 and died here in 1831.

Inver Nathaniel Gow, violinist and composer of *Caller Herrin'*, was born here on 28 May 1763 and died in Edinburgh on 19 January 1831.

Kinnesswood Michael Bruce, author of the hymn 'Behold, the Mountain of the Lord', was born in Kinnesswood on 27 March 1746 and died here on 5 July 1767.

Milnathort David Carmichael, composer of *Loch Leven Castle*, was born in Milnathort in about 1787 and died here on 19 July 1865.

Perth Catherine Glover, the 'Fair Maid of Perth', the subject of Bizet's opera, which was loosely based on Scott's novel *St Valentine's Day*, resided in Curfew Row, where her house was rebuilt in 1893.
David Kennedy, tenor singer, was born here on 15 April 1825 and died in Stratford, Ontario, on 12 October 1886. He is buried in the Grange Cemetery, Edinburgh.
Marjorie Kennedy-Fraser, singer, composer, folk-song collector and

daughter of David Kennedy, was born here on 1 October 1857 and died in Edinburgh on 22 November 1930. She collected and published 'Eriskay Love Lilt' and 'The Road to the Isles'.

Charles Mackay, author of the songs 'There's a Good Time Coming, Boys', 'To the West' and 'Cheer, Boys, Cheer!', was born here on 27 March 1814 and died in London on 24 December 1889.

Niccolò Paganini gave an evening concert here on 8 November 1831.

John Philip Sousa conducted his band at concerts in City Hall on 7 February 1903.

Straloch John Reid, general, musical benefactor and composer of *The Garb of Old Gaul*, originally entitled *Highland March*, was born here on 13 February 1721 and died in London on 6 February 1807.

Strath Braan Niel Gow, violinist and composer, was born here on 22 March 1727 and died at Inver on 1 March 1807.

Tulliemet Robert Mackintosh, composer and violinist, was born here in 1745 and died in London in February 1807.

Tummel Bridge Felix Mendelssohn stayed here on the night of 3 August 1829. 'The storm howls, rushes and whistles, doors are banging, and window-shutters are bursting open . . . tea, with honey and potato-cakes . . . the serving-girl came to meet us with whiskey.'

THE SOUTH-EAST

BEDFORDSHIRE

Bedford John Barnett, second cousin of Meyerbeer and composer of the opera *The Mountain Sylph*, was born here on 15 July 1802.

James Grassineau, compiler of the first British music dictionary, published in 1740, was born in London in about 1715 and died in Bedford on 5 April 1767.

John Philip Sousa conducted his band at a concert here on 14 February 1905.

Clapham Glenn Miller, bandleader and composer, took off from the RAF fighter base at Twin Woods Farm on 15 December 1944, the day of his fatal disappearance in the English Channel.

Colmworth Timothy Matthews, hymn composer, was born in Colmworth Rectory on 4 November 1826 and died at Tetney, Lincoln, on 5 January 1910.

Elstow John Bunyan, author of *The Pilgrim's Progress*, from which the hymn 'Who Would True Valour See' is drawn, was born here in November 1628 and died in London on 31 August 1688. Vaughan Williams's opera *The Shepherds of the Delectable Mountains*, based on *The Pilgrim's Progress*, was first performed in London on 11 July 1922; his opera *The Pilgrim's Progress* was staged in London on 26 April 1951.

Meppershall Thomas Salmon, writer on music, was born in London on 24 June 1648 and died in Meppershall in July 1706.

BERKSHIRE

Ascot Joseph Haydn visited Ascot and Windsor on 14 June 1792. 'These horse races are run on a large field, especially prepared for them, and on this field is a large circular track 2 English miles long and 6 fathoms wide . . . The riders are very lightly clad in silk, and each has a different colour, so you can recognize him more easily, no boots, a little cap on his head, they are all as lean as greyhounds and lean as their horses, each is weighed and a certain weight is allowed him, in proportion to the strength of the horse, and if the rider is too light he has to put on heavier clothes or else some lead is hung on him. The horses are of the finest breeds, light, with thin feet, the hair on their necks tied into braids, the hooves very delicate. As soon as they hear the sound of the bell, they immediately dash off with the greatest force, every stride of the horses is 22 feet long. These horses are very expensive. The Prince of Wales paid 8 thousand pounds for one some years ago and sold it again for 6 thousand. But he won 50000 pounds with it. Among other things a stall is erected, where the English place their bets. The King has his own stall at one side.'

Arthur Sullivan is probably the composer who visited Ascot most frequently; he usually stayed nearby. In June 1893 he was at Meadow Bank, Winkfield. Between 1894 and 1896 he owned two race horses, Cranmer and Blue Mark. Each was sold at a loss.

Bray Angus Morrison, pianist, was born here on 28 May 1902.

Frank Schuster, patron of music, who was born in 1852 and died on 26 December 1927, resided intermittently at The Hut (later called The Long White Cloud), next to Monkey Island. Edward Elgar was a frequent guest, writing part of his Violin Concerto here. Gabriel Fauré also came on a number of occasions and composed some of his songs at The Hut.

Cookham Dean Henry Walford Davies, composer of the *Royal Air Force March Past* and *Solemn Melody*, organist, educationist and Master of the King's Music, resided at High Meadow, Cookham Dean, 1932–9.

Crowthorne Arthur Christopher Benson, man of letters, author of 'Land of Hope and Glory', was born here on 24 April 1862 and died in Cambridge on 17 June 1925. He resided at The Old Lodge, Magdalene College.

Alan Murray, educationist, and composer of the songs *I'll Walk Beside You*, *Nut Brown Ale* and *The Cornish Witch*, resided during the 1930s and '40s at Firtrees, Crowthorne.

Curridge Geoffrey Shaw, composer and educationist, was born in London on 14 November 1879 and died there on 14 April 1943. He resided at The Cottage, Curridge.

Easthampstead Annie Fortescue-Harrison, composer of the song *In the Gloaming*, was born in 1850 and died on 12 February 1944. She resided at Easthampstead Park.

Eton Arthur Ainger, who was born in Blackheath on 4 July 1841 and died at Eton on 26 October 1919, wrote the hymn 'God Is Working His Purpose Out As Year Succeeds to Year' in 1894, while he was a master at Eton College.

Humphrey Lyttleton, trumpeter and writer, was born here in 1921.

Donald Tovey, music scholar, pianist and composer, whose Cello Concerto was first performed by Pau Casals, was born here on 17 July 1875.

Lambourn George Martin, organist and composer, was born here on 11 September 1844 and died in London on 23 February 1916. He is buried in St Paul's Cathedral.

Langley Elizabeth Poole, mezzo-soprano singer and actress, was born in London on 5 April 1820 and died at Langley on 14 January 1906.

Littlewick Green Ivor Novello, composer, dramatist, singer and actor, resided intermittently at his country home, Redroofs, from November 1927 until the time of his death in 1951. Much of his composing was done here.

Maidenhead John Philip Sousa conducted his band at a concert here on 10 February 1905.

Zerubbabel Wyvill, organist and composer of the hymn tune *Eaton*, usually sung to 'O, God, How Often Hath Thine Ear', was born here in 1763 and died in Hounslow on 14 May 1837.

Padworth Walter Ford, lecturer on music and teacher, was born in London on 20 March 1861 and died at Padworth on 21 August 1938.

Reading Hugh Allen, teacher, conductor and composer, was born here on 23 December 1869. His hymn tunes include *Midian*, sung to 'Christian, Dost Thou See Them', and *Kingley Vale*, sung to Buckoll's 'Lord, Dismiss Us With Thy Blessing'.

Basil Cameron, conductor, was born here on 18 August 1884 and died on 26 June 1975. He resided at 30 Ingelow House, Holland Street, Kensington, London.

Niccolò Paganini gave a recital in the Theatre Royal on 28 October 1833.

Robert Archibald Smith, composer of *Jessie, the Flow'r o'Dunblane* and *Bonnie Mary Hay*, was born here on 16 November 1780. He also wrote the hymn tune *Selma*, often sung to 'Fair Waved the Golden Corn'.

John Philip Sousa conducted his band at a concert here on 10 February 1905.

Johann Strauss senior led his orchestra in a concert in the Town Hall on 1 October 1838. He gave a second concert in the Town Hall on 5 June 1849.

Slough Friedrich Wilhelm Herschel, astronomer, discoverer of Uranus, oboist, organist and composer, was born in Hanover on 15 November 1738 and died at Slough on 25 August 1822.

Joseph Haydn visited him here on 15 June 1792 and inspected the telescope through which Herschel had sighted Uranus three years earlier.

Charles Harford Lloyd, composer of the hymn tune *Cosmos*, sung to 'I Praised the Earth in Beauty Seen', died here on 16 October 1919.

Thatcham Charles Lockey, tenor singer, was born here on 23 March 1820 and died in Hastings on 3 December 1901. He took part in the first performance of *Elijah* on 25 August 1846. Mendelssohn wrote to his brother Paul on the following day: 'A young English tenor sang the last aria with such wonderful sweetness that I had to exercise great self-control to avoid being overcome and keep a steady beat.'

Windsor Albert of Saxe-Coburg-Gotha, Prince Consort of England, statesman, organist and composer, was born in Rosenau, Bavaria, on 26 August 1819 and died in Windsor Castle on 14 December 1861. He is buried in Frogmore Mausoleum.

George Elvey, organist of St George's Chapel and composer, resided in The Cloisters 1835–82. Thalberg visited him here in 1839 and played his fantasy on Rossini's *Mosè in Egitto*.

Richard Farrant, composer of *Hide Not Thou Thy Face, O Lord*, was organist of St George's Chapel from 1564 until his death in 1581.

Edmund Horace Fellowes, music scholar and composer, was born in London on 11 November 1870 and died at Windsor on 20 December 1951. He resided in The Cloisters.

Nathaniel Giles, composer and organist, was organist of St George's Chapel from 1585 until his death on 24 January 1633. He is buried in the Chapel.

Edvard Grieg and his wife Nina played and sang for Queen Victoria at Windsor Castle in December 1897. 'She is so charming and interested,' the composer wrote to Julius Röntgen, 'that it's quite astonishing in somebody of her age.'

John Griesbach, composer, pianist and cellist, was born here on 20 June 1798 and died in London on 9 January 1875.

Joseph Haydn came here on 14 June 1792 and visited the Castle. He particularly admired St George's Chapel, 'a very old, but splendid building, the high altar cost 50,000 fl. It shows the ascension of Christ in stained glass. In the side altar to the right, a smaller one was completed this year, 1792, depicting Christ appearing to the shepherds. This small one is more highly valued than the larger. The view from the terrace is divine.'

Karl Friedrich Horn, organist and composer, who was born in Nordhausen, East Germany, was organist of St George's Chapel from 1824 until his death in Windsor on 5 August 1830.

Pelham Humfrey, composer and teacher of Purcell, was born in 1647 and died here on 14 July 1674.

Franz Liszt played for George IV at Windsor Castle in the early summer of 1825. His second visit was on 7 April 1886, when he appeared before Queen Victoria and other members of the Royal Family, performing an improvisation, a transcription of *The Miracle of the Roses* from *St Elisabeth*, a *Hungarian Rhapsody* and Chopin's Nocturne, Op 9 No 1. Princess Marie of Battenburg noted in her diary: 'The Queen greeted him very kindly, and I much appreciated the sight of the two figures as they stood facing one another. Both little, both white haired, both in black, both dignified and amiable, both a little embarrassed. She the ruler of the great British Empire, he ruler in the realm of music. Franz Liszt played for about half an hour, the notes falling from his fingers like pearls, while sounds as from another world floated through the room. The intellectual head and the soutane would have suited an organ well, although, with the Abbé Franz Liszt, the man of the world showed everywhere through the priestly garment. The Princess and I had armed ourselves with our birthday-books, in order to obtain Liszt's autograph, but when he was about to take leave of the Queen none of us could make up our minds to proffer our request; we all felt too bashful. In the end I was pushed forward, crossed the room, and boldly laid my book on the piano before the great man. He bowed smilingly and wrote his name in it, and also in those of the shy princesses, who were hanging back, and finally in that of Her Majesty herself . . .'

John Marbeck, composer, organist and Bible scholar, was born in about 1510 and died in about 1585. It is believed that he passed most of

Frank Bridge lived much of his life in what is now East Sussex. He was born in 1879 in Brighton, spending his childhood there. During his later years, he lived at Friston Field, Friston, near Eastbourne. He died in Eastbourne in 1941. Among the visitors to Friston Field was his pupil Benjamin Britten, whose *Variations on a Theme of Frank Bridge* was written in 1937 (*Courtesy of John Bishop*)

Claude Debussy photographing *la mer* from his balcony at the Grand Hotel, Eastbourne. He spent the latter part of the summer of 1905 there with Emma Bardac, whom he later married, this happy event being anticipated by their entry in the guest book. He completed *La Mer* during his stay and also worked on other compositions. *Reflets dans l'eau* was inspired by the reflections of sun and clouds in a fountain and ornamental pool in Devonshire Park. The radio programme 'Grand Hotel' was originally broadcast from the hotel's Palm Court (*Courtesy of Richard Langham Smith*)

John Ireland at his home, Rock Mill, in Washington, West Sussex, where he spent his final years. Shortly after taking up residence, in 1953, he wrote to a friend, 'It would be difficult to describe this place to you. It is wonderful and absolutely unique.' (*Courtesy of Mrs Norah Kirby*)

Bourne Park House, near Bridge in Kent. Wolfgang Amadeus Mozart and his mother, father and sister stayed here at the end of July 1765 with Sir Horace Mann. On 1 August, they embarked from Dover for Calais. Bourne Park House was left vacant a few years ago and deteriorated badly, becoming a refuge for tramps and vagrants. It is being restored by its present owner (*Author*)

his life here, being organist of St George's Chapel.

Pietro Mascagni conducted *Cavalleria Rusticana* at Windsor Castle on 15 July 1893. This was among Her Majesty's favourite operas and had previously been performed here at her command on 25 November 1891, five weeks after the British première.

John Mundy, organist and composer, died here in 1630. He is buried in St George's Chapel.

Jacques Offenbach, then 24 and a virtuoso cellist, gave a recital before Queen Victoria and Prince Albert at Windsor Castle on 6 June 1844. Also among the audience were the Emperor of Russia and the King of Bavaria. The composer received a diamond ring as a token of royal approval. 'Everything here is splendid, but cold,' he wrote to a friend in Paris.

Walter Parratt, organist, composer, educationist and Master of the Queen's and King's Music, was organist of St George's Chapel from 1882 until his death here on 27 March 1924.

Benjamin Rogers, organist and composer, was born here in May 1614 and died in Oxford in June 1698.

Anton Rubinstein played for Queen Victoria at Windsor Castle in May 1877. The baritone singer George Henschel also performed and later wrote about the occasion. 'After receiving us most graciously, Her Majesty seated herself near the tail-end of the piano, evidently in order to be able to see Rubinstein's face as he played. In the distance the only other listeners were seated, two or three ladies-in-waiting. The great pianist began with some Chopin nocturnes and other soft sweet things, which greatly pleased the Queen. After that I sang, and then Rubinstein played again, this time some louder things. I thought I could detect faint signs of uneasiness in Her Majesty's face as she seemed to realize the alarming nearness of the huge concert grand, the open lid of which threw the sounds back in the direction of Her Majesty's chair with redoubled force. Then I sang again, and then, to my dismay I confess, for I had heard him do it before, Rubinstein settled down to the playing of Liszt's arrangement of Schubert's *Erl-King*.' This was the piece with which the celebrated pianist had stunned audiences throughout Europe and America by unleashing the most awesome and ·ferocious power imaginable; to have heard his performance was to possess one of the memories of a lifetime. As the work progressed, Henschel eyed the Queen with concern, expecting her to ask him to close the lid; but she found a better solution. 'Every now and then she would, unnoticed by the player, gently push her chair farther and farther away from the piano, the sounds issuing from which were growing more and more terrific from bar to bar, until, during the last frantic ride of the horror-stricken father, keys, strings, hammers seemed to be flying through the air in all directions.' But, by now, the Queen had covered some distance and reached safety, greeting the conclusion of the performance with 'a charming smile of pleasure and relief'.

Camille Saint-Saëns twice visited Windsor Castle to play for Queen Victoria, in July 1880 and July 1898. On the first occasion, she greeted him 'with both hands extended to take mine and . . . addressed me with real cordiality'. At her request he played the organ of St George's Chapel and then the piano, and also accompanied Princess Beatrice in an aria from his opera *Étienne Marcel*. The Queen noted in her diary that Saint-Saëns 'plays and composes beautifully'. In 1898 he gave a little chamber concert with the Dutch violinist Johannes Wolff. 'We were lodged at a hotel, for the honour of sleeping at the Castle was reserved for V.I.Ps — an honour that need not be envied, since the sleeping apartments are actually servants' rooms. But etiquette demands it.' The concert took place after the Queen had dinner. 'I was heartbroken when I saw her enter, for she was almost carried by her Indian servant and clearly could not walk alone. But, once seated at a small table, she was just the same as ever, with her wonderful charm, her simple manner and musical voice. Only her white hair bore witness to the passing of the years.'

John Bernard Sale, bass singer, organist and composer, was born here on 24 June 1779 and died in London on 16 September 1856.

John Philip Sousa conducted his band at a royal command performance in Windsor Castle on 31 January 1903.

Nicholas Staggins, composer, and Master of the King's and Queen's Music, died here on 13 June 1700. He is buried in St George's Chapel.

Samuel Stone was curate of Windsor 1862–70, during which time he wrote the hymn 'The Church's One Foundation'.

Richard and Cosima Wagner were received at Windsor Castle on 17 May 1877 by Queen Victoria and her youngest son, Prince Leopold. 'Windsor makes a powerful impression,' Cosima wrote in her diary, 'though its interior furnishings are much out of keeping with its exterior; and even the lovely Van Dycks, the splendid Holbein, and the miraculous Rembrandt do not match it. How different the palaces in Italy!' Wagner had previously met Queen Victoria on 11 June 1855, when he conducted a Philharmonic Society concert, in the Hanover Square Rooms, which included, at her request, the overture to *Tannhäuser*. In his autobiography he mentions that, during their conversation, 'the question arose of putting my operas on the stage, and Prince Albert objected that Italian singers would never be able to interpret my music. I was amused when the Queen met this objection by saying that, after all, a great many Italian singers were really Germans.'

With regard to the Windsor visit, we may note that both the Wagners had previously been married and that Cosima's father, Franz Liszt, whom Victoria received nine years later, had never been married at all. The Queen was perhaps less rigid in her role of Defender of the Faith than is generally supposed.

Wokingham Arthur Sullivan, composer and conductor, stayed at Ashridgewood, Forest Road, during the summer of 1899, working on *The Rose of Persia*.

BUCKINGHAMSHIRE

Amersham Eric Coates, composer, wrote *Four Centuries* at Chalfonts, Longfield Drive, in 1941.

Sebastian Forbes, composer and conductor, was born here on 22 May 1941.

Walter Goehr, composer and conductor, who was born in Berlin on 28 May 1903, resided for several years at 17 Batchelor's Way.

Alexander Goehr, his son, composer, conductor and educationist, who was born in Berlin on 10 August 1932, spent much of his childhood at the same address.

Tim Rice, librettist of *Jesus Christ Superstar* and *Evita*, was born here on 10 November 1944.

Paul Schoeffler, baritone singer, was born in Dresden on 15 September 1897 and died in Amersham on 21 November 1977.

Aylesbury Rutland Boughton, composer, was born here on 23 January 1878.

Beaconsfield Edmund Waller, whose poetry inspired songs by Blow and Quilter, was born at the Manor House, Coleshill, in 1606 and died at his home, Hall Barn House, in 1687.

Frederick Gore Ouseley, music scholar and composer, was brought up at Hall Barn House.

Felix Mendelssohn was a guest at Hall Barn House in 1832 and played a piano duet with Ouseley, then six years old.

Malibran was a guest in 1833.

Chalfont St Giles John Milton, poet, who was born in London on 9

December 1608 and died there on 8 November 1674, resided at Milton's Cottage, his only surviving home, during 1665 and here completed *Paradise Lost*. His verses inspired works by Arne, Handel, Haydn, Henry Lawes, Elisabeth Lutyens, Mackenzie, Parry, Rubinstein, Spohr, Spontini, Stanford, Sullivan and Vaughan Williams. He is also the author of the hymns 'Let Us with a Gladsome Mind' and 'The Lord Will Come and Not Be Slow'.

Chesham Bois Eric Coates, composer, wrote the first movement of *The Three Elizabeths* at 3 The Woodlands in 1940.

Bruce Montgomery, composer, conductor and, as Edmund Crispin, author of detective novels, was born here on 2 October 1921.

Gerrards Cross Granville Bantock, composer and conductor, resided at Mead Cottage for much of the 1930s.

Phyllis Tate, composer, was born at Lexden, Gerrards Cross, on 6 April 1911.

Great Missenden Adam Carse, distinguished writer on the orchestra and orchestration, teacher and composer, died here on 2 November 1958.

High Wycombe Ivor Gurney, composer and poet, resided at 51 Queen's Road 1919–20, intermittently acting as organist at St Michael's.

William Havergal, composer, was born here on 18 January 1793 and died in Royal Leamington Spa on 19 April 1870.

Denis Stevens, music scholar, was born here on 2 March 1922.

Marlow Arnold Bax, composer and Master of the King's and Queen's Music, resided 1913–15 in Station Road and then moved to a nearby house, Riversleigh, near the bridge on the south side of the river.

Frederic Clay, composer of *I'll Sing Thee Songs of Araby* and *The Sands of Dee*, was born in Paris on 3 August 1838 and died in Marlow on 24 November 1889.

Mursley Thomas Beecham, conductor, impresario and patron of music, resided intermittently at Mursley Hall during his twenties.

Newport Pagnell Charles Sanford Terry, distinguished authority on Bach, was born here on 24 October 1864 and died in Westerton of Pitfodels, Grampian, on 5 November 1936.

Olney William Cowper, poet and hymn writer, came here in 1767 at the invitation of John Newton and remained until 1786, living at Orchard Side in the Market Place. During this time were published his hymns 'O for a Closer Walk with God', 'God Moves in a Mysterious Way', 'Hark, My Soul! It is the Lord', 'Jesus, Where'er Thy People Meet' and 'Sometimes a Light Surprises'. In 1785 he published 'The Diverting History of John Gilpin', which has been set to music by Frederic Cowen, Thomas Dunhill and Sidney Waddington.

John Newton, author of hymns, was curate here 1764–79, during which time he wrote 'Glorious Things of Thee Are Spoken', 'Amazing Grace' and 'How Sweet the Name of Jesus Sounds'. He died in London on 21 December 1807; his remains were reinterred at Olney in 1893.

Speen Edmund Rubbra, composer, resided at Valley Cottage 1933–61. Works written here include Symphonies Nos 1–7, *Festival Overture*, Viola Concerto, *Canterbury Mass, Missa in honorem Sancti Dominici* and *Festival Te Deum.*

Stokenchurch Richard Hickox, conductor, was born at The Vicarage, Stokenchurch, on 5 March 1948.

Taplow Thomas Arne came to Cliveden to supervise the first presentation, on 1 August 1740, of his music for the masque *Alfred*, performed before the Prince and Princess of Wales. The soloist in the masque's celebrated final number, *Rule, Britannia*, was the tenor Thomas Lowe who also gave the first performances of Arne's songs *Under the Greenwood Tree* and *Blow, Blow, Thou Winter Wind. Alfred* was staged in the gardens of Cliveden. (Lowe died in London on 1 March 1783.) A rehearsal took place a few days earlier at Drury Lane Theatre. Among the composers who have quoted from *Rule, Britannia* in their works are Handel, Beethoven and Wagner.

Arthur Sullivan, composer and conductor, stayed at Skindles Hotel on various occasions during the 1880s.

Wendover Edward Payne, lawyer, historian and authority on stringed instruments, was born in High Wycombe on 22 July 1844 and drowned at Christmas 1904 in the canal at Wendover. He resided at Holywell Lodge, Wendover.

Giacomo Puccini stayed at Halton House, Halton, in July 1900 as the guest of Alfred de Rothschild.

THE CHANNEL ISLANDS

Guernsey Philip Catelinet, conductor and composer, associated in particular with brass bands, was born in St Peter Port on 3 December 1910.

John David, composer of the hymn tune *Marienlyst*, sung to 'Captain of Israel's Host, and Guide', was born in Guernsey in 1837 and died here on 7 September 1902.

Fanny Davies, pianist and music scholar, pupil of Clara Schumann, was born here on 27 June 1861 and died on 1 September 1934 in London, where she resided at 52 Wellington Road, St John's Wood.

Robert Farnon, distinguished composer of music for films and television and of popular light orchestral works, who was born in Toronto on 24 July 1917, moved to La Falaise, St Martins, in June 1959.

Victor Hugo, poet, novelist and dramatist, resided in 1855 at 20 Hauteville, St Peter Port, and 1856–70 at Hauteville House. Between 1852 and 1855 he had lived at Maison Victor Hugo, St Luke's, Jersey. Works based on his writings include Donizetti's *Lucrezia Borgia*, Liszt's *Ce qu'on entend sur la montagne* and *Mazeppa*, Mendelssohn's overture *Ruy Blas*, Ponchielli's *La Gioconda*, Verdi's *Ernani* and *Rigoletto* and compositions by Berlioz, Bizet, Delibes, Fauré, Franck, Gounod, D'Indy, Lalo, MacDowell, Massenet, Mussorgsky, Rakhmaninov, Saint-Saëns, Ambroise Thomas and Wagner.

John Ireland resided in 1939 at The Royal Hotel, St Peter Port; Fair View, Jerbourg; Woodside, St Martins, and, October 1939–April 1940, at Fort Saumarez, L'Eree. In May 1940, on becoming organist of St Stephen's, St Peter Port, he moved to Birnam Court Hotel, but was evacuated to England on 22 June. The piano suite *Sarnia* derives from this stay on the island.

Arthur Jamouneau, composer of the hymn tune *Lynton*, often sung to 'Happy the Heart Where Graces Reign', was born here in 1865 and died in Yorkshire on 7 December 1927.

Alan Murray, educationist and composer of the songs *I'll Walk Beside You*, *Nut Brown Ale* and *The Cornish Witch*, was born here in 1890.

Ellen Orridge, contralto singer, was born in London on 14 August 1856 and died here on 16 September 1883. She is buried in Kensal Green Cemetery, London.

Jersey Barré Bayly, violinist, was born at Mount Orgueil House, St Helier, in 1850.

Claude Debussy stayed at St Helier in July 1904. He was working on

La Mer at the time. 'It's a lovely place,' he wrote to a friend. 'I am quiet, and what is even better, I work with perfect freedom, something that hasn't happened for a long time. The sea has been very good to me, showing me all her robes.'

John Ireland, composer, came here regularly between 1907 and 1912. Works inspired by these visits, often to Le Fauvic, include the song *Sea Fever*, the piano piece *The Island Spell* and the orchestral prelude *The Forgotten Rite*.

Edwin Lott, organist and composer, was born in St Helier on 31 January 1836.

Samuel Lover, composer, painter and author, died in St Helier on 6 July 1868. He is buried in Kensal Green Cemetery, London.

Clement Perrot, composer of the hymn tune *Morna*, sung to 'What Shall I Render to My God', was born here in 1842 and died in Ecclesall, South Yorkshire, on 16 July 1910.

HAMPSHIRE

Andover George Bennett, organist and composer, was born here on 5 May 1863 and died in Lincoln on 20 August 1930.

Ashmansworth Gerald Finzi, composer, resided at Church Farm from 1939 until his death in Oxford in 1956. Works completed here include *Let Us Garlands Bring, Lo, the Full, Final Sacrifice, God Is Gone Up, Intimations of Immortality, For St Cecilia*, Clarinet Concerto, Grand Fantasia and Toccata, *In Terra Pax* and Cello Concerto.

Ralph Vaughan Williams was a frequent visitor to Church Farm and wrote part of his Ninth Symphony here in 1956.

Barton Stacey Henry Balfour Gardiner, composer and conductor, was born in London on 7 November 1877 and died in Salisbury on 28 June 1950. He resided for some years at Moody's Down, Barton Stacey, where he was visited around 1902 by Percy Grainger and Cyril Scott.

Fareham John Goss, composer of the hymn tune *Praise, My Soul*, sung to 'Praise, My Soul, the King of Heaven', was born at 21 High Street on 27 December 1800. He died in London on 10 May 1880.

Farnborough Arthur Sullivan, composer and conductor, was a visitor during the 1880s and '90s to Farnborough Hill, the home of Empress Eugénie of France.

Fleet (near Farnborough) Arthur Sullivan, composer and conductor, wrote most of *The Yeomen of the Guard* at Booth Lodge during the summer of 1888.

Gosport Frank Walker, distinguished music scholar, was born here on 10 June 1907 and died in Tring, Hertfordshire, in March 1962.

Grayshott Rutland Boughton, composer, resided in a cottage on the Tarn Moor estate of his patron, Frederick Jackson, 1912–14. It was here that he composed his most important work, the opera *The Immortal Hour.*

Hardway Henry Lambeth, organist, conductor and composer, was born here on 16 January 1822 and died in Glasgow on 27 June 1895.

Liss Isaac Albéniz, who lived in London during the early 1890s, is likely to have stayed on various occasions at the country home, Stodham Park, East Liss, of his patron, Francis Money-Coutts, who gave him an allowance of about £1,000 a year.

Richard Dering, composer and organist, was born in about 1580. His birth may have taken place here, which is where his family home was. He died in London in March 1630.

Nether Wallop Leopold Stokowski, conductor, died at his home, Place Farm House, on 13 September 1977.

Petersfield William Harris, composer and organist, was born in London on 28 March 1883 and died here in September 1973. He resided at 64A Heath Road, Petersfield.

Portsea Johann Strauss senior led his orchestra at a concert in the Beneficial Society's Hall on 29 September 1838.

Portsmouth David Harries, composer, was born here in 1933.

Joseph Haydn was here on 9 and 10 July 1794. The dockyard, he wrote in his notebook, 'is of an enormous size and has a great many fine buildings. But I could not go there because I am a foreigner . . . Every ship-of-the-line or *Man of War* has 3 masts, similarly a frigate. Most of them have 3 decks/a brig has 2 masts/a cutter has only one mast. Every ship-of-the-line must have at least 64 cannons. A cutter has only 14 or at the most 16 cannons. A fire-ship has 2 masts . . .'

Franz Liszt played at a concert in the Green Row Rooms (demolished) on 17 August 1840.

Felix Mendelssohn and his father came here at the beginning of July 1833 to see the *Victory* and the dockyards.

Niccolò Paganini gave recitals here on 10 and 11 September 1832, in the Green Row Rooms and the Theatre Royal.

Joseph Reinagle, violinist and composer of *Dumfries Races*, was born here in 1762 and died in Oxford on 12 November 1825.

Johann Strauss senior led his orchestra at a concert in the Portsmouth Theatre on 7 September 1838.

Freda Swain, composer and pianist, was born here on 31 October 1902.

Purbrook April Cantelo, soprano singer, was born here on 2 April 1928.

Romsey Harvey Grace, writer on music, editor and organist, was born here on 25 January 1874 and died in Bromley, London, on 15 February 1944.

Frederick Westlake, pianist and composer, was born here on 25 February 1840 and died in London on 12 February 1898.

Southampton William Sterndale Bennett, composer, pianist and conductor, frequently spent the summer here. He was residing at 13 Hanover Buildings in July 1853 when he was offered the conductorship of the Leipzig Gewandhaus Orchestra, which he was obliged to decline because of other engagements.

Charles Dibdin, composer, singer and writer, was born here in 1745 and died in London on 25 July 1814. His song *Tom Bowling*, for which he wrote both words and music, was introduced by him at the Lyceum Theatre in London on 7 December 1789.

Joseph Haydn stayed the night here during the middle of July 1794.

Franz Liszt played at a concert in the Royal Archery Rooms (demolished) on 19 August 1840.

Richard Mant, author of the hymn 'Bright the Vision That Delighted', was born here on 12 February 1776.

Dominic Muldowney, composer, was born here in 1952.

Niccolò Paganini gave a recital here on 6 March 1832. He returned later in the year and gave concerts in the Long Rooms on 30 and 31 August and 7 September.

Anastasia Robinson, Countess of Peterborough, soprano singer, died at Bevis Mount in April 1755. She is buried in Bath Abbey.

John Philip Sousa conducted his band at a concert in the Palace of Varieties on 27 January 1905. He gave two further concerts, in the

Palace of Varieties and the Hartley Hall, on 13 February 1911. He stayed the night at the South Western Hotel.

Johann Strauss senior stayed at the Star Hotel 2–3 September, 9–11 September and 26–9 September 1838. He led his orchestra at the Royal Victoria Assembly Rooms in concerts on 3 and 10 September and at a ball on 28 September.

John Brande Trend, authority on Spanish literature and music, was born here on 17 December 1887 and died in Cambridge on 20 April 1958.

Mathilde Verne, pianist, pupil of Clara Schumann, teacher of Solomon, the Queen Mother and John Gielgud, was born here on 25 May 1865 and died in London on 4 June 1936. She resided at 194 Cromwell Road, Kensington and Hillside, Ramsdell, Hampshire.

Adela Verne, pianist and composer, pupil of Paderewski, sister of Mathilde Verne, was born here on 27 February 1877 and died in London on 5 February 1952.

Isaac Watts, author of numerous familiar hymns, was born here on 17 July 1674. A plaque in Vincent's Walk commemorates his birthplace. He spent the first sixteen years of his life in Southampton, went to school in London for four years and then returned for a further two years before leaving altogether. During his final period in the city it is believed that he wrote three of his finest hymns, 'How Bright These Glorious Spirits Shine!', 'When I Survey the Wondrous Cross' and 'There Is a Land of Pure Delight'. According to tradition, the idea for the last of these came to him as he was gazing one summer's day across Southampton Water towards the meadows near Netley ('Sweet fields beyond the swelling flood/Stand dressed in living green'). The idea that the 'sweet fields' were on the Isle of Wight is less likely.

Southsea Houston Stewart Chamberlain, Wagner propagandist, husband of the composer's daughter Eva and, according to Hitler, 'the ideal Englishman', was born here on 9 September 1855 and died at Haus Wahnfried, Bayreuth, on 9 January 1927.

David Heneker, composer of *Half a Sixpence* and other successful musicals, was born here on 31 March 1906.

Alec Robertson, writer on music, was born here on 3 June 1892.

John Philip Sousa conducted his band at a concert in Portland Hall on 26 January 1905. He gave two further concerts in Portland Hall on 12 February 1911.

Warsash Adelaide Kemble, soprano singer, was born in London in 1814 and died at Warsash House on 4 August 1879.

Winchester Jeremiah Clarke, organist and composer of the *Trumpet Voluntary*, was organist of Winchester College 1692–5.

Martin Cooper, music critic and editor, was born here on 17 January 1910.

Joseph Haydn visited here during the middle of July 1794.

John Holmes, organist of Winchester Cathedral and composer of the madrigal *Thus Bonny Boots the Birthday Celebrated*, died here in 1602.

Randolph Jewett, organist and composer, was born in about 1603 and died here on 3 July 1675.

Franz Liszt played at a concert in the St John's Rooms on 19 August 1840.

E. H. Moberly, enterprising amateur conductor, was born here on 20 October 1849.

Niccolò Paganini gave recitals in the St John's Rooms on 5 March and 4 September 1832.

Lionel Power, composer, died here on 5 June 1445.

Francis Toye, writer on music, was born here on 27 January 1883 and died in Portofino, Italy, on 13 October 1964.

Geoffrey Toye, conductor and composer, brother of Francis Toye, was born here on 17 February 1889 and died in London on 11 June 1942.

Thomas Weelkes, composer and organist, was organist of Winchester College around 1600.

Samuel Sebastian Wesley, composer and organist, was organist of the cathedral and of Winchester College 1849–65. He resided at 8 Kingsgate.

William Whiting, author of the great hymn for seafarers, 'Eternal Father, Strong To Save', written in 1860, was master of Winchester College Choristers School for some twenty-five years before his death here on 3 May 1878.

Charles Lee Williams, conductor, composer and organist, was born here on 1 May 1853 and died in Gloucester on 29 August 1935.

Yately Edward Caswall, author of the hymns 'Bethlehem, of Noblest Cities', 'Jesu, the Very Thought of Thee' and 'When Morning Gilds the Sky', was born here on 15 July 1814.

HERTFORDSHIRE

Ayot St Lawrence George Bernard Shaw, dramatist, novelist and music critic, whose plays inspired music by Auric, Blitzstein, Honegger and most notably Straus's *Der Tapfere Soldat* and Frederick Loewe's *My Fair Lady*, resided at Shaw's Corner from 1906 until his death here on 2 November 1950. His ashes were scattered in the garden.

Edward Elgar was a guest here on 6 January 1920 and subsequent occasions.

Berkhamsted William Cowper, poet and hymn writer, was born here on 26 November 1731.

Andrew Davis, conductor, was born in Ashridge Hospital on 2 February 1944.

Borehamwood Thomas Beecham, conductor, impresario and patron of music, resided intermittently at Highfields, Borehamwood, from 1906 until after World War I.

Frederick Delius resided at Highfields during 1915, sketching *Eventyr* here. Peter Warlock called upon him at this time.

Broxbourne Guy Bolton, author and librettist, was born here in 1884. He often collaborated with Jerome Kern, for whom he wrote the song 'Look for the Silver Lining'.

Elizabeth Maconchy, composer, was born at Silverleys, Broxbourne, on 19 March 1907.

Bushey Henry Wilde, conductor and composer, was born here on 22 May 1822 and died in London on 13 May 1890.

Cheshunt Joseph Speaight, pianist and composer, was born in London on 24 October 1868 and died in Cheshunt on 20 November 1947.

Isaac Watts, hymn writer, lived at Theobalds, the country house of Sir Thomas and Lady Abney, 1712–35, also staying here frequently until his death in 1748. His hymns 'Jesus Shall Reign Where'er the Sun', 'The Heavens Declare Thy Glory, Lord' and 'Our God, Our Help in Ages Past' date from his time at Theobalds. The emendation 'O God, Our Help in Ages Past' was made by John Wesley in 1737.

Chorleywood Henry Wood, celebrated conductor, resided intermittently at Apple Tree Farm House, Chorley Common, 1918–35.

Leoš Janáček visited him here on 2 May 1926.

Harpenden Alan Hyde, virtuoso horn player, was born here on 14 July 1905.

Hatfield Dennis Brain, virtuoso horn player, was born in London on 17 May 1921 and died here on 1 September 1957, having crashed into a tree while driving from the Edinburgh Festival to his home at Craigmore, 37 Frognal, Hampstead.

Hertford Hubert Parry, composer, resided at St Holme, Bengeo, 1873–4.

Hertingfordbury Joseph Haydn stayed with Nathaniel Brassey at Roxford from 4 August to about 8 September 1791. He is thought to have written much of Symphony No 93 here and possibly parts of Nos 94 and 98. His notebook relates: 'Mr Brassey once cursed because he had too easy a time in this world.' Not only did he curse, Haydn added, he threatened to shoot himself, calling for pistols. It is not clear whether he was intending to use more than one pistol or whether he wished to select a particular firearm from his arsenal.

Highfield Elizabeth Poston, composer and pianist, was born here on 24 October 1905.

Knebworth James Oswald, composer and music publisher, who was born in Scotland in about 1710 and died in January 1769, is buried here.

Little Berkhamsted Thomas Ken, author of the hymns 'Awake, My Soul, and with the Sun' and 'Glory to Thee, My God, This Night', was born here in July 1637.

Preston Joseph Haydn came here on 14 November 1794 as a guest of Sir Walter Aston.

Radlett Alan Bush, composer, resided at Derwent, The Rose Walk, 1931–5. He then moved to 25 Christchurch Crescent, where he wrote *Wat Tyler, Men of Blackmoor, The Sugar Reapers, Voices of the Prophets, Byron Symphony* and *The Man Who Never Died.*

John Ireland stayed with him for a few months in 1940, later moving for a brief time to Clifton, Loom Lane.

Sacombe Green Michael Balfe, composer, resided at Rowney Abbey from 1864 until his death at Sacombe Green on 20 October 1870. He is buried in Kensal Green Cemetery, London. There is a tablet to his memory in Westminster Abbey, a statue in Drury Lane Theatre, a bust in the National Gallery in Dublin and a window in St Patrick's Cathedral, Dublin.

St Albans William Henry Bell, composer, was born here on 20 August 1873 and died in Cape Town on 13 April 1946.

David Munrow, conductor, music scholar and composer, died here in 1976. He resided at 48 Lancaster Road.

Shenley Eduard Speyer, businessman and patron of music, was born in Frankfurt-am-Main on 14 May 1839 and died at his home, Ridgehurst, Shenley, on 8 January 1934.

Edward Elgar came here on several occasions, notably in 1910 when he stayed and worked on his Violin Concerto. Richard Strauss was also a frequent visitor. He and Elgar dined with Speyer on 5 December 1902. Elgar and Percy Grainger were fellow guests on 9 July 1911. Other visitors to Ridgehurst included Frank Bridge and Adrian Boult.

Ware Simon Ives, organist and composer, was born here in 1600 and died in London on 1 July 1662.

ISLE OF WIGHT

Bonchurch Elizabeth Sewell, novelist and author of the hymn 'O Saviour! When Thy Loving Hand', who was born in Newport on 19 February 1815, resided for many years at Ashcliff, Bonchurch. She died here on 16 August 1906.

Brighstone Thomas Ken is thought to have written his hymn 'Awake, My Soul, and with the Sun' at Brighstone Rectory in 1667.

Carisbrooke Albert Midlane, author of the hymns 'Revive Thy Work, O Lord' and 'There's a Friend for Little Children', was born here on 23 January 1825 and died in Newport on 27 February 1909.

Cowes Albert Ketèlbey, composer of *In a Monastery Garden, In a Persian Market, Bells across the Meadows, In the Mystic Land of Egypt* and *In a Chinese Temple Garden*, died here on 26 November 1959. He resided in Appley Road.

Anne Shepherd, author of the hymn 'Around the Throne of God in Heaven', was born here on 11 November 1809 and died in Blackheath, Greater London, on 7 January 1857.

Ernest Winchester, organist and composer, was born here on 22 May 1854 and died in Bexley, Greater London, on 21 February 1916.

Freshwater Trevor Harvey, conductor, was born here on 30 May 1911.

Alfred Tennyson, poet, resided intermittently in Farringford from 1853 until his death at Aldworth House, Kingsley Green, West Sussex, on 6 October 1892.

William Sterndale Bennett was his guest here in January 1862; Charles Villiers Stanford, in December 1879; Hubert Parry, in January 1892.

Ralph Vaughan Williams wrote part of *Hugh the Drover* at Samatt House in August 1911.

Newport Gerald Abraham, writer on music, was born here on 9 March 1904.

Frederick George Baker, composer of the hymn tune *St Saviour*, often sung to 'I Sing the Almighty Power of God', was born here on 19 May 1839 and died in Shanklin on 10 March 1919.

Alexander Groves, part-author of the hymn 'Break Thou the Bread of Life', was born here in 1842 and died in Henley-on-Thames, Oxfordshire, on 30 August 1909.

Jemima Luke, author of the hymn 'I Think, When I Read That Sweet Story of Old', was born in London on 19 August 1813 and died in Newport on 2 February 1906.

Mary Maude was wife of the vicar of St Thomas's in 1847, when she wrote the hymn 'Thine for Ever! God of Love' expressly for the girls in her Sunday School class.

Ryde James Charles Beazley, pianist, violinist and composer, was born here in 1850.

Allen Blackall, composer, was born here on 13 November 1877 and died in Canterbury on 3 April 1963.

William Knyvett, composer, was born in London on 21 April 1779 and died in Ryde on 17 November 1856.

Johann Strauss senior led his orchestra at a concert here on 8 September 1838.

Emma Toke, author of the hymns 'Glory to Thee, O Lord', 'O Lord, Thou Knowest All the Snares' and 'Thou Art Gone Up On High', died here on 29 September 1878.

Sandown Henry Temple Leslie, composer of the hymn tune *Ephraim*, usually sung to 'Earth, Rejoice, Our Lord Is King!', was born in 1825 and died here on 5 May 1876.

Shanklin Moritz Rosenthal stayed at the Royal Spa Hotel in May 1910.

Ventnor Edwin Lemare, organist and composer of *Andantino in D Flat*, subsequently better known as *Moonlight and Roses*, was born at The Mount on 9 September 1865 and died in Los Angeles on 24 September 1934.

John Sterling, author of the hymn 'O Source Divine, and Life of All', died here on 18 September 1844.

Whippingham Henry Prothero, composer, was born here on 4 November 1848 and died in Cheltenham, Gloucestershire, on 25 September 1906.

Wootton Joseph Haydn stayed with the Governor of the Isle of Wight at Fernhill (demolished), Wootton Creek, during the middle of July 1794. He landed at Ryde, visited Newport and Carisbrooke Castle and embarked for Southampton from Cowes. 'The Isle of Wight is 64 miles in circumference,' he recorded in his notebook. Newport people 'mostly have black hair'.

Edward Elgar spent his honeymoon, in May 1889, at Shanklin and Ventnor.

Edvard Grieg took a short holiday on the Isle of Wight around 20 May 1888, enjoying 'the turbulent sea'.

Franz Liszt, having been sick while crossing the Solent, played at a concert in Ryde Town Hall on 18 August 1840, stayed briefly at the Star Hotel and, later in the day, played on a cottage piano in another concert, at the Green Dragon Hotel, Newport, where he stayed the night. He embarked the next day from Cowes for Southampton.

Richard Strauss, convalescing from an illness, stayed on the Isle of Wight in June and July 1903 and completed the *Domestic Symphony*.

KENT

Aldington Noël Coward, dramatist, actor, writer, composer, director and singer, resided intermittently at Goldenhurst Farm 1926–55. Visitors to the farm included Richard Rodgers, Richard Addinsell and Fritz Kreisler.

David Fanshawe, composer, explorer, conductor, music scholar and writer, resided 1963–71 at Bourne Tap, Aldington.

Ashford David Moule-Evans, composer, was born here on 21 November 1905.

Malcolm Sargent, conductor, was born at Bath Villas on 29 April 1895.

Eric Thiman, composer and organist, was born here on 12 September 1900.

John Wallis, mathematician and writer on musical acoustics, was born here on 23 November 1616 and died in Oxford on 28 October 1703.

Bearsted Robert Fludd, philosopher and writer on music, was born here in 1574 and died in London on 8 September 1637.

Bethersden Frederick Keel, baritone singer and composer of *Salt-Water Ballads*, was born on 8 May 1871 in London and died in 1950, residing at Fridland, Bethersden.

Boughton Malherbe Henry Wotton, poet and author of the hymn 'How Happy Is He Born and Taught', was born at Boughton Hall on 30 March 1568 and died at Eton in December 1639.

Brabourne Lees George Frideric Handel was a guest of Sir Wyndham Knatchbull at Mersham-le-Hatch.

Bridge Wolfgang Amadeus Mozart, together with his father, mother and sister, stayed at Bourne Place, Bourne Park, 25–30 July 1765. The nights of 24 and 30 July were spent in Canterbury, where they also went to the horse races. Mozart's last night in England appears to have been in Dover, from which the family embarked for Calais at 10am on 1 August. The crossing took three and a half hours.

Karol Szymanowski visited Joseph Conrad at Bishopsbourne in December 1920.

Broadstairs Richard Rodney Bennett, composer and pianist, was born here on 29 March 1936.

Jennifer Vyvyan, soprano singer, who created roles in Britten's *Gloriana, The Turn of the Screw, A Midsummer Night's Dream* and *Owen Wingrave*, was born here on 13 March 1925 and died in London on 5 April 1974. She resided at 59 Fitzjohns Avenue, Hampstead.

Brompton Charles Oakley, author of the hymn 'Hills of the North, Rejoice', was born here on 9 January 1832.

Canterbury Vincent d'Indy visited here in May 1887.

George Elvey, organist and composer, was born in Union Street on 27 March 1816.

Orlando Gibbons, composer and organist, died here on 5 June 1625 and is buried in the cathedral.

Christopher Hassall, author, dramatist, poet, librettist and actor, was born in London on 24 March 1912 and collapsed and died in a train on 25 April 1963. He resided at Tonford Manor, Canterbury. He wrote the librettos of Walton's *Troilus and Cressida*, Bliss's *Tobias and the Angel*, Malcolm Arnold's *Song of Simeon* and Ivor Novello's *Glamorous Night, Careless Rapture, The Dancing Years* and *King's Rhapsody*.

Herbert Irons, composer of the hymn tune *Southwell*, sung to 'Jerusalem, My Happy Home', was born here on 19 January 1834.

Isaac Nathan, composer, singer, writer on music and friend of Byron, was born here in 1792. He was run over and killed by a tram in Sydney, Australia, on 15 January 1864.

Niccolò Paganini gave a recital here on 23 August 1832.

Trevor Pinnock, keyboard player and conductor, was born here on 16 December 1946.

William Shrubsole, composer of the hymn tune *Miles Lane*, sung to 'All Hail the Pow'r of Jesus' Name', was born here in January 1759 and died in London on 18 January 1806. He is buried in Bunhill Fields. *Miles Lane*, published in 1779, was regarded by Elgar as the finest of all English hymn tunes. Vaughan Williams called Shrubsole one of those 'who get a glimpse of the eternal glory once in a lifetime for a few moments and, like Gerontius, are blinded by it and turn their faces away for ever; but in that one moment these Shrubsolian composers may have achieved something which neither Beethoven nor Bach could have bettered'.

Igor Stravinsky came here on 31 May 1963, visited the cathedral and had lunch with Kenneth Clark at Saltwood Castle.

Thomas Tallis, composer and organist, was a lay clerk of the cathedral around 1541–2.

John Ward, composer, was born here in September 1571 and died in 1638.

Thomas Young, alto singer, was born here in 1809 and died in London on 12 August 1872.

Chatham George Enescu conducted a concert here on 17 September 1947.

John Philip Sousa conducted his band at a concert in the Town Hall on 23 January 1905.

Percy Whitlock, organist and composer, was born here on 1 June 1903 and died in Bournemouth on 1 May 1946.

Dartford Ivor Gurney, composer and poet, was admitted to the City of London Mental Hospital on 21 December 1922 as a result of his experiences at Passchendaele. He died here on 26 December 1937, while Europe prepared once more to sacrifice its young men. Ralph Vaughan Williams visited him here.

Joseph Maas, tenor singer, was born here on 30 January 1847 and died in London on 16 January 1886. Massenet especially wrote for him the scena *Apollo's Invocation*, which received its first performance at the Norwich Festival on 16 October 1884.

Deal Edward Fitzwilliam, composer, was born here on 1 August 1824 and died in London on 20 January 1857.

John Ireland, composer, wrote his *Concertino Pastorale* at Comarques, High Street, in 1939.

Dover Charlotte Barnard, composer of *Come Back to Erin* and *Golden Days*, was born on 23 December 1830 and died here on 30 January 1869.

Edenbridge Walter Alcock, composer and organist, who played the organ at the coronations of Edward VII, George V and George VI, was born here on 29 December 1861 and died in Salisbury on 11 September 1947.

Richard Streatfield, writer on music, was born here on 22 June 1866 and died in London on 6 February 1919.

Eynsford Peter Warlock, composer and writer on music, and Ernest John Moeran, composer, resided at the house marked with a plaque, opposite The Five Bells in the main street, 1925–8.

Arnold Bax, William Walton and Constant Lambert visited them here.

Farningham William Stockley, organist and conductor, was born here on 1 February 1830.

Faversham Edward Hay, composer and organist, was born here on 19 April 1889.

Frederick Read, organist, conductor and composer, was born here in December 1857 and died in Chichester on 28 January 1925.

Five Oak Green Arnold Cooke, composer, moved to Phyllis Cottage, Whetsted Road, in 1963. Works written here include Symphonies Nos 2 and 3 and the Piano Quintet.

Folkstone Enrique Granados embarked from here at 2pm, on 24 March 1916, for Dieppe on board the ss *Sussex*, which an hour later was torpedoed and sunk by a German submarine. The composer and his wife were among those lost.

Gravesend Pocahontas, legendary North American Indian princess and heroine, the subject of several operas, was born in Virginia, USA, in 1595 and died in Gravesend in 1617. She was buried in St George's Church.

Nikolay Rimsky-Korsakov, then an 18-year-old sea cadet, was anchored here, November 1862–February 1863, on board the *Almaz*, which was being fitted with new masts; some of the work was also carried out at Greenhithe. He spent much of the time reading French and English authors, including Macaulay and John Stuart Mill. He was granted permission to visit London a few times and went to Westminster Abbey, the Tower of London and the Crystal Palace. While here, he completed the slow movement of his First Symphony. 'I wrote it without a piano (we had none); I think once or twice I contrived to play the entire piece at a restaurant on shore.'

Harbledown Aphra Behn, dramatist and novelist, whose plays inspired music by Arne, Banister, Blow and Purcell, was born here in December 1640 and died in London on 16 December 1689. For a revival of her *Abdelazer* at Drury Lane in April 1695, Purcell composed the *rondeau* that is the subject of Benjamin Britten's variations in *The Young Person's Guide to the Orchestra*. She may also have contributed to the libretto of Blow's *Venus and Adonis*.

Hilden Park William Cornyshe, composer, poet, dramatist and actor, born in London, is thought to have died here in about October 1523.

Ightham Bertram Luard-Selby, composer and organist, was born here on 12 February 1853 and died in Glanford Brigg, Lincolnshire, on 26 December 1918.

Maidstone Walter Gilbert was organist at the Old Collegiate Church 1859–66, during which time he composed the hymn tunes *Maidstone*, sung to 'Pleasant Are Thy Courts Above', and *Thanksgiving*, sung to 'Hark! The Song of Jubilee'.

John Jenkins, composer, was born here in 1592.

John Philip Sousa conducted his band at a concert here on 9 February 1905.

Margate James William Davison, music critic, was born in London on 5 October 1813 and died in Margate on 24 March 1885.

Alfred Deller, counter-tenor singer, was born here on 30 May 1912 and died in Bologna in 1979.

Michael Kelly, tenor singer, actor and composer, the first Don Basilio and Don Curzio in *La nozze di Figaro*, friend of Mozart and Sheridan, died here on 9 October 1826.

Niccolò Paganini gave a concert in the Royal Hotel on 27 August 1832.

John Sinclair, composer and tenor singer, pupil of Rossini — who wrote for him the part of Idreno in *Semiramide*, presented in Venice on 3 February 1823 — was born near Edinburgh on 9 December 1791 and died in Margate on 23 September 1857.

Ramsgate Francis Burnand, editor of *Punch* 1862–1906, librettist of Sullivan's *Cox and Box* and *The Contrabandista* (revised as *The Chieftan*), was born in London on 29 November 1836 and died on 21 April 1917, residing at 18 Royal Crescent, Ramsgate.

Felix Mendelssohn stayed with his wife's relations the Beneckes at their country home here from about 2–5 September 1846, working on the piano arrangement of *Elijah.*

Stephen Philpot, composer and conductor, was born in London on 12 August 1870 and died in Ramsgate on 12 October 1950, residing at Watchester Lodge, Watchester Avenue.

Arthur Sullivan, composer and conductor, stayed at 3 Sion Hill in 1866.

Rochester John Alleyn, composer, died in 1373 and appears to have come from Kent, for a while holding livings here.

Royal Tunbridge Wells Roy Douglas, composer, virtuoso orchestrator, music editor, whom Vaughan Williams consulted over many of his later compositions, and orchestrator of Chopin's *Les Sylphides* and Addinsell's *Warsaw Concerto*, was born here on 12 December 1907.

Tyrone Guthrie, theatre and opera director, was born here on 2 July 1900.

George Frideric Handel took the waters in 1734 and 1735. In August

1758 he came here to be treated by the eye surgeon John Taylor. It is believed that he stayed in a lodging-house, once the home of Lord Egmont, at Mount Pleasant. By now he had been blind for five years, and Taylor was unable to help him regain his sight. Taylor had carried out an operation on Johann Sebastian Bach in Leipzig at the end of March 1750, claiming it to be a success, although Carl Philipp Emmanuel Bach later stated that it was not only a complete failure, but had seriously undermined his father's health.

Annunzio Mantovani, conductor, who was born in Venice on 15 November 1905, died in Royal Tunbridge Wells on 29 March 1980.

John Philip Sousa conducted his band at a concert here on 9 February 1905.

St Margaret's at Cliffe Noël Coward, dramatist, actor, writer, composer, director and singer, resided intermittently at White Cliffs 1945–50.

St Peter's Edward Heath, statesman, author, yachtsman and conductor, was born at 1 Holmwood Villas, Albion Road, on 9 July 1916.

Seal Elizabeth Maconchy, composer, resided at Chart Corner, Seal Chart, 1932–41, writing here the String Quartets Nos 1, 2 and 3.

David Wooldridge, conductor, composer and writer on music, was born here in 1931.

Sevenoaks Samuel Lover, composer and author, resided during the 1860s at The Vine. His grandson Victor Herbert, composer, conductor and cellist, spent some of his early years with him here.

Alfredo Piatti, cellist, was a visitor to The Vine.

Sheerness Henry Russell, pupil of Rossini, father of Landon Ronald and composer of *Oh, Woodman, Spare That Tree, The Wreck of the Hesperus, Cheer, Boys, Cheer!* and *A Life on the Ocean Wave*, was born here on 24 December 1812.

Speldhurst Francis Pott, author of several well-known hymns, died here on 26 October 1909.

Sundridge Edward Perronet, author of the hymn 'All Hail the Pow'r of Jesus' Name', was born here in 1726 and died in Canterbury on 2 January 1792.

Tankerton Ethel Hobday, pianist, died here on 10 July 1947, residing at 26 St Anne's Road.

Tonbridge Jean Stewart, viola player, was born here on 17 February 1914. Among the numerous works dedicated to her is Vaughan Williams's Second String Quartet, 'For Jean on her birthday', a present for her twenty-ninth birthday.

Walmer Robert Bridges, poet, author of the hymns 'Love of Love, and Light of Light' and 'Rejoice, O Land, in God Thy Might', whose verses inspired works by Frank Bridge, Finzi, Gurney, Holst, Moeran, Parry, Stanford and Vaughan Williams, was born at Roselands, now a convent, on 23 October 1844.

Woodchurch Sydney Nicholson, organist and educationist, was born in London on 9 February 1875 and died in Woodchurch on 30 May 1947, residing at Myrtle Cottage.

SURREY

Ashtead Henry Purcell, composer, gave harpsichord lessons to Katherine Howard of Ashtead Manor 1693–5.

Banstead Geoffrey Bush composed his overture *Yorick*, in memory of Tommy Handley, in 1949 at his home, 21 Hill Side.

Hamilton Clarke, composer and conductor, died on 9 July 1912 in Banstead Hospital, to which he had been committed in 1901.

Mary Gabriel, composer, was born here on 7 February 1825 and died in London on 7 August 1877.

Walter Midgley, tenor singer, died at his home here on 18 September 1980.

Beare Green Charles Woodhouse, violinist, was born in London in 1879 and died here on 2 May 1939.

Brookwood Thomas Beecham, conductor, impresario and patron of music, died in St Marylebone, London, on 8 March 1961. He is buried in Brookwood Cemetery.

Camberley David Fanshawe, composer, explorer, conductor, music scholar and writer, spent his childhood at Cedar Cottage, Watchetts Drive.

Caterham Mátyás Seiber, composer, conductor, cellist and writer on music, who was born in Budapest on 4 May 1905 and died in South Africa on 24 September 1960, resided at 169 Stafford Road, Caterham, during the 1940s and, towards the end of his life, at 51 Stafford Road.

Chilworth Edward Elgar, composer and Master of the King's Music, used to visit his daughter, Mrs Samuel Blake, at Lockner, Chilworth.

Chipstead Edgar Cook, organist and composer, died at Newlands, Chipstead, on 5 March 1953.

Hermann Grünebaum, conductor, was born in Giessen, West Germany, on 2 January 1872 and died at Chipstead on 5 April 1954.

Chobham John Addison, composer, was born in West Chobham on 16 March 1920. His score for the film *Tom Jones* won the Hollywood Academy Award for 1963, and that for *Sleuth* received a nomination in 1972.

Claygate John Moody, opera director, was born here on 6 April 1906.

Dorking Alan Hacker, virtuoso clarinettist, was born at Southsea House, Dorking, on 30 September 1938. He spent most of his childhood at 18 Morella Road, Wandsworth Common, London.

Robert Müller-Hartmann, composer, was born in Hamburg on 11 October 1884 and died in Dorking on 15 December 1950.

Ralph Vaughan Williams, composer, resided at The White Gates (demolished), Nutcombe Lane, Westcott Road, Dorking, 1929–53. Works written here include *Job*, the Oboe Concerto, *The Pilgrim's Progress*, the arrangement of *Greensleeves, Serenade to Music*, Partita for Double String Orchestra, Romance for Harmonica, *Dona Nobis Pacem, O Taste and See, Three Songs from Shakespeare, Silence and Music* and Symphonies Nos 4, 5, 6 and 7. Gustav Holst, Arnold Bax, Gerald Finzi, Arthur Bliss and Elizabeth Maconchy were among the visitors to The White Gates.

Vaughan Williams earlier stayed in Dorking, at Glorydene, St Paul's Road, during the latter part of 1928.

East Molesey John Orlando Parry, pianist, singer and composer of humorous songs, was born in London on 3 January 1810 and died in East Molesey on 20 February 1879.

Egham John Monsell, poet and hymn writer, was vicar of Egham when his hymns 'O Worship the Lord in the Beauty of Holiness' and 'Fight the Good Fight with All Thy Might' were published in 1863.

Elstead Victor Beigel, pianist, singing teacher and instigator of the Musicians' Benevolent Fund, was born in London on 19 May 1870 and died in Elstead on 7 January 1930.

Alan Patrick Herbert, author, librettist and dramatist, was born here on 24 September 1890 and died on 11 November 1971. He resided at 12 Hammersmith Terrace, Hammersmith, London.

Epsom Gustave Becker, pianist and composer, was born in Richmond, Texas, on 22 May 1861 and died in Epsom on 25 February 1959.

George Caldbeck, composer of the hymn tune *Pax Tecum*, often sung to 'Peace, Perfect Peace, in This Dark World of Sin?', died here on 29 January 1918.

Maurice Miles, conductor, was born here on 25 February 1908.

Kathleen Riddick, conductor, was born here on 17 July 1907.

Esher Jacques Offenbach visited the exiled Queen Marie-Amélie, widow of Louis-Philippe of France, at Claremont, now a girls' school, on 17 June 1857. He brought with him his company, who had been playing at the St James's Theatre, and they performed here *Les Deux Aveugles*, *Croquefer* and *Dragonnette*. Marie-Amélie was so moved by this evocation of the spirit of her beloved Paris, that she burst into tears during the finale of *Dragonnette*.

Montague Phillips, composer, who was born in London on 13 November 1885 and died on 4 January 1969, lived in Esher for more than fifty years. He resided at Clare Cottage, Clare Hill. His light opera *The Rebel Maid*, in which his wife Clara Butterworth played Lady Mary Trefusis and which includes the song *The Fishermen of England*, was presented at the Empire Theatre on 12 March 1921.

Ewell Petula Clark, singer and actress, was born here in 1934.

Margaret Glyn, composer and music scholar, was born in Ewell on 28 February 1865, lived at The Well House and died here on 3 June 1946.

Henry Heron, composer of the *Cornet Voluntary*, resided here towards the end of the eighteenth century.

David Sydney Morgan, composer and conductor, was born here on 18 May 1932.

Ewhurst Stopford Brooke, author of the hymns 'It Fell upon a Summer Day', 'Let the Whole Creation Cry' and 'When the Lord of

273

Love Was Here', died here on 18 March 1916. He resided at The Four Winds.

Farnham Colin Campbell, composer and conductor, was born in London on 12 March 1890 and died in Farnham on 24 June 1953.

Joseph Haydn stopped for 'a good dinner at Feernham' on his journey from Winchester to London during the middle of July 1794. H. C. Robbins Landon feels that this would have been at The Bush, the town's coaching inn. Another of Farnham's inns was The Jolly Farmer, where William Cobbett was born in 1763. On 26 August 1794 Haydn went to stay with Sir Charles Rich at Waverley Abbey.

Peter Pears, tenor singer, for whom Benjamin Britten wrote many of his most important works, was born in Searle Road on 22 June 1910. He spent much of his childhood in Storrington, West Sussex.

Arthur Sullivan, composer and conductor, stayed at Brightwells, the home of Patrick Paget, in 1865.

Augustus Toplady, author of the hymn 'Rock of Ages', was born at 10 West Street on 4 November 1740 and died in London on 26 July 1778.

Forest Green Ralph Vaughan Williams, composer, resided at Leith Hill Place 1875–95. Over the following sixty years he often stayed here and took part in the Leith Hill Festival. He collected here the hymn tune *Forest Green*, sung to 'What Service Shall We Render Thee', in 1903; this was traditionally known as *The Ploughboy's Dream.*

Frimley Ethel Smyth, composer and author, who was born in London on 23 April 1858, resided at Frimhurst, Frimley, 1867–94. She then moved to One Oak, a cottage nearby, where she remained until shortly before World War I.

Godalming Ernest Irving, composer and conductor, was born in The Pound on 6 November 1878 and died on 24 October 1953 in London, where he resided at The Lawn, Ealing Green. As music director at Ealing Studios, he conducted Vaughan Williams's scores for *The Loves of Joanna Godden* and *Scott of the Antarctic*; the *Sinfonia Antarctica* is dedicated to him. Ireland's music for *The Overlanders* was also performed under his baton. As a composer, he wrote the scores for many films, most notably *Whiskey Galore!* Among other works dedicated to him are string quartets by Rawsthorne and Walton.

Philip Radcliffe, composer and writer on music, was born here on 27 April 1905.

Clement Scholefield, composer of the hymn tune *St Clement*, sung to 'The Day Thou Gavest, Lord, Is Ended', died here on 10 September 1904.

Peter Warlock, composer and writer on music, is buried in Godalming Old Cemetery.

Great Bookham Carl Schloesser, pianist and composer, was born in Darmstadt, West Germany, on 1 February 1830 and died in Great Bookham on 10 November 1913. He resided at Paddocks.

Guildford John Monsell, poet and hymn writer, was rector of St Nicholas's at the time of his death on 9 April 1875, when he fell from the roof of the church while inspecting rebuilding operations.

Ernest Read, educationist, conductor and gifted trainer of young orchestral musicians, was born here on 22 February 1879 and died in London on 9 October 1965. He resided at 151 King Henry's Road, Hampstead.

John Philip Sousa conducted his band at a concert here on 7 February 1905.

Pelham Grenville Wodehouse, novelist, dramatist and librettist, working notably with Jerome Kern, for whom he wrote the song 'Bill', was born here on 15 October 1881 and died in Long Island, New York, on 14 February 1975.

Haslemere Arnold Dolmetsch, music scholar and instrument maker, was born in Le Mans on 24 February 1858 and died at his home, Jesses, Haslemere, on 28 February 1940.

Holmbury St Mary William Murdoch, pianist and writer on music, was born in Bendigo, Australia, on 10 February 1888 and died in Holmbury St Mary on 9 September 1942. He resided at High Lawns.

Ralph Vaughan Williams spent part of the summer of 1928 at The Old Barn, where he put the finishing touches to *Sir John in Love*. Gustav Holst was a visitor here.

Limpsfield Frederick Delius, composer, who died in Grez-sur-Loing, near Fontainebleau, France, on 10 June 1934, was buried in the cemetery of St Peter's, Limpsfield, on 26 May 1935. An oration was delivered by Thomas Beecham before a large crowd of mourners, among whom were Vaughan Williams and many other prominent musicians. It had been the composer's wish that he be buried in a country churchyard in the south of England, and Limpsfield was selected by his friends Beatrice and May Harrison, whose mother had been buried in Limpsfield. The original burial in Grez, on 12 June 1934, was a contrastingly dismal occasion, attended by a mere handful of mourners who included Delius's amanuensis Eric Fenby and the conductor Otto Klemperer. 'Better that he had been left in that cold graveyard at Grez,' Fenby later wrote, 'over there by the wall amongst the peasants whom he had known, than that he should rest with strangers in a strange place even in his native land.'

Oskar

Michael Tippett, composer, resided here 1929–51. He was initially at Chestnut Cottage, in the grounds of Hazelwood Preparatory School, where he taught for three years. He was at Whitegates Cottage, Grant's Lane, 1932–8. In 1938 he moved into Whitegates, a house he had had built nearby in Grant's Lane; he remained there until 1951. Works completed at Whitegates include the Concerto for Double String Orchestra, *Fantasia on a Theme of Handel*, *A Child of Our Time*, *Boyhood's End*, *Plebs Angelica*, *The Weeping Babe*, First Symphony, *Little Music for String Orchestra*; much of *The Midsummer Marriage* was also written here.

Nutfield Wilfred Sanderson, composer of the songs *Drake Goes West*, *Friend o'Mine*, *Shipmates o' Mine*, *Up from Somerset* and *Devonshire Cream and Cider*, died on 10 December 1935. He resided at Lone Oak, Nutfield.

Oxted Gerrard Williams, composer, was born in London on 10 December 1888 and died in Oxted on 7 March 1947.

Reigate Kenneth Joseph Ricketts, better known as Kenneth Alford, composer of *Colonel Bogey*, *The Thin Red Line*, *On the Quarterdeck*, *The Great Little Army* and *The Standard of St George*, was born in London on 21 February 1881 and died at his home, The Ridge, Blackborough Road, Reigate, on 15 May 1945.

Howard Talbot, composer of musical comedies which include *The Belle of Brittany* and *The Blue Moon*, was born in Yonkers, New York, on 9 March 1865 and died in Reigate on 12 September 1928. He resided at 35 Croydon Road.

Shamley Green Godfrey Thring, author of a number of familiar hymns, died at Ploncks Hill on 13 September 1903.

Stanwell James Nares, organist and composer of the anthem *The Souls of the Righteous*, was born here in 1715 and died in London on 10 February 1783.

Sunbury Arthur Hutchings, writer on music and composer, was born here on 14 July 1906.

Tadworth Ernest Newman, eminent writer on music, died here on 7 July 1959.

Walton-on-Thames Julie Andrews, soprano singer and actress, was born at 6am on 1 October 1935 at Rodney House Maternity Home. She spent her childhood at Threesome (later Foursome), Burhill Road.

Arthur Sullivan, composer and conductor, stayed during the summer of 1895 at River House, where he began work on *The Grand Duke*. He again stayed here in the summer of 1900.

Weybridge Colin Davis, conductor, was born at 45 The High Street on 25 September 1927.

Joseph Haydn stayed with the Duke of York at Oatlands House (demolished) on 24 and 25 November 1791. 'On the 2 days we played music for 4 hours in the evening, that is from 10 o'clock to 2 o'clock, then we had supper and at 3 o'clock went to bed.' Having apparently heard the name of the house mentioned only by the aristocracy, the composer entered it in his notebook as 'Eatland'.

Arthur Sullivan, composer and conductor, often came here for the summer during his later years. In 1889 and 1890 he stayed at Grove House (demolished), where he worked on *Ivanhoe* and *The Gondoliers*, and, between 1891 and 1893, at Dorney House, where he wrote much of *Utopia Limited*.

Pietro Mascagni visited him here during the summer of 1893.

Windlesham George Elvey, organist and composer, died at his home, The Towers, on 9 December 1893. He is buried at St George's Chapel, Windsor.

Witley John Chandler, author of the hymn 'Christ Is Our Corner-Stone', was born here on 16 June 1806 and was vicar of Witley from 1837 until his death in Putney, London, on 1 July 1876.

Woking Adelina de Lara, pianist and composer, who died on 25 November 1961, spent her final years at Adelina's Cottage, Woking.

Julian Herbage, conductor and writer on music, was born here on 10 September 1904.

Ethel Smyth, composer and author, resided for her last thirty years at Coign, Hook Heath. She died here on 8 May 1944.

York Town Arthur Sullivan, composer and conductor, spent several of his early years at Albany Terrace, London Road. He rented the house next door in the summer of 1886, it having been offered to him purely by chance. Much of *The Golden Legend* was written in the second house.

EAST SUSSEX

Beckley Humphrey Searle, composer, pupil of Webern and writer on music, notably on Liszt, spent much of his later childhood at The Firs, Beckley.

Bexhill Ruth Gipps, composer and pianist, was born here on 20 February 1921.

Boarshead Noel Mewton-Wood, pianist, who was born in Melbourne, Australia, on 20 November 1922 and committed suicide in London on 5 December 1953, resided at Little Renby, Boarshead.

Brightling William Shield, composer, violinist and Master of the King's Music, died here on 25 January 1829.

Brighton William Havergal Brian, composer, resided at 14A Marine Square from October 1920 to the summer of 1922. Joseph Holbrooke, composer, resided in the same building during this period.

Frank Bridge, composer, was born in North Street on 26 February 1879.

Hyam Greenbaum, conductor, violinist and composer, was born here on 12 May 1901 and died in Bedford on 13 May 1942.

Edvard Grieg took part in a concert here in early December 1897.

Franz Liszt took part in concerts here on 25 and 26 September 1840.

Charles Neate, pianist and friend of Beethoven, was born in London on 28 March 1784 and died here on 30 March 1877. He gave the first performances in Britain of Beethoven's Fifth Piano Concerto and Weber's *Konzertstück*.

Ray Noble, bandleader and composer of *Goodnight, Sweetheart, Love Is the Sweetest Thing* and *The Very Thought of You*, was born here in 1907 and died in London on 2 April 1978.

Niccolò Paganini took part in concerts in the Theatre Royal on 7 and 9 December 1831 and in The Old Ship Hotel on 27 August 1832.

Alexander Reinagle, organist and composer of the hymn tune *St*

Peter, sung to 'How Sweet the Name of Jesus Sounds', was born here on 21 August 1799.

Gioachino Rossini was presented to George IV in the Pavilion on 29 December 1823. They met again, in London, during the early months of the following year and sang duets, the composer accompanying at the piano.

John Philip Sousa conducted his band at a concert in the Dome on 25 January 1905. He gave two further concerts in the Dome on 11 January 1911. He stayed the night at the Metropole Hotel.

Leo Stern, cellist, who, under the composer's baton, gave the first performance of Dvořák's Cello Concerto, on 16 March 1896 in London, was born here on 5 April 1862 and died in London on 10 September 1904.

Johann Strauss senior stayed at the Hotel Royal 4–6 September 1838. He led his orchestra at a concert on 6 September. He gave two further concerts, in the Town Hall, on 7 and 8 May 1849.

Arthur Sullivan, composer and conductor, stayed at 2 Adelaide Crescent in October 1891.

Georgina Weldon, soprano singer and composer, was born at Tooting Lodge, Clapham, on 24 May 1837 and died in Brighton on 11 January 1914.

Burwash Rudyard Kipling, poet and novelist, who was born in Bombay on 30 December 1865 and whose verses and tales inspired works by Bantock, Boughton, Elgar, Grainger, Koechlin, Martinu, Quilter, Sullivan, Vaughan Williams and Weill, resided at Bateman's from 1902 until his death on 18 January 1936.

Crowborough Peter Wishart, composer, was born here on 25 June 1921.

Eastbourne William Sterndale Bennett, composer, pianist and conductor, frequently spent the summer here. He composed *The May Queen* at The Gilbert Arms (demolished) in July and August 1858. In August 1870 he stayed at 2 Adelaide Terrace. He often went to the Sunday morning services at Willingdon, East Dean, Jevington and Westham.

Claude Debussy stayed from 24 July to the end of September 1905 at the Grand Hotel, where he put the finishing touches to *La Mer* and worked on *Images*. 'The sea displays herself here with a strictly British correctness,' he wrote to a friend. He found Eastbourne 'a pleasant, even charming spot . . . a lovely place to cultivate one's egotism'. He was pleased by the lack of noise; moreover, there were 'no musicians discussing painting, and no painters discussing music'. He saw only one person who was poor, although 'he, too, looked pretty comfortably off . . . they must hide the poor during the holiday season'. By the end of August he was suffering from neuralgia and was losing his taste for Eastbourne; the town now seemed 'silly, as these places sometimes are. I shall have to leave, because there are too many draughts and too much music.'

Alexander Glazunov conducted a concert of his works here on 26 November 1931.

Michael Head, composer, singer and pianist, was born here on 28 January 1900 and died in 1976. He resided at 38 Asmuns Hill, Finchley, London.

Herbert Oakeley, organist, music scholar and composer, died here on 26 October 1903. He resided at 38 Marine Parade, Dover.

John Philip Sousa conducted his band at a concert here on 8 February 1905. He gave two further concerts, in the Devonshire Park Floral Hall, on 10 January 1911. He stayed the night at the Grand Hotel.

Friston Frank Bridge, composer, resided at Friston Field, Old Willingdon Road, from 1923 until his death in Eastbourne on 10 January 1941. Works written during this period include *Oration, Phantasm, Rebus*, Third and Fourth String Quartets, Second Piano Trio and *Divertimenti. Enter Spring*, dating from 1927, was originally entitled *On Friston Down*.

Benjamin Britten visited him here for lessons.

Glyndebourne John Christie, who founded the famous opera house on his estate in 1934, died here on 4 July 1962.

Hastings Anthony Collins, conductor and composer, was born here on 3 September 1893 and died in Los Angeles in 1963.

Edward Dannreuther, pianist and writer on music, was born in Strasbourg on 4 November 1844 and died in Hastings on 12 February 1905.

John Philip Sousa conducted his band at two concerts in the Royal Concert Hall on 9 January 1911. He stayed at the Queen's Hotel.

Winifred Wagner, daughter-in-law of Richard Wagner and director of the Bayreuth Festival 1930–45, was born here on 23 June 1897 and died in Überlingen, West Germany, on 5 March 1980.

Thomas Attwood Walmisley, composer and organist, was born in London on 21 January 1814 and died in Hastings on 17 January 1856.

Ralph Vaughan Williams at his home in Dorking, where he lived for more than twenty years. The slippered master produced a stream of great works here, including the Fourth, Fifth and Sixth Symphonies. The White Gates, which unfortunately has been demolished, was only a few miles from Leith Hill Place, where the composer spent his childhood. The Leith Hill Musical Festivals, with which he was so closely associated, began in 1905, when the principal concert took place in what was later to become Dorking Fire Station (*Allan G. Chappelow, courtesy of Mrs R. Vaughan Williams*)

Arthur Sullivan, left, and probably his nephew Herbert, right, sit outside Booth Lodge, Crookham Road, Fleet, near Farnborough, where practically all of *The Yeomen of the Guard* was written during the summer of 1888. The composer was a Londoner, but he frequently spent his summers in this part of the country, either in rented houses, like Booth Lodge, or at the homes of friends. Some of his childhood was passed in nearby Wokingham; another attraction of the area was its nearness to Ascot, where a proportion of his large earnings annually found its way back into general circulation (*Courtesy of Peter Joslin*)

Frederick Delius spent most of his life abroad and died at his home in Grez-sur-Loing, France, on 10 June 1934. He was initially buried there, but his wife was persuaded to have him reinterred in Limpsfield, Surrey, on 26 May 1935. Two days later, she herself died and was buried next to him (*Author*)

Hellingly Richard Redhead, composer and organist, died here on 27 April 1901. His best known hymn tunes are No 76, sung to 'Rock of Ages, Cleft for Me', and No 46, sung to 'Bright the Vision That Delighted'.

Hove Luigi Arditi, conductor and composer of the waltzes *Il Bacio* and *Parla*, was born in Crescentino, Piedmont, on 22 July 1822 and died here on 1 May 1903. He resided at 14 Gwydyr Mansions.

Michael Costa, conductor and composer, was born in Naples on 4 February 1808 and died in Hove on 29 April 1884.

Antonín Dvořák stayed at 7 Victoria Mansions (now 7 Grand Avenue), the home of the publisher Henry Littleton, on 18 and 19 August 1885. 'The lovely view of the sea from my room, the sight of thousands of people swarming everywhere, the lovely English women bathing (*and publicly*), together with the men and children, and also a countless number of boats large and small, and a band playing Scottish folk-songs, and goodness knows what else besides — everything is enchantingly beautiful, so that nobody who has seen it can ever forget it.'

Hamilton Harty, composer and conductor, died at 33 Brunswick Square on 19 February 1941.

Herbert Menges, conductor, was born here on 27 August 1902 and died in London on 20 February 1972.

Roger Quilter, composer, was born at 4 Brunswick Square on 1 November 1877.

Henry Wood, celebrated conductor, resided intermittently at 4 Grand Avenue at the time of World War II.

Lewes William Havergal Brian, composer, resided June 1919–October 1920 at 8 St Anne's Crescent and Emscote, Prince Edward's Road.

Nicholas Yonge, singer and music editor, was born here and died in London in October 1619. He is buried at St Michael's, Cornhill.

Moulsecoomb William Havergal Brian, composer, resided at 130 Hillside from the summer of 1922 to the summer of 1927, during which period he wrote most of *The Gothic Symphony*.

Ore Scott Goddard, music critic, was born here on 15 September 1895.

Peacehaven Felix Powell, composer of the song *Pack Up Your Troubles in Your Old Kit-Bag*, published on 23 November 1915, shot himself to death on 10 February 1942 while residing at Harley House.

Ratton Village Arthur Goring Thomas, composer, was born at Ratton Park on 20 November 1850.

Rottingdean Rudyard Kipling wrote the hymn 'God of Our Fathers, Known of Old', published in *The Times* on 17 July 1897 and entitled 'Recessional', at The Grange, 49 North End Road, the home of his uncle Edward Burne-Jones. He shortly afterwards moved into The Elms, where he lived until 1902.

St Leonards John Philip Sousa conducted his band at a concert in the Royal Concert Hall on 24 January 1905.

Ticehurst Francis Pott, author of several well-known hymns, was curate here 1861–6, during which period were published 'Angel Voices, Ever Singing' and 'The Strife Is O'er, the Battle Done'.
John Bacchus Dykes, one of the world's greatest hymn composers, died here on 22 January 1876.

Tidebrook Michael Tippett, composer, resided at Tidebrook Manor 1951–60, during which time he completed *The Midsummer Marriage* and wrote *Fantasia Concertante on a Theme of Corelli*, the Piano Concerto, the Second Symphony and much of *King Priam*.

WEST SUSSEX

Amberley John Ireland, composer, used to come here frequently to enjoy the beautiful views across the meadows. His piano piece *Amberley Wild Brooks* dates from 1921.

Arundel David McCallum, violinist, leader of prominent British orchestras, died on 21 March 1972. He resided at 75 Maltravers Street.

Ashington John Ireland, composer, frequently stayed here. *A Legend*, for piano and orchestra, inspired by a walk to Harrow Hill, was written in Ashington in 1933. In 1949 he was at Merios Farm and, in the following year, at the Old Rectory.

Bognor Regis Eric Coates, composer, resided at The Holdinge, Aldwick Avenue, from 1952 until he had a fatal stroke here on 18 December 1957. He died three days later in Royal West Sussex Hospital, Chichester. He was cremated at Golders Green.

Bosham Isidore Godfrey, musical director of D'Oyly Carte Opera, was born in London on 27 September 1900 and died in September 1977. He resided at Little Saxons, Crede Close, Old Bosham.

Camelsdale Tobias Matthay, distinguished piano teacher, was born in Clapham on 19 February 1858 and died at his home, High Marley, Camelsdale, on 14 December 1945.

Chichester Leonard Bernstein conducted the British première of his *Chichester Psalms* in the cathedral on 31 July 1965.

Gustav Holst's ashes are buried in the north transept of Chichester Cathedral.

Thomas Kelway, organist and composer, died here on 21 May 1749.

Franz Liszt played at a concert in the Assembly Rooms on 17 August 1840.

John Marsh, composer, was born in 1752 and died here in 1828.

Niccolò Paganini gave recitals here on 12 and 13 September 1832 in the Assembly Rooms.

Thomas Weelkes, composer and organist, was organist of Chichester Cathedral from around 1602 until his death in London on 30 November 1623. In 1617 he suffered a loss in standing and income when the Bishop of Chichester declared him to be 'a common drunkard and a notorious swearer and blasphemer'. Gustav Holst wrote of Weelkes: 'No one in any age or country has expressed so many different ideas and moods in pure choral music.'

George Weldon, conductor, was born here on 5 June 1906.

John Weldon, organist and composer, was born here on 19 January 1676 and died in London on 7 May 1736.

Crawley Anne Wood, contralto singer, was born here on 2 August 1907.

Eastergate John Ireland, composer, frequently stayed here during the first decade of this century. His hymn tune *Eastergate* was published in 1906.

East Grinstead John Mason Neale was warden of Sackville College from 1846 until his death here on 6 August 1866. Author of many of the world's best known hymns, he wrote during this period 'All Glory, Laud, and Honour', 'Around the Throne of God a Band', 'Brief Life Is Here Our Portion', 'Christian, Dost Thou See Them', 'Come, Ye Faithful, Raise the Strain', 'Light's Abode, Celestial Salem', 'Jerusalem the Golden', 'O Come, O, Come, Emmanuel' and 'O Happy Band of Pilgrims'. His great carol 'Good King Wenceslas' was written in 1853.

East Preston Richard Walthew, conductor, composer and pianist, was born in London on 4 November 1872 and died in East Preston on 14 November 1951. He resided at 1 Clarence Drive.

Felpham William Blake lived in the cottage now known as Blake's House 1800–3, writing 'Jerusalem' during his last year here. Those who have set his poems to music include Bantock, Britten, Griffes, Hindemith, Holst, Ireland, Moeran, Parry, Quilter and Tippett.

Fittleworth Edward Elgar, composer and Master of the King's Music, resided intermittently at Brinkwells, near Bedham, 1917–21, writing here the Cello Concerto, Violin Sonata, String Quartet and Piano Quintet.

Monk's Gate The hymn tune *Monks Gate*, sung to 'Who Would True Valour See', was adapted in 1904 by Vaughan Williams from the folksong *Our Captain Calls All Hands On Board Tomorrow*, which was performed for him by a singer from Monk's Gate. He also collected here the words and music of *On Christmas Night All Christians Sing*, known as the *Sussex Carol*.

Rustington Hubert Parry, composer, resided intermittently from 1882 at Knight's Croft, where he died on 7 October 1918. He is buried in St Paul's Cathedral. The incidental music to *The Birds*, including the celebrated wedding march, was written here.

Selsey Eric Coates, composer, had country homes here for almost three decades. His first visit to Selsey was in 1922. 'How often have we blessed the day when we discovered this unpretentious village, with its bathing, its glorious beaches and its life-giving air, which three features are beyond the powers of man to despoil.' From the main street, he and his family, he later recalled, 'would walk the two minutes to the beach and bathe in waters as clear and almost as warm as you would find in any South Sea lagoon'. From 1923 to 1926 he was at Stonecracker, East Beach. He occupied Summer Days, The Crescent, East Beach, 1926–33, where he wrote *By the Sleepy Lagoon*. He was at Erivan, now Orchard Crown, Hillwood Road, 1933–7, where he orchestrated *The Three Men*. He was further inland, at Ivy Grange, Sidlesham, 1937–9, composing *The Enchanted Garden* here. After World War II he moved briefly, in 1947, to South Lodge, Selsey, and then to Tamerisk Lodge. He resided at Tamerisk Cottage 1948–52.

Shipley John Ireland, composer, is buried here, opposite the south door of Shipley Church.

Shoreham-by-Sea William Havergal Brian, composer, resided 1958–68 at 1 Marlinespike, where he wrote his Symphonies Nos 13–30, and, during his last four years, at 11 Atlantic Court, Ferry Road, where he completed Symphonies Nos 31 and 32. He died at Southlands Hospital on 28 November 1972 and was cremated in Worthing.

Southdean Albert Sammons, violinist, was born in London on 23 February 1886 and died in Southdean on 24 August 1957. He resided at Pembridge, North Avenue.

Southwick Clara Butt, contralto singer, who gave the first performance of Elgar's *Sea Pictures* at Norwich on 5 October 1899, was born at 4 Adur Terrace on 1 February 1873.

Storrington Arnold Bax, composer and Master of the King's and Queen's Music, spent the last twelve years of his life at the White Horse Hotel.
  John Ireland frequently visited him here.

Warnham Percy Bysshe Shelley, poet, whose verses inspired works by Bantock, Samuel Barber, Boughton, Havergal Brian, Alan Bush, Butterworth, Delius, Dieren, Elgar, Gounod, Hindemith, Howells, MacDowell, Miaskovsky, Parry, Quilter, Rakhmaninov, Respighi, Rubbra, Schumann, Stanford and Vaughan Williams, was born at Field Place on 4 August 1792 and drowned near La Spézia, Italy, on 8 July 1822. His heart is buried in St Peter's Church, Bournemouth.

Washington John Ireland, composer, resided at Rock Mill from 1953 until his death here on 12 June 1962. The contents of the house have been transferred to the John Ireland Memorial House, High Street, Steyning.
  Arthur Bliss, Geoffrey Bush, Alan Bush and William Alwyn were among those who visited Ireland at Rock Mill.

Wisborough Green Benno Schönberger, pianist and composer, pupil of Liszt and Bruckner, was born in Vienna on 12 September 1863 and died in Wisborough Green on 9 March 1930.

Worthing Engelbert Humperdinck stayed at 1 Canterbury Villas in September 1898, prior to attending the Leeds Festival.

Edward Lloyd, tenor singer, was born in London on 7 March 1845 and died in Worthing on 31 March 1927.

John Philip Sousa conducted his band at a concert here on 8 February 1905.

WALES

CLWYD

Abergele Charles Oakley, author of the hymn 'Hills of the North, Rejoice', died here on 16 September 1865.
Mervyn Roberts, composer, was born here on 23 November 1906.

Colwyn Bay Joseph Parry's *Blodwen* received its first stage performance here on 29 April 1919.

Corwen Felix Mendelssohn visited here on 24 August 1829; it seems likely that he stayed overnight.

Denbigh John Parry, known as 'Bardd Alaw', composer, singer and conductor, was born here on 18 February 1776 and died in London on 8 April 1851.

Ffynnongroew Osian Ellis, distinguished harpist, was born here on 8 February 1928.

Hawarden Edward White Benson, author of the hymn 'The Splendours of Thy Glory, Lord', was born in Birmingham on 14 July 1829 and died in Hawarden on 11 October 1896.

Holywell Felix Mendelssohn stayed here on 20, 21 and 27 August 1829. On 3 September he attended a dinner in Holywell that was given for John Taylor, his host at Rhyd-y-mwyn, where he was a guest 28 August–4 September.
Rowland Huw Pritchard, composer of the hymn tune *Hyfrydol*, frequently sung to 'Alleluya, Sing to Jesus', died here on 25 January 1887.

Llanarmon Dyffryn Ceiriog John Ceiriog Hughes, known as 'Ceiriog', poet, farmer, stationmaster and author of 'Men of Harlech' and 'God Bless the Prince of Wales', was born here in 1832 and died at Glyn Ceiriog in 1887.

Llangollen Felix Mendelssohn stayed here on 25 August 1829. 'No national music for me! Ten thousand devils take all nationalism! Now I'm in Wales, and dear me! A harper sits in the hall of every so-called inn, ceaselessly playing so-called national melodies; that is to say, the most shocking, vulgar, out-of-tune trash, with a hurdy-gurdy going *at the same time*! It's . . . already given me toothache . . . Anybody like myself, who can't stand Beethoven's national songs, should come here and listen to them bellowed out by rough nasal voices, accompanied in the most awkward manner, and keep his temper . . . I'm getting angry and will have to leave off writing for the while.' The composer discovered on the following morning that the harper who had caused him such discomfort was a barber.

While in this locality he went up 'a high mountain, with a ruined convent on the summit. From there, I looked round into the blue distance and into dark, lonely valleys at the mountain's foot, walked down to one of those still vales, with the walls and windows of an ancient abbey, covered and filled up with tender green trees; a noisy brook rushes by, stones and rocky fragments are scattered everywhere. The choir of the church has been turned into a stable, the altar is a kitchen; the fretted window-arches are covered over by the tops of the beeches that stand in the nave. The sky was a monotonous grey. I composed some music . . . It was a good day.' The ruins described here are possibly those of the Valle Crucis Abbey and Castell Dinas Bran.

William Sidney Gwynn Williams, conductor, writer on music, and composer of the songs *Duw Wyr, My Little Welsh Home, Y Tylwyth Teg* and *Gwladgarwr*, was born in Plas Hafod in 1896.

Mold John Ambrose Lloyd, composer of the hymn tunes *Wyddgrug, Eifionydd, Henryd, Whitford, Wynnstay, Groeswen* and *Cromer*, the song *Y Blodeuyn Olaf* and the anthem *Teyrnasoedd y Ddaear*, was born here on 14 June 1815 and died on 14 September 1874 in Liverpool, where he is buried.

Northop Edith Wynne, soprano singer and actress, known as 'The Welsh Nightingale', was born here on 11 March 1842 and died in London on 24 January 1897. Her sister Kate, a contralto singer, also born in Northop, was called 'The Welsh Linnet'.

Overton Mary Maude, author of the hymn 'Thine for Ever! God of Love', was born in London on 25 October 1819 and died here on 30 July 1913.

Rhosllanerchrugog William Davies, composer, was born at 13 Smith Street, Pentrefelin, in 1859 and died in London in 1907. His song *O Na Byddai'n Haf o Hyd* was composed one summer evening while he was walking along Palace Street.

Arwel Hughes, composer and conductor, was born here on 25 August 1909.

Rhos-y-madoc Caradog Roberts, organist and conductor, was born here on 31 October 1878. He later resided in Osborne Street.

Rhyd-y-mwyn Felix Mendelssohn stayed with John Taylor and his family at Coed Du, now a hospital, 28 August–4 September 1829. 'My stay at the Taylors' was one of those times of which I shall never lose the flowery memory, and I shall always recollect the meadows and woods, the rivulet with its pebbles and rustling sound; we have become friends, I think, and I am truly fond of the girls and believe that they like me too, for we were very happy together. To them I owe three of my best piano pieces.'

Each of the *Three Fantasies*, Op 16, is dedicated to one of the Taylor daughters. The *Andante and Allegro in A minor* was written for the youngest, Anne; the *Capriccio in E minor*, for the eldest, Honoria; the *Andante in E major*, for the middle sister, Susan. Susan was Mendelssohn's favourite — 'She is *very* pretty' — and he took many rides and walks with her. They often stopped by the rivulet, on the Coed Du estate, that he said he would never forget. Her piece is subtitled *The Rivulet*, which the composer described as 'flowing and quiet and drowsily simple'.

Works that occupied his thoughts while he was here were the *Reformation Symphony, Scottish Symphony* and *Fingal's Cave*, although it seems unlikely that anything was committed to paper; part of the String Quartet, Op 12, seems, however, to have been written at Coed Du.

'I do nothing but flirt, and that in English!' he told his parents. The time went quickly, and he was sorry to leave. 'I drove away in the evening; the lights in the house sparkled through the bushes in the distance; in my open carriage I passed by several favourite places, the gentle rivulet already mentioned, the last hedge of the property, and then off I went at furious English speed.'

Ruabon John David Edwards, who was born in Dyfed on 19 December 1805, was vicar of Rhosymedre at the time he composed the hymn tune *Rhosymedre*, sung to 'Author of Life Divine'.

John Parry, blind harpist, whose playing inspired Thomas Gray to complete his poem 'The Bard', died here on 7 October 1782.

Ruthin Joseph David Jones, composer of the hymn tune *Gwalchmai*, sung to 'King of Glory, King of Peace', died here on 17 September 1870.

St Asaph Felix Powell, composer of the song *Pack Up Your Troubles in Your Old Kit-Bag*, was born here in 1878.

Wrexham Reginald Heber, author of numerous memorable and poetic hymns, visited his father-in-law Dr Shipley, Dean of St Asaph's and vicar of Wrexham, at Whitsun 1819. During the Saturday before Whit Sunday, Dr Shipley asked Heber for 'something for them to sing in the morning'. The author thereupon sat down and in a short time wrote out the hymn 'From Greenland's Icy Mountains', while his father-in-law conversed with friends on the other side of the room. The hymn was printed in Wrexham that evening and sung in St Asaph's on the following morning.

Elizabeth Randles, prodigy, who gave her first public piano recital at the age of one year, was born here on 1 August 1800 and died in Liverpool in 1829.

DYFED

Aberystwyth Béla Bartók took part in a chamber concert at the university on 16 March 1922, for which he was paid £15. He wrote to his mother: 'Here I am, on the west coast of England, or rather, of Wales. The 2 huge windows of my room look out over the sea — down below the waves roar, and it's marvellously sunny.' Apart from performing a Beethoven piano trio, Bartók also played some of his own works. At the conclusion of one of these, Walford Davies, the Professor of Music, was heard to exclaim: 'Perfectly baffling!'

Richard Samuel Hughes, composer of the songs *The Inchcape Bell, Y Dymestl, Llam y Cariadau, Arafa Don, Elen Fwyn* and *Suo Gan*, was born here on 14 July 1855 and died on 5 March 1893 in Bethesda, Gwynedd, where he is buried.

Ammanford Rae Jenkins, conductor, was born here on 19 April 1903.

Irwyn Walters, organist, conductor and composer, was born here on 6 December 1902.

Blaenannerch John Thomas, composer of the hymn tune *Blaencefn*, was born here on 11 December 1839.

Burry Port Tom Williams, baritone singer, was born here on 2 August 1902.

Capel Dewi Dafydd ap Gwilym, poet, whose verses have inspired works by countless Welsh composers, is thought to have been born in Brogynin in about 1340.

Cardigan David Lloyd-Jones, conductor, who was born in London on 19 November 1934, spent much of his childhood here.

Carmarthen Henry Brinley Richards, composer of *God Bless the Prince of Wales*, and friend of Chopin, was born in Hall Street on 13 November 1817 and died in London on 1 May 1885. He is buried in Brompton Cemetery.

Colby Catherine Barlow, later Lady Hamilton, keyboard player, whom Leopold Mozart praised, but who 'trembled at having to play in front of Wolfgang', was born here in about 1738 and died at Portici, near Naples, on 27 August 1782.

Cwm Cynfelin Isaac Williams, poet and author of the hymn 'Be Thou My Guardian and My Guide', was born here on 12 December 1802.

Cynwyl Elfed David Pughe Evans, tenor singer and composer of the songs *Hyd Fedd Hi gar yn Gywir*, *Y Ddwy Delyn* and *Cymru fy Ngwlad*, was born here in 1866.

Howell Elvet Lewis, poet and hymn writer, was born here on 14 April 1860 and died on 10 December 1953. He resided at Erw'r Delyn, Penarth, and is buried at Blaen-y-coed.

Devil's Bridge Geoffrey Bush composed his *Music for Orchestra* in 1967 at Cae Bach, Devil's Bridge. One of the work's themes spells out, in German notation, the name of the cottage.

Laugharne Dylan Thomas, poet, whose verses have inspired works by numerous composers and whose death in New York on 9 November 1953 is commemorated by Stravinsky's *In Memoriam Dylan Thomas*, Elisabeth Lutyens's *Valediction* and Daniel Jones's Fourth Symphony, resided here intermittently for the last fifteen years of his life. He is buried at St Martin's.

Llandovery William Williams, poet and hymn writer, was born at Cefn-y-coed on 11 February 1717. In 1748 he moved to Pantycelyn, Pentre-tŷ-gwyn, where he died on 11 January 1791. His great hymn 'Arglwydd, Arwain Trwy'r Anialwch', was published in 1745; it first appeared in English in 1771, as 'Guide Me, O Thou Great Jehovah', translated by Peter Williams. William Williams made his own translation a year later, though retaining in its entirety Peter Williams's version of the first verse. His other outstanding hymn, 'Dros y Bryniau Tywyll Niwliog' ('O'er the Gloomy Hills of Darkness'), was published in 1772.

Llanelli Donald Swann, composer and entertainer, was born on 30 September 1923 at 33 Coleshill Terrace.

Llangranog Edward Elgar, composer and Master of the King's Music, took a holiday at 'Llangringoggywoggypygwgssill', as he called it, in August 1901. During his stay, he heard a choir singing a melody that he later used in his *Introduction and Allegro*.

Milford Haven Helen Watts, contralto singer, was born here in December 1927.

Newcastle Emlyn David Emlyn Evans, composer of the hymn tunes *Eirinwg* and *Trewen* and the songs *Hen Wlad y Menyg Gwynion* and *Bedd Llywelyn*, was born in Pen'ralltwen on 21 September 1843. He is buried in Llandyfriog.

Pembroke Daniel Jones, composer, was born at Bank House, Main Street, on 7 December 1912. The bulk of his music, including the nine symphonies, has been written in Swansea.

Penllwyn John Roberts, known as 'Ieuan Gwyllt', composer of the hymn tunes *Moab*, often sung to either 'Thy Way, Not Mine, O Lord' or 'Who Dreads, Yet Undismayed', *Ardudwy*, often sung to 'When By Fear My Heart Is Daunted', *Liverpool, Rheidol, Lledrod* and *Llantrisant*, was born at Tanrhiwfelin on 27 December 1822.

St David's Thomas Tomkins, composer and organist, pupil of William Byrd, was born here in 1571 or '72.

Strata Florida Dafydd ap Gwilym, poet, whose verses have inspired works by countless Welsh composers, died towards the end of the fourteenth century and is presumed to be buried in Strata Florida Abbey.

Whitland William Mathias, composer, was born here on 1 November 1934.

MID GLAMORGAN

Aberdare John Philip Sousa conducted his band at a concert in the Market Hall on 19 January 1911.

Bargoed Alun Hoddinott, composer, was born here on 11 August 1929.

Bridgend W. T. Rees, composer, was born here in 1838.

John Thomas, harpist to Queen Victoria, conductor and composer, was born here on 1 March 1826. In 1861, at the Aberdare Eisteddfod, he received the title 'Pencerdd Gwalia'.

Thomas Thomas, harpist and composer, brother of John Thomas, was born here in 1829 and died in Ottawa in May 1913.

Cilfynydd Geraint Evans, celebrated baritone singer, was born here on 16 February 1922.

Cymmer Tudor Davies, tenor singer, was born here on 12 November 1892 and died at Penallt, Gwent, on 2 April 1958.

Dowlais Evan Thomas Davies, composer of the songs *Ynys y Plant* and *Baled Rhyfel Glyndwr*, was born here in 1878.

Harry Evans, conductor and composer, was born in Russell Street on 1 May 1873 and died on 23 July 1914 in Liverpool, where he is buried in Smithdown Road Cemetery.

John Hughes, composer of the great hymn tune *Cwm Rhondda*, sung to 'Guide Me, O Thou Great Jehovah', was born here on 22 November 1873.

Eos Morlais, tenor singer, was born here in 1841 and died in 1892. He is buried in Aberdulais, West Glamorgan.

Hirwaun David Wynne, composer, was born here on 2 June 1900.

Llangynwyd Will Hopkin, composer of *Idle Days in Summertime* and *Bugeilio 'r Gwenith Gwyn (Watching the Wheat)* and lover of the Maid of

Cefn Ydfa, was born in Llangynwyd in about 1700 and died here on 19 August 1741. Both he and the Maid are buried at Llangynwyd Church.

Llantwit Fardre John Hughes, who resided in Llantwit Fardre from 1874 until his death here on 14 May 1932, composed the hymn tune *Cwm Rhondda*, sung to 'Guide Me, O Thou Great Jehovah', which was first performed at the Baptist Singing Festival — the Cymangfa Ganu — in Pontypridd in 1905.

Merthyr Tydfil Joseph Parry, composer of *Blodwen*, the first opera in Welsh, the songs *Myfanwy, Y Marchog, Baner ein Gwlad, Yr Eos, Y Bachgen Dewr* and *Y Gardotes Fach* and the hymn tunes *Aberystwyth*, usually sung to 'Beth Sydd i mi yn y Byd' or 'Jesu, Lover of My Soul', *Merthyr Tydvil*, usually sung to 'He Dies! The Friend of Sinners Dies!' or 'These Things Shall Be! A Loftier Race', and *Dinbych*, sung to 'Thou Judge of Quick and Dead', was born at 2 Chapel Row, Cyfarthfa, on 21 May 1841.

John Philip Sousa conducted his band at a concert in the Drill Hall on 19 January 1911. Reaching the climax of the programme, he launched into *The Stars and Stripes Forever*, at which the conducting-stand collapsed through the stage, and he disappeared from sight, landing in a pile of debris and sending up clouds of dust. He later recalled: 'It is a breath-snatching sensation to fall 7 feet below the floor with nothing to catch on to.' However, sturdily built and not unlike Teddy Roosevelt in physique, he at once extricated himself from the wreckage, clambered up on to the stage and, in the spirit of San Juan Hill, bowed to the audience and said: 'We will now continue.' From a point of comparative safety, he then restarted the march and brought the concert to a triumphant conclusion.

Pontypridd Evan and James James were residing in Mill Street when they wrote *Hen Wlad fy Nhadau (Land of My Fathers)* one Sunday afternoon in January 1856. Evan, the father, wrote the words; James, the son, composed the melody. There is a plaque on their house, and in Ynysangharad Park stands a statue of them both.

Porth Geraint Jones, organist and harpsichordist, was born here on 16 May 1917.

Tonpentre Cory Workmen's Silver Band was formed here in 1884, originally as the Ton Temperance Band. It was subsidized by Sir Clifford Cory in 1895.

Tonypandy Megan Foster, soprano singer, was born here on 16 July 1898.

Tonyrefail Francis Russell, tenor singer, was born here on 12 December 1896.

Trecynon Griffith Rhys Jones, conductor, known as 'Caradog', was born here on 21 December 1834. There is an imposing statue of him in Aberdare.

Treforest Morfydd Llwyn Owen, composer and mezzo-soprano singer, was born here on 1 October 1891 and died in Swansea on 7 September 1918. She is buried in Oystermouth.

Lucas Williams, bass-baritone singer, was born here on 17 February 1852.

Tylorstown Mansel Thomas, conductor and composer, was born here on 12 June 1909.

Wick Robin Orr composed his Third Symphony at West House, Wick.

Ystrad Mynach Mervyn Burtch, composer, was born at 7 Davies Street on 7 November 1929.

SOUTH GLAMORGAN

Barry Robert Tear, tenor singer, was born here on 8 March 1939.

Grace Williams, composer, was born in Barry on 19 February 1906 and died here on 10 February 1977.

Cardiff Ivor Atkins, composer, organist and conductor, was born here on 29 November 1869. He was appointed organist of Worcester Cathedral in 1897, a post he retained until 1950. During that period he conducted the Three Choirs Festival when it was held in Worcester. He was friendly with Elgar, who dedicated to him *Pomp and Circumstance March* No 3. He died in Worcester on 26 November 1953.

Owain Arwel Hughes, conductor, was born here on 21 March 1942.

Ivor Novello, composer, dramatist, singer and actor, was born at Llwyn-yr-Eos, 95 Cowbridge Road, on 15 January 1893. His mother was the conductor and pianist Clara Novello Davies. The family later moved to 11 Cathedral Road.

John Philip Sousa conducted his band at a concert in Park Hall on 31 January 1905. He gave a further concert, in the Palace Theatre, on 21 January 1911.

Alec Templeton, blind pianist and composer of *Bach Goes to Town*, was born here on 4 July 1910 and died in Connecticut in March 1963.

Cowbridge Gabriel Fauré stayed at Llandough Castle, the home of the singer Elizabeth Campbell Swinton, in August 1898, composing part of his *Seventh Nocturne* here.

Penarth Haydn Draper, clarinettist, was born here on 21 January 1889 and died in London on 6 November 1934.

Kenton Emrys-Roberts, composer of incidental music for *Poldark* and other television programmes and films, was born here on 16 January 1923.

Joseph Parry, composer of *Blodwen*, the first opera in Welsh, the songs *Myfanwy, Y Marchog, Baner ein Gwlad, Yr Eos, Y Bachgen Dewr* and *Y Gardotes Fach* and the hymn tunes *Aberystwyth*, usually sung to 'Beth Sydd i mi yn y Byd' or 'Jesu, Lover of my Soul', *Merthyr Tydvil*, usually sung to 'He Dies! The Friend of Sinners Dies!' or 'These Things Shall Be! A Loftier Race', and *Dinbych*, sung to 'Thou Judge of Quick and Dead', died here on 17 February 1903. He resided at Cartref, Penarth.

WEST GLAMORGAN

Birchgrove Idris Lewis, conductor, and composer of *Bugail Aberdyfi*, was born here in 1888 and died in 1952.

Briton Ferry John Myrddin, tenor singer, was born here on 6 April 1901.

Cymmer Trefor Jones, tenor singer, was born here on 27 August 1901.

Landore David Hughes, baritone singer, was born here in 1863 and died on 18 November 1921. He is buried at Cwmgelli, Treborth.

Neath Jeffrey Lewis, composer, was born here on 28 November 1942.

Coed Du, Rhyd-y-mwyn, Clwyd, where Felix Mendelssohn stayed with the Taylor family in August 1829. His visit brought him some of the happiest moments of his life, expressed most notably in the piano piece *The Rivulet*, which was inspired by rambles along the Leet with one of the Taylors' pretty daughters. Coed Du is now a hospital (*J. Glynn Morris*)

Pant-y-celyn, the home of William Williams in Dyfed (*Welsh Tourist Board*)

Ivor Novello, who was born in Cowbridge Road, Cardiff, is pictured here with Dennis Price and Gisèle Préville, the stars in the film version of *The Dancing Years*, which was released in 1950, a year before the composer's death. His mother, Clara Novello Davies, was a distinguished choral conductor and singing teacher. Their house in Cowbridge Road was called 'Llwyn-yr-Eos' — 'Home of the Nightingales' (*Archives Department, Chappell International*)

Gabriel Fauré stayed here, at Llandough Castle, near Cowbridge, South Glamorgan, in August 1898 as the guest of Mrs George Campbell Swinton. Part of his Seventh Nocturne was composed during this visit. Mrs Campbell Swinton was a singer; her husband was an officer in the 71st Highland Light Infantry (*Royal Commission on Ancient & Historical Monuments in Wales*)

Pontardawe Ben Davies, tenor singer, was born here on 6 January 1858 and died in Oakhill, Somerset, on 28 March 1943. He took the title role in Arthur Sullivan's *Ivanhoe*, produced at the Royal English Opera House, now the Palace Theatre, in London on 31 January 1891.

Resolven David Evans, music scholar and composer of the hymn tunes *Pisgah*, sung to 'Unto Mary, Demon-Haunted', *Charterhouse*, usually sung to 'O Perfect Love, All Human Thought Transcending', *Maldwyn*, often sung to 'With Jesus for Hero, for Teacher and Friend', and *Yn y Glyn*, sung to 'Cilio Mae fy Hen Gyfeillion' or 'Son of God, Eternal Saviour', was born here on 6 February 1874 and died in Rhosllanerchrugog on 17 May 1948.

T. Hopkin Evans, conductor and composer, was born here in 1879 and died in Liverpool in 1940, being buried in Resolven.

Skewen David de Lloyd, composer and music scholar, was born here on 30 April 1883 and died in Aberystwyth on 20 August 1948.

Swansea David Pughe Evans, tenor singer and composer of the songs *Hyd Fedd Hi gar yn Gywir, Y Ddwy Delyn* and *Cymru fy Ngwlad*, died at his home in Eaton Crescent on 3 February 1897. He is buried in The Mumbles.

Cyril Jenkins, composer, was born here on 9 October 1889 and died in Hove, East Sussex, on 15 March 1978.

John Philip Sousa conducted his band at two concerts in the Albert Hall on 20 January 1911. He stayed the night at the Metropole Hotel.

Dylan Thomas, poet, whose verses have inspired works by numerous composers, was born at 5 Cwmdonkin Drive on 27 October 1914.

Ynysmeudwy Thomas Williams, composer of the hymn tune *Ebenezer*, sometimes sung to 'Through the Night of Doubt and Sorrow', was born here in 1869 and died in Llanelli on 24 April 1944.

Ystalyfera David Vaughan Thomas, music scholar, poet and composer of the song cycle *Saith o Ganeuon* and the songs *Berwyn, Can y Bardd wrth Farw* and *Enter These Enchanted Woods*, was born here on 15 March 1873 and died in Johannesburg on 15 September 1934. He is buried in Oystermouth.

GWENT

Blaina Arthur Fear, baritone singer, was born here in 1902.

Parry Jones, tenor singer, was born here on 14 February 1891 and died on 26 December 1963 in London, where he resided at 185 Old Brompton Road.

Monmouth Matilda Wilson, contralto singer, was born here on 7 April 1860 and died in Boscombe, Dorset, on 1 December 1918.

Newport Richard Roderick-Jones, composer and conductor, was born here on 14 November 1947.

John Philip Sousa conducted his band in a concert at the Stow Hill Rink on 21 January 1911. He stayed the night at the King's Head.

Albert Williams, composer and conductor, was born here on 14 March 1863 and died in Southsea, Hampshire, on 11 February 1926.

Pontnewynydd Gwyneth Jones, distinguished soprano singer, was born at Glenburn, Pentrepiod, on 7 November 1936. She spent much of her childhood at 81 Waunddu, Pontnewynydd.

Rhymney Tom Price, composer, was born here in 1857.

Tredegar William Aubrey Williams, composer, was born here on 28 July 1834 and died in Plymouth, Pennsylvania, on 3 July 1891.

GWYNEDD

Bala Rowland Huw Pritchard, composer of the hymn tune *Hyfrydol*, frequently sung to 'Alleluya, Sing to Jesus', was born in Graienyn on 14 January 1811.

Bangor Felix Mendelssohn stayed here on the night of 22 August 1829. It was his intention to visit Ireland, but the weather dissuaded him. 'Summer's gone, and we haven't had a single summer's day. Yesterday was a good day; that is to say, I got wet only three times, kept my cloak around my shoulders, and several times saw the sun through the clouds. A furiously driving storm has been blowing almost without interruption for four weeks . . . The trip to Ireland dissolved in Bangor and on the Isle of Anglesey. In spite of all the rain, I kept thinking I'd go over for a few days; then the steamers arrived, having been fifteen hours at sea instead of six, and when the seasick passengers came tottering off, wet, weak and swearing, I at once booked a seat on the coach. I've fought a good fight against the weather . . . But that's the end of it.'

William Shrubsole, composer of the hymn tune *Miles Lane*, sung to 'All Hail the Pow'r of Jesus' Name', was organist of the cathedral 1782–4. He was dismissed for 'frequenting conventicles'.

Beddgelert Felix Mendelssohn came here, from Bangor via Caernarfon, on 23 August 1829. He also visited the Vale of Ffestiniog.

Bethesda David Ffrangcon-Davies, baritone singer, was born here on 11 December 1855 and died in London on 13 April 1918.

John Henry Roberts, composer, was born here on 31 March 1848 and died in Liverpool on 30 July 1924.

Edward Stephen, known as 'Tanymarian', conductor, singer, poet, geologist and composer of *Ystorm Tiberias*, the first oratorio in Welsh, and the hymn tune *Tanymarian*, died on 10 May 1885 and was buried at Llanllechid.

Betws-y-coed Alfred Rodewald, conductor and patron of music, resided intermittently at Minafon, Betws-y-coed.

Edward Elgar was a frequent guest, writing much of *The Apostles* here in July 1903.

Caeathraw William Owen, who was born in Bangor on 12 December 1813 and died in Caernarfon on 20 July 1893, composed the hymn tune *Bryn Calfaria*, sung to 'Gwaed y Groes Sy'n Codi Fynny', while residing in Caeathraw, where he spent much of his life.

Caernarfon John Henry Roberts, composer, resided at 2 Uxbridge Square during the 1890s.

Capel Curig Felix Mendelssohn visited here on 23 August 1829; it seems likely that he stayed overnight.

Conwy Felix Mendelssohn stayed here on the night of 26 August 1829. 'I arrived perhaps wetter than I'd ever been in my entire life.'

Dyffryn Ardudwy Meirion Williams, composer and pianist, was born here on 19 July 1901.

Ffestiniog Edward Stephen, known as 'Tanymarian', conductor, singer, poet, geologist and composer of *Ystorm Tiberias*, the first oratorio in Welsh, and the hymn tune *Tanymarian*, was born in Rhyd-y-sarn in 1822.

Harlech Margaret More, composer, was born here on 26 June 1903.

Llandderfel Edward Jones, harpist and sometime Bard to the Prince of Wales, was born here on 29 March 1752 and died in London on 18 April 1824.

Llanddoget John David Edwards, composer of the hymn tune *Rhosymedre*, sung to 'Author of Life Divine', died in Llanddoget Rectory on 24 November 1885.

Llanfechell Robert Williams, blind basket-maker and composer of the hymn tune *Llanfair*, often sung to 'All the Toil and Sorrow Done, Alleluia!', was born at Mynydd Ithel, near Llanfechell, in 1781 and died there in 1821.

Llanfrothen J. R. Jones, who was born in 1762 and died in 1822, was minister here at the time he wrote the hymn tune *Ramoth*, sung to 'Christ Is Our Corner-Stone' and named after the nearby chapel.

Llangelynin John Williams, composer of the hymn tune *Brynhyfryd*, sung to 'Now Praise We Great and Famous Men', was born here on 26 December 1740 and spent much of his life in Dolgellau. He died on 11 March 1821. Lloyd George once described *Brynhyfryd* as the most beautiful melody he had ever heard.

Llanrwst Felix Mendelssohn walked along the Vale of Conwy, apparently from here, on 26 August 1829.

Maentwrog Edmund Prys, composer of the hymn tune *St Mary*, often sung to 'O Lord, Turn Not Away Thy Face', was born in Maentwrog in 1541 and died here in 1624.

Penmaenmawr Edward Elgar, composer and Master of the King's Music, came here for a holiday in August 1913, staying at a house named Tan-yr-allt, where he finished work on *Falstaff*.

Penygroes John Roberts, known as 'Ieuan Gwyllt', composer of the hymn tunes *Moab*, sung to either 'Thy Way, Not Mine, O Lord' or 'Who Dreads, Yet Undismayed', *Ardudwy*, often sung to 'When By Fear My Heart Is Daunted', *Liverpool, Rheidol, Lledrod* and *Llantrisant*, died at Fron on 6 May 1877. He is buried in Caeathraw.

Portmadoc John Henry, bass singer and composer of the songs *Gwlad Y Delyn* and *Galwad y Tywysog*, was born here in 1859 and died in Liverpool in 1914.

Rhiwddolion Griffith Hugh Jones, who was born at Ty Du, Llanberis, in 1849, was a teacher at the elementary school from 1869 until his death here on 26 July 1919, during which period he composed the hymn tune *Llef*, sung to 'That Day of Wrath, That Dreadful Day'.

Rhosgoch William Lloyd, composer of the hymn tune *Meirionydd*, sung to 'Pray When the Morn Is Breaking', was born here in 1786 and died here in 1852.

Talysarn John Jones, composer, who was born at Tan-y-castell on 1 March 1796, resided here for most of his life. He died in August 1857, and is buried in Llanllyfni. His hymn tune *Llanllyfni*, arranged by David Jenkins, is sung to 'Make Me a Captive, Lord'.

Tan-y-bwlch Granville Bantock, composer and conductor, owned a holiday home, Coed-y-bleiddeau, that he frequently visited during the 1930s. He took his early morning baths beneath a nearby waterfall. After his death in London on 16 October 1946, his ashes were scattered on Moelwyn Mawr.

Ynyscynhaern David Owen, known as 'Dafydd y Garreg Wen', harpist and composer of *Codiad yr Hedydd (The Rising of the Lark)* and *Dafydd y Garreg Wen (David of the White Rock)*, was born in 1720. He died in 1749 and is buried here.

POWYS

Abermule Peter Warlock, composer and writer on music, spent much of his life at his family home, Cefn Bryntalch, Abermule.

Béla Bartók stayed with him for a few days, from 17 March 1922 onwards.

Bryncrugog Joseph David Jones, composer of the hymn tune *Gwalchmai*, sung to 'King of Glory, King of Peace', was born here in 1827.

Cemmaes David Emlyn Evans, composer of the hymn tunes *Eirinwg* and *Trewen* and the songs *Hen Wlad y Menyg Gwynion* and *Bedd Llywelyn*, died here on 19 April 1913.

Craig-y-nos Adelina Patti, legendary soprano singer, was born in Madrid on 10 February 1843 and died at her home, Craig-y-nos Castle, on 27 September 1919.

Llandrindod Wells Edward German, composer, stayed here in 1904 when completing his *Welsh Rhapsody*.

Llanfihangel Ann Griffiths, hymn writer, was born at Dolwar Fechan in 1776 and died in 1805.

Llansantffraed Henry Vaughan, poet and author of the hymns 'They Are All Gone into the World of Light' and 'My Soul, There Is a Country', was born at Newton Farm on 17 April 1622 and died here on 23 April 1695. He is buried in Llansantffraed Churchyard.

Llansantffraid-ym-Mechain Henry Leslie, conductor and composer, was born in London on 18 June 1822 and died in Bryn Tanat on 4 February 1896.

Llanwrtyd Wells John Thomas, composer of the hymn tune *Blaencefn*, died here on 25 February 1921.

Montgomery George Herbert, poet, whose hymns include 'Come, My Way, My Truth, My Life', 'Let All the World in Every Corner Sing', 'Teach Me, My God and King' and 'The God of Love My Shepherd Is', was born here, possibly in the castle, on 3 April 1593.

Newtown Walford Davies frequently stayed at Gregynog Hall during the 1920s and '30s.
Edward Elgar was a guest at Gregynog Hall in June 1924.

Presteigne John Arkwright, author of the hymn 'O Valiant Hearts, Who to Your Glory Came', was born in Westminster on 10 July 1872 and resided here at Kinsham Court. He died in Presteigne on 19 September 1954.

Trecastle David Jenkins, conductor, writer on music and composer of the hymn tunes *Penlan*, often sung to 'In Heavenly Love Abiding', *Gnoll Avenue, Capel Tygwydd* and *Builth*, was born here on 30 December 1848. He died in Aberystwyth on 10 December 1915, and is buried in Trecastle.

Tregynon Thomas Olivers, author of the hymn 'The God of Abraham Praise' and composer of the hymn tune *Helmsley*, was born here in 1725 and died in London in March 1799.

Ystradgynlais Daniel Protheroe, conductor, baritone singer and composer of the cantatas *Milwyr y Groes* and *Drontheim* and the hymn tunes *Cwmgiedd* and *Hiraeth*, was born in Gough Buildings on 24 November 1866 and died in Chicago on 24 February 1934.

J. T. Rees, composer, was born here in November 1858.

THE WEST COUNTRY

AVON

Bath Nathaniel Davis Ayer, composer of *Oh, You Beautiful Doll*, was born in Boston, Massachusetts, in 1887 and died in Bath in 1952.

Thomas Bayly, composer of the song *Long, Long Ago!*, perhaps better known by a subsequent title, *Don't Sit Under the Apple Tree with Anyone Else but Me*, was born here on 13 October 1797 and died in London on 22 April 1839.

Ferruccio Busoni gave a concert here on 1 October 1907.

Thomas Chilcot, organist and composer, died here, November 1766.

Giovanni Cimadoro, composer, was born in Venice in 1761 and died in Bath on 27 February 1805.

William Croft, composer and organist, died here on 14 August 1727.

Charles Eulenstein, celebrated player of the Jew's harp, guitar and concertina, who was born in Heilbronn, West Germany, in 1802 and died in Styria, Austria, in 1890, lived here 1834–45.

John Field, composer, pianist, pupil of Clementi, teacher of Glinka, stayed here with his parents during the summer of 1793.

Percy Grainger took part in two concerts here in February 1902.

Thomas Haweis, composer of the hymn tune *Richmond*, sung to 'City of God, How Broad and Far', died here on 11 February 1820.

Joseph Haydn was here 2–6 August 1794. 'On 2 August 1794 I left at 5 o'clock in the morning for Bath . . . and arrived there at 8 o'clock in the evening, it is 107 miles from London. The Mail Coach does this distance in 12 hours, I stayed with H. Rauzzini . . . His summer house, where I stayed, is situated on a rise in the middle of a most beautiful neighbourhood, from which you can see the whole city. Bath is one of the most beautiful cities in Europe, all the houses are built of stone, these stones come from quarries in the surrounding mountains, it is very soft, indeed, it can be cut into any desired shape, it is very white; and the older it gets, once it has been taken from the quarry, the harder it gets. The entire city lies on a slope, and that is why there are very few carriages, instead there are many sedan chairs that will take you a good way for 6 pence. It's a pity there are so few straight roads; there are lots of beautiful squares, on which stand the most magnificent houses, but which cannot be reached by any vehicle . . .'

Haydn called on the composer Henry Harington at his home in Queen Square. He also appears to have visited Royal Crescent. 'Today, the 3rd, I looked at the city, and found halfway up the hill a building shaped like a half-moon, so magnificent, that I have seen nothing like it in London. The curve extends for 100 fathoms. . .'

Charles Edward Horn, tenor and baritone singer, composer and conductor, who was born in London on 21 June 1786 and died in Boston, Massachusetts, on 21 October 1849, came here in 1808 to study under Rauzzini. He composed *Cherry Ripe, I Know a Bank* and *The Deep, Deep Sea*.

Lady Caroline Keppel wrote the song 'Robin Adair' here ('What's this dull town to me?') in about 1757. She and Robin Adair were married on 22 February 1758. She died in 1769 at the age of 32, shortly after giving birth to the third of their children. It is said that her husband, who was then Inspector-General of Military Hospitals, dressed in mourning for the rest of his life. He died in 1790. The melody of *Robin Adair* was originally known as *Eileen Aroon* and is probably of Irish origin.

Elizabeth Ann Linley, celebrated soprano singer, daughter of Thomas Linley senior and wife of Sheridan, was born here on 5 September 1754 and died at Hotwells, Bristol, on 28 June 1792.

Thomas Linley junior, violinist, composer, brother of Elizabeth Ann Linley and friend of Mozart, was born here on 5 May 1756. His brothers, Ozias and William, and two further sisters, Mary and Maria, also achieved musical prominence.

Franz Liszt took part in concerts in the Theatre Royal on 1 and 2 September 1840.

Edward Loder, composer and conductor, was born here in 1813 and died in London on 5 April 1865.

Kate Loder, pianist, composer and cousin of Edward Loder, was born here on 21 August 1825 and died in Headley, Surrey, in 1904.

Thomas Tertius Noble, organist and composer, was born here on 5 May 1867 and died in Rockport, Massachusetts, on 4 May 1953.

Niccolò Paganini gave recitals in the Theatre Royal on 13, 15 and 16 December 1831 and in the Assembly Rooms on 6 January 1832. He spent Christmas here.

Louise Phillips, mezzo-soprano singer, was born here in 1857 and died in Exeter, Devon, in 1950.

Emilio Pieraccini, composer of the hymn tune *Trinity*, who was born in Italy in 1828, settled in Bath and died here in 1902.

Folliott Pierpoint, author of the hymn 'For the Beauty of the Earth', was born at Spa Villa on 7 October 1835 and died in Newport, Gwent, on 10 March 1917.

James Kendrick Pyne, organist, was born here on 5 February 1852 and died in Ilford, London, on 3 September 1938. He resided at 166 Cranbrook Road, Ilford.

Venanzio Rauzzini, composer and male soprano singer, for whom Mozart wrote his *Exultate, Jubilate*, K165, was born in Camerino, Italy, on 19 December 1746 and died here on 8 April 1810. He had a villa in Perrymead.

John Christopher Smith, composer, organist and Handel's amanuensis, who was born in Ansbach, West Germany, in 1712 and died in London on 3 October 1795, resided here during the last two decades of his life.

John Philip Sousa conducted his band at a concert in the Palace Theatre on 18 January 1911.

Johann Strauss senior led his orchestra at concerts in the Assembly Rooms on 13 June and 31 August 1838.

William Viner, composer of the hymn tune *Dismissal*, sung to Fawcett's 'Lord, Dismiss Us With Thy Blessing', was born here on 14 May 1790 and died in Westfield, Massachusetts, on 24 July 1867.

Harriet Waylett, soprano singer and actress, was born here on 7 February 1800 and died in London on 26 April 1851.

Bristol Eric Ball, distinguished composer and conductor of brass band music, was born here on 31 October 1903.

Elway Bevin, pupil of Tallis, organist and composer, was organist of Bristol Cathedral from about 1589 to 1637.

Ferruccio Busoni gave a concert here on 2 October 1907.

John Callcott, composer, organist and pupil of Haydn, was born in London on 20 November 1766 and died here on 15 May 1821.

William Child, organist and composer, was born here in 1606 and died on 23 March 1697 at Windsor, where he was organist of the Chapel Royal from 1632 until his death.

William Chatterton Dix, author of the hymns 'As with Gladness Men of Old' and 'Alleluya, Sing to Jesus', was born here on 14 June 1837 and died in Cheddar, Somerset, on 9 September 1898.

Joseph Haydn came here in August 1794. 'On the 6th I went from Bath 11 miles to Pristol to Mr Hamilton', who resided at Rodney Place, Clifton Hill. He found the city 'rather dirty', but 'the drinking water at Pristol is very sweet and pleasing. Visitors go to Pristol in the summer and to Bath in the winter.'

Edward Hodges, organist and composer, was born in Bristol on 20 July 1796 and died in Clifton on 1 September 1867.

Hubert Hunt, conductor and organist, was born in Windsor in July

1865 and died here on 7 October 1945. He resided at 14 Belgrave Road.

Franz Liszt played at a concert in Clifton on 3 September 1840.

Frank Merrick, composer and pianist, was born in Clifton on 30 April 1886. He was brought up at 7 Hughenden Road.

Anthony Milner, composer, was born here on 13 May 1925.

Dennis Noble, baritone singer, was born here on 25 September 1899.

Boris Ord, organist and conductor, was born in Clifton on 9 July 1897 and died on 30 December 1961.

Niccolò Paganini gave concerts in the Theatre Royal on 12 and 14 December 1831 and in the Assembly Rooms, Clifton, on 4 January 1832.

Robert Pearsall, composer of the hymn tune *Pearsall*, often sung to 'Jerusalem the Golden', was born in Clifton on 14 March 1795 and died in Germany on 5 August 1856.

Henry Phillips, bass singer and writer on music, was born here on 13 August 1801 and died in London on 8 November 1876.

William Phillips, organist, conductor and composer, was born here on 26 December 1816 and died in London on 19 March 1860.

Elizabeth Rainforth, soprano singer, was born on 23 November 1814 and died in Redland on 22 September 1877. On 8 January 1845 in London she gave the first performance of Mendelssohn's *Hear My Prayer*.

Thomas German Reed, theatrical manager, actor, composer and conductor, was born here on 27 June 1817 and died in Barnes, London, on 21 March 1888.

George Riseley, organist, conductor and composer, was born in Bristol on 28 August 1845 and died here on 12 April 1932. He resided at 11 Priory Road, Tyndalls Park.

Joseph Leopold Roeckel, composer, who was born in London on 11 April 1838 and died in Vittel, France, on 20 June 1923, resided in Clifton at the time he wrote the songs *Angus Macdonald, The Three Old Maids of Lee*, and *The Skippers of St Ives*.

Cyril Rootham, composer, conductor and organist, was born here on 5 October 1875 and died in Cambridge on 18 March 1938.

Julian Slade composed practically all of *Salad Days* in the prop room of the Bristol Old Vic in 1954.

John Philip Sousa conducted his band at a concert in the Victoria Rooms, Clifton, on 30 January 1905. He gave a concert in the Coliseum on 18 January 1911. He stayed at the Royal Hotel.

George Stansbury, tenor singer, conductor and composer, was born here in 1800 and died in London on 3 June 1845.

Johann Strauss senior led his orchestra at a concert in the Assembly

Rooms, Clifton, on 1 September 1838.

Charles Wesley, organist, composer and son of the hymn writer, was born here on 11 December 1757.

Samuel Wesley, composer, organist and son of the hymn writer, was born here on 24 February 1766.

Steuart Wilson, tenor singer and music administrator, was born in Clifton on 21 July 1889 and died on 18 December 1966. He resided at Fenn's, Petersfield, Hampshire.

Clevedon Gareth Morris, flautist, was born here on 13 May 1920.

East Harptree Some of the verses of 'The Holly and the Ivy' were collected here by Cecil Sharp.

Falfield Arthur Sullivan, composer and conductor, stayed at Eastwood Park in the early 1870s.

Great Badminton Thomas Linley senior, composer of *Here's to the Maiden of Bashful Fifteen* and conductor, was born here on 17 January 1733 and passed much of his early life in Bath. He later moved to London where he resided in Southampton Street. He died on 19 November 1795 and is buried in Wells Cathedral, Somerset.

Kelston Henry Harington, composer of the hymn tune *Harington*, sung to 'O Sweeter Than The Marriage-Feast', was born here on 29 September 1727. He became mayor of Bath and died in that city on 15 January 1816.

Midsomer Norton Reginald Thatcher, organist and educationist, was born here on 11 March 1888 and died in Cranleigh, Surrey, on 6 May 1957. He resided at Barnvale, The Common, Cranleigh.

Olveston Basil Harwood, composer of the hymn tunes *Luckington*, sung to 'Let All the World in Every Corner Sing', and *Thornbury*, sung to 'Thy Hand, O God, Has Guided', was born in Woodhouse on 11 April 1859 and died in London on 3 April 1949.

Peasedown St John John Bull, composer and organist, to whom it is reasonable to attribute his country's national anthem, was born, in the opinion of a number of scholars, in the Wellow parish of Peglinch in 1562.

Shirehampton Philip Napier Miles, patron of music, conductor and composer, was born here on 21 January 1865 and died in Kings Weston on 19 July 1935.

Ralph Vaughan Williams visited him at Kings Weston. Vaughan Williams's *The Lark Ascending* was first performed on 15 December 1920 in the Public Hall, Shirehampton.

Stowey The hymn tune *Stowey*, sung to 'When a Knight Won His Spurs, in the Stories of Old', was collected here by Cecil Sharp.

Thornbury Charles Harford Lloyd, composer of the hymn tune *Cosmos*, sung to 'I Praised the Earth in Beauty Seen', was born here on 16 October 1849 and died in Slough, Berkshire, on 16 October 1919, in accordance with Psalm 90.

Westbury on Trym Joseph Cooper, pianist and television programme presenter, was born at Southdene, Southfield Road, on 7 October 1912. He spent his childhood at Denehust, Southfield Road.

Weston-super-Mare Lance Dossor, pianist, was born here on 14 May 1916.

Wrington Henry Walford Davies, composer of the *Royal Air Force March Past* and *Solemn Melody*, organist, educationist and Master of the King's Music, died here on 11 March 1941.

William Leeves, composer of *Auld Robin Gray*, was born in London on 11 June 1748 and died in Wrington on 28 May 1828.

CORNWALL

Camborne Henry Tonking, organist, violinist and composer, was born here on 17 January 1863 and died in Glasgow on 7 June 1926.

Devoran Lady Mary Lygon, who is said to be enshrined in the thirteenth variation of the *Enigma Variations*, resided for some years at Porthgwidden, Devoran, where Edward Elgar stayed with her in July 1910, at the time he was writing his Violin Concerto.

Egloshayle Henry Shuttleworth, author of the hymn 'Father of Men, in Whom Are One', was born here on 20 October 1850 and died in London on 24 October 1900.

Falmouth Edward Osler, author of the hymns 'O, God, Unseen, Yet Ever Near' and 'Worship, Honour, Glory, Blessing', was born here on 30 January 1798 and died in Truro on 7 March 1863.

Elizabeth Philp, composer, was born here in 1827 and died in her home, at 67 Gloucester Crescent, Camden Town, London, on 26 November 1885.

Fowey Noël Goodwin, music critic and writer on music, was born here in 1927.

Godolphin Cross Sidney Godolphin, poet and author of the hymn 'Lord, When the Wise Men Came from Afar', was born at Godolphin House in 1610.

Helston Eaton Faning, conductor and composer, was born here on 20 May 1850 and died in Brighton on 28 October 1927.

Landrake William Beale, composer and organist, was born here on 1 January 1784 and died in London on 3 May 1854.

Liskeard John Matthews, organist and composer, was born here on 27 March 1856.

Looe Daniel Jones composed his Piano Sonata in C Sharp Minor here in 1939.

Lostwithiel Thomas Tomkins, organist and father of his more famous son, was born here in about 1545 and died in Gloucester in about 1627.

Mithian John Julian, author of the monumental and matchless *Dictionary of Hymnology* and of the hymn 'Father of All, to Thee', was born here on 27 January 1839.

Newquay David Willcocks, conductor and organist, was born here on 30 December 1919.

Padstow Edward Dayman, author of the hymns 'Almighty Father, Heaven and Earth' and 'O Lord, Be With Us When We Sail', was born here on 11 July 1807 and died in Shillingstone, Dorset, on 30 October 1890.

Par Gerald Knight, organist and composer, was born here on 27 July 1908.

Penzance William Tregarthen, organist at the age of 11 to General Booth's mission in Whitechapel, was born here on 17 September 1856. After being a pupil of Samuel Sebastian Wesley, he emigrated to South Africa.

William Viner was organist of St Mary's 1838–59, during which time he composed the hymn tune *Dismissal*, sung to Fawcett's 'Lord, Dismiss Us With Thy Blessing'.

Perranarworthal Jane Crewdson, author of the hymn 'There Is No Sorrow, Lord, Too Slight', was born here on 22 October 1809 and died in Greater Manchester on 14 September 1863.

Redruth Thomas Haweis, composer of the hymn tune *Richmond*, sung to 'City of God, How Broad and Far', was born here on 1 January 1734.

Benjamin Luxon, baritone singer, was born here on 24 March 1937 and spent his childhood in Camborne.

Fanny Moody, soprano singer and opera impresario, was born here on 23 November 1866.

St Agnes Daniel Jones composed his Seventh String Quartet here in 1937 and his Sonata for Three Non-Chromatic Kettledrums Unaccompanied in 1947.

St Ives George Lloyd, composer, was born here on 28 June 1913. His first opera, *Iernin*, was staged in Penzance on 6 November 1934.

St Keverne Charles Incledon, celebrated tenor singer and composer of *Black-Ey'd Susan*, was born here in 1763 and died in London on 18 February 1826.

St Merryn Malcolm Arnold, composer, resided at Primrose Cottage during the latter part of the 1960s and early '70s.

Peter Warlock visited D. H. Lawrence at Porthcothan, St Merryn, in 1916. He visited him at Higher Tregerthen, Zennor, in 1917.

Saltash Frederick Crouch composed the song *Kathleen Mavourneen* near here in 1835. 'I jotted down the melody on the historic banks of the Tamar. On arriving at Plymouth, I wrote out a fair copy of the song, and sang it to Mrs Rowe, the wife of a music publisher of that town.'

Moura Lympany, pianist, was born here on 18 August 1916. She spent her early childhood at 10 Barnpark, Teignmouth.

Sennen Frederick Delius, composer, stayed here for about two months in the spring of 1919.

Tintagel Edward Elgar visited Alice Stuart-Wortley here on 3 April 1910. The first movement of his Second Symphony, written during the following year, is associated with memories of his visit.

Arnold Bax's symphonic poem *Tintagel*, composed in 1917, portrays 'the castle-crowned cliff of Tintagel, and more particularly the wide distances of the Atlantic as seen from the cliffs of Cornwall on a sunny but not windless summer day'.

Igor Stravinsky visited here on 17 August 1957.

The second act of *Tristan und Isolde* is generally understood to be set in Tintagel. Wagner is not specific in his stage directions, but in Gottfried von Stassburg's *Tristan*, on which the opera is largely based, King Marke's castle is situated at Tintagel. Wagner merely indicates that the castle is in Cornwall.

Gilbert Vinter, conductor and composer, died on 10 October 1969. He resided at St Mabyn, Trethevy.

Tregony Archer Gurney, author of the hymn 'Christ Is Risen! Christ Is Risen!', was born here on 15 July 1820 and died in Bath on 21 March 1887.

Truro Ralph Dunstan, composer, was born in Truro on 17 November 1857 and died here on 2 April 1933.

John Lemon, composer, was born here in 1754 and died in Polvellen on 5 April 1814.

Washaway James Robinson Planché, librettist of Weber's *Oberon*, stayed at Pencarrow in 1868 as the guest of Lord and Lady Molesworth.

Arthur Sullivan, composer and conductor, stayed at Pencarrow in August 1882, writing most of the first act of *Iolanthe* here.

DEVON

Barnstaple Hubert Bath, composer of *Cornish Rhapsody*, was born here on 6 November 1883 and died in Harefield, London, on 24 April 1945. *Cornish Rhapsody* was written in 1944 for the film *Love Story*; the piano part on the sound track was played by Harriet Cohen.

John Gay, poet, dramatist, librettist of *The Beggar's Opera* and Handel's *Acis and Galatea*, was born at 35 High Street (replaced by a supermarket) in September 1685 and died in Old Burlington Street, Mayfair, London, on 4 December 1732. He is buried in Westminster Abbey.

John Wreford, author of the hymn 'Lord, While for All Mankind We Pray', was born here on 12 December 1800 and died in London on 2 July 1881.

Bideford Richard Mudge, composer, was born here in 1718 and died at Packington Park, near Little Packington, Warwickshire, on 3 April 1763.

Bovey Tracey Jane Campbell, author of the hymn 'We Plough the Fields, and Scatter', died here on 15 November 1878.

Cuthbert Girdlestone, music scholar, was born here on 17 September 1895.

Arthur Henry Fox Strangways, writer on music, lived at The Hut, Bovey Tracey, during the 1940s.

Brixham Francis Henry Lyte, hymn writer, was curate of All Saints' Church from 1823 until his death in Nice on 20 November 1847. He lived at Whitegates, Burton Street, until 1833 and thereafter at Berry Head House, now a hotel, where he wrote 'Abide with Me' on 4 September 1847, knowing he was dying from tuberculosis. In 1834 he published two other familiar hymns, 'Praise, My Soul, the King of Heaven' and 'God of Mercy, God of Grace'.

Broadhembury Augustus Toplady was vicar here 1768–78, during which time he wrote the famous hymn 'Rock of Ages', which was published in March 1776. This was Gladstone's favourite hymn; Prince Albert also greatly admired it, reciting some of the verses on his death-bed. Toplady may, or may not, have found inspiration for the hymn while sheltering from a storm in Burrington Combe, near Blagdon, Avon.

Chagford Sidney Godolphin, poet and author of the hymn 'Lord, When the Wise Men Came from Afar', died here in 1643, killed, so men say, at The Three Crowns, an inn that stood near the churchyard. He is buried in Okehampton.

Henry Ley, composer of the hymn tune *Ottery St Mary* and organist, was born here on 30 December 1887 and died on 24 August 1962. He resided at Combewater Cottage, Metcombe, Ottery St Mary.

Cheriton Fitzpaine George Body, author of the hymn 'Father, Who Dost Thy Children Feed', was born here on 7 January 1840 and died in Durham on 5 June 1911.

Churston Ferrers William Sloane Sloane-Evans, heraldist and composer, was born here on 21 August 1823 and died in Stoke Fleming on 4 March 1899. He is buried in Dartmouth.

Clovelly Edward German, composer, drew inspiration for some of his *Romeo and Juliet* music through witnessing in 1894 a fisherman's funeral procession toiling up the steep and narrow main street in Clovelly. He is further linked to the county by his song *Glorious Devon*.

Colyton Lawrence Tuttiett, author of the hymns 'O Grant Us Light, That We May Know' and 'Father, Let Me Dedicate', was born here in 1825 and died in St Andrews, Fife, on 21 May 1897.

Crediton Samuel Chapple, blind organist and composer, was born here in 1775 and died in Ashburton on 3 October 1833.
    Charles Smith, baritone singer, organist and composer of *The Battle of Hohenlinden*, was born in London in September 1786 and died in Crediton on 22 November 1856.

Dartington Igor Stravinsky, attending the Dartington Hall Music Summer School in 1957, resided at 8 Warren Lane 7–21 August. He spent 9–12 August in London. He was at a concert of his works here on 14 August.
    Aaron Copland came to the Summer School in 1958, staying at Dartington Hall. Other composers who have visited Dartington for the Summer School include Stefan Wolpe in 1958 and 1959; Luigi Nono in 1960, 1961 and 1962; Bruno Maderna in 1960, 1961 and 1962; Luciano Berio in 1961 and 1962; Virgil Thomson in 1961 and 1965; Witold Lutoslawski in 1964; William Walton in 1965; Alexander Tcherepnin in 1967 and 1973. Benjamin Britten stayed at Yarner Farm, Dartington, in 1959 and 1962.

Dartmouth Elizabeth Codner, author of the hymn 'Lord, I Hear of Showers of Blessing', was born here in 1824 and died in Croydon, London, on 28 March 1919.
    John Eustace Giles, author of the hymn 'Hast Thou Said, Exalted Jesus?', was born here on 17 June 1805 and died in Clapham, London, on 24 June 1875.

Dawlish Charles Abdy Williams, organist, writer on music and composer, was born here on 16 July 1855 and died in Milford on Sea, Hampshire, on 27 February 1923.

Dean Prior Robert Herrick, poet and author of the hymns 'When Virgin Morn Doth Call Thee To Arise', 'In This World, the Isle of Dreams' and 'Here a Little Child I Stand', whose verses inspired works by Bax, Blow, Havergal Brian, Frank Bridge, Britten, Geoffrey Bush, Delius, Hindemith, Holst, Maconchy, Moeran, Parry, Quilter, Rubbra, Stanford, Sullivan, Warlock and Grace Williams, was born in London in 1591 and resided in Dean Prior for many years. He died here in October 1674 and is buried in the churchyard.

Devonport William Medlen Hutchings, author of the hymn 'When Mothers of Salem', was born here on 28 August 1827 and died in Camberwell, London, on 21 June 1876.

Dittisham Francis Rous, author of the hymn 'The Lord's My Shepherd, I'll Not Want', was born here in 1579 and died in Acton, London, on 7 January 1659.

Eggesford John Christie, founder of Glyndebourne Opera House, was born at Eggesford House (in ruins) on 14 December 1882.

Exeter George Baker, organist and composer, was born here in 1768 and died on 19 February 1847.

Sabine Baring-Gould, historian, novelist, composer, folk-song collector and author of 'Onward, Christian Soldiers', was born here on 28 January 1834.

John Bowring, statesman, philologist, traveller, economist, advocate of the decimal system in coinage, prison reformer, poet and author of the hymns 'In the Cross of Christ I Glory' and 'Watchman, Tell Us of the Night', was born in Heavitree on 17 October 1792 and died there on 23 November 1872.

Margaret Campbell, author of the hymn 'Praise Ye Jehovah, Praise the Lord Most High', was born in Alphington in 1808 and died there on 6 February 1841.

Thomas D'Urfey, poet, dramatist and musician, was born here in 1653 and died in London on 26 February 1723. Among the composers who provided incidental music for his plays or set his poems as songs or odes were Blow, Jeremiah Clarke and Purcell. John Gay drew on D'Urfey's collection of songs and ballads, 'Wit and Mirth, or Pills To

Purge Melancholy', published in 1719, for *The Beggar's Opera*.

Walter Gilbert, organist and composer of the hymn tunes *Maidstone*, sung to 'Pleasant Are Thy Courts Above', and *Thanksgiving*, sung to 'Hark! The Song of Jubilee', was born here on 21 April 1829 and died in Headington, Oxfordshire, on 2 March 1910.

William Jackson, author, painter and composer, who was born in Exeter on 28 May 1730, was organist of the cathedral from 1777 until his death here on 12 July 1803. During this time he composed the hymn tune *Exeter*, sung to 'Father of Men, in Whom Are One'.

Joseph Kemp, composer and organist, was born here in 1778 and died in London on 22 May 1824.

Richard Langdon, organist and composer, was born in Exeter in about 1729 and died here on 8 September 1803.

Franz Liszt took part in concerts here on 28 and 29 August 1840.

Matthew Locke, composer, was born here in about 1630.

John Macdonald, writer on music and son of the legendary Flora Macdonald, was born in New York in 1759 and died here on 16 August 1831.

Niccolò Paganini gave recitals here on 20, 21 and 22 December 1831. He generously returned £50 to the theatre manager, owing to poor receipts.

Robert Parsons, composer, was born here and died in Newark-on-Trent, Nottinghamshire, on 25 January 1570, having drowned in the Trent.

Kellow John Pye, pianist, composer and wine merchant, was born here on 9 February 1812 and died in Exmouth on 22 September 1901.

William Randall, composer and organist, died here in about 1604.

John Philip Sousa conducted his band at a concert in New Queen's Hall on 16 January 1911. He stayed at the People's New London Hotel.

William Spark, organist and composer, was born here on 28 October 1823 and died in Leeds on 16 June 1897.

Robert Stone, composer, was born in Alphington in 1516 and died in London on 2 July 1613.

Igor Stravinsky spent the day here on 8 August 1957.

Arthur Sullivan and William Schwenck Gilbert met at the Half Moon Hotel towards the end of August 1882 to reconstruct the first act of *Iolanthe*, with which Sullivan was dissatisfied. The work was first performed on 25 November of that year. The Half Moon, demolished in 1912, stood on the south corner of High Street and Bedford Street.

Samuel Sebastian Wesley, composer and organist, was organist of the cathedral 1835–42. He is buried in the Old Cemetery, Exe Street.

Exmouth Editha Knocker, distinguished violin teacher, writer on the violin and pupil of Joachim, was born here on 2 March 1869 and died in Glenuig, Highland, on 19 September 1950.
  Franz Liszt played at a concert here on 24 August 1840.

Halberton Edmund Hooper, composer and organist of Westminster Abbey, was born here in about 1553 and died in Westminster on 14 July 1621.

Holne Charles Kingsley, novelist, poet and author of the hymn 'From Thee All Skill and Science Flow', was born at the old vicarage on 12 June 1819 and died at Eversley, Hampshire, on 23 January 1875. His poems have been set to music by Gounod, Stanford and Holst.

Ivybridge Franz Liszt stopped for a mid-morning cream tea here on 28 August 1840, while travelling from Plymouth to Exeter.

Killerton Arthur Troyte, composer, was born here on 3 May 1811 and died in Bridehead, near Dorchester, Dorset, on 19 June 1857.

Kingsbridge Louisa Vinning, soprano singer and harpist, who made her public début at the age of 2 in Plymouth, was born here on 10 November 1836 and died in London in 1904.

Lew Trenchard Sabine Baring-Gould lived here from 1881 until his death on 2 January 1924.

Morwenstow Robert Stephen Hawker, poet and eccentric, who was born in Stoke Damerel on 3 December 1804 and died in Plymouth on 15 August 1875, was vicar here 1835–74, during which time he wrote the hymns 'Sing to the Lord the Children's Hymn' and 'Welcome, That Star in Judah's Sky'.

Newton Abbot Joyce Jellen, contralto singer, was born here in 1925.

Ottery St Mary Arthur Coleridge, lawyer and Bach scholar, was born at Heath's Court on 1 February 1830 and died in London on 29 October 1913. He was the grand-nephew of Samuel Taylor Coleridge.
  Samuel Taylor Coleridge, poet and essayist, whose verses inspired works by Bantock, Havergal Brian, Coleridge-Taylor, Griffes, Mackenzie, Parry, Stanford and Vaughan Williams, was born here on 21 October 1772 and died in London on 25 July 1834.

Paignton David Fanshawe, composer, explorer, conductor, music scholar and writer, was born at Manor House on 19 April 1942.

Arthur Sullivan's *The Pirates of Penzance* received its first performance, in front of an audience of sixteen, at the Bijou Theatre in Hyde Street on 30 December 1879, thereby, for copyright reasons, pre-empting the New York première by a single day.

Plymouth Stanley Bate, composer, was born here on 12 December 1911 and died in London on 19 October 1959.

Ambrose Blatchford, author of the hymn 'A Gladsome Hymn of Praise We Sing', was born here in 1842 and died in Bideford on 24 April 1924.

Samuel Clarke, author of the hymn 'Great Giver of All Good, to Thee Again', was born here on 6 January 1821 and died in Penzance on 22 February 1903.

Ron Goodwin, composer of numerous highly successful film scores, was born here on 17 February 1925.

John Jenkins Husband, composer of hymn tunes, notably of *Revive Us Again*, better known as *Hallelujah, I'm a Bum*, was born here in 1760 and died in Philadelphia, USA, in 1825.

John Albert Jeffrey, composer of the hymn tune *Albany*, was born here in 1855 and died in Brookline, Massachusetts, in 1929.

Franz Liszt played at a concert here on 26 August 1840. He remained in the city for the next day and night and left for Exeter at 8am on the 28th. A projected concert on the 27th was cancelled when only seven people bought tickets.

Herman Löhr, composer of *Little Grey Home in the West*, was born here in 1871 and died in Tonbridge, Kent, in 1943.

Marian McKenzie, contralto singer, was born here in 1858.

Richard, Earl of Mount-Edgcumbe, writer on music and composer, was born here on 13 September 1764 and died in Richmond, London, on 26 September 1839.

George Prynne, who was born in West Looe, Cornwall, on 23 August 1818, was vicar of St Peter's, Plymouth, from 1848 until his death here on 25 March 1903, during which time he wrote the hymn 'Jesus, Meek and Gentle'.

Thelma Reiss, cellist, was born here on 2 July 1906.

John Philip Sousa conducted his band at two concerts in the Guildhall on 17 January 1911. He stayed at the Royal Hotel.

Henry Wendon, tenor singer, was born here on 7 January 1900.

Sidbury William Cummings, organist, composer and music scholar, was born here on 22 August 1831 and died in London on 6 June 1915.

Sidmouth William Hoyte, organist and composer, was born here on 22 September 1844.

Franz Liszt played at a concert here on 22 August 1840.

William Speer, organist and composer of *The Jackdaw of Rheims*, was born in London on 9 November 1863 and died in Sidmouth on 31 May 1937.

Stoke Damerel John Masterman, author of the hymn 'Almighty Father, Who Dost Give', died here on 25 November 1933.

Stonehouse John Patey, baritone singer and music publisher, was born here in 1835 and died in Falmouth on 4 December 1901.

Tavistock Elisabeth Charles, author of the hymn 'Never Further Than Thy Cross', was born here on 2 January 1828 and died in London on 28 March 1896.

Christopher Willing, composer of the hymn tune *Alstone*, sung to 'O Grant Us Light, That We May Know', was born here on 28 February 1830 and died in Southgate, London, on 1 December 1904.

Teignmouth Franz Liszt played at a concert here on 24 August 1840.

Elias Parish-Alvars, noted harpist, composer and chamber musician to the Austrian emperor, was born here on 28 February 1808 and died in Vienna on 25 January 1849.

Tiverton Samuel Reay was organist of St Peter's Church 1847–54, during which time he wrote for the Tiverton Vocal Society the part-songs *The Clouds That Wrap the Setting Sun* and *The Dawn of Day*. On 2 June 1847, for the wedding of Tom Daniel and Dorothea Carew at St Peter's, he played Mendelssohn's *Wedding March*; this appears to be the first occasion on which the march was performed at such a ceremony. Reay is also the composer of the hymn tune *Stamford*, sung to 'Father of Everlasting Grace'. On 27 October 1879 in London, he conducted the British premières of Bach's *Coffee Cantata* and *Peasant Cantata*.

Topsham John Pridham, pianist and composer, was born here on 1 October 1818 and died in Taunton in August 1896.

Torquay Astra Desmond, contralto singer, was born here on 10 April 1898.

John Ellerton, author of the hymns 'The Day Thou Gavest, Lord, Is Ended', 'Saviour, Again to Thy Dear Name We Raise', 'Throned upon the Awful Tree' and 'Behold Us, Lord, a Little Space', was born in London on 16 December 1826 and died here on 15 June 1893.

John Henley, author of the hymn 'Children of Jerusalem', was born here on 18 March 1800 and died in Weymouth, Dorset, on 2 May 1842.

Franz Liszt stayed here on 25 August 1840. He had intended to take part in a concert, but this had to be cancelled because he was too unwell to perform.

John Philip Sousa conducted his band at a concert in the Bath Saloons on 16 January 1911.

Anna Thillon, soprano singer, who created the role of Catarina in Auber's *Les Diamants de la couronne* on 6 March 1841 in Paris and also appeared in the initial productions of the same composer's *Le Duc d'Olonne* and *La Part du diable*, was born in 1819 and died here on 5 May 1903.

William Wotton, bassoonist and the earliest British saxophone virtuoso, was born here on 6 September 1832 and died in Deal, Kent, on 3 May 1912.

Totnes Evelyn Hingston, composer, was born in Totnes in 1876 and died here on 7 July 1941.

John Old, composer of the opera *Herne the Hunter*, conductor, pianist, pupil of Thalberg, was born at Rowton Hall on 28 May 1827 and died in Reading on 4 February 1892.

Karol Szymanowski gave a recital here at the beginning of November 1934.

Ugborough John Harris, author of the hymn 'Light Up This House With Glory, Lord', was born here on 8 March 1802 and died in Hampstead, London, on 21 December 1856.

Upton Hellions John Davy, composer, was born here on 23 December 1763 and died in May's Buildings, St Martin's Lane, London, on 22 February 1824. His song *The Bay of Biscay* comes from the comic opera *The Spanish Dollars*, presented in London in May 1805.

Willand Hugh Tracey, collector of African folk-songs, was born here on 29 January 1903 and died in Johannesburg on 22 October 1977.

Woolacombe William Busch, composer and pianist, was born in London on 25 June 1901 and died here on 30 January 1945.

Gustav Holst, pictured here shortly before his death in 1934 (*Courtesy of John Gay and the Holst Birthplace Museum Trust*)

Gustav Holst was born in Clarence Road, Cheltenham, in 1874. His birthplace became the Gustav Holst Birthplace Museum and Period House in 1975. The Borough Council has taken great pains to restore the building and to furnish it in mid-Victorian style, consistent with the composer's childhood. Letters, manuscripts, photographs and other souvenirs of his life are on display, including the piano that he used when writing *The Planets* (*Author*)

The Old Vicarage, Down Ampney, Gloucestershire. Ralph Vaughan Williams was born here in October 1872. After his father died in 1875, his mother took the family to live at Leith Hill Place in Surrey. The composer's magnificent hymn tune *Down Ampney*, to which the words of 'Come Down, O Love Divine' are sung, has taken the name around the world and led to the p in Ampney generally being pronounced, when it should ideally remain silent. For much of the nineteenth century, the village was known as Down-Amney (*Author*)

A garden party at Highnam Court, Hubert Parry's house near Gloucester. The occasion was the Three Choirs Festival, possibly in 1910. On the extreme left in the upper row is somebody bearing a resemblance to Ralph Vaughan Williams. The enlarged section shows, among the seated figures, Parry at the extreme left and Edward Elgar at the extreme right. After many years of neglect, Highnam Court is now being restored and will soon become one of Britain's most beautiful and comprehensive centres for music and the other arts (*Courtesy of Tom Fenton*)

Michael Tippett's house in Corsham, Wiltshire, where he lived during the 1960s. Born in London, he previously had homes in Suffolk, Surrey and East Sussex. Among the works completed at Corsham are *King Priam*, *Songs for Ariel* and Concerto for Orchestra. Much of *The Knot Garden* was also written here (*Author*)

The home of Peter Maxwell Davies during the mid-1960s in Tollard Royal, Wiltshire. Here, at Kimbers Cottage, he completed the *Second Fantasia on a Theme of John Taverner*, *Ecce manus tradentis* and *Revelation and Fall*. In 1966, he moved four miles away, to Charlton, near Shaftesbury (*Author*)

DORSET

Blandford Forum Franz Liszt played at a concert in the Assembly Rooms on 20 August 1840.

Bournemouth Ferruccio Busoni played at a concert in the Winter Gardens on 25 October 1919.

Frederic Curzon, composer of *The Boulevardier*, was born in London in 1899 and died in Bournemouth in December 1973. He resided at 15 St Winifred's Road.

Dan Godfrey junior, first conductor of the Bournemouth Symphony Orchestra, who introduced Tchaikovsky's First and Second Symphonies to Britain, was born in London on 20 June 1868 and died on 20 July 1939 in Bournemouth, where he resided at Dannholme, Alumhurst Road.

John Keble, after whom the Oxford college is named and author of numerous hymns, including 'Sun of My Soul, Thou Saviour Dear' and 'New Every Morning Is the Love', died here on 29 March 1866.

Hubert Parry, composer, was born here on 27 February 1848.

Simon Preston, organist, conductor and composer, was born here in 1938.

Jean Sibelius conducted his Third Symphony, *Finlandia* and *Valse triste* at a concert in the Winter Gardens on 17 February 1921.

Constantin Silvestri, conductor and composer, was born in Bucharest in 1913 and died on 23 February 1969. He resided at Flat 4, Addiscombe, Cranborne Road, and is buried near Dan Godfrey in St Peter's Churchyard.

John Philip Sousa conducted his band at concerts in the Winter Gardens on 28 and 29 January 1905, and on 14 January 1911. He had a great affection for Bournemouth, which he amusingly called 'the hub of the musical universe'. He once addressed a letter to Dan Godfrey as follows:

> In Bournemouth by the sea
> A gentlemanly he,
> Besides he's every inch a music man.
> Dan Godfrey is his name,
> So, postman, quickly hustle this to Dan.

The letter safely reached its destination. In January 1911 he stayed at the Royal Bath Hotel.

Henry Twells, author of the hymns 'At Even Ere the Sun Was Set' and 'Not For Our Sins Alone', was born on 23 March 1823 and died here on 19 January 1900.

Paul Verlaine, poet, whose verses inspired works by Casella, Chabrier, Gustave Charpentier, Chausson, Debussy, Delius, Dieren, Fauré, Honegger, Ireland, Koechlin, Loeffler, Ravel and Stravinsky, resided 1876–7 at 2 Westburn Terrace, now part of the Sandbourne Hotel, and taught at St Aloysius's School, now 24 Surrey Road.

John Wilbraham, trumpeter, was born here on 15 April 1944.

Branksome Park Annunzio Mantovani, conductor, resided during the late 1970s until shortly before his death, at 12 Burton Road.

Bryanston Paul Hindemith stayed at Bryanston School in August 1948, and taught at the Bryanston Summer School.

George Enescu also stayed here, teaching at the Summer School in August 1949, August 1950 and August 1952.

Canford Cliffs Ralph Vaughan Williams stayed at The Brown House, Cliff Drive, during January 1929.

Child Okeford William Kethe, author of the hymn 'All People That on Earth Do Dwell', who died in Dorset in 1594, was vicar here for many years. It was the singing of this hymn in St Paul's in 1851 by the massed choirs of Charity Children that so moved Hector Berlioz. 'My emotions were deeply stirred,' he wrote, by 'the five thousand little singers . . . It is hopeless to attempt to give you any notion of the effect this produced.'

Cranborne Edward Thorne, composer of the hymn tune *St Andrew*, sung to 'Jesus Calls Us; o'er the Tumult', was born here on 9 May 1834 and died in London on 26 December 1916.

Dorchester Francis Galpin, authority on ancient musical instruments, was born here on 25 December 1858 and died in Richmond, London, on 30 December 1945.

John Ireland, composer, was inspired by a visit to Maiden Castle to write the symphonic rhapsody *Mai-Dun*, completed in 1921.

Sydney Smith, composer, was born here on 14 July 1839 and died in London on 3 March 1889.

Christopher à Becket Williams, composer and novelist, was born here on 2 July 1890 and died in Chandler's Ford, Hampshire, on 3 November 1956.

Fontmell Magna Newman Flower, writer on music, publisher and collector, was born here on 8 July 1879 and died on 12 March 1964, at his home, Tarrant Keyneston House, Tarrant Keyneston.

John Eliot Gardiner, conductor, was born on 20 April 1943 at Springhead, where he spent his childhood.

Iwerne Minster Muzio Clementi, composer and pianist, resided at Stepleton House, the home of his patron Peter Beckford, 1766–73.

Lyme Regis Franz Liszt played at a concert here on 22 August 1840.

Shaftesbury Peter Maxwell Davies, composer, resided at Barters Town (now Barters Lane Cottage), Charlton, 1966–9. Works written during this period include *Notre Dame des fleurs, Antéchrist, Missa super l'homme armé, St Thomas Wake, Worldes Blis, Eight Songs for a Mad King* and *Vesalii icones.* Much of the opera *Taverner* was also composed here.

Shillingstone Arthur Sullivan, composer and conductor, composed the hymn tune *St Gertrude*, sung to 'Onward, Christian Soldiers', in 1871 at Hanford House, the home of Ernest Clay Ker-Seymer, after whose wife Gertrude the tune is named. The first performance of 'Onward, Christian Soldiers' took place in the chapel next to Hanford House, which has since become Hanford School. Sullivan's hymn tune *Hanford* was composed here during another visit.

Wareham William Knapp, composer of the hymn tune *Wareham*, sung to 'Rejoice, O Land, In God Thy Might', was born here in 1698 and died in Poole in September 1768.

Weymouth Franz Liszt played at a concert here on 21 August 1840.

Wimborne Minster Christopher Le Fleming, composer, was born here on 26 February 1908.

GLOUCESTERSHIRE

Berkeley Joseph Bennett, eminent writer on music, was born here on 29 November 1831 and died at Purton on 12 June 1911.

Bourton-on-the-Water Gustav Holst, composer, resided here in

1892, having been appointed conductor of the town's Choral Society and organist and choirmaster at Wick Rissington.

Edwin Ransford, baritone, actor, composer and music publisher, was born here on 13 March 1805 and died in London on 11 July 1876.

Brookthorpe Alexander Brent Smith, composer, was born in Brookthorpe on 8 October 1889 and died here on 3 July 1950.

Cheltenham John Barnett, second cousin of Meyerbeer and composer of the opera *The Mountain Sylph*, died here on 17 April 1890.

Ferruccio Busoni played at a concert here on 3 October 1920.

Robert Elliott, harpsichordist, organist and educationist, was born here on 4 June 1932.

Fanny Frickenhaus, pianist, was born here on 7 June 1849 and died in London on 8 August 1913.

Edvard Grieg took part in a concert here in early December 1897.

George Frideric Handel took the waters here in June 1751.

Gustav Holst, composer, was born on 21 September 1874 at 4 Clarence Road, formerly 4 Pittville Terrace. The house is now the Gustav Holst Birthplace Museum and is open 11am–5pm, Tuesday to Saturday. Holst later moved to 1 Vittoria Walk (demolished) and 46 Lansdown Crescent.

Dyneley Hussey, writer on music, was born in Deolali, India, on 27 February 1893 and died on 6 September 1972. He resided at Hawksworth, Albert Road.

Franz Liszt took part in a concert at the Assembly Rooms (demolished and replaced by Lloyd's Bank, on the corner of High Street and Rodney Road) on 4 September 1840. He played at another concert, in the Rotunda, on the following day, and stayed at the George Hotel (demolished and replaced by Marks and Spencer in the High Street). Among the works he performed at the first concert was his transcription of the overture to *William Tell*.

Agnes Nicholls, soprano singer and wife of Hamilton Harty, was born here on 14 July 1877 and died in London on 21 September 1959.

Charles Wilfred Orr, composer, was born here on 31 July 1893.

Niccolò Paganini gave recitals here on 20 and 21 July 1831 in the Assembly Rooms. He stayed at the Plough Hotel.

Emily Shinner, violinist and pupil of Joachim, was born here on 7 July 1862 and died in London on 17 July 1901.

Jean Sibelius conducted his works at a concert here in October 1912.

John Philip Sousa conducted his band at a concert in the Town Hall on 24 January 1911.

Charles Speer, organist and composer, was born here on 21 November 1859 and died on 27 October 1921.

Johann Strauss senior led his orchestra at concerts in the Assembly Rooms on 11 June, 14 June and 30 August 1838; on 2 October, he played at a ball. He gave a final concert here, at the Royal Old Wells, on 30 June 1849.

Chipping Campden The music and most of the words of *The Holly and the Ivy* were collected here by Cecil Sharp.

Cirencester Peter Maxwell Davies, composer, resided at The Apple Loft, Oxford House, 1960–2. Works written during this period include *O Magnum Mysterium*, the First String Quartet, *Te Lucis Ante Terminum*, the *First Taverner Fantasia, Frammenti di Leopardi* and the Sinfonia for Chamber Orchestra.

Sebastian Bach Mills, organist and pianist, was born here on 13 March 1839 and died in Wiesbaden, West Germany, on 21 December 1898.

Didbrook Peter Warlock, composer and writer on music, stayed at Didbrook Vicarage in February 1913.

Down Ampney Ralph Vaughan Williams, composer, was born at The Old Vicarage, Down Ampney Road, on 12 October 1872. He spent only his first two and a half years here.

Ebrington William Henry Hadow, eminent writer on music, was born here on 27 December 1859 and died on 9 April 1937 in London, where he resided at 13 Belgrave Road.

Fairford John Keble, after whom the Oxford college is named and author of numerous hymns, including 'Sun of My Soul, Thou Saviour Dear' and 'New Every Morning Is the Love', was born here on 25 April 1792.

Fretherne Seymour Whinyates, violinist, was born here on 4 December 1892.

Gloucester John Dykes Bower, organist, was born here on 13 August 1905.

Geoffrey Brand, conductor, music administrator and authority on brass band music, was born here on 9 May 1926.

Ivor Gurney, composer and poet, was born in a house, since demolished, in Queen's Way, then Queen Street, on 28 August 1890. Shortly afterwards his family moved to 19 Barton Street, where they lived above his father's shop, on the corner of Clarence Terrace. This building was demolished in the early 1970s. In 1922 he was a patient at Barnwood House, Barnwood, a private asylum, from which he escaped on 8 November of that year and went to the local police station, where he was detained. After his death in Dartford, Kent, his body was brought to Twigworth Churchyard, where he was buried on 31 December 1937.

Donald Hunt, composer, conductor and organist, was born here on 26 July 1930.

Niccolò Paganini gave a recital in the Bell Assembly Rooms on 29 April 1834.

Camille Saint-Saëns conducted the world première of his oratorio *The Promised Land* in the cathedral on 11 September 1913. On the previous day Jean Sibelius's *Luonnotar* was given its world première in the Shire Hall.

John Stafford Smith, organist, tenor singer and composer, to whom the melody of *The Star Spangled Banner* is attributed, was born here in 1750 and died in London on 21 September 1836.

John Philip Sousa conducted his band at a concert in the Shire Hall on 24 January 1911. He stayed the night at the Bell and County.

Herbert Sumsion, organist, conductor and composer, was born here on 19 January 1899.

Samuel Sebastian Wesley, composer and organist, son of Samuel Wesley, was born in London on 9 September 1810 and died here on 19 April 1876. He is buried in Exeter.

Charles Wheatstone, physicist, founder of modern telegraphy, cryptographer, inventor of the automatic telegraph, the kaleidophone, the stereoscope and the concertina, was born here in February 1802 and died in Paris on 19 October 1875.

George Whitefield, author of the lines 'Hark, the Herald Angels Sing, Glory to the New-Born King', which have generally been preferred to the opening couplet of Charles Wesley's 'Hark, How All the Welkin Rings', was born here on 16 December 1714 and died in Newburyport, Massachusetts, on 30 September 1770.

Hasfield Edward Elgar, composer and Master of the King's Music, was a frequent visitor to Hasfield Court, the home of his friend William Meath Baker, who is characterized in the fourth variation of the *Enigma Variations*.

Highnam Hubert Parry, composer, spent his childhood at Highnam Court. He resided here intermittently throughout his life.

Since 1977 Highnam Court has been undergoing extensive restoration, instigated by April Cantelo, Roger Smith and Michael Procter, who intend making the house a leading centre both for music and other arts.

Huntley Richard Webster, composer of *Bonnie Jeanie Gray*, was born here in 1783 and died in Glasgow on 26 December 1848.

Kilcot Rutland Boughton, composer, resided here from 1927 until his death in London on 25 January 1960.

Ralph Vaughan Williams visited him here in September 1956.

Lydney Herbert Howells, composer and educationist, was born here on 17 October 1892.

Painswick Gerald Finzi, composer, resided at King's Mill 1922–6.

Robert Watkin-Mills, bass-baritone singer, was born here on 5 March 1856 and died in Toronto in December 1930.

St Briavels Robert Bryson, composer, died here on 20 April 1942. He resided at Yewtree Cottage.

Siddington Henry Buckoll, author of the hymn 'Lord Dismiss Us with Thy Blessing, Thanks for Mercies Past Receive', was born here on 9 September 1803.

Stanway Percy Grainger stayed at Stanway Hall, the home of Lady Elcho, on several occasions between 1907 and 1909. He met H. G. Wells here.

Stinchcombe Isaac Williams, poet and author of the hymn 'Be Thou My Guardian and My Guide', died here on 1 May 1865.

Stow-on-the-Wold Edmund Chilmead, music scholar, was born here in 1610 and died in London in February 1654.

Winchcombe Cornelius Cardew, composer and music scholar, was born here in 1936.

SOMERSET

Alford Godfrey Thring, author of a number of familiar hymns, was born here on 25 March 1823. He was rector of Alford 1858–76, during which time he wrote 'Fierce Raged the Tempest o'er the Deep' and 'Jesus Came—the Heavens Adoring'.

Babington Dora Bright, composer and pianist, resided here during the 1930s and '40s, the last two decades of her life.

Bridgwater Franz Liszt took part in a concert here, before an audience of thirty people, on 31 August 1840. He played with a bandage on his hand, which he had cut in Taunton earlier in the day.

Downside Joseph Mazzinghi, organist and composer, pupil of J. C. Bach, was born on 25 December 1765 in London, where, at the age of 9, he became organist of the Portuguese Chapel. He died in Downside on 15 January 1844.

Frome Edwin George Monk, composer of the hymn tune *Angel Voices*, sung to 'Angel Voices, Ever Singing', was born here on 13 December 1819.

William Henry Reed, violinist, conductor, composer and close friend and biographer of Elgar, was born here on 29 July 1876 and died in Dumfries on 2 July 1942.

Glastonbury Rutland Boughton, composer, moved here in 1914, his opera *The Immortal Hour* receiving its first perfomance on 26 August of that year in the Assembly Rooms. He resided at Shapwick 1920–1. He left Glastonbury in 1927 after the disbanding of the Glastonbury Festival Players.

Igor Stravinsky came here on 19 August 1957, also visiting Bath and Wells on that day.

Hambridge The hymn tune *Hambridge*, sung to 'The Year Is Swiftly Waning', is an arrangement by Vaughan Williams of a folk melody collected here by Cecil Sharp.

Holford Frederic Norton, composer of *Chu Chin Chow*, resided in Holford. He died here on 15 December 1946.

Hungerford Harry Plunket Greene, bass-baritone singer, biographer of Stanford and soloist in the first performances of Stanford's *Songs of the Sea* and *Songs of the Fleet* and Elgar's *The Dream of Gerontius*, resided intermittently during his later years at Chefford Woodlands House. He died in London on 19 August 1936.

Langport Hugh Ross, organist and conductor, was born here on 21 August 1898.

Minehead Peter Hurford, composer and organist, was born here on 22 November 1930.

Odcombe Charles Draper, clarinettist, was born here in 1869 and died in London on 21 October 1952.

Penselwood Arthur Bliss, composer and Master of the Queen's Music, resided intermittently at his country home, Pen Pits, 1934–55.

Portishead Frederick Weatherly, author of the songs 'Danny Boy', 'Nancy Lee', 'Roses of Picardy', 'When We Are Old and Grey', 'Darby and Joan' and 'Up from Somerset', was born here on 4 October 1848 and died in London on 7 September 1929. He resided at 1 Hare Court, Temple.

Shepton Beauchamp Cecil Sharp collected the song 'Tarry Trousers' here in 1904. It had already been known for some years, since Dickens quotes from it in *Dombey and Son*, published in 1847. The song's melody, now known as *Shepton-Beauchamp*, is often sung to 'Fight the Good Fight with All Thy Might'.

Somerton James Turle, organist of Westminster Abbey 1831–75 and composer of the hymn tune *Westminster*, sung to 'My God, How Wonderful Thou Art', was born here on 5 March 1802 and died in London on 28 June 1882.

Taunton William Crotch, organist, pianist, painter and composer of the *Westminster Chimes*, died here on 29 December 1847. He is buried at Bishop's Hull.

Alexander Ewing, composer of the hymn tune *Ewing*, sung to 'Jerusalem the Golden', died here on 11 July 1895. He is buried in the nearby village of Trull and lies next to his wife, Juliana, who wrote *The Brownies* and other favourite tales for children.

Edward Harper, composer, conductor and pianist, was born here on 17 March 1941.

John Isaac Hawkins, inventor of the upright piano, was born here in 1772 and died in Elizabeth Town, New Jersey, in 1855.

John Hotchkis, composer and conductor, was born here on 22 November 1916.

Franz Liszt stayed here on the night of 30 August 1840 and took part in a concert on the following day.

Wells Charles Ives, after visiting Bath on 17 June 1933, spent the following two days here. Sunday evening service in the cathedral seems to have been taken faster than he preferred. His diary mentions, 'A horse race at Wells Cathedral Evensong.'

John Jackson, organist and composer, died here in March 1688.

John Okeover, organist and composer, died here in 1663.

Edward Plumtre, who was born in London on 6 August 1821, was Dean of Wells from 1881 until his death here on 1 February 1891. He wrote the hymns 'Thine Arm, O Lord, in Days of Old', 'O Lord of Hosts, All Heaven Possessing' and 'Thy Hand, O God, Has Guided'.

Thomas Welsh, bass singer and composer, was born here in about 1780 and died in Brighton on 31 January 1848.

Witcombe Ivor Gurney, composer and poet, resided at Cold Slad, Dryhill, during the summer of 1920.

WILTSHIRE

Aldbourne Gerald Finzi, composer, resided intermittently and later permanently at Beech Knoll 1933–9. During this period he completed *Dies Natalis, Two Milton Sonnets* and *Earth and Air and Rain.*

Bemerton George Herbert, poet and hymn writer, died here on 1 March 1633. He is buried in St Andrew's. His best known hymns include 'Come, My Way, My Truth, My Life', 'Let All the World in Every Corner Sing' and 'The God of Love My Shepherd Is'.

Bradford-on-Avon Joseph Knight, composer of the songs *Rocked in the Cradle of the Deep* and *She Wore a Wreath of Roses*, was born here on 26 July 1812 and died in Great Yarmouth on 2 June 1887.

Bromham Thomas Moore, poet and songwriter, resided at Sloperton Cottage from 1818 until his death here on 26 February 1852. He is buried in the nearby churchyard.

Corsham Michael Tippett, composer, resided at Parkside, 36 High Street, 1960–70. He completed *King Priam* here and also wrote *Songs for Ariel*, Concerto for Orchestra, *The Vision of Saint Augustine, Songs for Dov* and *The Knot Garden*, and began work on the Third Symphony.

Dauntsey Walter Stanton, composer, was born here on 29 September 1891.

Dinton Henry Lawes, composer, was born here on 5 January 1596.
   Arthur Henry Fox Strangways, writer on music, died here on 2 May 1948.

Landford Adrian Boult, conductor, resided intermittently during the 1920s, '30s and '40s at Northlands.

Longleat Thomas Ken, author of the hymns 'Awake, My Soul, and with the Sun' and 'Glory to Thee, My God, This Night', died here on 19 March 1711. He is buried in Frome, Somerset.

Malmesbury William Wallace, composer, writer on music, editor, dramatist and ophthalmic surgeon, died here on 16 December 1940.

Marlborough Ralph Vaughan Williams wrote part of *Hugh the Drover* at Sheepshanks Cottage in July 1911.

Mere Thomas Norris, composer, organist and tenor singer, was born here in 1741.

Milston Joseph Addison, poet, essayist and politician, was born here on 1 May 1672. His hymn 'The Spacious Firmament On High' was published in *The Spectator* on 23 August 1712. He died at Holland House in Kensington, London, on 17 June 1719.

North Tidworth John Philip Sousa came here on 25 June 1930 and, in a special ceremony, conducted the Second Battalion of the Royal Welch Fusiliers in the British première of his second *Royal Welch Fusiliers* march, commemorating the association of the Fusiliers and the US Marines during the Boxer Rebellion. He then presented the manuscript of the march to the commandant, Lieutenant-General Sir Charles Dobell. This is preserved in the regimental museum at Caernarfon Castle, Gwynedd.

Oare Ralph Vaughan Williams composed much of *Flos Campi* here, at the home of Mary Fletcher, during the summer of 1924.

Quidhampton William Walton began writing his First Symphony around the beginning of March 1932 at The Daye House, the home of Edith Oliver. Other visitors here included Constant Lambert and Rex Whistler.

Rushmore George Webb, composer of the hymn tune *Morning Light*, sung to 'Stand Up, Stand Up For Jesus', was born at Rushmore Lodge on 24 June 1803 and died in Orange, New Jersey, on 7 October 1887.

Salisbury Joseph Corfe, organist and composer, was born in Salisbury on 25 December 1740 and died here on 29 July 1820.

George Frideric Handel was a guest of the author James Harris in The Close.

Maurice Handford, conductor, was born here on 29 April 1929.

William Lawes, composer, was born in The Close in 1602.

Franz Liszt played at a concert in the Assembly Rooms on 20 August 1840 and visited Stonehenge.

Edward Lowe, organist and composer, was born here in about 1610 and died in Oxford on 11 July 1682.

Charles Lucas, cellist, organist, conductor, publisher and composer, was born here on 28 July 1808 and died in London on 30 March 1869.

John Philip Sousa conducted his band at a concert in County Hall on 27 January 1905.

Michael Wise, composer of the anthems *Prepare Ye the Way* and *The Ways of Sion* and of the hymn tune *Congleton*, often sung to 'Here, O My Lord, I See Thee Face to Face', was probably born in Salisbury in 1648; he died here on 24 August 1687 after quarrelling first with his wife and then with a nightwatchman, who clubbed him to death.

Stapleford Ralph Vaughan Williams composed part of his Fifth Symphony at Rose Cottage during the early 1940s.

Swindon Arthur Carron, tenor singer, was born here on 12 December 1900.

Tilshead Walter Emery, organist and music scholar, was born here on 14 June 1909 and died in June 1974.

Tollard Royal Peter Maxwell Davies, composer, resided at Kimbers

Cottage 1964–5. Works written at this time include the *Second Taverner Fantasia, Shakespeare Music, Ecce Manus Tradentis, Revelation and Fall* and *The Shepherd's Calendar.*

Warminster Ernest Ford, conductor and composer, was born here on 17 February 1858 and died in London on 2 June 1919.

Wilton Davis Mell, violinist, was born here on 15 November 1604 and died in London, possibly in the 1660s.

Hubert Parry composed *Blest Pair of Sirens* at Wilton House in 1887.

INDEX

(Page numbers in **bold type** indicate entries for the birth or death of a musician.)

INDEX

Faring, Eaton, 314

INDEX

345

INDEX

351

INDEX

352